THE 23rd DIVISION

1914-1919

.

Recipients of the Victoria Cross.
23rd Division.

2 Lt. John Scott Youll
11th N. Fusiliers.

2 Lt. Donald Simpson Bell
late 9th Yorks. Regt.

No. 13820. Serjt. William McNally, M.
8th Yorks. Regt.

1st Lt. Charles Edward Hudson, D.S.O.M.C.
11th Sherwood. Foresters.

2 Lt. Henry Kelly
10th Duke of Wellington's Regt.

No. 17524. Pte. Thomas Kenny
13th D.L.I.

No. 12067. Pte. William Short
late 8th Yorks. Regt.

2 Lt. Frederick Youens
late 13th D.L.I.

No. 59812. Pte. Wilford Wood
10th N. Fusiliers.

THE 23rd DIVISION

1914-1919

BY

LIEUT.-COLONEL H. R. SANDILANDS
C.M.G., D S.O.
NORTHUMBERLAND FUSILIERS

William Blackwood and Sons
Edinburgh and London
1925

FOREWORD.

At the close of the Great War both officers and men of the 23rd Division expressed a wish to commemorate the honoured memory of their gallant dead, and at the same time to record the great deeds performed by the Division. The difficulties of erecting a memorial in a suitable locality were apparent from the large area in which the Division was recruited, the numerous countries and battlefields on which it fought, and the desire to avoid expense during the difficult period which followed demobilisation. After due consideration, it was decided that this history should serve to commemorate the fallen, and to recall to the living the comradeship of those great days.

Lieut.-Colonel H. R. Sandilands, C.M.G., D.S.O., was invited to undertake the work, and to his whole-hearted and devoted efforts we owe this graphic story. His task has been carried out under difficult circumstances, for the greater part has been written during the hot weather, first in Mesopotamia, and latterly in India, while commanding his battalion. The writing of a Divisional History under the most favourable conditions is a difficult task, but when 6000 miles separate the author from his principal sources of information, voluminous correspondence and long delays are inevitable. Never for one moment has Colonel Sandilands grudged time or trouble spent upon work which has been a real labour of love.

It was agreed that the history should be a serious record of the events it portrays, and, though not aspiring to military history, it should present to future generations a true picture of the military significance of the part played by the 23rd Division.

Space has prohibited a detailed record of the work of the administrative services; but the success of the fighting arms invariably reflects the efficiency of the services on which it depends. Never was a Division better served by its administrative units than was the 23rd.

It will be seen that many difficulties were encountered in the early days of the Division. That these were successfully overcome was due in the main to the cheerfulness and indomitable spirit of the men themselves. The Division was fortunate during its period of training to be under the command of General Sir Archibald Hunter, G.C.B., G.C.V.O., D.S.O., than whom no one has constantly been in closer sympathy with the soldier.

In due course of time the Division crossed over to France, and took its place in the battle line. Already that *esprit-de-corps* which was so marked a feature of the Division, and which was described by a very distinguished officer as "magnificent," had taken firm root. It was the bright reflection of comradeship and mutual help, added to the true discipline under which the Division had been brought up. One of the many evidences of this spirit occurred after an action on the Somme. On visiting the wounded I was met with the one question: "Were we successful?" Pain and wounds were for the moment forgotten, and I only hope that the good news I was able to give helped them a little in the days that followed.

In this story many a gallant action is recorded; many another, doubtless, passes unnoticed. Recorded or not, however, they remain treasured in proud memory by those who served with the Division in those great days, and who witnessed stupendous deeds performed under conditions that no words can adequately describe.

At the last we read of the dispersal of a body of men who had been true comrades in the best sense of the word. We are not told of the scenes at the entraining station for England, though many witnessed them, where men who had passed through the rough and hardening school of war said "Good-bye" with tears running down their faces.

May this story of my gallant and loyal comrades inspire those who follow after to uphold at all times the freedom of our country as nobly as did the citizen soldiers of our day.

J. M. BABINGTON, *Lieut.-General.*

PREFACE.

AT least once in the course of writing this history I expressed to General Babington doubts as to my being equal to the work I had undertaken at his request. To these misgivings I received the simple but uncompromising reply : " You can do it ! "

In that I have written a History of the 23rd Division he has been justified ; but it is left to the reader to decide to what extent I have done justice to my subject.

On general matters I have occasionally expressed opinions with which all may not be in agreement. In some of the smaller details it is nearly inevitable that I may at times be found inexact. But the more important events I believe to be accurately related, and I can claim to have done my utmost faithfully to set down the truth without bias.

A difficult question presented to the writer of a history of this kind is that of the mention of names. To include the names of all who performed distinguished service is only less impossible than to record those of all who served in the Division. Three alternatives remain : to mention no names ; to record a few ; to include as many as possible. In deciding on the last alternative I have hoped to add human interest to my subject, but the amount of detail necessary to its adoption has extended the book to a length which I realise may be regarded by some as excessive for the history of a division. Of the three alternatives offered, moreover, that adopted lends itself least to even treatment ; many more names would have been mentioned had they appeared in the records placed at my disposal. I suggest that this defect may be remedied by the reader noting in the margin the name of any anonymous figure he recognises.

During the war the application of different terms in different armies and corps to the areas occupied by the various units and formations in defence often led to confusion. The terms I have applied are those which, I believe, were employed in the First Army in 1916—viz., Corps Front, Divisional Sector, Brigade Section, Battalion Sub-section.

Finally, I must gratefully acknowledge the very great help I have received from the many officers of the 23rd Division who have assisted me in various ways in my work.

The several parts of the History as first written were sent to Lieut.-General Sir James Babington, K.C.B., K.C.M.G.; Major-General H. F. Thuillier, C.B., C.M.G.; Brig.-General D. J. M. Fasson, C.B., C.M.G.; and Lieut.-Colonel A. K. Hay, D.S.O., O.B.E., for their criticism. The suggestions I received from them were most valuable, and the manner in which they were offered most encouraging.

This criticism formed but a small part of the work done by Lieut.-Colonel Hay. It was he who collected and filed for my use the mass of unofficial material—diaries, narratives, maps, &c.,—without which I should have been solely dependent on bare, and sometimes barren, war diaries. The task of arranging maps and appendices, under my instructions, and of indexing the book, was also undertaken by him. In this he has been assisted by Captain Hely-Hutchinson, M.C., who by a coincidence arrived in England simultaneously with a letter in which I had expressed a wish that he of all men was available to help in the work.

Many others have supplied me with valuable material of every kind, and I would like to express my thanks to all who have helped in this way.

For the written life of the 23rd Division to be worthy of its deeds, greater skill than mine was needed. But I trust that this History will recall to those who served in the Division the events in which they took part, and the comrades with whom they share its high traditions.

H. R. S.

FYZABAD, U.P., *September* 1923.

CONTENTS.

ILLUSTRATIONS.

MAPS.

(At end of Book.)

Full-size copies of the following Etchings, by Lieut.-Colonel B. Buchanan, *may be obtained from* Messrs BROMHEAD CUTTS & CO., 18 Cork Street, W. 1. :—

PART I. ENGLAND

THE FIRST YEAR

FORMATION OF THE 23RD DIVISION—EARLY DAYS IN ENGLAND.

AUGUST 4, 1914, TO AUGUST 23, 1915.

THIS is the story of the life of the 23rd Division. It is a history of the Great War commenced in 1914 only in so far as the Division was associated to a greater or less degree with certain events in the immense cataclysm into which the world was plunged.

Those, then, who would study the events which led up to the declaration of war by Great Britain against the German Empire on August 4, 1914, must refer elsewhere. For it is at this date that our history commences : when subtle argument and diplomatic negotiation had failed to avert the catastrophe, and when it was enough for the patriotic citizen that he had confidence in the justice of his country's cause, and that the country had need of his services.

But as in dealing with the life of an individual the biographer strives to reproduce the atmosphere in which his subject was born, as inevitably influencing his character, and relates the events of his childhood, as providing clues to his actions in later life, so it is no less necessary for an appreciation of the spirit, character, and actions of a division that the circumstances of its birth and early being should be understood.

For future generations to gain a full understanding of how the divisions of the New Army were raised, and trained to stand up on equal terms against the trained soldiers of the German Empire, it will be necessary for them to realise to the full, not only the patriotism that filled the ranks, but also the individual sacrifice which enhanced this patriotism.

For this, too, it is necessary for a moment to consider the conditions under which the British people had been living for the century

preceding the war, and the outlook of the average citizen during that
period.

Unlike those in a continental country with the anxiety of a land
frontier, where lurked a potential enemy watching and waiting the
chance to descend on their land, the British citizen through three generations had experienced a sense of complete security under the joint-
protection of the British policeman and the strongest navy in the world.
At the close of the nineteenth century his complacency had for a moment
been disturbed by the reverses suffered in the South African War. But
the necessary number of volunteers to put things right had then been
found without difficulty ; the families of the working-classes had not
been seriously involved, and it was generally considered that we had
attained in South Africa as great a military effort as we should ever
be called on to make in the future. These events, moreover, were but
a dim recollection to the younger generation.

The Army was outside the national life. It can perhaps be said
that the average Englishman knew less of it than of any other profession. It is doubtful if one in a hundred thousand knew the name
of a military leader beyond those of Lord Roberts and Lord Kitchener
—that they knew the latter was to mean much. At the same time
they acknowledged the Army as a British institution, and, except when
it talked nonsense about a war with Germany, trusted it.

If some prophet had told any fifty young Englishmen in the early
summer of 1914 that they would be millionaires before they died, he
would have been honoured. Had he predicted that they would be
soldiers before the close of the year, he would no less surely have been
stoned. This attitude prevailed up till the very outbreak of hostilities.
That it was due to ignorance and not to apathy was made clear when,
with the declaration of war, an immediate appeal was made for 100,000
volunteers. The sudden realisation of the country's need crowded the
recruiting-offices throughout the land. The first rush was made by the
unfettered youth of the country, those who, owing to their financial
position or freedom from family ties, were at liberty to offer their services at the first call. But there were others in their thousands whose
spirit was no less keen, but who, in this sudden and unforeseen emergency, were compelled first to secure the position of those dependent
on them.

It was from this latter class that the 23rd Division was raised, to form with the 21st, 22nd, 24th, 25th, and 26th Divisions the Third New Army.

The infantry of the Division was to be formed of battalions of north country and midland county regiments, the bulk being drawn from the north. These were organised to form the 68th, 69th, and 70th Infantry Brigades. The composition of brigades and their commanders were as follows :—

68TH INFANTRY BRIGADE.

Commander—Colonel G. H. OVENS, C.B.

> 10th Northumberland Fusiliers.
> 11th Northumberland Fusiliers.
> 12th Durham Light Infantry.
> 13th Durham Light Infantry.

69TH INFANTRY BRIGADE.

Commander—Brig.-General F. S. DERHAM, C.B.

> 11th West Yorkshire Regiment.
> 8th Yorkshire Regiment.
> 9th Yorkshire Regiment.
> 10th Duke of Wellington's Regiment.

70TH INFANTRY BRIGADE.

Commander—Brig.-General Sir D. A. KINLOCH, Bart., C.B.

> 11th Sherwood Foresters.
> 8th York and Lancaster Regiment.
> 9th York and Lancaster Regiment.
> 8th K.O. Yorkshire Light Infantry.

The following battalions, detailed as Army Troops, were also to be attached to the Division :—

> 8th Leicestershire Regiment.
> 9th Leicestershire Regiment.
> 9th South Staffordshire Regiment.

Of these, the first two were to leave the Division before it proceeded overseas ; the last, as will be seen, was to be converted to a pioneer battalion, and to form part of the Division throughout the war.

The 89th and 90th Field Companies R.E. were to form part of the Division on its formation, but were later to be replaced by its permanent field companies. The Divisional Artillery was yet to be formed.

It remained for a commander to be appointed to the Division. He also was found in the north, just across the border.

Colonel (Hon. Major-General) James Melville Babington, C.B., C.M.G., on whom the choice fell, had seen considerable service. Joining the 16th Lancers in 1873, he had later commanded that regiment. He had served in the Bechuanaland Expedition of 1884-85 and in the South African War, being mentioned in despatches for his services in both these campaigns. He had served as A.A.G., Sirhind District, 1896-1899, and later as colonel on the Staff, Cavalry Brigade, Colchester, 1899. After the South African War he had been appointed to the New Zealand Defence Force, which he had commanded from 1902 till 1907.

He had retired from the service in 1907, but commanded the Lowland Mounted Brigade from 1908-13. At that time he was colonel of the 16th Lancers and of the 5th Mounted Rifles (Otago Hussars), N.Z.

General Babington at this date was in his sixty-first year, and, though more active than many men ten years his junior, the fact that the most brilliant period of his military career still lay before him could have seemed, early in 1914, scarcely less remote to him than the idea of shouldering a musket to the hitherto peaceful citizens who were to know him as their commander.

The next few months were to be spent in the gradual creation of order out of chaos.

The concentration of the Division was to commence on September 16, the 68th Infantry Brigade assembling at Bullswater, and the 69th and 70th Infantry Brigades at Frensham.

But few officers had yet joined their units ; others had been delayed by an error in orders. That mistakes should occur in the orders emanating from the hard-pressed War Office was not surprising ; that so few occurred must always stand to the credit of a staff nigh overwhelmed with work in those anxious days.

When the 68th Infantry Brigade assembled in camp at Bullswater,

Lieutenant-General Sir James Melville Babington, K.C.B., K.C.M.G.
G.O.C. 23rd Division.
Aug. '14 – Oct. '18.
and subsequently G.O.C. XIVth Corps.

and the 69th and 70th Infantry Brigades and Field Companies R.E. arrived at Frensham, though other ranks were plentiful, officers were scarce. This shortage of officers continued during the early weeks, and added to the difficulties of those who were present.

On September 18 General Babington, accompanied by Major H. J. Bartholomew, D.S.O., who had been appointed G.S.O. 2, reached Frensham, and established his headquarters at the Pond Hotel, prior to moving under canvas on October 4.

The difficulties in issuing orders and in opening communication with units necessitated command being exercised at first on the most primitive lines. No trained clerks were available, and orders were issued verbally by the staff (Major Bartholomew) to the adjutants of units. Men with experience of clerking in civil life were, however, hastily collected from the ranks of the various units ; typewriters, office stationery, and two motor-cars soon became available, and, with the valuable assistance of the Boy Scouts of a local company, who acted as orderlies, things rapidly improved.

But where one can make shift in issuing orders, there are other needs in dealing with a mass of human beings which are not so easily met. Where one may find a hundred men among the ranks of Englishmen with experience as clerks, one would be lucky to find one even passable cook. Trained cooks were non-existent in the Division. This situation was saved by a contract made with Messrs Lyons & Co. to arrange for the messing of the troops. This arrangement, which proved most satisfactory, continued till the Division had trained its own *chefs* early in December. Officers were provided for in brigade messes, managed by a caterer.

Only second in importance to the provision for the inner man was the question of clothing. A company on parade presented the most motley and grotesque appearance. An officer tells of the pride he took in the smart appearance of one of his men who wore a bowler hat, khaki jacket, blue trousers, and a pair of smart brown boots. Another records the value of the variety of costume in enabling him to distinguish between the men. But the men, very naturally, had come in their oldest civilian clothing and boots, and these were being rapidly reduced to rags.

To remedy this, General Babington obtained permission to expend £17,000 on clothing. Two officers connected with the clothing trade were despatched to Yorkshire and the north with orders to purchase 20,000 suits of underclothing and boots. This relieved matters considerably; but it was not till mid-October that any sort of uniform, in the shape of emergency blue clothing, began to be available.

The troops were accommodated thirteen to fourteen in a tent, and for a considerable time no tent boards were available. But, fortunately, the weather during the early weeks was fine.

Military custom and etiquette cannot be picked up in a day even with the best will in the world. The vague bewilderment in which the men lived at this period is illustrated by an incident related of a visit by the Divisional Commander to one of the Yorkshire battalions. It was the custom of General Babington, who was one of the few who possessed uniform at this time, to walk round and talk to the men. One day, after he had been in conversation with a group of men, an officer reproved them for not standing to attention, asking if they did not know who it was who had been speaking to them. After consideration, one of them replied, " I doan't rightly know who 'e be, but I reckon 'e be one o' t' Directors."

As early as September 29, H.M. the King, accompanied by the Queen and Princess Mary, inspected the troops at work. The encouragement given by this visit of His Majesty was manifest in the enthusiastic cheering of the troops at the time of his departure.

To maintain this immense collection of enthusiasts in health and in such moderate degree of comfort as was possible, hard task though it was, formed but part of the labour that lay before commanders and all others. In the high spirit and goodwill which enabled the men to accept without murmur the discomforts of a life entirely strange to the great majority, the few experienced officers saw the ideal qualities of the good recruit. Given all facilities, such material would soon be trained to take their place in battle. But the Divisional Commander was faced by two tremendous difficulties in the training of his Division : firstly, the shortage of trained instructors ; secondly, lack of equipment.

Battalions in the First New Army had been supplied with as many as six regular serving officers ; the battalions of the 23rd Division had, on an average, less than one. Commanding officers and senior majors were, in most cases, retired officers of the British or Indian services, or retired officers of the old Militia. There had been great developments in military training in the years preceding the war, and such ex-service N.C.O.'s as were with battalions, having in many cases left the service many years before, had dropped behind the times.

For long it was a fixed idea with many of the officers of the New Army, and may still be with some, that the Old Army N.C.O. was always a fatherly old gentleman of this type. The impression was created in those who had seen these patriotic old soldiers, but had never known the vigorous young sergeant-majors who went to France with the Expeditionary Force at the start of the war.

In October 100 obsolete Lee-Metford rifles were issued to each battalion for drill purposes. But it was not till November that L.M.E. service rifles became available for instruction, and then it was only in the proportion of eight per battalion. At this time, too, 400 sets of old buff equipment—waistbelt, scabbard, and bayonet—were issued to each battalion. Old pattern water-bottles and white haversacks did not arrive till December. One wonders from what secret caches of the Army Ordnance all these ghosts of old equipment were raised to make our new Division feel more like soldiers, and what far-seeing purpose had prevented its destruction in the previous century.

In the meantime, while odds and ends of equipment came to hand, and as straw hats, bowlers, and check trousers gave place to a " horrible blue-serge uniform, which we found impossible to smarten except by brightening it up with brass buttons," units were training from eight to ten hours a day. In the degenerate days after the war, it is recalled as a dream that " we sometimes did two hours' battalion drill before breakfast, and *we liked it.*" In the early days, owing to lack of equipment, training was necessarily confined to squad drill, physical training, running, marching, night work, and entrenching.

Training at this high pressure was continued until it became evident that it would not be possible to equip the Division for overseas before the following spring; it was then so far relaxed as to make Sunday a day of rest.

Early in November the 23rd Divisional Artillery was formed at Mytchett Camp, Aldershot. The description of its formation, as given by an officer who took part in it, serves so well to illustrate the birth of units at this period that it deserves quotation in some detail. " We arrived," he tells us, " to find the camp deserted but for a sergeant of

the Ordnance Corps, who informed me that the Divisional Artillery
was not being formed till Monday—*i.e.*, November 9, adding that a
gentleman in ' civvies ' had been looking round the camp that day."
Gentlemen in civvies were not so rare in those days as later in the war,
but the officer, finding himself seated at table that evening at a hotel
with a gentleman answering to the description, drew a bow at venture,
and discovered that his fellow guest was none other than Colonel (later
Brig.-General) Elmslie, who was to command the 23rd Divisional Artillery. " On Monday," he continues, " we proceeded to Mytchett Camp,
where we found four more 2nd lieutenants wandering round. Whilst
Colonel Elmslie was introducing himself to these, a sixth 2nd lieutenant
appeared. The colonel then called us to a marquee, gave us a brief
outline as to what the formation of a Divisional Artillery meant, and
detailed the four senior officers each to take a brigade, the commands
falling to—

> 102nd Brigade—2nd Lieutenant Darwin.
> 103rd Brigade—2nd Lieutenant Moss.
> 104th Brigade—2nd Lieutenant Kusel.
> 105th Brigade—2nd Lieutenant Hewitt Taylor.

The responsibilities to which these young officers had been called
were, however, not quite so heavy as they might at first sight appear,
since there were no guns, nor was there any food. Fortunately also, in
view of the last consideration, there were still no men. The men
commenced to arrive on the following morning ; the camp was
divided into four parts, each man was given blankets and a basin,
the necessary rations had arrived, and the 23rd Divisional Artillery
was formed.

On November 15 General Ovens was transferred to the command
of the 67th Infantry Brigade, being replaced in command of the 68th
Infantry Brigade by Major-General B. J. C. Doran.

On November 23 that fine old Indian warrior, Maharajah Sir Pertab
Singh, visited the troops at Frensham.

The weather had now become very wet and cold. A gale on November
30 blew down the mess tents and the Y.M.C.A. tents, and inflicted very
great discomfort on the troops. The two Y.M.C.A. tents, which had
been established at Frensham in October, were a great boon to the

men, and many residents of the surrounding district were untiring in
their efforts at this period to relieve the hardships of the troops.

On December 1 and 2 the Division moved into barracks at Aldershot,
the 68th and 69th Infantry Brigades being accommodated in North
Camp, where the Field Companies R.E. were already situated, the
70th Infantry Brigade taking up its quarters in Stanhope Lines. Divisional headquarters were established on Queen's Parade, while the staff
took up their residence at the Queen's Hotel.

The following letter was received by the Divisional Commander on
moving to the new area :—

DEAR GENERAL BABINGTON,—Now that the troops under your
command have left Farnham, will you allow me, on behalf of the Committee which has run the Recreation Room in Farnham and also on
behalf of the Farnham people in general, to wish officers, N.C.O.'s and
men God-speed and good luck? We very much appreciate the consistent excellent behaviour of the troops, and it has been a great pleasure
to have had the opportunity to do something in a small way for their
pleasure whilst at Farnham. Again I say good luck to them all.—Yours
sincerely,

(Sd.)   EDGAR KEMPSON,
Chairman, Farnham Urban District Council.

The Divisional Artillery were shortly afterwards moved to barracks,
the 102nd and 103rd Brigades to Ewshott, the 104th and 105th Brigades
to Lille Barracks, Aldershot. The special training of the artillery had
hitherto been confined to gun-pit digging. For practice in this, brigades
would go out for the whole day, every man carrying a pick, spade, and,
to the amusement of onlookers, the inevitable pudding-basin. To assist
in training, a number of senior N.C.O.'s had now been posted to the
Divisional Artillery ; among these Sergeant-Major Clutterbuck will be
remembered by those who served with the 105th Brigade in the early
days as a staunch friend and helper in their trials. To his bitter disappointment and to the sorrow of all in the brigade, this veteran soldier
was later deprived by the age-limit of the privilege of going overseas
with the units for whose efficiency he did so much.

The equipment of the artillery was, if anything, less in advance even
than that of the infantry. It is related that a guard used to be supplied
with one bandolier. Proudly equipped in this, the first sentry would

be mounted, handing it over in turn to his relief, together with a large stick, which represented the sole means of defence.

Shortly after the formation of the Divisional Artillery, Brig.-General Elmslie had presented a flag, which was handed over on a full parade at the end of each month to the best all-round brigade. Competition for this acted as a keen stimulant to training, and the excitement was great when, shortly before moving to Aldershot, orders were received to send parties to collect real guns. The twenty-seven guns which arrived proved to be old French 90 mm. guns, which had certainly seen better days, but the sight of them appealed greatly to the artillery spirit. There were still no horses, and man-handling was the order of the day.

Shortly after arrival in barracks, however, the first batch of re-mounts turned up, equipment began to arrive, and driving drill commenced in earnest. The 2nd lieutenants had now been relieved by senior officers of their responsibilities as artillery brigade commanders, and the Divisional Artillery was fast developing.

Early in December Major-General Sir F. Howard, K.C.B., Inspector of Infantry, inspected two infantry brigades of the Division, and ex-pressed his pleasure in witnessing the high standard of efficiency that had been attained.

On December 6 the 101st, 102nd, and 128th Field Companies R.E., which were to form part of the Division throughout the war, replaced the 89th and 90th Field Companies.

For the purpose of carrying out battalion training, the Division was now allotted an area north of the canal, extending to Basingstoke on the west, Ascot on the east, and bounded on the north by the Reading-Wokingham-Ascot railway. To save the time that would be wasted in marching to and from this ground, it was decided to billet two brigades in the vicinity. The 68th Infantry Brigade, accordingly, moved on December 7 into billets in the Swallowfield-Arborfield-Hartley Row-Shinfield-Mattingly area, while the 69th Infantry Brigade were accom-modated in Eversley, Blackwater, Camberley, and Bagshot. In the former area in particular adequate billets were difficult to get, and in many cases troops had to be content with rough barns ; but all ranks, mindful of what their comrades were undergoing in France and Flanders at this period, made the best of these somewhat inhospitable quarters.

Bad weather continued throughout December, heath and moorland were waterlogged, and the submersion of road bridges by floods at times made communication and the delivery of rations matters of great difficulty ; but in spite of this much useful work was done, the Divisional Commander inspecting two or more units daily at their work.

On December 16 Christmas leave was opened, every man being granted seven days' leave and a free return warrant to his home. A very few fortunate men had received their khaki uniform before this event, but the vast majority had to suffer the chagrin of visiting their friends in the blue-serge horror which they so cordially disliked.

The 9th South Staffordshire Regiment were at this time quartered in Talavera Barracks. The policy had been adopted of forming one pioneer battalion for each division. To select battalions for this a census of the trades of the men was taken in the various battalions of divisions. In the 23rd Division the 9th South Staffordshire Regiment was found to contain the highest percentage of men with qualifications for pioneer work, and from this date it became the Pioneer Battalion of the Division.

On January 14 the whole Division was again assembled at Aldershot. On January 22 the Division was inspected by M. Millerand, the French Minister of War, and Lord Kitchener. It is a day that few who took part in it will ever forget. The inspection was timed for 2.30 P.M., but M. Millerand had, unfortunately, been delayed, and did not arrive till 3.30 P.M. Snow fell during the morning, and was lying four inches deep on the parade-ground at 12 noon, when heavy rain set in. The men, in their blue-serge uniform and civilian greatcoats, were soaked to the skin. The infantry, armed with D.P. rifles, were formed up in line of battalions in mass. It was a most trying day for all concerned. At its conclusion General Babington personally visited many of the units after the troops, drenched and chilled, had returned to their barracks. Since the weather had broken in November there had been a good many cases of pneumonia in the Division, particularly among the older men. The men who paraded this day represented the stronger men who had survived the rigours of life under service conditions, and fortunately no evil resulted from the appalling circumstances under which the parade was held.

On January 16 the 23rd Divisional Train was formed from the 190th, 191st, 192nd, and 193rd Companies R.A.S.C., under command of Major (later Lieut.-Colonel) A. Northen, R.A.S.C.

Towards the end of January the 68th and 69th Infantry Brigades again moved to billets near the training area, and battalion training was resumed. Shortly after this the 8th and 9th Battalions Leicester-shire Regiment were transferred to another division to form part of a Leicester Brigade.

The Division was now ordered to the Shorncliffe area, for which it started to march in three columns on February 24.

Immediately prior to this the long-looked-for khaki was issued. The secret of the diplomatic coup which secured this can now for the first time be made public. To relate it in General Babington's own words : " The issue came about in this wise. I happened to be in the C.O.O.'s office, and found him talking on the telephone to his chief at the War Office. I said, ' Tell him to let us draw khaki.' The answer was, ' Impossible.' I then said, ' Tell him Lord K. is going to inspect us.' We got the khaki at once ! " Discretion forbids too close an inquiry as to the grounds the Divisional Commander had at the time for his statement. Lord Kitchener did, in fact, inspect two of the columns on the march near Maidstone on February 28, but the official notification of his intention to do so was only received late on the preceding day. His visit was to be kept secret, but the short notice at which the tele-gram announcing it was received necessitated cancelling certain orders already issued for the following day. The adjutant of one of the bat-talions guessed the reason of this alteration in orders, with the horrify-ing result that Lord Kitchener's secret visit was announced that evening on the screen of the local theatre. It was confidently anticipated that half the countryside would turn out next day, but, thanks probably to no hour having been mentioned, none of the inhabitants appeared, and all was well. Lord Kitchener expressed his warm approval of the troops he saw.

The Division arrived in the Shorncliffe area on March 1 and 2, and was quartered at Ashford, Canterbury, Shorncliffe, Folkestone, and Rye, forming part of the Third Army, under the command of Lieut.-General Sir Leslie Rundle, who inspected the 69th and 70th Infantry Brigades on March 9.

The next months were characterised by hard training and frequent inspections. On April 8 and 9 the infantry were inspected by Major-General L. Drummond, Inspector of Infantry ; on May 7 by General Sir A. Paget, Commanding the Southern Command ; and on May 11 and 12 by Major-General Sir A. Murray, Chief of the Imperial General Staff. All expressed their entire satisfaction with the progress that had been made.

Training in manœuvre was now sufficiently advanced for divisional field days to be carried out ; but that there was still scope for individual training is apparent from the record of a battalion scheme carried out at this time. This was designed to give practice in that fascinating operation of war, the encounter battle. Two half-battalions, placed at a distance of six miles from each other and so directed that encounter would be inevitable, commenced their movement. Encounter took place at a sharp bend in the road, where the opposing forces came face to face in column of route, the scouts of both sides having failed entirely to discover the enemy. But it is from such incidents rather than in the hard school of war, as is generally supposed, that lessons are learnt. Nor had the pioneers (if the secret of the unit may be disclosed) recently had much opportunity for practising scouting, as they had been employed during the latter part of April and early May on the defences of London, and had been hard at work on trenches between Westerham and Knockholt. During this time the 9th South Staffordshire Regiment was quartered at Bromley, in Kent, before returning to their previous billets at Folkestone.

Infantry battalions were also employed on work on the outer defence of London between May 1 and 10, being billeted for this purpose at Maidstone and elsewhere.

On May 24 the Division moved by rail to the Bordon area. The conduct of all ranks while in the Shorncliffe area had been as exemplary as it had been throughout. Before leaving, the Divisional Commander received the following letter of generous appreciation from the Mayor of Folkestone :—

TOWN HALL, FOLKESTONE,
21st April 1915.

DEAR GENERAL BABINGTON,—Now that the troops who for the past few weeks have been billeted in Folkestone are leaving, I should like to express for myself and for the inhabitants of the town our appreciation of the exemplary behaviour of the men whilst they have been amongst us.

Their earnest yet cheerful demeanour has aroused our admiration ; and we are deeply grateful for all that they are doing and are prepared to do for their king and country.

May God bless and protect them in all their dangers.—Yours very faithfully,

STEPHEN PENFOLD, *Mayor.*

On arrival in the Bordon area the Divisional Headquarters and the 70th Infantry Brigade were accommodated in Bordon Barracks ; the remainder of the Division were placed in hutments, with the exception of the Pioneer Battalion, which went into camp near Oxney Farm. The huts of the 68th and 69th Infantry Brigades were at Bramshot Common.

Hitherto the appointment of G.S.O. 1 of the Division had been held by Colonel D. J. M. Fasson, C.B. This officer now took over the duties of C.R.A. from Brig.-General Elmslie, being replaced as G.S.O. 1 by Colonel A. Blair, D.S.O., of the K.O. Scottish Borderers.

The training of the artillery will always remain one of the most remarkable features of the war, and the services of General Elmslie, who first fashioned the artillery brigades of the 23rd Division from raw material, were pre-eminent. Another change took place in the Division at this time, owing to the promotion of Major-General Doran to the command of the 25th Division ; his place in command of the 68th Infantry Brigade was taken by Brig.-General Pearce-Serocold, D.S.O., of the 60th Rifles.

Several artillery officers now returned from a three weeks' tour in France, during which they had been attached to the artillery of divisions in the line. 18-pdr. guns and 4.5 howitzers were fast arriving to replace our old friends the 90 mm. guns, and the Divisional Artillery, under strenuous training, was gaining form every day.

The infantry at this period was allotted to battalion commanders three days a week, and underwent two days' brigade and one day's divisional training. The last included bivouacking : troops marched out in division to a given rendezvous, bivouacked for the night, and carried out combined operations the following day before returning to quarters.

Frequent lectures were given to officers in the camp theatre ; many of these were greatly enjoyed, but some proved trying after the long day of strenuous training. It is even recorded that " on one occasion an officer actually fell asleep after being on duty all the previous night, and was reprimanded by the lecturer ! " Some years' experience in the Army persuades one that a long night's duty is not essential to this effect being produced by certain lectures ; the reprimand of the lecturer, one imagines, was prompted by knowledge of that fact. That the incident should be recorded as something unusual and rather disgraceful indicates, however, the almost religious respect paid to matters of training in the Division at the time.

The infantry had now attained a high standard of efficiency in all except one most important respect : their knowledge of rifle-shooting was still mainly theoretical. These men who had now been under hard military training for ten months had little practical experience of the weapon with which they were armed. But supply was gradually overtaking demand, and the munition factories were growing capable of arming the New Armies, while at the same time coping with the continual wastage at the front. In June service rifles were issued to the Division, and musketry practice was immediately commenced on the Woolmer and Longmoor ranges.

In the course of the month Divisional and Brigade Staffs spent a week in France visiting the trenches, and receiving general instruction at the front.

During the winter the general idea had prevailed that the war would be finished and Germany crushed before the Division was equipped. This optimistic view had been frequently expressed in the most pessimistic tones. But now it was realised throughout that all the hard work that had been done would not serve merely to cow Germany into submission by the knowledge of the vast trained reserves available for the British Army, but that the Division was to stand the test of war. Enthusiasm grew daily ; all were impatient to get overseas. The artillery were hard at it in a practice camp on Salisbury Plain. In vain did the C.R.A. open one of his lectures by asking them if " they realised they couldn't *damned well shoot.*" They were past heeding such admonition. Their shooting on Salisbury Plain might be open to criticism, but give them Germans in front of them, and they would quickly show that they could shoot *damned well !*

B

At the end of July all ranks were given seven days' leave. This was divided into two periods, and was finished by the second week in August. During this period mobilisation stores, G.S., and limbered waggons were received, and the troops were practised in loading waggons and in entraining horses. Still there was no news of embarkation.

On August 16 the Division formed up on Hankley Common, and, presenting a magnificent appearance, was inspected by His Majesty the King, who was accompanied by the Queen. His Majesty was graciously pleased to express his very warm appreciation of all he saw. The cheers with which the 23rd Division acclaimed their King at the conclusion of the parade will live in the memory of all who were present that day.

On the following day orders were received for the Division to embark for France. Three days later, on August 20, the first advanced troops entrained for their ports of embarkation.

On August 22 the following gracious message was received from His Majesty :—

OFFICERS, NON-COMMISSIONED OFFICERS, AND MEN, — You are about to join your comrades at the Front in bringing to a successful end this relentless War of over twelve months' duration.

Your prompt patriotic answer to the Nation's Call to Arms will never be forgotten. The keen exertions of all ranks during the period of training have brought you to a state of efficiency not unworthy of my Regular Army.

I am confident that in the Field you will nobly uphold the traditions of the fine regiments whose names you bear.

Ever since your enrolment I have closely watched the growth and steady progress of all units. I shall continue to follow with interest the fortunes of your Division.

In bidding you farewell, I pray that God will bless you in all your undertakings.

22nd August 1915.

To this the Divisional Commander replied :—

I desire very respectfully to express, on my own behalf and that of the Division I have the honour to command, my very great thanks for His Majesty's most gracious message. The deep interest taken by him in the 23rd Division is most keenly felt and appreciated by all ranks, who respectfully beg to assure His Majesty of their devotion and loyalty, and of their earnest determination to do their utmost to uphold the honour of their King and country.

BORDON, 23/8/15.   .

The long weary months of training, with their humours and hardships, were over. The Division had come to the day it had worked and waited for. On August 23 the troops commenced to embark for France. Many, alas! were never to see the full fruit of their sacrifice ; but the spirit in which they had trained for war, and the determination expressed to the King by General Babington, were to endure in the Division to the end.

The following pages are written with the aim of showing in what way the 23rd Division justified the words of their commander.

PART II. FRANCE

THE SECOND YEAR

CHAPTER I.

THE entrainment and embarkation of the Division was carried out Map. No. 1. without hitch. Certain of the conscripts of the Division—the horses —gave some trouble by refusing to drag their waggons to the station, but these were successfully man-handled while their teams sullenly followed in rear.

The artillery, mounted personnel, and transport of the Division embarked at Southampton for Havre ; staffs and infantry brigades embarked at Folkestone for Boulogne.

The spirits of the conscripts revived during the perfect passage across the Channel to an extent that prompted one of these to plunge into the dock on arrival at Havre. The horse proved to be an expert swimmer, and having been secured to a raft was hauled ashore. But for this incident disembarkation at both ports passed off as smoothly as had embarkation in England.

Orders had been issued for the Division to concentrate in the Tilques area, in the neighbourhood of St Omer.

Concentration was completed by August 31, when the Division was included with the Guards and 24th Divisions to form the XI. Corps, whose headquarters were at St Omer.

More fortunate than Divisions which earlier in the war had of necessity been thrown almost straight into battle on disembarkation, the 23rd Division now had a few days in which to settle down on foreign soil. Advantage was taken of this period to collect the few stores still necessary to complete the equipment of units, and to carry on training

before engaging in the serious business of war. The officers of the Royal
Engineers and of the Pioneer Battalion made a tour of inspection of the
defences of the Second Army, and a Field Company, together with 1150
men drawn from infantry battalions, was employed in the construction
of rear defences.

On August 27 the 23rd Division Signalling Company, commanded
by Major F. A. Iles, laid their first line in France, the first of hundreds
of miles to be reeled out by a unit whose services to the Division during
the war were unsurpassed.

Training was influenced by the species of warfare that had resulted
from the opposing armies having been brought face to face in assault
positions on the whole length of the Western Front, with their flanks
resting on neutral territory in the south and on the sea in the north.
The observer who attempted to view the enemy's trenches by daylight
from above his own parapet became a certain prey to the sniper. The
infantry holding the forward defences on both sides remained, therefore, concealed in deep trenches while the front was watched through
periscopes. So protected, the enemy could only be attacked by high-
angle fire. The rifle, which had served us so well in the early phase of
the war, had lost its rôle, and it had come to be neglected more and
more in favour of the trench-mortar and bomb. We were no longer
dependent on disused jam-tins filled with explosives as a means of reply-
ing to the German bomber. Stick-bombs had been available for a considerable time, and the Mill's bomb had since been introduced ; but
there was still to be a great development both in the hand and rifle-
grenade. The trench-mortar in use was still crude.

During the hours of daylight, throughout the hundreds of square
miles over which the forward defences of the opposing Armies lay, no
living thing was seen above ground ; but if at midnight the world by
a sudden twist had brought the light of the sun on this same area a very
different scene would have been disclosed. In the moments that followed
such a phenomenon the heads of sentries all along the line would have
been seen to duck below their parapet ; wiring parties and patrols, sent
out under cover of darkness, would have been witnessed rushing to
safety from No Man's Land ; parties bringing forward rations and
ammunition would have been found leaping to the protection of the
nearest cover. After dark the area was peopled with targets for direct

fire. But here again the rifle was at a disadvantage as compared with the machine-gun, with its greater accuracy in night firing. The machine-gun at this period was mainly employed in sweeping the enemy's parapet by night, and in preventing the repair, under cover of darkness, of the gaps in the wire made by the artillery during the day.[1]

Senior officers and battalion machine-gun officers were then sent straightway to a course at the G.H.Q. Machine-gun School to learn the latest methods, and arrangements were made for others to attend bombing and trench-mortar schools.

On September 5 orders were received for the attachment of the Division to the III. Corps, whose front lay east and south-east of Armentières. On the following day the Division moved to the Haze-brouck-Arques area, with headquarters at Renescure, and continued the march on September 7 to the Borré-Vieux Berquin area, where Divisional Headquarters were established at Merris. This two days' march, carried out in oppressive heat, proved the Division to be still somewhat raw. There was a good deal of straggling and lack of the march discipline on which the Division in later days was to be congratulated on more than one occasion. But the test was severe, some units covering as many as twenty-one miles a day in full marching order, and much of it on pavé roads.

Trench training commenced on September 8 with the attachment to the 20th and 27th Divisions of the Divisional Artillery, the 101st and 102nd Field Companies R.E., and the 70th and 71st Field Ambulances. On the same day the infantry of the Division was inspected by Lieut.-General Pulteney, commanding the III. Corps.

On September 9 " A " and " Q " Staff of the Division and the 68th Infantry Brigade were attached to the 20th Division, the General Staff of the Division, R.A. Staff, and the 69th and 70th Infantry Brigades, to the 27th Division.

On September 12 Brig.-General Sir David Kinloch, who had gained the deep respect and affection of the 70th Infantry Brigade by his constant devotion to their interests from the date of their formation, was relieved by Brig.-General L. Philips of the 60th Rifles.

Its tour of attachment having been completed, the Division received orders to take over the left sector of the III. Corps front from the

---

[1] Machine-guns still formed part of the establishment of an infantry battalion.

27th Division. The front of this sector, which had a length of some 4500 yards, extended from a point 300 yards south of the Ferme Grande Flamengrie to the Armentières-Wez Macquart road.

At this time it was regarded as a " peaceful " front ; but such peace as had hitherto been enjoyed was shortly, as will be seen, to be disturbed.

On September 14 the 70th Infantry Brigade relieved the 82nd Infantry Brigade in the left section, with headquarters at Rue Marle, just south of Armentières, and on the following day the 69th Infantry Brigade took over the right section, with headquarters at Erquinghem.

On the 16th General Babington assumed command of the sector, and established his headquarters at Croix du Bac.

On the 17th the 68th Infantry Brigade and 9th (Pioneer) Battalion South Staffordshire Regiment rejoined the Division, the 68th Infantry Brigade being placed in Divisional reserve in billets and bivouac between l'Hallobeau and Erquinghem, the pioneers taking over billets at Fort Rompu.

The defensive system consisted of a front line, which, except for a short length of trench on the right, was formed by a continuous line of breast-work ; a close support line of trench, wired throughout and furnishing dug-outs for 75 per cent of the front-line garrison ; and the Bois Grenier (reserve) line, a continuous line of breast-work, 1000 yards in rear of the front line, partially wired, with fire bays at intervals, and containing dug-outs. Six main communication trenches connected the Bois Grenier line to the front line. There were, in addition, numerous short lengths of communication trench between the front and support line.

The defence was continued in rear by the La Vesée and l'Armee branches, chains of fortified posts, which formed switches to the Bois Grenier line.

The enemy had considerable advantage in observation. Our gun positions, which were mostly in hedges or orchards, and, on the left of the line, among houses and brick-stacks, were very exposed, and concealment of flashes was difficult.

Infantry brigades in the line held the front line with two battalions, of which the bulk was disposed in the front and close support lines. Machine-guns of these battalions were sited mostly in the front line. Remaining battalions were disposed in reserve, in occupation of the fortified posts in rear. The Bois Grenier line was garrisoned mainly by machine-guns; included in these were guns of No. 6 Motor Machine-gun Battery, which, together with the 17th and 21st Trench Howitzer Batteries and two cars of No. 14 Squadron R.N.A.S., had been attached to the Division.

One Field Ambulance, with headquarters at Fort Rompu, was made responsible for clearing the whole line. Casualties were brought down communication trenches from regimental aid-posts by the Field Ambulance bearers to an advanced dressing-station situated in the cellars of a house in Bois Grenier. Thence they were cleared by car after dark to a dressing-station established in a good barn and the out-houses of a farm at Fort Rompu.

Provided time is unlimited and ground favourable, the advantages of trenches over breast-works are manifest. But the defensive system now taken over had been developed during the dry weather of the late spring and summer. Even without the experience gained in the previous winter, a heavy thunder-shower was sufficient to prove the necessity for making provision for the approaching autumn and winter, when this low-lying country would be water-logged by heavy rains. Work was directed, therefore, to the construction of above-ground communication avenues and of a new breast-work support line. The defended localities, which constituted the rear lines of defences, were to be organised for all-round defence by the construction of breast-work; in the several buildings which existed in the sector, house-to-house cellar defence was to be arranged. Throughout special attention was to be given to drainage.

To assist in the forward work one company of pioneers was attached to each brigade in the line, while the 102nd and 128th Field Companies R.E. were allotted to the right and left sections respectively for super-vision of work and for the construction of rear defences.

A weak point in the sector, both from an offensive and defensive point of view, lay in the restriction to movement across the River Lys, which was confined to the Erquinghem road bridge. Preparations were accordingly made for the construction of three pontoon bridges for forward and two for rearward movement. Material for these was col-lected ready to hand, the footings of the bridges placed in position, and the 101st Field Company detailed to be prepared to construct the bridges should occasion require.

The optimist, or at any rate the lazy optimist, was doubtless impatient with all this work on defences. How many infantrymen have not reflected during the long hours of digging, sand-bagging, and carrying interminable rolls of barbed wire—" What's the use of patching up these filthy old trenches when we're going to leave 'em all behind in a few days' time ? " Indeed it was difficult at times, with your eyes strained to Berlin and your heart on the Tyneside, to go on digging yourself in in the Bois Grenier !

For there had been vague rumours of a coming British offensive —rumours which came to a head on September 19 with the receipt of an order from III. Corps.

By this it was learnt that the First Army, assuming the offensive, was to advance between Lens and La Bassee Canal towards the line Henin Lietard-Carvin. Corps north of the canal were to engage the enemy to prevent withdrawal of troops for counter-attack. With this intention the 8th Division, in the centre of the III. Corps, was to capture the enemy's line between Corner Fort and Bridoux Fort ; while on its right and left the 20th and 23rd Divisions were to co-operate by fire, and to be prepared to exploit success by an assault of the trenches on their front.

The attack of the battle of Loos was to be delivered on September 25. It was to be preceded by a four days' bombardment. At a conference held at the headquarters of the 8th Division, arrangements were made for the attachment of the 103rd and 105th Brigades R.F.A. to the 8th Division to assist in their operation.

The total number of rounds allotted per gun calculated on the basis of four days' bombardment, two days' battle, and four days' subsequent fighting, was—

	H.E.	Shrapnel.
For 18-pdr. guns	112	338
4.5" howitzers	336	15

On September 21 the artillery bombardment opened on the enemy's wire, front line, and support line. In considering the enormous expenditure of artillery ammunition later in the war, the ammunition allotted per gun for September 21 is interesting.[1] It reads :—

---

[1] Compare expenditure during period July 5 to August 14, 1916, recorded later in this book —viz., 480 rounds per gun in four and a half hours as a common occurrence, and 30,000 rounds fired in twelve hours by the 18-pdrs. of 23rd Divisional Artillery alone.

H. Oakley.

A DUG-OUT IN
RESERVE TRENCHES
ARMENTIERES SECTOR
1915.

For batteries shooting at salients .   . 30 H.E.
    12 S.
For other batteries .   .   .   .   . 12 H.E.
    50 S.
C/102 counter-battery   .   .   . . 30 S.

The enemy replied feebly during the 21st and 22nd, but his field artillery became more active on September 23.

The weather on September 24 continued fine, but with a light wind and haze. About 5 A.M. the enemy was active with rifle-bombs, but limited his action for the remainder of the day to a desultory artillery fire. At 4 P.M. Divisional Headquarters moved to La Rolanderie Farm, where an advanced headquarters had been prepared for the purpose both of offensive and defensive battle. Brigade Headquarters took up advanced positions in the Bois Grenier, and near the Chapelle d'Armentières.

At 7 P.M. " A," " B," and " C " pontoon bridges were thrown across the Lys. At 10 P.M. two armoured cars, attached to the Division, moved forward to a position near Burnt Farm, and opened a burst of fire on the German trenches with their 3-pdr. guns. To this the enemy made no reply.

On the night of September 24-25 the infantry of the Division was disposed as follows :—

In the right section the 10th Duke of Wellington's Regiment and 8th Yorkshire Regiment occupied the front line ; the 9th Yorkshire Regiment were in support in the Bois Grenier line ; the 11th West Yorkshire Regiment was in reserve some 3000 yards in rear of the right of the front line at Rue Delettre.

In the left section the front line was held by the 11th Sherwood Foresters and the 8th K.O. Yorkshire Light Infantry ; the 8th York and Lancaster Regiment, in support, occupied the Bois Grenier line ; while the 9th York and Lancaster Regiment, in reserve, held two companies in a central position 2000 yards in rear of the front line in the La Vesée branch, and two companies at Rue Marle, about two miles in rear of the left.

Zero hour for the operation on the front of the 23rd Division had been fixed for 4.50 A.M. Six minutes after zero a smoke barrage was to be opened along the whole front, and maintained for twenty-eight minutes. This barrage was to be formed by the primitive means of smoke-candles and of smoke-bombs hurled by hand and giant catapult. The latter ingenious device, borrowed from the early Romans, was more the terror of the operator than of the enemy. The new lease of life to which it had been resuscitated proved short, and its future revival is improbable.

At 3.30 A.M. orders were received postponing zero hour till 5.50 A.M. Except for the artillery bombardment, the first action taken by the 23rd Division would now not occur till just one and a half hours after the assault of the 8th Division, which had been fixed for 4.30 A.M.

The morning was misty and dark. Little more than the outline of the enemy's trenches was visible at 4.25 A.M., when the artillery bombardment opened. A mountain artillery gun, sited in our front-line parapet, opened a rapid fire on a salient in the hostile front line. The vicinity of this gun was later heavily shelled by 4.2 and 77 mm. shells, but it is thought that this was by chance, and that its position was not observed.

At 4.30 A.M. the 25th Infantry Brigade of the 8th Division assaulted, and two minutes later had carried the enemy's front-line trenches.

The enemy's artillery retaliated heavily on the right section of the 23rd Division, but the left section remained fairly quiet throughout the day.

At 5.56 A.M. the smoke-candles were set in action, and the barrage was maintained for the next half-hour by steadily throwing forward the 1900 smoke-bombs which had been supplied to each brigade for the purpose. No sooner had our barrage cleared than the Germans retaliated with a smoke barrage from their side. The wind is a vital factor in smoke operations. That it was possible for a smoke-screen to be formed in the narrow limits of No Man's Land from opposite directions, within so short a space of time, shows what a shifty and doubtful factor the wind was on the day of the battle of Loos.

At 9 A.M. good reports were received of the progress of the main attack of the First Army. But by then aeroplane reports had also been received of the arrival of ten trains in Lille, and of considerable movement westward of German reinforcements.

Artillery work had been hampered from the first by bad visibility. Mist continued to hang over the ground all day, not only making observation practically impossible, but communication a matter of the greatest difficulty, as telephone wires were continually cut.

Though the 8th Division had been unable to maintain their position in the enemy's trenches, hostile artillery fire had slackened considerably by 10 A.M. Two of the batteries lent to the 8th Division were returned before noon. Except for some shelling of Water Farm, on the extreme right of the sector, the situation on the 23rd Division front quietened during the afternoon, and there was no event to record for the remainder of the day.

This was the first occasion on which the 23rd Divisional Artillery supported an infantry attack. The brigades attached to the 8th Division had in particular done good work. A/105 Battery (Major Shaw) had been heavily shelled, and suffered severe casualties. A direct hit destroyed their No. 1 gun, and killed the greater number of its detachment. The first decorations awarded for gallantry to the Divisional Artillery (and, it is believed, to the Division) were won this day, Lieutenant Van Grutten, who had acted as F.O.O. to the 103rd Brigade, receiving the Military Cross, and Battery Sergeant-Major Keeley of the 105th Brigade the Distinguished Conduct Medal.

To his great chagrin the officer commanding the 105th Brigade ammunition column, in recognition of *his* services on September 25, was at a later date awarded a fine of 250 francs. The circumstances which led to this lack of appreciation were as follows. Warned to move at short notice and finding his transport inadequate, he procured three large French farm-carts, which were loaded sky-high with fuel and 4.5 ammunition boxes. Had his energy and initiative stopped there, all might have been well. But the spirit of commandeering once roused is not easily quelled. Finding a fashionable " Victoria " lying idle, he could not resist adding it as a finishing touch to his caravan. After distinguished service in battle, the " Victoria " appeared a few days later in Armentières in all the pride of a new coat of service grey paint and smart postilions. Despite its disguise it was immediately identified by a zealous gendarme as the carriage of no less a person than the Mayor of Armentières, and was dragged back to lead its old dull humdrum existence. In assessing the damages no consideration was given either to the exigencies of the service or the new coat of paint.

September 26 opened with fog, but at 10 A.M. the weather turned

bright, and remained fine till 5 P.M., when mist again fell. Except for
some shelling by the German heavy artillery, the day remained quiet.
During the day the 68th Infantry Brigade was detached to the 20th
Division, together with one company of the 23rd Divisional Train.
In the event of the main attack of the First Army meeting with
such complete success as to carry the line forward to the Haute Deule
Canal, an advance by the III. Corps had been contemplated. In this
case the 23rd Division had been prepared to exploit success by an attack
on the Bois Blanc, and subsequently on Trois Fétus, which was to be
carried by the 69th Infantry Brigade. The right flank of such an attack
would be secured by an advance of the 8th Division on Maisnil and
Radinghem, while on the right again the 20th Division would advance
with the Aubers Ridge as their objective.

Events, however, had not justified these further operations, and on
September 27 orders were received to husband ammunition. Divisional
Headquarters returned to Croix du Bac, and the pontoon bridges across
the Lys were removed. The 68th Infantry Brigade rejoined the Division
on the following day, but were again sent to reinforce the 20th Division,
who had been called on to extend their front to the right. Active operations in connection with the Loos offensive, so far as the 23rd Division
was concerned, were at an end.

All detached artillery had now returned, and Divisional Artillery
was organised again into two groups to cover the front. " A " Group,
in support of the right section, was formed by the 102nd Brigade (less
" C " Battery), and the 103rd Brigade (less " B " Battery). " B " Group,
in support of the left section, consisted of the 104th Brigade, B/103,
and C/102 (counter-battery). The 105th (Howitzer) Brigade remained
under the orders of the C.R.A., but was at the direct call of either group
commander in case of emergency.

No one who has studied the field of Loos, where troops of the New
Armies were engaged in their first big battle, can fail to be impressed
by the magnitude of the task set them, or to realise the determination
and valour that enabled the troops to accomplish what they did. The
open Le Rutoire Plain and the succession of glacis slopes across which
lay the advance to the German forward positions; the town of Loos,
with its cellars and dug-outs; and the commanding position of Hill 70,
which lay beyond, all combined to render attack a most formidable

operation. The artillery bombardment, though regarded in those days
as heavy, could in no way compare with the devastating fire which in
the later days of the war prepared the way for the infantry attack. The
capture of the German positions on September 25 must always rank as
one of the finest feats of the war. The success gained was due to the
spirit of the troops engaged ; failure to exploit this success was due to
causes for which the troops were in no way responsible.

The 23rd Division played only a subsidiary part in the battle ; only
if success had been more complete would it have been called on to play
a more important rôle. But for the Division the battle of Loos had this
great significance—it had shown what the soldiers of the New Army
could accomplish.

For the rest, the fact that greater results had not been obtained now
chiefly affected the 23rd Division in persuading the optimist that he
must be reconciled to remain a while longer in the Bois Grenier, and
so heartening him to get on with his digging and wiring. There was
ample scope for work. Names such as Wine Avenue, Cowgate, Shaftes-
bury Avenue, and Park Row must be indelibly graven on the memory
of Lieut.-Colonel A. G. Bremner, who at this time took over the responsible duties of C.R.E. from Lieut.-Colonel P. J. Radcliffe on the
appointment of the latter to G.H.Q.

The 68th Infantry Brigade returned from the 20th Division on October
4 to relieve the 69th Infantry Brigade in the right section. The latter
brigade, on withdrawing to Divisional reserve, detached the 11th West
Yorkshire Regiment and the 9th Yorkshire Regiment to strengthen the
20th Division. This arrangement, by which two battalions of the reserve
brigade were placed at Estaires at the disposal of the 20th Division,
continued during the next month.

The early part of the month was marked by occasional gusts of anger
on the part of the enemy's artillery. On October 3 some sixty shells
were fired into the front line of the left section, and a week later a light
bombardment was continued on our whole front for one and a half
hours. But the first three weeks of October passed, on the whole, very
quietly. Our ammunition supply was now sufficiently plentiful to return
two shells for every German one.

Advantage was taken of such hostile artillery fire as occurred to
locate the German batteries. Counter-battery work, as organised later

C

in the war, with its elaborate system for locating guns by sound-ranger and flash-spotting, was not yet practised ; aeroplane photography was in its infancy. Special night observation posts were, however, established to locate the flashes of the enemy's guns, and precautions were at the same time taken to conceal the flashes of our own by thickening hedges, and by placing single guns at some distance from battery positions at night. The efforts of our artillery were so far successful as to have located fairly definitely nine hostile batteries by the end of the month by means of sound, flash, shell-hole bearings, fuzes, and photographs.

In these days co-operation between Divisional Artillery and the Heavy Artillery was mainly carried out by mutual arrangement. The Division was fortunate in having very helpful Heavy Artillery commanders to deal with, among whom Lieut.-Colonel Logan, in charge of counter-battery work, was conspicuous.

A scheme was now instituted for the training of the new troops in the III. Corps by their association with those of more experienced units. By this the composition of the Division was to undergo a slight alteration during the ensuing nine months. This was the only alteration made in the composition of the Division throughout the war, till towards the end of the final year it was deprived of three of its infantry battalions. In pursuance of this scheme, the 70th Infantry Brigade was transferred on October 18 to the 8th Division, where its battalions were temporarily exchanged with others of the brigades of that Division. It was replaced in the 23rd Division by the 24th Infantry Brigade (Brig.-General Oxley), which was composed of the 1st Worcestershire Regiment, 2nd Northants Regiment, 2nd East Lancashire Regiment, and 1st Sherwood Foresters. The two last-named battalions were temporarily transferred to the 68th and 69th Infantry Brigades respectively, being replaced in the 24th Infantry Brigade by the 13th Durham Light Infantry and 10th Duke of Wellington's Regiment.

This scheme of interchange of battalions continued till November 14, when brigades resumed their normal composition. The 70th Infantry Brigade, however, remained detached from the 23rd Division till July 16, 1916.

The advantage of the arrangements were not all on one side. The 8th Division had passed through the miseries of the winter of 1914 and the ordeal of Neuve Chapelle ; and Lieut.-Colonel B. C. M. Western, later of the 23rd Division, but at that time with the 8th, relates how the arrival of the keen and enthusiastic 23rd Division acted like a tonic to the war-worn weary men who had been holding the enemy for months while the New Army was being trained and equipped. "They" (the 23rd Division), he writes, "were never happy unless they were patrolling No Man's Land, sniping, or arranging some special 'hate' in the form of trench-mortaring or rifle-grenading. They also introduced to the 8th Division the Lewis-gun, and we were greatly impressed with its usefulness."

At this date there were only four Lewis-guns in each infantry battalion. The Division was still armed with long rifles ; misfires were frequent, and a great amount of attention was needed to keep them serviceable. A partial issue of short rifles to the infantry was arranged early in October by withdrawing these from the personnel of the R.A., A.S.C., A.O.C., and A.V.C., but the infantry were not rearmed throughout till the following February. In his struggle to rearm the Division and to obtain the various articles of new equipment which were being introduced, Major W. S. G. Bishop, the D.A.D.O.S., had a hard time. Steel helmets, thigh gum-boots, trench braziers, tube-helmets were among the many requirements for protection against the onslaughts of the enemy and the weather.

Tube-helmets replaced respirators at the end of September. One wonders whether the designers of anti-gas appliances were influenced solely by ideas of protection, or if they also sought the same moral effect in which the bearskins and busbies of the old European armies had their origin. The open countenance of the young British soldier is certainly not calculated to inspire terror in the enemy ; the addition of a respirator merely suggested that he was asthmatic. But with his head tied up in a tube-helmet he presented a truly terrifying aspect, though this again was mild in comparison with the monstrous appearance lent by the final box-respirator.

Though the enemy's artillery had become more active towards the end of October, our artillery bombardments as a rule evoked little retaliation. The weather had become unsettled during the month, and November opened with heavy rains. The misery of mud and of flooded trenches and gun positions increased daily.

A party of eight munition workers from the Division's recruiting districts visited the trenches on November 8. It was perhaps as well that life in the trenches should not be presented in its rosiest colours to these, or to the eight Members of Parliament who floundered in the mud of the sector five days later.

That resource is a no less valuable quality in an officer on such occasions than in battle was illustrated by an incident during the latter visit. An artillery officer had been detailed to demonstrate the perfect arrangements that existed for the response of the guns to an S.O.S. call. The first call was answered with the most amazing promptitude. As the shells came whistling overhead the demonstrator was moved to give a second exhibition. With more experience he might have known that he was tempting Providence. The second call produced no result. Not a gun spoke to break the silence which had fallen on our own and the enemy's lines. It was an embarrassing situation, in which many would have become flustered. Not so our artillery officer, who, quite unperturbed, turned to the company and remarked, "There! I have shown you one instance of how things should be done, and one of how they should not."

For instruction in "how things should be done and how they should not," a Divisional School of Instruction was established about this time at Steenwercke. This necessitated the transference of the headquarters of the reserve brigade to Erquinghem.

The front of the III. Corps had now been shortened, and it was decided to hold it with two divisions instead of the three hitherto employed. On November 23 the 8th Division was withdrawn from the centre, and the 23rd Division extended its right some 1200 yards to join up with the 20th Division, who made a similar extension of its left. Shortly before, the 21st Division had relieved the 50th Division on our left.

A short spell of fine weather about the middle of the month had ended with a hard frost, followed by rain. The weather turned bitterly cold, with frequent fog. The enemy's infantry remained very quiet, and his artillery action was confined to occasional bombardments.

Despite the weather conditions patrolling was carried out nightly in the narrow muddy stretch of ground which separated the German from the British lines. The first Victoria Cross awarded to the 23rd

Division was earned in the course of this work by Private Kenny of the 13th Durham Light Infantry. An account of his action will illustrate the conditions under which patrolling was carried out and the danger of the work.

When on patrol in a thick fog on the night of November 4, Lieutenant Brown of the same battalion came up against some Germans who were lying in a ditch in front of their parapet. These opened fire, and wounded Lieutenant Brown through both thighs. Kenny, who accompanied him, took the officer on his back, and, though heavily and repeatedly fired upon, crawled about for over an hour with his burden trying to find his way through the fog to our trenches. More than once Lieutenant Brown begged him to leave him and return alone, but he refused to do so.

At last, coming to a ditch which he recognised, he placed the officer in it and went to look for help. He found an officer and a few men of his battalion at a listening post, and guided them back to where Lieutenant Brown lay. The Germans again opened heavy rifle and machine-gun fire, and hurled bombs at a range of thirty yards, but with the assistance he had gained Private Kenny brought the officer safely to the British lines.

Early in December very bad weather, with wind and rain, set in. The one bright sunny day, the 8th, was marred by a heavy hostile bombardment, when Erquinghem for the first time received the attention of the German artillery. Forty 5.9 shells were fired into the village, but the casualties were, fortunately, not heavy.

By the 12th the continual rain had produced serious results. The River Laies, a tributary of the Lys, which ran through the sector, was six feet deep, and the Lys itself was in the highest flood known for twenty years. The most arduous labour was necessary to maintain the sector in a condition in any degree habitable, and the Royal Engineers had to be taken off the work of constructing huts in the reserve area to assist in work on the front line.

Conditions in the back areas were only less appalling than in the trenches. Artillery waggon lines and transport lines generally had been converted into a sea of mud. The lot of the officers who were in charge of these was far from enviable. In their efforts to keep their animals in comfort and themselves out of trouble they found themselves between the devil and the deep sea. " There was more than a touch

of the miser in the C.R.E. as regards hoarding material," we are told
by the C.R.A. "Very little could be obtained from his store." The
alternative was to acquire derelict or, more properly speaking, un-
guarded material wherever found.[1] Court-martial threatened any one
caught in the act of adopting this alternative. Nor did the righteous
escape censure if substantial progress in the construction of standings,
cook-houses, harness-rooms, &c., was not found by higher authority in
its periodical visits—slackness and lack of initiative were some of the
milder epithets applied to the unfortunate officer whose conscience
had forbidden him to "find things lying about."

The perennial question "to clip or not to clip," which was to form
a subject of heated controversy in each successive winter of the war,
had already been dealt with by the Divisional Commander, who had
no hesitation in deciding on the second alternative. The appearance
and condition of the horses in the following spring were to prove the
wisdom of his decision. There were few commanders better qualified
to advise on matters of horsemastership than General Babington, and
the animals of the Division owed no less than the men to his constant
care. In the hands of Lieut.-Colonel A. Northen, who was to remain
with the Division till the final year of the war, the heavy draught-horses
of the Divisional Train were second to none. Major F. L. Melhuish,
A.V.C., as D.A.D.V.S. at this period, was responsible for the care of
the sick animals.

The Germans had long since been suspected of conducting mining
operations against this front, and a detachment of the 108th Tunnelling
Company had been attached to the Division during October. The
knowledge that one is possibly directly over an enemy mine adds not
a little to the discomfort of trench life. On the early morning of December
19 the Germans exploded a mine on the front of the 21st Division, about
1100 yards from our left, and an hour later commenced to bombard
the Lille-Armentières road and the left of the 23rd Division. By 12 noon
our artillery succeeded in silencing their bombardment. Later in the
day the Germans attempted to occupy the crater, but failed.

Christmas Day in the line passed very quietly. Plenty of good
things had been sent out for the troops from home ; football matches

[1] It would be interesting to hear the comments of Colonel Bremner, the C.R.E., on the
C.R.A. and the Divisional Artillery at this period.

and sing-songs were organised for those out of the line, and the prospect of home leave, which had by now started in earnest, served in no
small degree to counteract the depressing influence of the weather.
As an expression of goodwill, the enemy's long-range guns shelled the
artillery waggon lines around the Erquinghem Canal.   Many of the
shells fell in the canal, their explosions bringing up a quantity of fish.
Fried fish and chips formed an unexpected extra to several Christmas
suppers.

The first number of the 'Dump,' the 23rd Division's Christmas
Annual, appeared at this time.

Recently a new feature had been introduced into trench warfare,
which in the future course of the war was to bring into prominence
the courage, coolness, and resource of the young British officer.   Hitherto
attack had been confined to operations for the capture and retention of
some hostile position.   The idea of the raid had now occurred almost
simultaneously to ourselves and the Germans : a minor operation,
carefully planned and rehearsed, designed to enter the enemy's trenches
by surprise, to destroy his garrison and defences, secure prisoners, and
withdraw.

Though several such enterprises had already been undertaken both
by the British and Germans, it seemed that the enemy in certain portions
of the line were still unprepared for this form of attack.   Trenches had
been entered where officers and men were found without equipment,
and where a general slackness was apparent.

Plans had been made to raid the German trenches on the 23rd Division
front on the night of December 31 and January 1.   In preparation for
this the artillery had been employed during the preceding week in cutting wire at selected spots, and in destroying suspected machine-gun
emplacements in the enemy's lines.

The objects of the operation were laid down as :—

1. To kill Germans.   2. To capture prisoners.   3. To destroy important work in the trenches.

To assist in the third object a party of the Royal Engineers with
explosive charges were to be included in the raiding party.   Any idea
of attaining this to the extent desired had, however, to be abandoned,
owing to a most unfortunate incident on the afternoon of December 31.
Lieutenant E. W. Ruse, R.E., was superintending the preparation of

gun-cotton for demolitions, in the field store of the 128th Field Company R.E., when an explosion occurred which resulted in the death of this officer and four of his men, and the wounding of twenty-eight others.

The operation was to take the form of simultaneous raids on two salients in the German front line. That on the right, on the front of the 68th Infantry Brigade, lay opposite the Ferme de la Flamengerie ; that on the left, on the front of the 69th Infantry Brigade, was situated just north of German House, a ruined building in the enemy's front line on the eastern edge of the village of Rue du Bois, and about 500 yards east of the Armentières-Wavrin railway.

When darkness fell on December 31 the night was still and starlit. The enemy appeared very alert. Flares were rising continually from all along the hostile line, and three searchlights, sweeping No Man's Land, added to the difficulties of the raiders.

The raiding party of the 68th Brigade, which was composed of 6 officers and 110 other ranks of the 10th Northumberland Fusiliers, under the command of Captain Norfolk, was divided into three parties. A covering party, under Lieutenant Hird, was already in position when the party detailed for the assault, under Lieutenant Allan, left our trenches at 12.25 A.M. It was followed five minutes later by a blocking party under Lieutenant Jacobs. Cautiously and very slowly the raiders crept toward the hostile line. At 1.10 A.M. Jacobs' party was, unfortunately, observed. The enemy's searchlights swept down on the raiders. Red and white lights sprang from the German lines, and intense rifle and machine-gun fire was opened on the attack, followed shortly by artillery fire. Captain Norfolk was wounded, and it was realised that it would be useless to proceed with an enterprise which had depended on surprise for success. The raid was abandoned, and the party withdrew, bringing back their killed and wounded.

Though this party had failed to attain its main object, its action, by distracting the attention of the enemy, assisted the raid which was being carried out in the meantime on the front of the 69th Infantry Brigade.

The party operating on this flank was composed of 5 officers and 100 other ranks of the 9th Yorkshire Regiment, under the command of Major Prior. It had been ascertained that the wire covering the enemy's line at the proposed point of entry had not been completely cut. At

9.30 P.M. 2nd Lieutenant Armitage was sent forward with Sergeant Crowther and Privates Dixon, Gettings, and Kett to clear the way. At 11.30 P.M. the officer, leaving his men in position, returned to report that a five-foot gap had been cut, and that the way was clear up to the enemy's front line. At 12.15 A.M. the raiders filed out of the trenches to their position of assembly, and commenced to crawl towards the German lines, picking up the wire cutters, who were to act as guides.

At 1.33 A.M. our artillery put down a barrage on the enemy's support line and flank barrages on either side of the point of entry, and the infantry rushed the front line. A large number of the raiders lost direction, and only some thirty-five men actually entered the trenches. One party, under Lieutenant Gibson, turned right, in accordance with plan. They found the trench sparsely occupied, but accounted with bomb and bayonet for four of the enemy. A second party, under Captain Thomson, turning left, encountered some resistance. This was speedily overcome, and fifteen Germans were killed. At 1.48 A.M. the whole raiding party withdrew under heavy rifle fire, covered by the fire of our artillery, whose programme had worked to perfection in support of the operation.

The casualties suffered by the raiding party were very light, amounting to a total of seven men slightly wounded ; but some twenty-four casualties, including one officer and three other ranks killed, were sustained from hostile artillery fire brought on to our trenches in retaliation. This fire was so heavy that many of the raiders were unable to gain their lines till, in response to the slackening of our artillery fire, the enemy's fire died down.

As a means of concealment and also of identifying friend from foe, the raiders' faces were blackened on this occasion. A further precaution was taken in adopting the historic name of " Charlie Chaplin " as a password.

This was the first of many successful raids carried out by the 23rd Division during the war, the term " raid " being used in the sense of an operation undertaken with the object of entering but not of holding the enemy's trenches, and distinct from the action of fighting patrols against hostile parties in No Man's Land. It had attained its first object —the killing of Germans. Its third object had been rendered impossible before the operation commenced. That the raiders had failed to secure prisoners is not surprising. The capture of prisoners in such an operation is a difficult matter, requiring more experience than the killing of men. In a short hand-to-hand struggle in the dark, when hesitation to kill one's opponent may mean the loss of one's own or a comrade's life, to secure prisoners demands considerable skill and judgment. It was apparent as the war continued that, with greater experience and a better appreciation of the value of prisoners, the number captured in such operations increased.

Those who took part in these raids paraded on January 5 before the Corps Commander to receive his congratulations.

The first weeks of January were uneventful. In the reciprocal artillery fire that continued without cease we seldom fired less than four shells to each shell of the Germans. A 6-inch gun had been sited well forward in order to shell Lille by night. Our 18-pdrs. were employed in firing from open positions simultaneously with this big gun, in order to distract attention from its flash.

Two smoke demonstrations were carried out—one on January 9 by the 24th Infantry Brigade, in conjunction with an operation of the 20th Division ; the other, on the left of the sector, on January 14 induced the enemy to line his parapet, and so to afford targets for the artillery.

Towards the end of the month hostile artillery fire greatly increased, as many as 2000 shells being distributed all over the area on the 27th and again on the 28th. There was further heavy shelling on January 29 ; but on this, as on every occasion, our ammunition expenditure in reply was made to exceed the enemy's. This was the only form of protest which really appealed to the Germans, but it did not invariably appeal to our own "next highest formation" to the same degree. It will be remembered that the C.R.A. did not favour "miserliness" ; an interview before breakfast with the Corps Commander after the generous response to the Germans on January 29 persuaded him that if he did not curb his spendthrift proclivities he might expect a free ticket to England. He exercised great restraint after this, till the next time !

The Divisional Artillery now had a new brigade-major. Major A. K. Hay, who was to serve on the staff in the Division almost to the end of the war, had recently arrived to fill the place of Captain Clibborn,

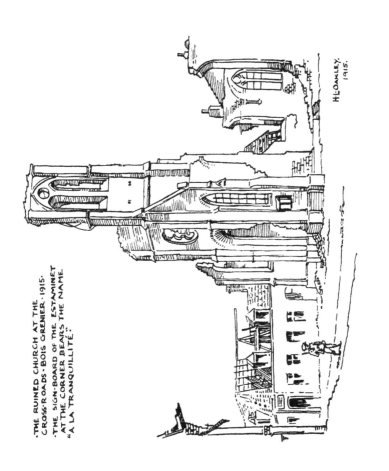

·THE RUINED CHURCH AT THE
CROSS-ROADS · BOIS GRENIER · 1915·
·THE SIGN-BOARD OF THE ESTAMINET
AT THE CORNER BEARS THE NAME.
"A LA TRANQUILLITÉ."

H.L.OAKLEY.
1915.

a charming and most promising officer, who had unfortunately been killed by a chance shell while going round the front trenches.

On January 20 Colonel Blair, who had come out to France with the Division as G.S.O. 1, was forced by ill-health to return to England. He was replaced by Major C. F. Watson, hitherto G.S.O. 2 on the Divisional Staff.

The weather continued cheerless, with fog and mist. But the Division's first tour in the trenches, which had lasted over five months, was drawing to a close. Relief by the 34th Division had been ordered; but before they took over the sector it was necessary for the units of the Division, which had only recently arrived in France, to undergo a course of trench training. The 23rd Division had already played the part of instructors to a party of senior officers from the Irish command, and now performed the same office for the units of the 34th Division, whose attachment was carried out between January 26 and February 8.

On relief all units of the Division did not move direct to rest. A certain amount of marching and counter-marching took place ; the reasons for this have not been discovered, but the nature of the movements ordered seem to indicate an uncertainty as to the enemy's intentions on the III. Corps front.

On February 10 the 9th South Staffordshire Regiment, on relief by the pioneers of the 34th Division, were required to detach two companies to the 8th Division. The artillery reliefs commenced the following day. The 102nd Brigade R.F.A. on withdrawal were ordered to relieve certain batteries of the Guards Division, which were covering the 8th Division, to whom D/104 and C/105 Batteries were also lent. Headquarters of the Divisional Artillery moved back to Lynde.

Infantry reliefs at first followed a normal course. The 69th Infantry Brigade on relief was withdrawn from Divisional reserve to Vieux Berquin, and thence to Steenbecque, four miles south-west of Hazebrouck. Reliefs in the front line were completed on February 21 and 22, the 24th Infantry Brigade having been withdrawn by the latter date to Vieux Berquin, and the 68th Infantry Brigade to Divisional reserve. On the 22nd orders were received for the 68th Infantry Brigade to stand fast, and for headquarters of the Division and the Divisional Artillery, the 69th Infantry Brigade, and the 128th Field Company R.E. to move forward to Estaires.

These orders were carried out on the two following days. It looked as if the Division was to be given a "side slip" on this flat and dreary front in place of the rest which they had confidently expected. A snow-storm on February 25 did not serve to relieve the gloomy prospect. But on the 26th fresh orders directed the movement of the whole Division to the III. Corps Reserve area. Divisional Headquarters were established at Blaringhem on the following day, when further orders were received for the concentration of the Division in the Bruay area and its attachment to the IV. Corps.

It was in the course of these movements that Brig.-General H. Page-Croft assumed command of the 68th Infantry Brigade, which had been vacated by Brig.-General Pearce-Serocold.

Divisional Headquarters moved on February 29 to Bruay, where the 24th Infantry Brigade was also accommodated. It was the first time since its arrival in France in November 1914 that this brigade had been farther back than Divisional reserve. The 68th Infantry Brigade was billeted in Marles-les-Mines, the 69th Infantry Brigade at Ruitz, and the Royal Engineers at Camblain Chatelain (more familiar to the British soldier as "Charlie Chaplin"). The Divisional Artillery marched to Pernes, where they were joined on March 1 by the batteries which had been detached to the 8th Division.

At this time the officers of the Division had the privilege of attending a lecture given by the IV. Corps Commander, Lieut.-General (later Field-Marshal) Sir Henry Wilson, on the European situation in the present and before the war. His light style and keen wit, while never obscuring his deep knowledge of the matters on which he spoke or leaving any in doubt of the strength of his convictions, held his audience from the outset. But the late Sir Henry Wilson owed his brilliance as lecturer, above all, to his keen perception of the manner in which his words were affecting his hearers. On this occasion the appreciation of his audience was acknowledged by him in the following kind and characteristic letter :—

DEAR BABINGTON,—Could you convey to your officers how much I appreciated their most kind and courteous bearing this afternoon? I have seldom, if ever, had so charming an audience.—Very sincerely yours,

HENRY WILSON.

The weather was now very cold, and snow fell during the first few days, making warm billets the more appreciated in a country which to many in the Division had a peculiarly homely aspect. For they were now in the centre of a mining district, and General Page-Croft tells us that the pitmen of the 68th Infantry Brigade were not content till they had taken a turn at their old trade in the pits.

But warm billets and the neighbourhood of friendly pit-shafts were not to last for long. A southward extension of the British front had been arranged, and on March 3 orders were received for the Division to relieve the 17th French Division in the Carency sector on the Souchez front.

CHAPTER II.

THE SOUCHEZ FRONT.

MARCH 5 TO JUNE 16, 1916.

Map No. 1. THE front to which the 23rd Division had now been ordered had been the scene of the heroic and bloody battles of 1915, in which the French had driven the Germans from the spur of Notre Dame de Lorette across the Souchez Valley to the Vimy Ridge beyond. Fierce fighting had ensued for the crest of the Vimy Ridge, from which the French, unable to maintain their position, had recently been forced back to a line on the near slope.

Front-line defences on either side, where they existed at all, were of the crudest description. In a portion of the line they were represented by hastily organised positions in the craters created by the mine warfare which had been in force ; opposing outposts were, in places, within twenty yards of each other.

The front of the sector to be taken over, which extended from the Boyau de l'Ersatz on the right to the Souchez river, had a length of roughly 2000 yards, and lay on either side of a straight line drawn on the map to join the villages of Souchez and Givenchy. In addition to holding this sector, the Division would be responsible for garrisoning the defences of Notre Dame de Lorette, to the left and in rear of the Vimy position, from which it was separated by the valley of the Souchez river flowing north-east.

In defence of this position the Division was to be disposed in depth. In accordance with the orders for relief, the 69th Infantry Brigade would take over the forward defences, the 24th Infantry Brigade (less one battalion) would take up a position in support, and the 68th Infantry

Brigade would be disposed in reserve. The fourth battalion of the supporting brigade would occupy the Lorette defences.

On the 6th the 9th Yorkshire Regiment relieved the French in the left of the sector, and the 1st Sherwood Foresters took over the Lorette defences. The remainder of the 69th Infantry Brigade moved to the Servins area, and the artillery reliefs commenced.

Having regard to the organisation of the French artillery, the C.R.A. considered that it would facilitate relief to organise the 23rd Divisional artillery covering the position into three groups, each composed of three 18-pdr. and one 4.5 howitzer battery, and to retain a mixed brigade in reserve.

Gun positions, some of which were greatly exposed, were sited in the valleys about Carency and Ablain St Nazaire and in the Bois du Bouvigny. Howitzer positions had been found in the ravines cutting the southern slope of the Lorette Spur, which flanked the exposed road running forward through Ablain to Souchez. The batteries about Carency and Ablain St Nazaire were subjected to severe shelling, as the result of which A/103 lost a very gallant battery commander, Captain L. Jones Bateman.

On March 7 the 8th Yorkshire Regiment and the 11th West Yorkshire Regiment relieved the French in the right and centre of the line, and the 10th Duke of Wellington's moved to Villers au Bois in brigade reserve. Headquarters of the 69th Infantry Brigade were established in the shattered remains of Ablain St Nazaire, in whose ruins the 101st and 102nd Field Companies R.E. were also accommodated.

The 24th Infantry Brigade (less one battalion) occupied the Servins area, with headquarters at Chateau de la Haie.

The 68th Infantry Brigade moved to the reserve area on March 8. Headquarters were established at Fresnicourt, battalions disposed in Verdrel, Estrée Cauchie, and Hermin. On the same day the 128th Field Company R.E. moved to Carency, and, relief being complete, General Babington assumed command of the sector, with headquarters at Chateau de la Haie.

In this sector, which the 23rd Division was the first British division to occupy, the most perfect observation was open to both the enemy and ourselves. The advantage, perhaps, was on the side of the Allies, as the Lorette Spur, which overlooked the enemy's position, was farther removed from the front line than any position of equal value to the Germans. It was not, however, immune from the enemy's artillery fire, which proved to be active in shelling the observation posts established on the Spur and the Souchez and Carency valleys. Some trouble was also experienced in the front line from aerial torpedoes, but otherwise the sector was at this time quiet.

Indeed, the situation in the front line lent itself little to any activity on either side beyond a feverish effort to construct defences. Such situations had occurred before in the war, when the impossibility of carrying on trench warfare without trenches had led almost to a truce. The peace which had reigned on the front prior to our arrival was exemplified shortly after we took over. A tin of bully beef having been thrown into No Man's Land (an incident which would have been recognised as normal by Germans accustomed to being in front of the "starving" British soldiery), a German soldier emerged to retrieve what he took to be a peace-offering. The simultaneous arrival on the scene of a heavy trench-mortar bomb, however, could not be accepted in the same spirit. Fortune favoured the disillusioned Boche in its proving to be a "dud," and he escaped to his hole in record time, having suffered nothing worse than the fright of a lifetime.

Tunnelling work was at this time becoming increasingly important, not only for offensive and defensive mining, but for the construction of deep-mined dug-outs for the protection of trench garrisons. The Division, rich in miners, was required at the beginning of March to find the personnel for the formation of a Tunnelling Company.

On March 10 Brig.-General Derham, who had commanded the 69th Infantry Brigade since its first formation, handed over command of the brigade to Brig.-General T. S. Lambert. A change had also occurred in the Divisional Staff a few days earlier, Lieut.-Colonel Burne having been succeeded as A.A. and Q.M.G. by Bt. Lieut.-Colonel H. B. de V. Wilkinson, Durham Light Infantry.

The stay of the Division in the Carency sector was very short. The 24th Infantry Brigade had just relieved the 69th Infantry Brigade in the line, when orders were received for relief of the 23rd by the 47th Division. The 23rd Division was not to be withdrawn to rest, however, but was to take over the Noulette sector from the 2nd Division, immediately north of its present position.

Relief by the 47th Division commenced on March 13. Preparatory to taking over the new sector, the 23rd Division was withdrawn to the Bruay area, Divisional Headquarters being established at Bruay on March 16 on completion of the relief.

The front of the Noulette sector extended from the Souchez river on the right, across the lower slopes of the eastern point of the Lorette Spur, to just north of the mining village of Calonne. The general area of defence lay to the north of and below the Lorette Spur. It was divided into three sections—the Souchez (right), Angres (centre), and Calonne (left),—the length of front requiring the Division in occupation to place all three infantry brigades in the line.

The conditions of the defences compared favourably with those just vacated in the Carency sector, but little beyond this could be said for them. Throughout the sector there was urgent need of development, and a vast amount of work was required on the trenches, particularly in the right and centre sections.

The defensive system planned, and already partially dug, by the French had considerable depth. In addition to the front, support, and reserve lines occupied by battalions in the line, there were two rearward lines situated forward of Brigade Headquarters—the Bajolle line and the strongly sited Maistre line. The latter, which was the rearmost line for the maintenance of which the Division was responsible, ran down southwards from Maroc into the Divisional sector, and, skirting the east edge of Noulette Wood, passed over the Lorette Spur to the south.

On relief by the 47th Division, the 68th Infantry Brigade had been moved to Hersin. This town was now made the staging area for each brigade as it moved up to take over the new front.

On March 17 the 68th Infantry Brigade relieved the 6th Infantry Brigade in the Calonne section. Two days later the 69th Infantry Brigade took over the Angres section. The 24th Infantry Brigade, whose battalions had been inspected in their billeting areas at Beugin, Ourton, and Divion by the Commander-in-Chief on March 18, completed the infantry reliefs by taking over the Souchez section on the 21st. Infantry Brigade Headquarters, from right to left, were situated at Aix Noulette, Bully Grenay, and Calonne. Calonne, through whose eastern outskirts the front line ran, later proved too hot for Brigade Headquarters of the left section, which were ordered back to Bully Grenay.

On March 22 General Babington assumed command of the Noulette
sector, with headquarters in Sains en Gohelle. The Divisional cyclists
were also accommodated in this village. The Divisional cavalry were
stationed at Hersin.

On completion of artillery reliefs, the C.R.A. established his headquarters at Boyeffles. The 24th Siege Battery R.G.A. was attached to
the Division.

The observation open to both sides on the Carency front has already
been referred to. Here, while the Lorette Spur still gave us unique
advantages for watching the German front, the observation open to the
Germans was even more favourable to them than farther south. South
of the Souchez river, the northern point of the Vimy Ridge, known as
the Pimple, completely dominated the Noulette sector, which was also
overlooked by other points in German occupation farther back from the
front line. Aix Noulette itself was concealed in a hollow, but the ground
a few hundred yards in front and in rear of the village was exposed.
Bully Grenay and the western approaches to Calonne were under
observation.

Movement above ground could only be safely carried out in this area
if the utmost caution was exercised. That it was dangerous rather than
impossible was proved by D Company of the 9th South Staffordshire
Regiment on first moving to the line. These innocent " braves " marched
gaily in broad daylight right into Calonne in column of fours, followed
by their first-line transport. Presumably this event occurred at the
German observer's dinner-hour. Otherwise it is certain that, though
the steaming cooker which accompanied them might have induced the
Germans to think our railhead had been moved forward, a shortage
of pioneers in the Division would have been the inevitable consequence.
The experiment was not repeated after the situation in Calonne had
been revealed.

The hostile artillery was from the first very active in this sector ;
continual bombardments took place, which included both the front-
line trenches and the back areas. Aix Noulette, where certain of our
guns were in position, suffered in particular from the enemy's artillery
fire. But the chief feature of the warfare at this period was the incessant duel carried out between the trench-mortars and rifle-grenades in
the opposing lines.

Two medium trench-mortar batteries, X/23 and Y/23, were already in existence ; two further batteries were now formed from personnel drawn from the Divisional artillery. These, named Z/23 and A/23, were armed with 58 mm. French weapons.

The officer who commanded the latter battery relates that these mortars " afforded a certain amount of amusement in the early stages." But, as he further admits that " one never knew to 100 yards where the torpedo would fall," it will be realised that there were occasions when, for a full appreciation of the joke, the infantry in our own line required a quite exceptional sense of humour. Not that the vagaries of these weapons affected the front line alone, as is shown by an incident told by the same officer, ". . . the fuse had been lighted, and we retired some three or four yards away, as was our custom with this weapon. Not hearing the usual report on discharge of the bomb from the mortar, I stepped into the trench, and was astonished to find the torpedo lying in the trench with the fuse pointing at me. Hastily retiring to cover again, I waited a minute or two, during which nothing happened. I then recharged the mortar, picked up the torpedo very gingerly, replaced it in the mortar, and fired again—this time with great success, a *splendid detonation* resulting."

The moral and material effect of these " splendid detonations " was undoubtedly great when the bombs reached the German trenches. But it is seen that, to gain this effect, a strong nerve of the lion-tamer order was required in trench-mortar personnel at this date. The heavy bombs themselves were effective enough ; it was in the means of propelling them that great improvements were to be effected in the future. The medium trench-mortar in use was the 2-inch mortar firing the " Toffee Apple " bomb, which resembled a large football attached to a long steel bar. The 3-inch light Stokes mortar had recently been introduced, and was to be taken into full use during the next month or two.

On April 10 a feint was made on the front of the 68th Infantry Brigade, in conjunction with operations carried out on the fronts of the 47th Division on the right and the 1st Division now on the left. Action had been taken for some days to induce the enemy to expect attack. The Divisional artillery had been cutting wire, and the gaps created had been kept under machine-gun fire by night. Dummy assembly trenches had been dug on the 8th. For three hours prior to zero, which had been fixed at 4.30 P.M., the Divisional artillery carried out a bombardment, in which the 6-inch howitzers of the 49th Siege Battery and a 9.2 howitzer of the Corps Counter-Battery Group co-operated. At one minute before zero the bombardment became intense, and was joined by the fire of heavy trench-mortars, two Stokes mortars, and forty-eight rifle grenadiers.

At zero a red rocket gave the signal for the artillery to lift to the hostile support line, as if to clear the way for infantry assault, and 200 smoke-candles were set in operation. In the meantime a display of scaling-ladders had been made in our forward trenches, and a "stage army" had shown their bayonets in the reserve line.

The Germans were thoroughly alarmed, and manned their parapet, shouting, "Gas, gas!" This was the effect desired. Snipers took advantage of the targets offered. Green rockets signalled the artillery to shorten and bring their fire again on the front line, where the German infantry had assembled to resist assault.

The bulk of the hostile artillery was directed on the threatened front in the Calonne section. Here protection was good, and our casualties were insignificant. On the other hand, there is little doubt that the Germans must have sustained a great number of casualties. In drawing the hostile artillery fire from the ill-protected Carency sector, where the 47th Division was operating, the diversion had also proved of great value.

Work on the defences was very heavy in the Noulette sector; for in addition to the large amount of construction that was needed, incessant repair work on trenches and wire became necessary owing to the destructive fire of the enemy's artillery and trench-mortars. The infantry and pioneers worked on the forward system, while the improvement of the Bajolle and Maistre lines was placed in the hands of the Royal Engineers. Deep-mined dug-outs were urgently required in the Souchez and Angres sections. The construction of the number necessary for the accommodation of the garrison was beyond the power of the Tunnelling Companies unaided, and thirty men from each battalion had been attached at the beginning of April to the 176th Tunnelling Company for this work.

On April 12 orders were received for the relief of the Division by the 2nd Division, which began to take over the sector on the 14th. Two Field Companies R.E. and three companies of the Pioneer Battalion remained attached to the 2nd Division for work in the sector. The former were to be employed on the construction of a pipe line for water supply to the trenches, a work which, when completed, would effect a great economy in labour at all times, and, in the event of a prolonged hostile bombardment, would save the many casualties to which water-carrying parties were liable on such occasions.

Command of the Noulette sector passed to the G.O.C. 2nd Division on April 19. On withdrawal the 23rd Division was again accommodated in the Bruay area. During the period of rest that ensued each infantry brigade in turn carried out a week's training in the First Army manœuvre area—Matringhem sur Lys, Beaumetz, Laires—about ten miles south-east of Aire. The remainder of the Division was billeted in and about Hersin, Divion, and Ruitz.

On May 7 orders were issued for the Division again to take over the Noulette sector. The front of the sector was to be reduced by the inclusion of the Calonne section in the front of the 1st Division on the left. In consideration of this reduction, however, the Noulette sector would now include the defences of the Lorette Spur, hitherto garrisoned by the division holding the Carency sector.

The 24th and 69th Infantry Brigades took over the Souchez and Angres sections between May 10 and 13. Command of the sector passed to the G.O.C. 23rd Division on the latter date.

The 68th Infantry Brigade was still in the First Army manœuvre area. On May 18 twelve guns of the 68th Machine-Gun Company and the 12th Durham Light Infantry were sent forward to take over the Lorette defences from the 47th Division. Headquarters of this battalion were established at Ablain St Nazaire. A battalion of the 47th Division, stationed at Bouvigny huts, was further available to reinforce this position in case of need.

On May 19 the remainder of the 68th Infantry Brigade moved, dismounted personnel by rail, to Divisional reserve in the area Verdrel, Fresnicourt, Barlin, and Coupigny, with Brigade Headquarters at Fresnicourt.

Mining and counter-mining were active on the front. Sounds detected by our listeners indicated that the Germans were searching for one of our galleries in the Angres section, and were dangerously close to it. It was necessary to blow a mine without delay. The length of the gallery made the laying of the charge most difficult, but it was successfully accomplished. At 6 A.M. on May 19 the mine was blown close to the hostile front line. A large crater was formed, the enemy's gallery destroyed, the wire in front of his trenches blown away, and the German front line itself was much damaged. Simultaneously with the explosion of the mine, the Divisional artillery and medium and heavy trench-mortars opened on the enemy's trenches.

The situation south of the Souchez river was now giving rise to some anxiety. The German artillery and minenwerfer had been very active on the front of the 47th Division ; farther to the right continual crater fighting was in progress on the front of the 25th Division. On the afternoon of May 19 our aeroplanes reported the arrival of thirteen trains in Billy Montigny behind the German front.

An extension of the 47th Division front was made on the night of May 19/20, by which they took over from the 25th Division the Berthonval section, in which the trenches, where they existed at all, were of the poorest description. On May 20 the enemy's artillery and trench-mortar fire increased on the 47th Division front, and intermittent shelling, mainly of the Berthonval section, continued during the following morning. The hostile artillery was also active in the early morning on the front of the 23rd Division, the Angres section in particular being heavily shelled. There was then a lull till 3.40 P.M., when an intense bombardment was opened on the whole front of the 47th Division, the left of the 25th Division, and the battery positions in rear.

About 4.30 P.M. the enemy commenced to shell the front line of the 68th Infantry Brigade on the right of our sector with gas-shell, and to bombard Aix Noulette heavily. Almost immediately communication with Divisional Headquarters was cut off. The 24th Infantry Brigade in Divisional reserve was ordered to be in readiness to move at short notice.

By 6 P.M. the bombardment on the 23rd Division front slackened, and the situation here became normal. But there was no slackening of the fire on the 47th Division front, and at 7.30 P.M. orders were received from the IV. Corps for the 23rd Divisional Artillery to assist in preventing an attack developing on that front by directing their fire on the enemy's front system opposite the 47th Division. The tasks to effect this were to be apportioned by the 47th Division.

At 7.45 P.M. the hostile artillery lifted to the Zouave Valley and Cabaret Rouge, and the German infantry assaulted the right and centre of the 47th Division and the left of the 25th Division.

The right of the enemy's attack was repulsed, but in the poorly protected Berthonval section the few British infantry that had escaped the bombardment were overwhelmed by the Germans. The centre of the attack having thus succeeded, the trenches on either flank became exposed, and the garrisons were forced to withdraw. Immediate counter-attack failed to eject the enemy.

The situation on the front of the 23rd Division still remained fairly quiet.

At 12.40 A.M. on the 22nd orders were received for the artillery to continue the same rate of fire day and night till further orders. At 2 A.M. orders were issued for C/104 Battery to move at 8 A.M. to Caucourt, where they were to report to the O.C. 34th Brigade R.F.A. of the 2nd Division, which was moving forward to take up a position near Ablain St Nazaire in reinforcement of the 47th Divisional Artillery; and for A/104 and C/103 Batteries to move up from reserve at Thieuloye and Barlin to the Divisional area.

At 2.45 A.M. the 47th Division requested our batteries to cease fire and stand on their present lines; but twenty minutes later they were asked to reopen fire.

During the morning the headquarters of the 24th Infantry Brigade moved forward from Fresnicourt to Hersin. B/103 and D/103 Batteries were now placed under the Corps Heavy Artillery for counter-battery work, though still remaining at the call of the Division to resist attack on its own front. Two companies of the 9th South Staffordshire Regiment were placed at the disposal of the 47th Division, and moved to Villers au Bois.

The recapture of the trenches lost was ordered for the night of May 23. From 4 P.M. on the 22nd the enemy front south of the Souchez river was subjected to bursts of fire by the Field Artillery, while 6-inch howitzers bombarded selected points in the trenches. Hostile artillery was very active throughout May 23, back areas, and particularly gun positions, being heavily shelled. The 1st Sherwood Foresters of the 24th Infantry Brigade were brought forward during the morning from Verdrel to Fosse 10 (Bully Grenay); later this place and Aix Noulette were both heavily bombarded.

At 8.45 P.M. the 47th Division, assisted on the right by the 25th Division and by the 23rd Divisional Artillery, attacked. The objectives were gained on both flanks, but the attack broke down in the centre. Shortly before midnight a report was received from the 47th Division that the situation was again the same as had existed before the attack.

On May 24 orders were issued from G.H.Q. for the counter-offensive to be discontinued. There was heavy hostile artillery fire of all natures during the morning. Aix Noulette, Hersin, and Sains en Gohelle were all subjected to heavy bombardment, which included a number of 13 cm. shells on the two last-named places. The fire of both sides, however, gradually died down during the day.

The extent of ground gained by the enemy in these operations had been small. It has been suggested that, fearing our mines, his object had been to gain the mine-shafts. If this was his sole object, he could claim success for his operation. Apart from the action of the artillery, the chief interest of the operations to the 23rd Division lay in their having so recently occupied a part of the front on which the attack was delivered, which enabled them to appreciate the difficulties which beset the 47th Division in defence.

On May 25 the detached companies of pioneers returned to the Division. On the 26th the 2nd Division relieved the 47th Division on our right.

Artillery and trench-mortar bombardments had become part of the normal routine on this front, and a quiet day was rare. But quiet days did occur, and in this sector and at this time of year could bring more refreshment than could be found in the winter in the watery wastes of the Armentières front.

In the defences themselves even, as summer came on, relief to the ugliness of trench and parapet could be found in the mass of wild flowers which sprang up from the overturned chalk soil. The long Arras road communication trench was flanked on either side by a bright herbaceous border of poppies and other wild flowers. While, looking far out across and beyond the German line from the summit of the Lorette Spur, one could almost forget the war, till, stumbling on some ghastly relic of 1915, one was brought back to the grim realities of the present. Speaking of this period, an officer of the Division recalls a lovely day in the early summer, when " . . . as I came down the wooded slope on the north side of the Notre Dame de Lorette Spur I could see the whole plain as far as La Bassée. Lens was quite distinct, and the flash of a gun firing near Loos was visible, though the report could not be heard. Birds all round were singing, and but for that one gun, the only sign of war, all seemed perfect peace. Very pleasant it was, too, to reach the village as the men's breakfast was being cooked. The whole village was fragrant with the aroma of frying bacon, and I reflected that at that hour a similar fragrance must exhale from the whole British line.''

The scent of honeysuckle or wallflower may bring a pang to the heart of an English exile ; but there is a poetry in the smell of frying bacon more potent to stir the heart of the British soldier than can be found in any garden.

On the night of June 1 the 2nd Division, which had recently relieved the 47th Division on our right, attacked to recover part of the line lost on the Vimy Ridge. The 23rd Divisional Artillery assisted this operation by counter-battery work, to which the enemy replied by shelling most of the batteries, in some cases very severely.

A very real danger which has to be guarded against in trench warfare is the effect which the inaction of their life may have on the *morale* of the infantry holding the line. During the periods which intervened between the big battles in the old days there was ample opportunity in camp or billets for a man who had had quite enough for one day at Marathon or Malplaquet to restore himself to a proper appreciation of his heroism on the field of battle, and for him to persuade himself that, however unkind fortune may have been in the past, he would prove a better man than his enemy next time.

In long weeks of trench warfare the painful present precludes much thought about the future, beyond a vague speculation as to when and where the next 5.9 or heavy trench-mortar bomb will arrive, and a pious hope that the event may occur on the next company's front and not on one's own. When the cursed projectile arrives and is followed by another and another, and the parapet, restored only the previous night by hours of labour, is blown sky-high, the infantry cannot hit back. The most they can do is to punish the unfortunate unoffending infantry in the opposite line with a shower of rifle-grenades, and call on their artillery and trench-mortars for further retaliation, trusting devoutly that the latter action will not bring additional trouble on their heads.

If a man shows himself he is sniped. But cover from this is not sufficient; the garrison must be protected as far as possible against the enemy's heavy artillery. No one on first entering a deep dug-out quite realises all that he is leaving behind. But few emerge for their duty in the trenches without feeling they are not quite so sure of themselves as they were before they had experienced its comforts.

So by degrees this unseen enemy, from whom one has everlastingly to protect oneself, becomes uncanny. His blows are felt; the return blows are given blindly; he is seldom *seen* to suffer. His powers may become exaggerated.

There is a sure way of overcoming such exaggeration : to meet him, and find he is not only a human but an inferior human at that.

The trench raid can be viewed from three points. To the Higher Command it provides the means of establishing the enemy's line of battle. The capture and identification of a prisoner by a small fighting patrol proved on occasion during the war of quite inestimable value to the Intelligence branch. It provided, perhaps, the one link missing in a chain of evidence affecting two theatres of war.

As a means of lowering the *morale* of the enemy, repeated successful raids must always be effective. This unseen uncanny British enemy suddenly appears out of the dark, more terrible even than he had come to be pictured ; a few short minutes of confusion and chaos and he disappears, leaving havoc behind him. Even if raids are not uniformly successful, the constant apprehension of attack robs the enemy of rest.

(Viewed from this point, it may be said that the British private soldier has a sterling virtue. No apprehension will rob him of rest when it is his turn to go to sleep. Unfortunately, he has the no less sterling vice of declining to wake up for anything short of the last trump when he knows he has done his last turn of sentry-go.)

But the whole value of the trench raid to the battalion commander lies in the effect it has in maintaining the *morale* of his men. Underlying the keenness of the officers and men who carried out these raids during the war was a restlessness, not only a vague desire for action, but a definite wish to be given the opportunity of proving, above all

to themselves, that they were as anxious as ever to meet the Boche
face to face, and as confident of the result of the encounter.

Such an opportunity was given to a party of the 13th Durham Light
Infantry on the night of June 3/4. The point selected for raiding the
German line lay opposite to the Souchez section, at a distance of about
seventy yards from our own front line. Lieutenants D. H. Clarke [1]
and N. A. Target and twenty-one other ranks were selected to carry
out the operation. They were organised into four parties—an attacking
party of one officer and five other ranks ; a dug-out clearing party of
one officer and six other ranks ; two blocking parties, one of five men,
the other of three, each commanded by a sergeant. The attacking
party would force an entry ; the second party would bomb the enemy's
dug-outs ; while the blocking parties would form posts on either flank
of the line carried, to protect the others from counter-attack from the
flank.

The operation was to be supported by the fire of four 18-pdr. batteries
and two 4.5 howitzer batteries of the Souchez Group R.F.A., and of six
medium and six light trench-mortars. No systematic wire-cutting was
carried out by the artillery for fear of giving warning to the enemy ;
but to cover the registration of mortars, which had been moved to
special positions for the operation, a short artillery bombardment was
opened at 7.30 P.M.

At 1 A.M. the artillery and trench-mortars opened an intense bombardment on the hostile front line, lifting after one minute to the support line to clear the way for the infantry assault.

The raiders in the meantime had found a small gap cut in the wire
by the trench-mortars, and, immediately the artillery lifted, were into
the enemy's front line. Most of the Germans were still sheltering in
their dug-outs from the artillery bombardment, but a few were found
guarding the trench. Of these, one was immediately shot by Private
Sanderson, another bayoneted by Private Brankstone, who then proceeded to bomb dug-outs, described as " lined with men."

Sergeant White, leading the right blocking party to the position
assigned to him, bayoneted three Germans in quick succession, and

---

[1] This was an early episode in a most distinguished career in the 23rd Division. Ultimately
this officer, as Lieut.-Colonel Clarke, D.S.O., M.C., commanded the 13th D.L.I. at the early
age of twenty-two.

established his post. The dug-out party heavily bombed five dug-outs.

Bombed dug-outs will not, however, furnish identification. Private Gowland, mindful of the requirements of the Higher Command, spotting a particularly fine specimen of German at the entrance of a dug-out, seized him.

In such a contest weight tells. This was all on the side of the German, and Gowland, to his dismay, found himself being dragged into the dug-out by his prisoner. At the critical moment Lance-Corporal Etherington, with his bayonet, which had already accounted for two of the enemy, robbed Gowland of his embarrassing prize.

Three minutes after the trench had been carried the signal for return was given, and the raiders regained our lines. The only casualties suffered were two men slightly wounded by the back splash of our own bombs. In addition to the heavy casualties sustained by the Germans in the dug-outs, at least twelve had been shot or bayoneted, but no prisoner was brought back.

The relief of the Division had now been ordered, and it was determined to make another attempt to obtain an identification of the enemy before leaving the sector.

With this object plans were made for a party of one officer and twelve other ranks of the 11th Northumberland Fusiliers to raid an enemy sap, which was believed to be garrisoned at night. The raid was to take place on the night of June 8. At 11 P.M. that night the sap was reported to be full of men. The raiders advanced, but when within fifteen yards of the sap one of the party tripped over a wire, and gave the alarm. The enemy opened a heavy fire, to which our men retaliated by hurling bombs at the sap. But success depended on surprise, and, since this had not been attained, withdrawal was ordered. Under cover of machine-gun fire the party regained the British line without casualty.

Beyond blowing a camouflet on the night of June 7, which did some slight damage to our mine galleries, the enemy's activities during the past weeks were confined to artillery and trench-mortar fire. The latter had in particular proved troublesome, and will probably remain as the chief recollection of the Division's experience in the Noulette sector.

During this, their last tour in the sector, the casualties sustained by the Division amounted to 4 officers and 85 other ranks killed, 7 officers and 426 other ranks wounded.

The relief of the Division by the 47th Division commenced on the 11th, when the 141st Infantry Brigade moved to Hersin as Divisional reserve in place of the 68th Infantry Brigade, which moved to the Pernes area, and thence to the Lisbourg-Prédefin area.

The 24th Infantry Brigade, relieved in the Angres section on the 12th, spent one night in Divisional reserve at Hersin before moving the following day to Pernes. Infantry reliefs were completed on the 13th, and the 69th Infantry Brigade, staging at Barlin, Oldhain Wood, and Fosse 10, moved to the Divion area. On June 14 command of the sector passed to the G.O.C. 47th Division, and 23rd Divisional Headquarters were established at Bruay.

On June 16 the Division concentrated in the Bomy area ; Divisional Headquarters, Bomy (eight miles south-west of Aire) ; 24th Infantry Brigade, Flechin ; 69th Infantry Brigade, Estrée Blanches ; Royal Engineers, Matringhem ; 68th Infantry Brigade remaining in the Lisbourg-Prédefin area, with headquarters at Delette.

The Divisional Artillery, whose relief in the line had been carried out during June 15 and 16, were accommodated partly at Camblain Chatelain, partly in the Therouanne area.

The whole Division being now " at rest," intensive training commenced.

After some inspired genius had coined the word "intensive," it was applied sooner or later to every department of the soldier's life except one. It is not recorded that a division was ever ordered to take an "intensive rest."

It was soon discovered, however, that the length of a rest period was generally in indirect ratio to the intensity of the training ordered for the soldier's repose.

On this thesis it was now calculated that the Division would not sojourn long in the Bomy area.

CHAPTER III.

THE SOMME BATTLES.

JUNE 17 TO AUGUST 14, 1916.

THE factor of surprise had perhaps never had greater importance in any war than it had in the Great War ; to maintain secrecy with regard to large-scale operations had certainly never been so difficult. The gigantic concentration, particularly of artillery, necessary to a grand offensive, and the extended reconnaissance made possible by aircraft, made the complete concealment of plans, both from friend and foe, nigh impossible. It can be said, perhaps, that from the time that the armies grappled in trench warfare, no complete surprise was effected on the Western Front till the battle of Cambrai in the autumn of 1917.

Rumours of a coming British offensive had long since reached the Division, and the purpose with which they had been withdrawn from the line was no mystery to them. When instructions were received on June 20 to be prepared to entrain in four days' time, the Divisional field days held to practise attack on a large scale were accepted as the natural corollary.

During June 24 and 25 the Division entrained at Lillers, Berguette, and Aire for a seven hours' journey to Longueau and Amiens.

On arrival at these destinations units marched to the Vaux area, where the concentration of the Division was completed on June 26.

Divisional Headquarters had been established at Vaux on June 24 ; headquarters of formations were situated as follows :—

Divisional Artillery at Belloy ; Royal Engineers, Yzeux ; 24th Infantry Brigade, St Sauveur ; 68th Infantry Brigade, St Pierre ; and 69th Infantry Brigade, Tirancourt.

THE ROAD TO ALBERT.

(From an etching by Lieut.-Colonel B. Buchanan, 23rd Divisional Artillery.)

The Division was held in G.H.Q. reserve, in readiness to move at
twenty-three and a half hours' notice. The artillery bombardment in
preparation for the coming attack had already commenced, and the
thunder of the guns continued without cease night and day. During
the next few days artillery reconnaissances were made about Albert and
in front of Fricourt, and infantry brigadiers reconnoitred the approaches
to the British lines.

On June 30 the Division moved forward to the Rainneville area.
The advance was continued during the night of July 1/2 to the Baizieux
area. On arrival of Divisional Headquarters at Baizieux on the following morning, orders were received for the Division to be ready to move
eastward again the same night.

In the meantime the largest operations hitherto undertaken by the
British Army had opened on the morning of July 1, on a front of over
fifteen miles, against a position the natural strength of which the Germans
for the past two years had laboured to render impregnable.

The British attack had been delivered against the German line from Map No. 2.
Maricourt on the south to a point opposite Serre, north of the River
Ancre. The attack to the north of the Ancre was in the nature of a
holding attack, the main offensive being directed south of the river
opposite Thiepval and on either side of the German salient at Fricourt.

The nature of the operations in which the 23rd Division was shortly
to be engaged, and particularly the direction in which its attacks were
to be delivered, had their origin in the events of this opening attack of
July 1 on the Fricourt salient. It is necessary, therefore, to consider
briefly the development of the situation in this salient resulting from the
simultaneous attacks delivered against its southern and western sides
on the first day of the great Somme offensive.

Regarding Fricourt as the apex of an isosceles triangle, of which the
one side extended easterly to a point in the German trenches opposite
Maricourt, the other to a point just north of Ovillers, the 11,000-yard
base will be found to pass roughly just west of Montauban, and thence
through the southern extremities of Mametz Wood and the village of
Contalmaison. The central point of this base will be found at a point
in Mametz Wood, about 1700 yards south-east of Contalmaison.

Contalmaison is situated at the northern point of a flat-topped ridge
whose crest slopes gently southwards for a distance of 800 yards, when

it descends more steeply towards Fricourt. The eastern and western slopes of the ridge fall somewhat steeply to valleys, separating it on the one hand from the ridge over which Mametz Wood is spread ; on the other, from the high ground standing between it and La Boisselle. Horse-Shoe Trench and Lincoln's Redoubt were sited on this latter high ground some 1200 yards south-west of Contalmaison. At the head of the western valley stood Bailiff Wood.

Attack from the west—*i.e.*, the direction of La Boisselle—would, it will be seen, meet the Contalmaison and Mametz Wood ridges as successive positions ; attack from the south would find each position flanking the other, and would necessitate the simultaneous capture of both.

The opening attack delivered on either side of Fricourt had failed to progress in the north between Ovillers and River Ancre. In the narrower limits of the triangle which has been described above, the attack had been completely held up opposite the village of La Boisselle (due west of Contalmaison). North of this point, however, some slight progress had been made, while south, between La Boisselle and Fricourt, the attack had penetrated far more deeply to a point some 1200 yards south-west of Contalmaison. From this point a defensive flank had been thrown back to join the old British line just south of La Boisselle. The attack on the western side of the salient had then only met with partial success, and this mainly in its southern quarter.

The attack delivered east of Fricourt against the southern side of the salient had, on the other hand, succeeded along its whole extent, and had carried the British line northwards beyond Montauban and the village of Mametz to within 1000 yards of the southern edge of Mametz Wood.

Fricourt, situated now in a sharp narrow salient, was captured on July 2 by the 17th Division of the XV. Corps, who pushed their advance forward towards the south of Contalmaison, and so brought the British forces on a line running roughly east and west from north of Montauban to just south of La Boisselle.

The situation had, accordingly, so developed that the general direction of advance lay northwards, and that Contalmaison was threatened from the south.

This was roughly the situation on July 3, when, in accordance with orders received from the III. Corps, in which the Division was now included, the 69th Infantry Brigade was placed at the disposal of the 34th Division, preliminary to the relief of the latter by the 23rd Division.

During the evening the 11th West Yorkshire Regiment and the 9th Map No. 3. Yorkshire Regiment moved forward to relieve units of the 101st and 102nd Infantry Brigades of the 34th Division in the front line from the north end of Round Wood to just west of Point 26. 69th Infantry Brigade Headquarters relieved 101st Infantry Brigade Headquarters in the Usna-Tara line about 1500 yards east of Albert. The 8th Yorkshire Regiment and the 10th Duke of Wellington's were held in reserve in the Usna-Tara line and Bécourt Wood respectively. The 101st and 128th Field Companies R.E. were placed under the orders of the 34th Division at Bellevue Farm about half a mile south-east of Albert.

At the same time the 68th Infantry Brigade was moved to a position in trenches just south of Albert.

These movements were carried out in heavy rain, which continued throughout the night. The relief in the front trenches, which were taken over after dark, was a trying experience for troops unaccustomed as yet to the aftermath of a great battle. The trenches, now battered to bits, had been the scene of terrific carnage. They were literally choked with dead bodies, which it was impossible to avoid treading underfoot, and the sensations of the young soldier, conscious that he was shortly to enter battle himself, can be readily realised.

The battalions in the line were in close contact with the enemy. Constant bombing attacks by both sides took place during July 4, the 9th Yorkshire Regiment on the left gaining some ground towards Lincoln Redoubt. The 11th West Yorkshire Regiment, on the right, made some progress during the afternoon, but were driven back by counter-attack before nightfall.

General Babington had now taken over command from the G.O.C. 34th Division, and had established his headquarters during the afternoon at Vivier Mill about one mile south of Albert.

The 17th Division of the XV. Corps was in the line on the right, the 19th Division of the III. Corps on the left.

The 17th Division was to attack at 12.30 A.M. on the following morning from the line Bottom Wood-Birch Wood. At 6.45 P.M. orders were received for the 23rd Division to co-operate by the capture of the line of the Horse-Shoe Trench and of Lincoln Redoubt, in order to protect the left flank of the 17th Division. This task was allotted to the 69th Infantry Brigade, who were ordered to attack at 4 A.M. on July 5.

In the meantime some progress had already been made towards the capture of La Boisselle, but the eastern outskirts were still occupied by the enemy in considerable strength. The 19th Division was to complete the capture of the village during the night of July 4/5, and the 24th Infantry Brigade was placed at their disposal for the purpose of this attack. The 1st Sherwood Foresters of this brigade were moved forward from Henencourt to La Boisselle on the evening of July 4 to take part in these operations.

At nightfall on July 4 the situation of the Division was, then, that the 69th Infantry Brigade was in occupation of the line taken over the previous day in preparation for attack ; the 68th Infantry Brigade was in position south of Albert ; the 24th Infantry Brigade was temporarily detached to the 19th Division. Orders for the 23rd Divisional Artillery, in support of the front, had been issued, but these had later been cancelled, and they were now to come into action west of Fricourt during July 5 and 6, in order of brigades from east to west—102nd, 103rd, 104th, 105th. On completion of this movement both the 34th and 23rd Divisional Artillery would be in support of the 23rd Division, under command of the C.R.A. 23rd Division, with headquarters at Vivier Mill. In to-morrow's operation, however, the 69th Infantry Brigade would be supported by the 34th Divisional Artillery alone.

Frequent and heavy showers continued, and the ground over which troops were to operate, churned up by shell-fire, was becoming hourly more unfavourable to infantry attack.

At 4 A.M. on July 5 the main attack was opened by the 10th Duke of Wellington's, who at that hour advanced through Point 74 to capture Point 56 in Horse-Shoe Trench, while the 11th West Yorkshire Regiment co-operated on their left. The objective was gained, but, shortly afterwards, counter-attack drove back the 10th Duke of Wellington's. Later the 11th West Yorkshire Regiment, heavily counter-attacked from the north and north-east, were forced back to Scots Redoubt. Here, reinforced by one company and a Lewis-gun section of the Duke of Wellington's, they maintained their position. Attacks and counter-attacks, chiefly by bombers, continued throughout the day.

The first attempt to capture Horse-Shoe Trench had failed. A fresh attack was ordered for 6 P.M. Hitherto trench-bombing tactics had been employed ; an attack across the open by the 10th Duke of Wellington's, 8th Yorkshire Regiment, and 9th Yorkshire Regiment in line from right to left was now to be attempted. Four machine-guns and two Stokes mortars were assigned to each battalion.

To ensure the success of this operation, it was necessary first to put out of action a machine-gun which had been located on the left flank in a position from which it would enfilade the attack. An effort to destroy this gun was made by Lieutenant Gibson, the bombing officer of the 9th Yorkshire Regiment, who, with a party of bombers, endeavoured to approach it along a communication trench leading to its position. Unfortunately their approach was detected by the enemy. Lieutenant Gibson, leading the party, was riddled with bullets ; the remainder of the party succeeded in withdrawing to safety.

Acquainted with what had occurred, 2nd Lieutenant Donald Bell of the same battalion immediately, and on his own initiative, crept up a communication trench, and then, followed by Corporal Colwill and Private Batey, rushed across the open and attacked the machine-gun, shooting the firer with his revolver, and destroying the gun and the remainder of its crew with bombs.[1]

With a view to carrying out the fresh attack on Horse-Shoe Trench, the 8th Yorkshire Regiment was now sent forward to relieve the 11th West Yorkshire Regiment. But before the hour ordered for attack, and while this relief was still in progress, the Duke of Wellington's and West Yorkshire Regiment had already gained ground, and had effected the capture of 80 prisoners. The enemy was badly shaken, and was beginning to break. His demoralisation was completed by a gallant advance of the 9th Yorkshire Regiment, who, sweeping across the open on the left, carried all before them, and captured Lincoln Redoubt, together with over 100 prisoners and many machine-guns.

---

[1] Accounts received of the action of 2nd Lieutenant Bell on this occasion conflict slightly in detail. It has been recounted here in the words of the official report accompanying the recommendation for the Victoria Cross, which was awarded for his gallantry. Corporal Colwill and Private Batey were awarded the D.C.M. for their gallant conduct in the affair.

At 7 P.M. Horse-Shoe Trench had been occupied and cleared of the enemy. The 101st and 128th Field Companies R.E. undertook the construction of strong points in the consolidation of the position. Both these companies had the ill-fortune to lose their commanders, Major J. J. Connor of the 101st, who had brought the company to France, and Major J. N. F. Armstrong of the 128th Field Company being both killed during the day.

The 102nd Field Company in reserve was employed on the maintenance of tramways and in the construction of communication trenches across the original No Man's Land of July 1.

South of Peake Wood the brigade was in touch with the 17th Division on the right, who had captured Quadrangle Trench to its junction with Shelter Alley ; but repeated efforts failed to gain touch with the 19th Division on the left. Later it was ascertained that the latter division had been unable to push forward to the point where it had been arranged to obtain contact. Junction was effected, however, by the morning of the 6th at a point some 400 yards west of Lincoln Redoubt.

Hampered by rain and mud, the troops had been fighting in unknown and broken trenches for fifteen hours. The enemy's artillery and machine-gun fire had, at times, been very heavy ; bombing attacks and counter-attacks had been incessant. The success attained was due, in the first place, to the stubborn perseverance of the troops first engaged. These, despite initial failure, had refused to admit defeat, and, together with elements of the 8th Yorkshire Regiment, had secured the upper hand at the end of the day. The completion of success was due to the brilliant assault of the 9th Yorkshire Regiment under command of Lieut.-Colonel Holmes.[1]

Two companies of the 10th Northumberland Fusiliers, borrowed from the 68th Infantry Brigade, had been held in support during the day by the 69th Brigade.

During the late evening the 11th West Yorkshire Regiment and 10th Duke of Wellington's were withdrawn to reserve at Bécourt Wood.

July 6 was spent in strengthening the captured line. In the evening the 69th Infantry Brigade was relieved by the 68th Infantry Brigade, and withdrawn to billets and bivouac near Albert.

[1] For casualties on July 5 see page 81.

The total of unwounded prisoners taken by the Division up till midnight, July 5/6, was 211.

The attack was to be continued on July 7 for the capture of Contalmaison, the objective allotted to the Division being from the cutting just north-east of the village, westwards along the northern edge of Contalmaison and Bailiff Wood, to the road junction 400 yards west of the wood. The 19th Division was to continue the attack on the left to a line running south-west from the road junction.

On the right the 17th Division (XV. Corps) was to capture Mametz Wood.

The attack of the 23rd Division was to be carried out by the 24th Infantry Brigade, which had now rejoined the Division, with objective Contalmaison, and the 68th Infantry Brigade, with objective Bailiff Wood. The boundary between brigades in attack would run, roughly, south-west from the northern point of Quadrangle Trench to Round Wood. The right boundary of the Division would run from the cutting, past the cemetery, along Shelter Alley, to Shelter Wood (all inclusive to 23rd Division).

The left divisional boundary would run, roughly, from the road junction, west of Bailiff Wood, past the east corner of Lincoln Redoubt to west of Scots Redoubt.

In order to dispose divisions on their base of attack, the 19th Division took over a portion of the front held by the 68th Infantry Brigade as far as Lincoln Redoubt ; while the 24th Infantry Brigade, moving up from Dernancourt, took over the front of the 52nd Infantry Brigade of the 17th Division preparatory to moving to a forward position of assembly, which will later be referred to.

The 101st and 128th Field Companies were moved forward on July 6 in readiness to consolidate Contalmaison after its capture. Owing to the death of Majors Connor and Armstrong on the previous day, these companies were placed under the command of Major J. P. Ouchterloney of the 102nd Field Company, which was to remain in reserve.

In preparation for the attack a French 75 mm. battery at 5.30 A.M. would bombard Contalmaison Wood with gas-shell. At 6.30 A.M. Contalmaison itself would receive 100 incendiary shells. At 7.20 A.M. the Heavy Artillery was to open an intense bombardment on Contalmaison and on a line running westerly from the north-eastern corner of Bailiff Wood, lifting gradually as the infantry attack developed. At the same hour the 23rd Division Artillery [1] would bring an intense bombardment on Contalmaison, Quadrangle Trench to the west of the village, the near edge of Bailiff Wood, and the trench just west of the wood. At 8 A.M. they would lift to form a barrage to prevent enemy supports being brought forward, and at this hour the infantry would advance to the attack.

The arrangements for the attack of the 23rd Division were interfered with at the outset. The 17th Division was to deliver an attack at 2 A.M. on Pearl Alley and Quadrangle Support. These objectives having been captured, Pearl Alley was to be handed over to the 24th Infantry Brigade as a jumping-off line for its attack on Contalmaison.

Unfortunately, not only did this preliminary attack by the 17th Division fail to secure its objective, but a heavy hostile counter-attack forced back their left to the line Birch Tree Wood—north end of Bottom Alley. The 1st Worcestershire Regiment, on the right of the 24th Infantry Brigade, became involved in the fighting to hold up this German attack. This check to the 17th Division delayed the advance of the 24th Infantry Brigade on Contalmaison ; this in turn delayed the advance of the left wing on Bailiff Wood.

In the meantime the artillery programme had been carried out according to plan. Though the incendiary shell, so far as incendiary results were concerned, proved a failure, the general effect of the bombardment, according to the German prisoners taken later in the day, was very great. But the material effect of artillery in weakening the defence, however great it may be, will seldom if ever entirely overcome it. One half of the support given to its infantry in attack lies in the moral effect of the artillery bombardment on the defence—the despair seizing infantry subjected to slaughter by a weapon to which they are powerless to reply. To gain the full value of this support, the infantry attack must follow the artillery bombardment immediately before the infantry and machine-guns of the defence realise that they have been released from the misery of artillery fire.

Any alteration at the last moment in prearranged artillery bombardments or barrages proved throughout the war to be a matter of the

[1] The 34th Divisional Artillery were included under the command of the C.R.A. 23rd Division at this time. On July 14 they were replaced by the 25th R.F.A. Brigade (1st Division), and on July 16 the 175th Brigade R.F.A. (34th Division) again came under his command.

greatest difficulty. On this occasion, moreover, it is admitted that the possibility of delay in the infantry advance had not been considered.

Owing to the delay resulting from the German counter-attack, it was not till 9.15 A.M. that the 11th Northumberland Fusiliers, under command of Lieut.-Colonel Caffin, advanced to attack Bailiff Wood. Throughout this day the troops, dragged down by the weight of sodden equipment and blinded by torrents of rain, were operating over flooded ground, water-filled craters, and trenches waist-deep in mud.

The enemy's artillery had now placed a heavy barrage across the line of the advance, filling the valley leading northwards to Bailiff Wood with the smoke of bursting shells. But the battalion moved steadily forward, passed through the barrage, and secured the southern edge of the wood. Here they came under a heavy enfilade machine-gun and rifle fire from the north and north-east, and were shortly afterwards forced to retire.

Seeing that this withdrawal had uncovered the right flank of the 19th Division, the 12th Durham Light Infantry now pushed forward and dug in on a line immediately south of Bailiff Wood, and further succeeded in capturing the German trenches at the south-west corner of the wood.

In the meantime the situation resulting from the German counter-attack of the early morning having cleared, the 24th Infantry Brigade had advanced on Contalmaison—the 1st Worcestershire Regiment on the right, the 2nd East Lancashire Regiment on the left.

The right of the attack made rapid progress. The village was entered from the south-east, and the troops succeeded in penetrating almost to its northern edge. The 2nd East Lancashire Regiment, however, were less fortunate. Their advance was held up by heavy machine-gun fire from Peake Wood. Checked in this direction, the battalion moved to the right, in the hope of approach being possible east of Quadrangle Trench. But here again they were held up by a heavy artillery barrage.

The position of the 1st Worcestershire Regiment in Contalmaison, with both flanks exposed and heavily shelled by the enemy, had now become untenable. They were forced to abandon the ground they had captured, and to withdraw to a line between Shelter Alley and Peake Wood.

The 2nd Northamptonshire Regiment was brought forward on the left during the afternoon, the 1st Sherwood Foresters moved to Shelter Wood in support, and the 10th Duke of Wellington's and 11th West Yorkshire Regiment, placed at the disposal of the G.O.C. 24th Infantry Brigade, were held in reserve.

Conditions were appalling. The flooded trenches, where men could scarcely drag along, were now congested with killed and wounded. Nevertheless, continuous efforts were made to establish posts at the southern end of Contalmaison. But every fresh attempt failed under heavy hostile fire.

The casualties were cleared by hand to Fricourt, where Lieut.-Colonel Nimmo Walker of the 69th Field Ambulance, with a bearer division and a tent subdivision, had established an advanced dressing-station. Here the wounded were tended in the tents and under tarpaulins which had been rigged up under shelter of a bank, which afforded scanty protection from the enemy's artillery fire. Lieut.-Colonel Walker showed the most conspicuous gallantry and devotion to duty during this and the following days in supervising the collection of the wounded under heavy fire.

Nightfall on July 7 found the 24th Infantry Brigade established on a line south of Contalmaison, while the 68th Infantry Brigade, who, though unable to make further progress, had maintained the position captured in the morning, held the southern edge of Bailiff Wood, with their right flank thrown back towards Peake Wood.

The 19th Division, on the left, had secured their objective, but the experience of the 17th Division on the right had been similar to our own, and though their advanced troops had at one time got as far forward as Acid Drop Copse, they had later been forced to withdraw.

The capture of Contalmaison and Bailiff Wood had not been effected, but the grip on Contalmaison had tightened.

On July 8 the 19th Division, extending their right, took over the trenches south-west of Bailiff Wood from the 12th Durham Light Infantry, who were moved back to Bécourt Wood. The 11th West Yorkshire Regiment, reverting to the command of the G.O.C. 69th Infantry Brigade, were withdrawn to the same place. The 10th Duke of Wellington's remained for the present with the 24th Infantry Brigade.

Reports were received of the evacuation of Bailiff Wood, but patrols sent out by the 13th Durham Light Infantry, who had relieved the 11th Northumberland Fusiliers on this front, proved these to be false. The

wood was still strongly held by the enemy, and here, as in Contalmaison and Quadrangle Trench, machine-guns were discovered to be
in great strength.

The exact position of our own troops and of the enemy at several
points was not clear. Captain Pye Smith, R.A.M.C., ignorant at the
time whether or not the Germans were in occupation of Peake Wood,
gallantly led a party of bearers into the wood and rescued four of our
wounded.

A gallant assault by the 1st Worcestershire Regiment succeeded,
during the afternoon, in reaching the southern edge of the village, but
they were later driven back by heavy machine-gun fire.

A fresh attack on Contalmaison was now ordered for July 10. But
in view of the casualties sustained by the 24th and 68th Infantry Brigades
and of the severe strain to which they had been subjected under the
weather conditions of the past two days, the operation was entrusted to
the 69th Infantry Brigade (less the 10th Duke of Wellington's Regiment).

The task assigned to the 24th and 68th Infantry Brigades was to
make every effort, in the meanwhile, to secure points whose occupation
would facilitate the attack.

There was to be a radical alteration in plan for this fresh attack.
In outlining the operations of July 1 earlier in this chapter, it was shown
how the varying fortunes in the attack on the flanks of the Fricourt
salient had resulted in bringing the general direction of the British
advance northward. By a brief description of the natural features
of the ground surrounding Contalmaison, an attempt was also made
to show the different relations in which the Contalmaison and Mametz
Wood Spurs would stand, the one to the other, in meeting an attack
from the south and an attack from the west.

The ground gained by the 68th Infantry Brigade and by the 19th
Division on the left now made an attack on Contalmaison from the
west a practical proposition. Contalmaison in British hands would
prove as great a support, as in the enemy's hands it had proved an
obstacle, to attack on Mametz Wood.

It was from the west, therefore, that the next attack against Contalmaison was to be directed.

Shortly after dawn on July 9 report was received that the Germans
were massing for attack in Contalmaison. Artillery opened on the

village, and succeeded in dispersing the enemy. Similar concentrations, reported at intervals throughout the day, were similarly dealt with.

The 68th Infantry Brigade now decided to make a further attempt to capture Bailiff Wood. The task was allotted to the 12th Durham Light Infantry, who arranged for one company to bomb along the trench on the line of the road north of the wood while one platoon cleared the wood itself. A second company in support would carry material and assist in the consolidation of the eastern edge of the wood.

The operation was timed to start at 6 P.M., and at this hour the supporting artillery opened fire. Unfortunately, just as the infantry were about to advance, a false alarm was raised of a hostile attack on the brigade on the left. This delayed the advance of the Durham Light Infantry for over two hours, and much of the value of the artillery fire was thereby lost. Nevertheless, after a fierce hand-to-hand struggle in the dark, they succeeded in carrying their objective, and in capturing three damaged field guns, together with 300 rounds of gun ammunition. The eastern edge of the wood was occupied, and the line of the road to the north consolidated and held as a protection to the left flank.

A further point of vantage for the coming attack was secured during the night by a determined bombing attack by parties of the 10th Duke of Wellington's, who succeeded in establishing a post immediately to the south of Contalmaison, from which the greater part of the village could be swept by machine-gun fire.

Throughout July 9 the infantry, both in the forward area and in support, suffered severely from artillery. At this period the Germans were notably weaker in artillery than the British; but, paradoxical though it may seem, our infantry probably suffered from this very weakness, which prompted the Germans to neglect counter-battery work in favour of concentrating their artillery fire on the infantry.

At midnight on July 9/10 orders were received for the relief of the 23rd by the 1st Division. This relief, however, was not to be completed till the morning of July 11, and would in no way interfere with the 69th Infantry Brigade's attack.

During the morning of July 10 our heavy artillery bombarded Contalmaison, Contalmaison Wood to the north, the cutting north-east of the village, the western edge of Mametz Wood and Quadrangle Trench, and the two copses on the western flank of the village.

By 3.30 P.M. the infantry of the 69th Infantry Brigade had assembled
for attack. On the left, and considerably in advance of the remainder
of the brigade, two companies of the 11th West Yorkshire Regiment
were in position some 300 yards due west of Bailiff Wood. The 8th
and 9th battalions of the Yorkshire Regiment (right and centre of attack)
were to have formed on a line extending southwards about 500 yards
in rear of the West Yorkshire Regiment, but the trenches selected for
their assembly were found to be either unsuitable, owing to their direction not corresponding with that shown on the map, or so damaged
by shell-fire as to be useless. The commanding officers, accordingly,
had to improvise the best arrangements possible at the eleventh hour
before attack.

The remaining two companies of the 11th West Yorkshire Regiment
were held in reserve at Scots Redoubt.

Thanks to the action of the 68th Infantry Brigade on the previous
night, posts had already been established in and around Bailiff Wood.
The possession of this wood, however, was so vital to the security of
the left flank of the attack that it had been made the duty of the two
companies of the West Yorkshire Regiment, detailed for attack, to
establish themselves, together with four Stokes mortars, on its eastern
and northern edges.

The 8th and 9th battalions Yorkshire Regiment, with the centre of
the attack directed on the village church, were to advance for the capture of Quadrangle Trench between the two roads running from Peake
Wood and Bailiff Wood to Contalmaison. Having secured this line,
a further advance would be carried out for the capture of the village.

To cover the infantry advance, the 23rd and 34th Divisional Artillery
were to keep a barrage on the line of the objective from 4 P.M. to 5 P.M.,
and to bombard Contalmaison. Trenches leading from the north-east
and south-east corners of Bailiff Wood to the village would also be
subjected to fire up till 4.30 P.M. At 5 P.M., the hour fixed for assault,
the artillery would lift from the objective to a line 200 yards in rear.

At 4 P.M. the infantry advanced to the attack. Ten minutes later
some 200 Germans attempted a counter-attack from the north against
Bailiff Wood, but were stopped with heavy casualties by our machine-
guns.

By 4.30 P.M. the companies of the West Yorkshire Regiment, under

Lieut.-Colonel Barker, had entered Bailiff Wood ; at the same time some hundreds of the enemy, driven from Contalmaison by our artillery fire, came under a heavy fire of rifles and machine-guns. Shortly afterwards a second attempt was made by the enemy against the northern edge of Bailiff Wood, in the form this time of a trench-bombing attack directed from the east ; this was repulsed without difficulty by Lewis-gun fire. The troops detailed for the reinforcement of the northern edge of the wood now wheeled left, and took up their position. Bailiff Wood was securely held.

In the meanwhile the arrangements improvised by Lieut.-Colonel Vaughan and Lieut.-Colonel Holmes for the assembly of their battalions, and the skilful leading of their officers, had brought the 8th and 9th battalions Yorkshire Regiment forward on their correct alignment in readiness for the main assault.

The ground over which lay the early stage of their advance, though heavy with mud and broken by shell-holes, was level. On leaving their assembly trenches the troops, though not fully in view, were yet under observation from Contalmaison. Immediately they moved forward both battalions came under heavy fire of artillery, rifles, and machine-guns, but the men continued to advance with the most perfect steadiness. As the advance progressed the attacking troops became increasingly exposed, till, descending to the valley which separated them from their objective, they came in full view of Quadrangle Trench, sited on the opposite slope, which rose to Contalmaison.

Crossing the light railway which marked the bottom of the valley, the 9th Yorkshire Regiment on the left pushed forward up the farther slope to the assault. The garrison of Quadrangle Trench had here been so thoroughly dealt with by our artillery as to prove incapable of resistance. By 5 P.M. the battalion had secured the whole line of trench allotted to its attack. But on the southern flank the 8th Yorkshire Regiment, on descending to the valley, found their advance hampered by wire, which in places was almost intact.[1] The ground to be traversed

---

[1] A memorial stone will be found, as far as can be remembered, on the eastern slope of the valley, inscribed as follows :—

IN MEMORIAM
FRANCIS
DODGSON
CAPTAIN
8TH YORKS REGT.
WHO HERE FELL
10-7-16.

On visiting the battlefields in December 1921 it seemed to the writer that this stone must approximately mark the point of junction of the two battalions in their advance.

was a quagmire of flooded shell-holes ; wire and débris lay everywhere. Under fire from the front and left flank men were falling every second, and advance was only possible by rushes in small groups for a few yards at a time.

Swept by a continuous hail of rifle bullets and shrapnel, the attack in face of such difficulties might well have failed but for the personal qualities of the commander, the gallant leading of his officers, and the superb courage of all ranks.

By 5.25 P.M. the 8th Yorkshire Regiment had gained their whole objective, reduced now to a muddy ditch three feet deep, providing little protection from the enemy's fire from the village.

At 5.30 P.M. the artillery barrage lifted, and the infantry moved forward to attack the village. The ground on the left and centre of the attack was fairly level, but presented a considerable slope on the right. The 9th Yorkshire Regiment, driving the enemy before them, and killing or capturing any who offered resistance, wheeled left and occupied the northern edge of the village. As this movement was made, search parties were detached to deal with those of the now thoroughly demoralised enemy who had taken refuge in the cellars and dug-outs which abounded among the ruined buildings of the village.

Upwards of 100 prisoners were here captured, together with two machine-guns and large quantities of ammunition. The latter proved useful, as our own ammunition had run short. Captured machine-guns and rifles were turned on the routed enemy, while Lieut.-Colonel Holmes, heartening all ranks by his coolness and courage, reorganised his battalion, reduced now to some 6 officers and 120 other ranks.

The natural strength of Contalmaison had been apparent from the first ; but its full strength was only realised later, when there was opportunity to examine the numerous cellars and dug-outs, and to reckon the immense garrison for which it could afford protection from artillery fire. The amount of work which had been expended on its defences by the Germans gave the measure of the importance that they must have attached to this position.

It seems that the greater proportion of the enemy's machine-guns had been massed in the south-east quarter of the village, leading to the supposition that the Germans anticipated attack from this direction. The position of the machine-guns in this quarter made them readily available to oppose the advance of the 8th Yorkshire Regiment on the right of the attack. The line of the battalion's advance lay up a slope pitted with shell-holes, and covered with the débris of battle and the killed and wounded of the enemy.

Despite the difficulties of the ground, the attacking infantry advanced in face of intense fire to the outskirts of the village. Here the fatigued and breathless troops were held up by a hedge and a line of wire-netting. This check to their advance told heavily against the battalion. Four of their officers were shot dead at this point, and 50 per cent of the casualties suffered on this day by the 8th Yorkshire Regiment occurred between the trench from which they had just advanced and this obstacle.

Such a check at the critical moment of assault might even now have turned the scale against less determined troops, but the 8th Yorkshire Regiment never wavered. The obstacle was overcome, and the battalion entered the village, where, taken in rear by unexpected machine-gun and rifle fire, they suffered further losses.

The situation was critical. The battalion, led by its commanding officer, was now reduced to 4 officers and 150 men. But the spirit which had carried the men through their costly advance still sustained them, and they continued to fight their way through the village. At the sight of these troops, so confident of victory, 8 German officers and 160 unwounded men surrendered. In addition to these, some 100 wounded Germans were discovered in dug-outs and cellars, and six machine-guns, together with thousands of rounds of ammunition, were taken.

Contalmaison had been finally captured.

So far, the action of the infantry has alone been dealt with ; for the movement of the infantry rules the sequence of the battle, and in their hands lies ultimate success.

But the success of the most determined infantry must always be dependent on the support of the other arms co-operating. On July 10 victory was in no small degree due to the action of the artillery. Artillery support had been perfect, and had been none the easier since the rapid advance of the infantry had made it necessary for the batteries more than once to modify their programme. The difficulties and anxieties of the artillery observing officer on such occasions are not always appreciated by the infantry ; it may, perhaps, be said that they are less realised when the work is so faultless as to appear simple. Three forward observing officers of the artillery entered Contalmaison on the heels of the infantry, and a protective barrage was put down round the exposed sides of the village and maintained throughout the night.

The four Stokes mortars with the two companies of the West Yorkshire Regiment in Bailiff Wood did valuable work in covering the advance of the bombers up the trenches and in protecting the left flank from counter-attack. Two other mortars of the 69th L.T.M. Battery, in position south of the village, supported the assault of the 8th Yorkshire Regiment on Contalmaison by high-angle fire, which was maintained up till the close approach of the infantry to their objective.

Guns of the 69th Machine-Gun Company rendered great assistance throughout the day in supporting the attack, resisting counter-attack, and inflicting heavy casualties on the retiring enemy. Two guns were posted some 250 yards west of the north-west corner of Bailiff Wood ; two guns near the junction of Shelter Alley and Pearl Alley ; four guns at Birch Wood fired on the cutting north-east of the village ; while the remaining guns were held at Willow Patch in brigade reserve. Of the last, four were later sent forward for the defence of Contalmaison.

The true military spirit which leads men to march to the sound of the heaviest fighting was exemplified this day by the conduct of Private H. Smith of the 10th Duke of Wellington's. This worthy, alone and without special orders, walked with a basket of pigeons through a heavy barrage, and reported, at a critical moment, to Major Western of the 8th Yorkshire Regiment in Contalmaison. His opportune arrival enabled the first message, asking for much-needed reinforcements and ammunition, to be sent back and acted on. The companies of the 11th West Yorkshire Regiment in brigade reserve were sent forward, and orders were dispatched to Lieut.-Colonel Haynes, commanding the 10th Duke of Wellington's, to reinforce the troops in Contalmaison. The latter battalion, which had been holding trenches for long hours under intense fire, was promptly led forward through a heavy hostile barrage.

In the meantime, under cover of the protective artillery barrage, the consolidation of the captured positions had been taken in hand. Sufficient troops were not available for holding the whole outer line of Contalmaison. The trench on the northern edge of the village was, therefore, occupied, and the defensive line drawn back from there southwards through the chateau in the centre of the village.

Two attempts were made by the Germans to regain a footing in Contalmaison. The first, made by a party of the enemy which emerged from the cutting north-east of the village, was immediately dispersed by the fire of a German machine-gun which had been captured by the 8th Yorkshire Regiment. Pending the arrival of reinforcements, the reduced number of the Yorkshire battalions allowed only a dangerously thin defence. When, therefore, at 9 P.M. a party of about forty of the enemy opened a rapid fire from the shelter of a hedge at the south end of the village, the situation gave rise to some anxiety. Major Western, second in command of the 8th Yorkshire Regiment, under the fire of the enemy, hastily constructed a barricade across the road, and collected the few men that could be spared from the two battalions to reinforce the threatened point. The fire of these sufficed to hold the enemy in check, while a bombing party was organised under the leadership of 2nd Lieutenant Donald Bell of the 9th Yorkshire Regiment. This party, with extreme gallantry, then attacked, and, at the cost of several casualties, drove back the enemy. For the second time within a few days the splendid valour of this young officer had saved a critical situation. But now, alas! the inspiration of his example alone survived, for on this occasion he sacrificed his life.

The reinforcing troops now commenced to arrive, and our position in Contalmaison became increasingly secure.

Relief of the 23rd Division (less artillery) by the 1st Division had commenced in the course of the day. During the afternoon the 24th Infantry Brigade had been withdrawn to Bresle on relief by troops of the 1st Infantry Brigade. The 68th Infantry Brigade, also relieved by units of the 1st Infantry Brigade, withdrew during the night to Albert, where they came under orders of the G.O.C. 34th Division, which two days previously had relieved the 19th Division on the left of the 23rd Division.

The companies of the West Yorkshire Regiment holding Bailiff Wood, having joined up with the 9th Yorkshire Regiment, were relieved under cover of darkness by the Cameron Highlanders of the 1st Division.

The consolidation of the defences at Contalmaison continued throughout the night, and by dawn the position was secure, though the work could not have been accomplished without the assistance given by two companies of the Black Watch of the 1st Division. These companies, after a long and tiring march, carried forward stores hour after hour through a heavy barrage, and did all that was in their power to help the 69th Infantry Brigade.

During the afternoon of the 10th the Royal Engineers of the 23rd Division had endeavoured to get forward, but, blocked by infantry in Quadrangle Trench, they had come under a hostile barrage. Infantry reinforcements were given priority, and the sappers had to withdraw to clear the way. On the morning of the 11th, the 101st, 128th, and two sections of the 102nd Field Companies succeeded in getting forward to Contalmaison. They set to work constructing strong points in the buildings and open machine-gun emplacements, and by unceasing labour completed the defences of the village by 6 P.M.

The following message was addressed to the G.O.C. 69th Infantry Brigade by General Babington after the action :—

Please convey at the earliest opportunity to all ranks of the 69th Infantry Brigade my very great admiration of their most gallant conduct during to-day's operations. For yourself, please accept my very best thanks.

Brig.-General T. S. Lambert, whose conduct of the operation had achieved this first noticeable success for the 23rd Division, in his report of the action, pays a just and generous tribute to the 24th and 68th Infantry Brigades, but for whose gallant efforts during the previous day his task, he claims, would have been far more difficult.

In the attack on Contalmaison the casualties of the 69th Infantry Brigade amounted to—

				Officers.	Other ranks.
Killed	.	.	.	11	51
Wounded	.	.	.	27	606
Missing	.	.	.	1	159

In the attack for the capture of Horse-Shoe Trench the Brigade had already lost—

				Officers.	Other ranks.
Killed	.	.	.	10	50
Wounded	.	.	.	26	453
Missing	.	.	.	1	57

F

Making a total effective loss in the brigade, in the two actions, of 1452 all ranks.

On July 10 the bearers of the 69th Field Ambulance were sent forward to Scots Redoubt ; the wounded were taken here on their way to Fricourt, where the A.D.S. still remained. From Fricourt casualties were evacuated by ambulance-cars.

Following the capture of Contalmaison, the 17th Division carried Quadrangle Support and Wood Support at 11 P.M. on the night of July 10, joining hands with the 38th Division, who were now advancing northwards through Mametz Wood. These divisions had been engaged in heavy and continuous fighting throughout July 7, 8, and 9, but their most determined attacks had failed to progress.

At 10.30 A.M. on July 11 command of the right sector of the III. Corps front passed to the G.O.C. 1st Division, and headquarters 23rd Division withdrew to St Gratien, eight miles north-east of Amiens.

During the night of the 11th/12th the 1st Infantry Brigade relieved the 69th Infantry Brigade, which moved to Albert, and thence to Franvillers. By July 12 the 1st Division had joined up at Mametz Wood with the 21st Division, which had now relieved the 17th Division.

The following message from General Rawlinson was forwarded on July 12 by the G.O.C. III. Corps :—

Please convey to 23rd Division my hearty congratulations on their capture of Contalmaison. They have acquitted themselves right well, and I desire to thank them most heartily for their gallantry and the fine fighting spirit displayed by all ranks.

As illustrating the fighting spirit of the Division, it is worthy of record that the sick-list, always remarkably low throughout its service, was reduced on July 14 to the astonishing figure of one man. The sick report of that day has been preserved by General Babington.

Orders were now received for the return to the 8th Division of the 24th Infantry Brigade, which had been with the 23rd Division for the past nine months, and for the 70th Infantry Brigade to rejoin the 23rd Division.

The 70th Infantry Brigade had taken part in the attack of the 8th Division between Thiepval and Ovillers on July 1, when all its battalions had suffered terrible casualties. The 8th York and Lancaster

CLEARING THE ROAD THROUGH CONTALMAISON.

Regiment, the leading battalion on the left of the attack, had alone lost all its officers that day, 18, including the commanding officer, Lieut.-Colonel Maddison, being killed, and 5 wounded. Of 608 men that went forward to the attack, 68 only had returned. Since then the brigade had been in the Bruay area.

To effect this exchange the 24th Infantry Brigade, which had been accommodated in the Molliens-au-Bois area, moved to Longeau, where they entrained on July 15.

The 69th Infantry Brigade took their place on July 13 in the Molliens-au-Bois area, where they were inspected by the G.O.C. III. Corps on July 15.

On the following day the 70th Infantry Brigade, now commanded by Brig.-General H. Gordon, joined the Division in the Poulainville area, moving thence on July 17 to Pierregot and Miruaux.

While these moves were in progress the 68th Infantry Brigade, Map No. 2. still detached to the 34th Division, had been moved forward to take part in an attack on Pozières. Preliminary to the attack on the village, which had been ordered for the 18th, it was found necessary to capture a continuous line of trench which lay between the village and the British line. An attack on this trench was carried out by the 12th Durham Light Infantry on the night of July 17/18, but broke down under intense machine-gun fire from the enemy's position. Attack on Pozières was then postponed, and the 68th Infantry Brigade, relieved by a brigade of the 1st Australian Division, rejoined the 23rd Division on July 20 at Franvillers.

The Division was now to enter the line again, and on July 21 Divisional Headquarters moved to Henencourt, 69th Infantry Brigade to the Millencourt area, and the 70th Infantry Brigade to Baizieux Wood. The 71st Field Ambulance established an advanced dressing-station at Bécourt Chateau on the following day.

The fighting of the past seven days had carried forward the British advance along the whole line of attack. In the centre, Bazentin-le-Petit had been captured, and the British line ran forward of Bazentin-le-Petit Wood. West of the wood progress had been made, but Pozières still remained in the hands of the enemy. The 23rd Divisional Artillery had played a prominent part in these operations in support of the 1st Division. High appreciation of their action in connection with a successful attack on the night of July 16/17 was expressed both by the G.O.C. 1st Division and by the Corps Commander. In preparation for the infantry attack on this occasion twenty-six 18-pdr. guns and eight 4.5 howitzers had been brought in direct enfilade on what were at that time the German second-line trenches, those known as O.G. 1[1] and O.G. 2 running north-west from the south-western edge of Bazentin-le-Petit Wood. Later the registration of the German " Switch Line " had entailed battery commanders lying for hours in front of the British trenches under fire of hostile snipers and in danger of being rounded up by some enterprising patrol. Telephone wires were continually cut. The patience required for this work can be judged from the fact that for every half-hour's registration three hours were spent in mending wires.

The 23rd Division was to relieve the 1st Division in the left sector of the III. Corps front, which lay between Bazentin-le-Petit and Pozières, covering Bazentin-le-Petit from the north. The right sector of the corps front was held by the 19th Division, while the 1st Australian Division occupied the sector to the left of the III. Corps, opposite Pozières.

The sector to be taken over lay on either side of the Contalmaison-Martinpuich road, and had a frontage of about 1600 yards. It was held by two infantry brigades distributed in depth, with one infantry brigade held in Divisional reserve in Albert and just east of Bécourt Wood. The boundary between brigades in the line ran along Gloster Alley and O.G. 2 to the Contalmaison road, thence east of Contalmaison and west of Birch Tree Wood.

On July 25 the 70th Infantry Brigade relieved the 1st Infantry Brigade in the right section. One battalion occupied Lancashire Trench, 70th Avenue, and 6th Avenue ; a second battalion was placed in close support in K.O.Y.L.I. Trench, O.G. 1, and O.G. 2 ; while a third battalion was in support east of Contalmaison. Brigade Headquarters were established in Shelter Wood just east of Birch Tree Wood, where the fourth battalion was held in brigade reserve.

On the following day the 68th Infantry Brigade relieved the 3rd Infantry Brigade in the left section, with headquarters in Contalmaison. One battalion was disposed in O.G. 1, The Hoop, and O.G. 2 ; two battalions were placed in support at Contalmaison and Peake Wood ; the fourth battalion was held in brigade reserve at Scots Redoubt.

[1] " O.G." stood for "old German " trench.

On the same day, July 26, General Babington assumed command Map No. 2. of the sector, with headquarters at Albert.

The 69th Field Ambulance, with headquarters at Fricourt, was made responsible for clearing the whole line. An advanced dressing-station was established at Contalmaison Chateau, and another post at the edge of Mametz Wood.

At this period the main British effort was being made against Longueval and Delville Wood and southward of these points, in order to straighten out the salient caused by the sharp southerly bend in the line which occurred at Longueval. Further advance west of Longueval was not contemplated for the present, but it was necessary to maintain pressure all along the line to prevent the enemy reinforcing the front opposite our main offensive. In carrying out the action necessary to this, it would be possible to secure points of tactical importance to future operations.

In reading of the events in which the troops of the Division were concerned in the next few weeks, it should be borne in mind that operations, which in a history of the war on the Western Front represented a mere nibbling process, were seen in a different perspective by those who took part in a "nibble." Such "nibbles" in a war of lesser magnitude would have been classed as grand battles. Raids may be regarded as distinct; for, however violent the experience might be, it was short and sharp. But it may well be that the operation which looms largest in the recollections of a regimental officer is one in which a single brigade or battalion was engaged for hours or even days, but one which cannot hope to receive more than the most casual notice in a general history of the war.

Before relief of the 1st Division had been completed, Pozières, which Map No. 4. had so long resisted British attack, had been captured by the Australians on July 25. During past weeks determined efforts had been made by the 1st Division to gain possession of Munster Alley opposite the left of the sector. The last of these had been made by the 2nd Welch Regiment just prior to relief by the 68th Infantry Brigade. They had succeeded in capturing the trench, but had later been forced to withdraw.

These attempts to drive the enemy from Munster Alley were continued by the 68th Infantry Brigade. Stiff bombing fights by the 13th

Durham Light Infantry during the night of July 26/27 established posts 200 yards up the trench. On the 28th our troops were forced back, but during the day regained the ground lost. Bazentin-le-Petit area was very heavily shelled, but there was no infantry action on this flank.

The 69th Infantry Brigade now relieved the 68th Infantry Brigade in the left section, and the 10th Duke of Wellington's Regiment was ordered to attack on the night of July 28/29 for the capture of Munster Alley and the forward portion of Gloster Alley. The whole battalion was to be employed. One company was to capture Munster Alley, a second company to advance up Gloster Alley as far as the German switch line, a third company would act in support, and the fourth be held in reserve.

Of the first company, one platoon advanced from the south-west end of the trench to bomb their way up the trench, while three platoons attacked across the open from The Hoop.[1]

The latter platoons met with heavy fire. Desperate fighting ensued, in which all the officers, the company sergeant-major, and many N.C.O.'s were hit, and the attack was finally driven back by a hostile counter-attack. The bombing attack in the meanwhile continued, but little progress was made, though the final barricade established in Munster Alley was slightly in advance of that previously held. In the fighting on this flank the most valuable assistance was given by the 17th Australian Battalion in filling sand-bags and sending up bombs and S.A.A.

On the right the attack on Gloster Alley made good progress, and succeeded in establishing a post some twenty-five yards short of the switch line, from which good observation overlooking Martinpuich was obtained. The official photographer alone was able to overcome the scepticism of Army Headquarters on this point, the report being regarded till then as a pleasing hallucination.

The casualties sustained in this operation amounted to—

	Killed.		Wounded.		Missing.	
	Officers.	O.R.	Officers.	O.R.	Officers.	O.R.
10th D. of W. . .	2	31	5	127	1	44
69th M.G. Coy. . .	..	..	..	2	..	..
69th L.T.M. By. . .	..	2	..	2	..	2

[1] This trench is shown on some maps as The Loop.

Such a heavy toll testifies to the desperate nature of the fighting. On the following day a deputation of Australian officers came over to the 10th Duke of Wellington's to express their admiration for the efforts they had made, and to offer them their congratulations on the fight they had put up. The Australian is not prone to empty compliments, and the congratulations of men on the spot were perhaps more deeply felt than those even of high commanders.

From this day the most friendly relations existed between our infantry and the Australians. As an expression of their friendship, some of them about this time insisted on establishing themselves in our support line. On being politely requested to move, they immediately complied —by going up into the front line ! It was the Division's first experience of these gallant soldiers, who were in 1917 to fight alongside the 23rd Division in one of its greatest battles.

On the night of 30th/31st the 70th Infantry Brigade co-operated with Stokes mortars in an attack by the 19th Division. The enemy shelled our line the whole night with gas-shells, followed by tear-shells at dawn. On the following day the 34th Division relieved the 19th Division on our right.

Few things, perhaps, tend to affect the *morale* of troops more than steadily dwindling numbers. The figures for July 1916 show the very great difficulty at this period in maintaining establishments up to strength.

The casualties in the 23rd Division during this month, which doubtless compared favourably with those sustained by many other Divisions, amounted to 212 officers and 4461 other ranks killed and wounded, 28 officers and 709 other ranks sick. Reinforcements during the same period totalled only 138 officers, 2862 other ranks.

At the beginning of August a temporary reorganisation was made in the Division to allow of the relief of battalions in the line without involving the relief of brigade headquarters.

In accordance with this arrangement two battalions of the 68th Infantry Brigade relieved two battalions of the 70th Infantry Brigade in the right section, and came under command of Brig.-General Gordon

Brig.-General Page-Croft assumed command of the left section with two of his own battalions and two of the 69th Infantry Brigade.

Brig.-General Lambert commanded a composite brigade in reserve the infantry of which consisted of two of his own battalions and two of the 70th Infantry Brigade.

Completion of these reliefs on August 2 found the 12th and 13th Durham Light Infantry holding the front line in the right and left sections respectively.

Shortly after the 68th Infantry Brigade had moved forward to take up these dispositions, a disaster overtook their headquarters, still in Albert. A heavy shell struck the house which they occupied, killing Captain Hurd Wood, the staff captain, who had been with the brigade since the outbreak of war, and two other officers, and mortally wounding Lieutenant de Mandiagues, a French officer interpreter, who had greatly endeared himself to all who knew him.

On the night of August 3/4 the 34th Division on our right were to capture a short length of trench opposite their left flank, and the 70th Infantry Brigade were ordered to join up Lancashire Trench to the left of the 34th Division objective at about Point 76.

Hostile shelling was very heavy on the left section and on Contalmaison during August 3, and, continuing after dark, became intense about 10 P.M. The right flank, however, where the operation was to be carried out, was not troubled to the same extent.

A party of the 9th South Staffordshire Regiment and a party of the 8th Yorkshire Light Infantry had been detailed for the work of joining up with the 34th Division in conjunction with their attack. The pioneers sapped forward up to the German line, but junction could not be effected with the troops on the right, as their attack had, unfortunately, been driven back. Private Nolan of the 9th South Staffordshire Regiment, however, having finished his digging, entered the German trench, and, followed by three other pioneers, bombed his way down the trench, and captured and brought back a German machine-gun. The operation, therefore, was not barren of result.

An attack had been planned for the following night by the Australians on our left. In co-operation with this, the 68th Infantry Brigade was to endeavour to secure Munster Alley up to its junction with Torr Trench, and to join the latter to The Hoop. An artillery bombardment in preparation for the attack was carried out during the day. To this the enemy replied by heavily shelling our trenches, including those about The Hoop, where the company of the 13th Durham Light Infantry detailed for the attack were to assemble. The troops suffered considerably from this artillery fire before they moved forward to attack. At 9.16 P.M. they advanced in two waves at fifty yards distance, covered by an artillery barrage. Immediately they came under a heavy rifle fire from Torr Trench and machine-gun fire from a barricade in Munster Alley. The attack faltered; the smoke and dust, drifting back from the Australian bombardment on the left, added to the confusion caused by the enemy fire, and the men lost sight of their leaders.

Captain Austin, the company commander, pushed forward with a second wave, and succeeded with a few men in gaining a footing in Torr Trench, but this gallant officer was never seen again. The attack across the open had failed; but after the second wave had crossed Munster Alley, a party succeeded in bombing their way up this trench for a distance of eighty yards, where they were held up by a strong wired block. A bombing fight continued till 2.15 A.M., and while this was in progress further frontal attack on Munster Alley was inadvisable.

Desperate efforts were made to force the enemy from his block, but without success, and a block was eventually formed at a distance of eighteen yards from the Germans.

On the following day, August 5, the 69th Infantry Brigade relieved the 68th Infantry Brigade in the left section.

During this relief Lieut.-Colonel Vaughan, commanding the 8th Yorkshire Regiment, was wounded, and command of the battalion fell to Major B. C. M. Western of the East Lancashire Regiment, who had been acting as his second-in-command.

This battalion was now ordered to make a further attempt against Munster Alley, with the object of seizing its junction with Torr Trench, and establishing blocks in both trenches fifty yards beyond the junction. If possible, a further advance would be made up Munster Alley to the German switch. One company was detailed to carry out the operation, under the personal supervision of Major Western. The attack was to be led by a party of picked bombers, volunteers, led by 2nd Lieutenant Lister. Following these would come one platoon under 2nd Lieutenant Lawson, which would be followed by another platoon under 2nd Lieutenant Cole.

At 4.10 P.M. the attacking party moved forward up Munster Alley. The enemy was at once encountered at the trench junction, and driven back 170 yards, with the loss of two prisoners. Strong opposition was now met, and in the bombing fight which ensued our men were forced back some twenty yards to a point where a block was formed. During all this time the enemy shell-fire was very heavy. Continual counter-attacks were made, but were driven off with great loss. Private W. Short, one of the leading party, though wounded in the foot, refused to leave his post. Later, his other leg was shattered by a shell, but he continued, as he lay in the trench, to adjust detonators and straighten the pins of bombs for his comrades. The action of this soldier, who shortly after died of his wounds, was but a notable example of the gallantry displayed by many this night.[1] The Australians on our left again gave splendid assistance, keeping up a continual supply of bombs to meet the heavy expenditure required. Lister having been wounded, 2nd Lieutenant Watson assumed command, and organised the defence of the captured trench with great ability. About 9 P.M. the 8th Yorkshire company, which had been bombing and attacking for five consecutive hours, was relieved by the 11th West Yorkshire Regiment. Fighting continued till dawn on August 7, but no part of the captured trench was lost. Between twenty and thirty prisoners had been taken, and the ground surrounding Munster Alley and Torr Trench was covered with German dead, half-buried and trodden under foot during the operation. Two Lewis-guns had been brought up to cover the block in Munster Alley and Torr Trench. The latter trench had been practically blotted out of existence by shell-fire, but it had been possible to establish a post about fifty yards from the junction, and the Australians undertook to clear the remainder of it. Arrangements were made to join up Torr Trench to The Hoop during the following night.

Munster Alley, so far as it provided positions for enfilade fire on the British line, had at last been wrested from the Germans. The efforts expended towards the capture of this trench in relation to its actual length can scarcely have been exceeded in any operation during the war. In addition to the attacks made by the 1st Division and to the constant bombing attacks of a minor nature, three carefully-planned attacks by troops of the 23rd Division had been made before the position was captured.

[1] The V.C. was awarded to Private Short after his death for his gallant conduct on this occasion.

The casualties sustained daily during the past fortnight had brought heavy work on the bearers of the R.A.M.C.

The relief of the Division by the 15th Division was now ordered. On August 7 the 46th Infantry Brigade relieved the 70th Infantry Brigade in the right section, and the 69th Infantry Brigade was relieved by the 45th Infantry Brigade the following day.

Command of the sector passed to the 15th Division on August 8, and 23rd Divisional Headquarters were moved to Baizieux, in the neighbourhood of which the Division was assembled prior to moving north.

In addition to the fighting in which the Division had been engaged during the past fortnight, an enormous amount of work had been carried out in the reconstruction and consolidation of the defences in the line so recently won from the Germans.

On orders being issued for the Division to leave the Fourth Army, General Rawlinson addressed a letter [1] to the Divisional Commander, of which the following is an extract :—

> The attack and capture of Contalmaison and Munster Alley were fine feats of arms, of which the Division may be justly proud, and I congratulate them not only on these successes, but also on the vigorous and determined manner in which they advanced our trench line by offensive digging. Both the infantry and artillery of the Division have performed their respective tasks admirably, and it is most satisfactory to see the two arms working in such close sympathy and unison.

On August 10 the mounted personnel and transport of the Division (less artillery) moved by road to the area about Ailly-le-Haut-Clocher, where Divisional Headquarters were established the following day on the detrainment of the dismounted portion of the Division, which moved to the area by rail.

On August 12 the Division commenced to entrain for the V. Corps area, where Divisional Headquarters were established on the 13th at Fletres.

The 23rd Division owed so much to *esprit de corps* that it is a dangerous thing to breathe a word against this sentiment in a history which we trust may be read by many who served in the Division. But it is undeniable that the 23rd Division—perhaps there were others like it

---

[1] Fourth Army G.S. 241, dated 9th August 1916.

—believed that *their* artillery was *the* artillery, and were not quite comfortable if supported by any other, however good an imitation they might be of the real thing. If *esprit de corps* were open to attack at all, it might be here. In compensation, however, it may be said that it is open to question if the infantry of the Division, in common again perhaps with that of other divisions, were seriously agitated with what their artillery was doing when they themselves were out of the line.

The 23rd Divisional Artillery had now been left behind. They had been continuously in the line since July 5. For the first ten days after coming into action the enemy's counter-battery work had been feeble, and casualties had been confined chiefly to forward observing officers and telephonists. But from July 15 onwards shelling of batteries had become increasingly heavy, the worst sufferers being the 102nd and 103rd Brigades, and the 25th Brigade, which was attached. Casualties during the period had amounted to 25 officers and 310 other ranks.

Batteries had fired continuously by night, and except for short periods during the greater part of the day. At times a rapid and intense fire had to be maintained for long periods ; for example, six rounds a minute per gun for twenty minutes, followed by two rounds a minute for one hour, followed by one round a minute for four hours. On one occasion the 18-pdr. guns of the 23rd Divisional Artillery alone fired 30,000 rounds in twelve hours. The sheer physical strain of this at a practice camp, if such a performance in peace time were conceivable, would be immense ; under the conditions in which it was carried out it is nigh incredible.

The artillery had not been grouped with infantry formations, but was under Divisional control throughout. Front-line battalions, however, each had a direct line to one Field Artillery brigade, on which they could call for support in case of emergency. An artillery liaison officer was with the headquarters of each infantry brigade, and a forward observing officer with each front-line battalion. In case of special operations extra F.O.O.'s were detailed to go forward of battalion headquarters.

It is reasonable to suppose that the infantry of the Division were to a certain extent unconscious of the above facts. But, now they learnt that they were to relieve the 41st Division in the line, they shared the satisfaction of the artillery in the relief of the latter by the 47th

Divisional Artillery on August 14, which was to enable them to join the Division.

A tale is told by an officer of the 23rd Divisional Artillery of the lack of appreciation of the infantry officer. Fifty rounds of 4.5 howitzer high-explosive shell had been allotted to knock out an enemy post located by the infantry in the line. The gunner officer sent up to observe was met by an eager young infantry officer, who pointed out the post that was to be dealt with. Range could be calculated quite easily by a registered target near-by.

No. 1 gun fired. For an opening shot it was a beauty, not more than fifty yards to the right, not more than twenty yards over. The gunner looked round for approval. But his infantry friend's face was simply desolate.

" You didn't hit it ! " he said dismally.

" No ; but there's one more shot in the locker, perhaps."

" My men," retorted the infantryman, still under the shock of his disillusion, " could hit that first shot every time, and just with a rifle ! " [1]

---

[1] Article in 'The Gunner,' by Lieutenant F. Fox, 23rd Divisional Artillery.

CHAPTER IV.

PLOEGSTEERT AND LATER SOMME BATTLES : MARTINPUICH,
DESTREMONT FARM, LE SARS.

AUGUST 15 TO OCTOBER 9, 1916.

Map No. 1. IN war, perhaps, more even than in peace, everything in this world
is comparative. In the war on the Western Front " Plug Street " will
always be connected with peace. The Ploegsteert sector represented
the nursery to which many divisions were sent on their first arrival
in France, and a haven of rest to tired divisions, both of ourselves and
the enemy. It was on this front that the Division was to take over
the line. The right of the sector, which was the right sector of the IX.
Corps front, was situated at a point about half a mile south-west of
Frélinghien, two miles north-east of Armentières. Thence the line ran
west of Frélinghien along the eastern edge of Ploegsteert Wood to a
point just south of the Neuve Eglise-Warneton road, 2000 yards due
south of Messines. The high ground of Haubourdin Hill lay behind the
left flank. The frontage of the sector was about 5000 yards.

Relief commenced on August 15, when the 70th Infantry Brigade,
moving up through Steenwercke, relieved the 122nd Infantry Brigade
in Divisional reserve. On the following day the 10th Northumberland
Fusiliers and the 13th Durham Light Infantry moved to Le Bizet and
Armentières respectively, and the Field Companies R.E. moved up
to the forward area. On August 17 the 68th Infantry Brigade relieved
the 123rd Infantry Brigade in the right section, and the 70th relieved
the 124th Infantry Brigade on the left. General Babington assumed
command of the sector on the same day, with headquarters at Steenwercke.

The New Zealand Division was on the right, and the 36th Division on the left.

Headquarters of the right infantry brigade were situated about 1500 yards north-west of Armentières on the Nieppe road ; headquarters of the left infantry brigade were in Ploegsteert Wood.

With the relief of the 124th by the 69th Infantry Brigade in Divisional reserve on the 18th, and of the 41st by the 23rd Divisional Artillery on August 20, the Divisional relief was complete.

The defences of the sector were formed by a continuous front line at an average distance of some 200 yards from the German trenches. From 500 to 700 yards in rear of this ran a main support line (Hunter Avenue), containing strong-points at intervals varying from 100 to 250 yards. 1000 yards in rear of this again an irregular line of strong-points had been constructed.

Each brigade held two battalions in the front-line defences, one battalion in the support line, and one battalion in brigade reserve. Machine-guns were distributed throughout the defence, the greater number being sited in the support line.

The state of the defences was exceptionally good on the left, and very fair in the centre ; but on the right they were in a poor state of repair. Concrete machine-gun emplacements were in the course of construction.

No greater contrast could be imagined than that between the conditions prevailing on this front and those of the battlefield of the Somme, from which the Division had just come. Where in Albert, 5000 yards in rear of the nearest point in the British front line, one lived in shattered ruins under shell-fire and the continuous roar of our own artillery ; here in Armentières, little more than a mile from the German line, one found a café and shops, where French civilians still plied a brisk trade with the British soldier.

Till within six weeks of the arrival of the Division, the farm of Grand Babécoue had been occupied within one mile of the line. It had only then been vacated by its proprietors on account of one of the family being killed by a stray shell while cutting hay ! Hayfields, where on the Somme nothing would have been found but the desolation of mud and shell-holes !

One might well think that such conditions would have been entirely

restful after the experience of the preceding six weeks. But this very
silence in close proximity to an enemy, whose presence was only made
manifest by occasional rifle-grenades and trench-mortar bombs and by
machine-gun fire at night, brought a certain strain on nerves accustomed to the din of the battle in the south.

Moreover, an ever-present danger was lurking on this front, which
in the interests of their safety the front-line garrison could never be
allowed to forget. The 9.2 shell is a terrible fellow, but he is gentleman
enough to announce his approach, and declares his arrival in manly
fashion. Strange though it may be, the average soldier will find a frank
and childish amusement in the terrific burst of a big shell—if it is not
too near him. Bairnsfather's drawings alone testify to that. But no
soldier has ever laughed at that true invention of the devil himself—
the gas which creeps silently and without warning over its victim, and,
having dealt the most horrible death, creeps on.

This was declared a "gas sector," and continual precautions had to
be taken. The direction of the wind was carefully noted, and when the
direction was dangerous, ears were unconsciously strained to detect
the warning note of the Strombus horn announcing the approach of a
gas cloud.

In the end, however, it was from our side that the first gas attack
was made. A hostile gas attack is perhaps the only thing which a British
soldier dislikes more than one from his own side. No one with experience of our gas services can fail to recognise the pluck, perseverance,
and self-sacrifice of the gas personnel or their skill at fighting the enemy
at his own hellish game. But it must be confessed that, quite apart
from moral principles, the "gas monger" was not generally popular.
His appearance invariably meant trouble. Even if spared the delights
of carrying gas-cylinders up narrow communication trenches to the
front line, the infantry in the line often spent days—sometimes weeks—
—with these undesirable companions, praying that a hostile bombardment might not burst them, and so spread their evil contents among
the front-line garrison. At last, when the wind, after days of perversity,
turned favourable, the foul stuff was let loose. As a rule, the full results
were not witnessed, but the one result which could be reckoned on was
the enemy's retaliatory bombardment.

During the end of August there was a considerable amount of rain, accompanied at times by strong wind. The weather, however, cleared during the night of the 30th/31st, and at 1.30 A.M. gas was released from cylinders which had been installed all along the line, the intervals between cylinders being filled by smoke from smoke-candles. There had been no preliminary artillery bombardment, for fear of warning the enemy. But four minutes after the release of gas our artillery and trench-mortars opened with the intention of catching the enemy as they were manning their front-line parapet and putting on their gas-masks. The enemy's S.O.S. signal was not fired till five minutes after zero, and it was reckoned that the operation had accomplished its purpose.

This was later confirmed by a raiding party. One hour after the release of gas four parties, two on the front of each infantry brigade, attempted to reach the enemy's line. On the left they were held up by wire and by machine-gun fire, but on the right a party of the 10th Northumberland Fusiliers succeeded in gaining the enemy's trench unobserved, and found the Germans standing-to. Four of this party entered the trench, killed a sentry, and threw some twenty bombs, causing much damage. They also discovered gruesome evidence of the effect of our gas. They regained our trenches with the loss of two other ranks killed and nine wounded. The remaining parties returned without casualty.

Provoked, presumably, by this breach of the "Plug Street Peace," the enemy's artillery and trench-mortars considerably increased their activity on September 1. But it was not to be known for how long this would be sustained. For on the same day instructions from the IX. Corps reached Divisional Headquarters, which had been moved to Bailleul a few days earlier, that the Division was to be relieved at once by the 19th and 51st Divisions. During the period of relief, however, which was carried out during the next few days, both our own and the enemy's artillery and trench-mortars were hard at it.

On September 2 the 70th Infantry Brigade, in Divisional reserve, was relieved by the 154th Infantry Brigade of the 51st Division, and withdrew to the Anzac training area near Bailleul, whence they moved on the following day to the Staple-Wallon Cappell area, to Arques on September 4, and to Lumbres on the 5th. The 68th Infantry Brigade, commanded now by Brig.-General G. N. Colville, D.S.O., who had taken over command from Brig.-General H. Page-Croft, C.M.G., on August 18, was relieved in the right section of the line by the 154th

Infantry Brigade on September 3. Staging in the Anzac training area and at Meteren, they moved on September 5 by tactical trains to St Omer, whence they marched to the Nordesque area.

The 69th Infantry Brigade, relieved in the left section by the 56th Infantry Brigade of the 19th Division on September 4, moved on the 6th by tactical trains to the Moulle area.

Divisional Headquarters moved on the same day to that same Tilques from which they had moved forward exactly one year before to join battle with the enemy. Peace had been coming before Christmas then, as it had been in 1914. Peace was still coming before Christmas. The more advanced optimists had indeed hoped to await the celebration of the event in the Ploegsteert area. This idea had perhaps stimulated the work on hutments and the general preparations in the area for comfort in the following winter ; but it is hoped that the division which eventually reaped the benefit of our labours regarded the work done as purely altruistic.

The withdrawal from "Plug Street," unexpected by many, augured fairly clearly that before Christmas Day, 1916, the Division was to be called on to maintain the reputation it had already established during its first year of war.

The Division was now in the Second Army. Orders were received on September 7 for it to rejoin the III. Corps of the Fourth Army.

On September 10 Divisional Headquarters moved to Allonville, and the Division (less artillery) commenced entrainment. On arrival in the new area on the following day the 70th Infantry Brigade was sent to Bresle in Corps reserve, and detached two battalions to the 15th Division on September 12. On the same day the remainder of the Division moved forward to the Baizieux area.

The Divisional Artillery had in the meantime been relieved on the Ploegsteert front, and moved south. On arrival, the 102nd Brigade R.F.A. was attached to the 15th Division, the 103rd Brigade to the 47th Division. On the same day (September 13) the 128th Field Company and two companies of the pioneers were detached, half to the 15th Division and half to the 50th Division.

Map No. 2.   The offensive continued by the Fourth Army in the early part of September had succeeded in carrying Guillemont, Ginchy, and Delville Wood, and so in reducing the salient on the right of the British line.

Westwards of Delville Wood the line had been carried forward in front of Bazentin and Pozières to High Wood and south of Martinpuich and Courcelette.

The 47th, 50th, and 15th Divisions of the III. Corps now occupied the line from the southern edge of High Wood to opposite Martinpuich.

A further attack had been arranged for September 15. Lest it should prove necessary to reinforce attacking divisions, the 68th Infantry Brigade was placed in readiness to move at ten minutes' notice from 6.20 A.M., the hour at which operations were to commence.

The attack of September 15, notable for being the first operation in which tanks were employed, proved a complete success on the whole front of the Fourth Army, and effected the capture of Le Flers, Martinpuich, and Courcelette.

During the day the 68th Infantry Brigade was moved forward to Bécourt Wood from Millencourt, where they were replaced by the 69th Infantry Brigade.

The 70th Infantry Brigade was moved to Black Wood. Later, the 13th Durham Light Infantry were placed at the disposal of the 47th Division, and were moved to Fricourt Circus.

A troop (1 officer and 26 other ranks) of the Duke of Lancaster's Own Yeomanry, the old Divisional Cavalry, reported for duty at Divisional Headquarters during the day.

On September 17 the Division received orders to take over the front which had been fixed as the left sector of the III. Corps front. This entailed relief of the 15th Division and taking over a small portion of the line held by the 50th Division.

The sector had a front of some 2000 yards, and ran from the junction Map No. 4. of Starfish and Prue Trenches round the north-easterly outskirts of Martinpuich to a point just east of the Bapaume road, and 350 yards south-east of Courcelette. The Division was to be disposed in depth. One infantry brigade would occupy the line, with headquarters in Villa Wood ; one infantry brigade would be in support in trench areas north and north-west of Bazentin-le-Petit, with headquarters in Contalmaison ; the third infantry brigade would be held in Divisional reserve at Contalmaison, Scots Redoubt, and Shelter Wood.

Reliefs in accordance with these arrangements were carried out on the 18th and 19th—the 69th Infantry Brigade taking over the line, the 68th Infantry Brigade being placed in support, and the 70th Infantry Brigade in reserve. Relief on the right of the line by the 9th Yorkshire Regiment, which was carried out by daylight on the 19th, was not completed till 12 noon, and was observed by the enemy. Shortly after they had taken over the line their most advanced post was surrounded on three sides by the Germans, who attacked heavily with bombs, inflicted many casualties, and rushed the post. About an hour later the enemy attacked again, and made further progress. The 9th Yorkshire Regiment then counter-attacked, and regained all the ground lost.

General Babington assumed command of the sector during the morning of September 19. The 50th Division was on the right of the 23rd Division, and the 1st Canadian Division was holding Courcelette on the left.

As is often the case after an attack, the exact position of the enemy and our own troops was somewhat obscure. A further advance was contemplated, but postponement of operations was forced by the bad weather, which had so consistently hampered British operations throughout the 1916 campaign.

Efforts in the meantime were directed to reconnoitring, improving our position by seizing points of vantage, and maintaining touch with divisions on the flanks. There was considerable activity in these days on the Canadian front, and incessant heavy fire was heard in the direction of Courcelette.

On September 21 a party of the 69th Infantry Brigade raided the enemy's line north of Martinpuich, where they succeeded in establishing posts ; but they were later driven from the position by machine-gun fire. Contact had now been definitely gained with the 50th Division in Starfish Line. On the following night patrols found 26th Avenue had been vacated by the enemy, but the G.O.C. 69th Infantry Brigade was averse to occupying it till the Canadians had improved the position on his left. Patrols of the 50th Division at the same time reported that there were no enemy on this side of Eaucourt l'Abbaye (1½ mile north-east of Martinpuich). This situation, in the light of subsequent events, seems to indicate that the enemy must have been in two minds at this time as to the line and the extent of resistance to be put up in this area.

The 68th Infantry Brigade relieved the 69th Infantry Brigade in

ALBERT CATHEDRAL.

the line during the afternoon of September 22. Orders were issued to the brigade the same day with reference to their action preparatory to an attack to be made by the Canadians on the 25th. Such action was to be directed to digging new trenches to connect with an advance post of the 50th Division on the right, and to the main road to connect with the Canadians on the left. Reconnaissance was to be made of the trenches in front of our position, and—an interesting point—the brigadier was to be prepared to discuss the question of holding this line for the winter.

On September 23 the Canadians reported that they had captured a labyrinth of trenches to the east of Courcelette, and asked the 23rd Division if they would now join up. This was agreed to, providing 26th Avenue was still found unoccupied. The 68th Infantry Brigade attacked at 4 P.M., and found the enemy had reoccupied the position. They succeeded, however, in occupying 26th Avenue for a distance of 200 yards west of Point 73, but were unable to progress farther to the left.

An advanced dressing-station had been established by the 69th Field Ambulance at Martinpuich in a very large dug-out containing bunks and several galleries. The headquarters of the ambulance were at Contalmaison Chateau. Here Lieut.-Colonel A. Nimmo Walker was killed by shrapnel on September 24.[1] He was succeeded in command of the 69th Field Ambulance by Lieut.-Colonel G. H. L. Hammerton.

An attack was now ordered for the capture of 26th Avenue on September 25. It was to be made by two companies of the 10th Northumberland Fusiliers. Two tanks, operating one on either flank, would assist the attack, in which the 11th Northumberland Fusiliers, in occupation of the portion of the trench already captured, would co-operate from Point 53 on the right of the objective.

By 12.15 P.M. on September 25 the attacking companies were in their assembly positions, concealed by a ridge which lay between them and their objective. One of the tanks had broken down on its way to the starting-point, but the other, detailed for the right of the attack,

---

[1] Lieut.-Colonel Walker was buried in the grounds of the chateau. The writer could only spend a short time at this cemetery, which contains a great number of graves, and there was a dense fog on the day of his visit. Other graves found here were those of :—
   Private Short, V.C., 8th Yorks. ; killed 6/8/16.
   2nd Lieutenant C. Armstrong, 12th D.L.I. ; killed 21/9/16.
   2nd Lieutenant J. Bollom, 12th D.L.I. ; killed 24/9/16.

now moved forward. Its object was to advance on Point 53, and then to work left towards the centre of the objective.

At 12.20 P.M. the tank was seen to top the rise. Four minutes later rockets were fired from the enemy's line, and at 12.30 P.M. heavy fire was opened by the hostile artillery. At 12.35 P.M. the infantry advanced in two waves at fifty yards' distance in face of terrific artillery and machine-gun fire—" A " Company on the right, " B " Company on the left. At the same time Captain Constable, commanding " A " Company, with two platoons of his company in file, worked up Push Alley on the right flank.

The tank got within 200 yards of the objective and opened fire. Turning, it then moved 100 yards to the left, when it was hit, and backed out of action across Push Alley.

In the meantime the first wave of the infantry, after an advance of 500 yards, had gained the crest of the ridge some 150 yards from the objective. Here they came under a withering fire from the enemy's trenches.

On the right 2nd Lieutenant Calder, already wounded, led forward the few men left with him. Wounded again twice, he continued to advance till, within 60 yards of the objective, he was killed. 2nd Lieutenant Lock brought forward the second wave. Wounded three times, he struggled gallantly on till killed within 150 yards of the enemy's trench. 2nd Lieutenant Noble was then ordered to lead the two platoons in Push Alley across the open. He at once rushed forward to comply with this order, but was killed as he climbed the parapet. Captain Constable then, with the assistance of Sergeant Bell, withdrew these platoons again to Push Alley, and proceeded to bomb up towards Point 53. Here he continued the fight till relieved by the 12th Durham Light Infantry at 5.15 P.M. Then, mounting from the trench to reorganise his company, Captain Constable was shot dead.

On the left " B " Company had made no better progress. The first wave pushed to within seventy yards of its objective ; here the officer in command, finding only a few men left with him, dug in. The following wave met with no better success, and was forced to dig in and wait for dark. The battalion commander sent forward Captain Ellis with two platoons to endeavour to carry forward the attack on this flank. This officer was last seen gallantly leading forward the reinforcing platoons, together with some of " B " Company, close to the enemy's lines.

The casualties suffered by the 10th Northumberland Fusiliers in this costly and abortive operation amounted to : killed—5 officers, 42 other ranks ; wounded—4 officers, 135 other ranks ; missing—1 officer, 18 other ranks.

These casualties alone prove that if success had been possible by the method of attack employed it would have been attained this day. But it must be remembered that there was no reason to expect that the Germans would be found in such strength, or that they would put up such a strong resistance on a line which they had vacated only a few days previously. The result of the attack provides an example of the strength of a reverse slope position against frontal attack in any but overwhelming numbers. The weakness of such a position lies in its restricted field of fire. If it is to be held against attack, this weakness will be counteracted by placing a large number of rifles and machine-guns in defence. The attack must therefore anticipate an intense fire from the defence by advancing in such strength as to ensure sufficient weight remaining after being weakened by the numerous casualties which will inevitably occur. Against a staunch defence the operation must always be costly.

The Canadian attack east of Courcelette had in the meantime been cancelled, owing to the two tanks which were to co-operate having both been hit. No further attempt was, accordingly, to be made to capture 26th Avenue for the present.

The final occupation of this line was effected in a most remarkable way. On September 27, two days after the desperate attack which has just been related, a patrol reconnoitring the right portion of 26th Avenue found it unoccupied, though fresh bread was discovered in the trench. Major Shaw, R.F.A., who happened to be in the line, together with an infantry subaltern, walked right down the line to the Bapaume road, found it vacated, and established touch with the 2nd Canadian Division.

The 70th Infantry Brigade then occupied the trench, and commenced to push up towards the north-east.

It is concluded that the Germans had been holding 26th Avenue as a rearguard position to cover their withdrawal to Le Sars and the Flers line. If this was their intention, it seems that on this, as on other occasions, their withdrawal was carried out farther than was intended. Patrols

of the 50th Division reached Flers line and Le Sars without difficulty,
and early on September 25 a patrol of the 70th Infantry Brigade reported Destremont Farm unoccupied. A platoon was sent forward
at 4 A.M. to occupy the farm, but by then the Germans had strongly
occupied the position. The platoon was met by heavy rifle and machine-
gun fire, and was unable to get forward. About the same time the
50th Division reported that the Germans had now occupied the Flers
line covering Le Sars in strength.[1]

The whole of 26th Avenue was now held, but touch had been lost
with the left of the 50th Division. This was said to be situated at a
point in a trench to the north-west of and parallel to 26th Avenue. The
70th Brigade, in reply, declared the whole of this trench to be occupied
by Germans. The discussion which ensued was typical of many that
raged between neighbouring brigadiers ; the responsibility for these, it
is feared, lay with the makers of maps.

The occupation of Destremont Farm was an essential preliminary to
future plans. A second attempt by the 70th Infantry Brigade on the
28th having failed to secure the position, the 8th York and Lancaster
Regiment, under command of Lieut.-Colonel S. L. Whatford, was ordered
to attack on September 29 for the capture of the farm.

The infantry attack was to be supported by the Divisional Artillery.
Assault of the farm was entrusted to Captain Barlow's [2] company,
while a second company would act in support of the operation.

The assaulting company was assembled on a line some 700 to 800
yards distant from their objective. At 5.30 A.M., moving forward in
two waves at fifty yards distance, they closed upon the artillery barrage
which covered the advance. Steadily advancing, the attacking lines
approached to within fifty yards of the enemy's position. The artillery
then lifted to clear the way for the assault. Immediately the German
garrison opened an intense fire with rifles and machine-guns on the
attack. But they were too late ; answering the call of their officers,
the 8th York and Lancasters charged the position with loud cheers,
killed a large number of the enemy, and drove the remainder in great

---

[1] The first evacuation of 26th Avenue on September 22 also appears to have been contrary
to their plan.

[2] This very gallant young officer, whose name occurs several times in this History, was as-
sassinated by Arabs in 1920 at Tel Afar, forty-five miles west of Mosul, where he was Assistant
Political Officer.

disorder from the farm. One machine-gun, a thousand bombs, many thousands of rounds of S.A.A., and a large number of rifles were captured. Later an important engineer dump was discovered near the farm. Patrols were sent out, and touch was gained with the Canadians on the left in the course of the day.

The German artillery very soon became acquainted with the turn of events, and commenced a heavy bombardment of the farm. This rendered the organisation of the defence a matter of the greatest difficulty. To avoid casualties three platoons were withdrawn ; the duty of consolidating and defending the position was left to the remaining platoon, assisted by two machine-guns. The platoon so left was relieved at intervals throughout the day and the following night.

There are few occasions when a cool-headed leader is of greater value than during the period following a successful assault, when the sight of a routed enemy flying in disorder seems to make resting on one's laurels not only preferable but more reasonable than " digging like the devil " to resist counter-attack. Consolidation on this occasion was largely due to the example set by Lieutenant T. H. Searle, who, by setting to work himself and by cheering his men's exertions, secured the position before he was eventually severely wounded.

Misty weather favoured work, and a much-needed communication trench, connecting the south-east end of the farm to 26th Avenue, was practically completed by noon. Trenches on this line were needed not only for communication but for the assembly of troops for future operations. An attempt was made by the Pioneer Battalion and by troops of the reserve brigade to dig another trench in front of the farm to 26th Avenue. But shelling was so intense that little progress could be made, and the short length completed was entirely obliterated the following day. On the night of September 30, however, a second trench was successfully dug immediately in rear of that already completed.

Under the continuous fire of the enemy's artillery, Destremont Farm was held by the 8th York and Lancaster Regiment and 2nd Lieutenant Lorraine's section of the 70th Machine-Gun Company from 6 A.M. on September 29 till 9.30 on October 2, when they were relieved by the 10th Duke of Wellington's.

Headquarters of the Division and of the C.R.A. had been moved forward during September 30 to Shelter Wood. The capture of the

Flers front and support lines, in co-operation with an attack by the 50th Division on the right, was now ordered for October 1. These trenches, called for convenience Flers 1 and Flers 2 respectively, running down from the north-west, covered the village of Le Sars from the west, and were continued east and south-eastwards to connect the defences of Le Sars with those of Flers, which had been captured by the Fourth Army on September 15.

The 70th Infantry Brigade was ordered to effect the capture of the portion of these trenches allotted as the objective of the 23rd Division, which lay astride the Bapaume road on a frontage of 800 yards. The plan of attack of the Brigade detailed two battalions for the capture of the objective, a third battalion to support the attack, while the fourth battalion was to be held in reserve. Having captured the hostile position, a defensive flank was to be thrown back from the left of the line to connect with the Canadians north-west of Destremont Farm.

In preparation for this attack the artillery commenced to cut the enemy's wire. Experiencing difficulty in obtaining observation of the wire, Major W. H. Powell crept before dawn to a shell-hole in close proximity to the German wire, where he lay for the best part of two days directing the fire of his battery. Under constant and heavy shell-fire, which incessantly interrupted his telephonic communication, Major Powell succeeded in his task at the cost of several casualties to his telephonists. For this and a subsequent gallant action Major Powell was awarded the D.S.O.

On the morning of October 1 the 11th Sherwood Foresters and 8th K.O. Yorkshire Light Infantry, detailed for the assault, assembled in the trenches prepared for the purpose between Destremont Farm and 26th Avenue. The 9th York and Lancaster Regiment, in support, took up position in trenches some 1100 yards in rear; the 8th York and Lancaster Regiment were held in reserve just north of Martinpuich, with elements in occupation of Destremont Farm.

The 70th Machine-Gun Company, co-operating in the attack, had detailed Nos. 2 and 3 Sections to bring overhead fire on Le Sars; No. 4 Section was divided—two guns under 2nd Lieutenant Gibson were to advance with the Sherwood Foresters, two guns under 2nd Lieutenant Osborne Jones with the Yorkshire Light Infantry; No. 1 Section was detailed to strengthen the defensive flank.

At 3.15 P.M. an artillery barrage opened to cover the advance, and simultaneously the infantry moved forward to the attack in four waves at close distance. The Germans were quick to realise the situation, and, four minutes after the advance had commenced, a heavy artillery barrage fell on the area of our assembly. But it was too late to effect its purpose, for our infantry were already beyond the danger zone, and within six minutes of zero they had closed on their own artillery barrage.

The moment of assault had arrived. As the artillery lifted to clear the way, the Sherwood Foresters rushed the hostile front line, over-powered the garrison, and, pushing forward, carried the right of the Division's objective in Flers 2. The advance of the Yorkshire Light Infantry on the left had proved more difficult. The position of their assembly trenches in relation to their objective had necessitated an oblique advance, and in the smoke of the artillery barrage the right of their attack lost direction. The battalion, more particularly on the left, had suffered heavily in the advance, but they none the less succeeded in carrying their objective in the enemy's front line, except in a portion on either side of the Bapaume road, which, owing to the loss of direction, had remained free from frontal attack.

The enemy on this flank put up a very stiff resistance against further advance to Flers 2, but 2nd Lieutenant Cooke, though wounded, forced his way forward with fifty men, and occupied 200 yards of this trench. In the meantime 2nd Lieutenant Roddle bombed his way down Flers 1, and secured and blocked the left flank. Here he was joined later in the day by ten men of the Canadians. Between dusk and 11 P.M. these two young officers with their men repulsed seven separate bombing attacks, in one of which eight bays of trench were captured by the enemy and retaken.

The machine-guns with the Yorkshire Light Infantry suffered severely in the attack. Five minutes before the assault one gun had been put out of action, and 2nd Lieutenant Jones had been wounded. 2nd Lieutenant Smellie, taking his place, was immediately wounded ; Sergeant Fiegehen then assumed command, and, advancing with the remaining gun, did good work till a bomb put the gun out of action and killed several of the team.

At 4.15 P.M. a company of the 9th York and Lancaster Regiment had been sent forward to capture the centre of the objective of the

Division—the trenches immediately north and south of the Bapaume road, which were still in occupation of the enemy. The whole uncaptured portion of Flers 1 was successfully carried, but Flers 2, covered as it was by the fire of rifles and machine-guns from the village, presented a more difficult task, and it was only found possible to occupy the portion south of the road and to form a block on the southern side of the road to protect the left flank. At 7.15 P.M. a second company was sent forward to join up with and reinforce the Yorkshire Light Infantry.

It had been intended, if no great resistance was encountered, to exploit success by the capture of Le Sars. But the enemy had been found in such strength as to make it clear that a separate operation would be necessary to effect the capture of the village. The positions secured were accordingly consolidated, while a company of the pioneers laboured throughout the night at the construction of a communication trench to connect up the right of the captured line with the rear.

Daybreak on October 2 found the 23rd Division in occupation of Flers 1 on its whole front ; Flers 2 was held south of the road. On the right the 50th Division had captured its objectives, and continued the line to the south-east.

In the action of October 1 the 70th Infantry Brigade lost 30 officers and 770 other ranks killed and wounded. Every man who survived the assault claimed to have killed several Germans. Though reliable estimates cannot always be derived from such sources, it is certain that the enemy suffered severely at the hands of the infantry ; his losses from artillery and machine-gun fire were, no less surely, very heavy.

The 70th Infantry Brigade, which had been relieved by the 69th Infantry Brigade during the night following their attack, was withdrawn on October 2 to Divisional reserve about Fricourt. The 68th Infantry Brigade was moved to a position in support in and around Contalmaison.

Hitherto the weather had been fine, but rain now set in, and the condition of the trenches and the surrounding ground, churned up as it was by artillery fire, became increasingly bad. Orders had been issued for the capture of Le Sars by the 23rd Division in co-operation with an attack by the 47th Division, on their right, directed on the Butte de Warlencourt. The incessant rain had, however, reduced the ground to such a condition as to render operations on a large scale impossible for the present, and the attack was postponed till October 7.

But as a preliminary to this big attack the G.O.C. 69th Infantry Brigade determined to endeavour to improve his position by two small operations, designed to capture the portion of Flers 2 still held by the enemy, and a short length of Flers 1 to the south of the Bapaume road, in which the enemy had again obtained a footing.

On the evening of October 3, following artillery preparation, two companies of the 10th Duke of Wellington's attacked Flers 2 north of the Bapaume road, while a party of the 8th Yorkshire Regiment carried out a simultaneous bombing attack against the enemy in Flers 1.

To gain their objective the Duke of Wellington's had but 100 yards to cross. But their advance lay across mud and mire of the most appalling description, and was met by a withering fire of rifles and machine-guns. Following their leaders, among whom 2nd Lieutenants Stafford, Harris, and Kelly were conspicuous in the example they set, the men pushed forward with the greatest gallantry, and gained the enemy's wire. Here they were held up. To cross a greater distance under these conditions would have been scarcely possible, but the distance of the assembly trenches from the objective had been insufficient to enable the artillery to deal effectively with the wire. Stafford and Harris were killed, and the attack broke down.[1]

In the meantime the bombing attack of the 8th Yorkshires had succeeded in occupying the objective in Flers 1. This point, however, was destroyed by artillery fire on the following day, and had to be evacuated.

These small operations, which had thus failed to secure the object desired, had been carried out at heavy cost. The 10th Duke of Wellington's had lost 3 officers and 25 other ranks killed, 2 officers and 80 other

---

[1] On November 29, 1916, the Corps Commander decorated Lieutenant (later Captain) Kelly with the ribbon of the Victoria Cross. In the official record of the action for which it was awarded no date appears, but it is believed that it was on this occasion that this officer, whose gallantry was conspicuous throughout the war, won the Victoria Cross. The official record is as follows : "For most conspicuous bravery in attack. He twice rallied his company under the heaviest fire, and finally led the only three available men into the enemy trench, and there remained bombing until two of them had become casualties and enemy reinforcements had arrived. He then carried his Company Sergeant-Major, who had been wounded, back to our trenches, a distance of seventy yards, and subsequently three other soldiers. He set a fine example of gallantry and endurance."

ranks wounded, 29 other ranks missing. The 8th Yorkshire Regiment lost 2 officers and 5 other ranks killed, 3 officers and 50 other ranks wounded.

In anticipation of the impending attack on Le Sars, General Babington had been ordered to assume command of the front held by the 50th Division on the afternoon of October 3. During the night the 149th Infantry Brigade, occupying this portion of the line, was relieved by the 68th Infantry Brigade. The 23rd Division now held Flers 1 for 1000 yards south of the Bapaume road, and 400 yards north of the road ; in front of the centre and right of this line Flers 2 was held for a distance of 1000 yards from a point just south of the road.

These lines were to form the " jumping-off " line of the Division in its attack on Le Sars. Before considering the plan of attack, it will be necessary to study somewhat carefully the direction in which they ran, since this to a large degree influenced the plan.

The task allotted to the 23rd Division included, in addition to the capture of the village, a northward extension of our hold on Flers 1 and Flers 2 for a distance of 800 yards from the point where the left of the Division now rested in the former trench. This extension would be carried out in conjunction with an attack by the Canadian Corps, with whom junction was to be effected. But since the Canadians had decided not to attack till the morning of October 8, this part of the 23rd Division's operations would not be carried out in full till the day following the capture of Le Sars.

The village of Le Sars was strung out along either side of the Bapaume road. The greater portion of the Divisional front, which crossed this road at right angles, ran in a south-easterly direction. But 500 yards from the right flank of the Division the Flers trenches took a sharp bend to the east. It will be seen, therefore, that while a direct frontal advance from the left and centre of the line would move parallel to the road, and through the length of the village, a similar advance from the right would converge in the direction of the north-eastern or farther quarter of Le Sars.

Before reaching the village on this line of advance the right attack would be confronted by two formidable obstacles—a tangle of trenches due east of the centre of the village, and a sunken road leading to Le Sars from the east, just beyond these trenches. It was recognised, moreover, that this right attack would be threatened with enfilade fire from the southern quarter of the village so long as this was in the occupation of the enemy.

The attack was to be carried by the 68th Infantry Brigade on the right and the 69th Infantry Brigade on the left, battle headquarters of each brigade being established at Martinpuich. Each brigade was to employ two battalions in the first line of attack, the remaining battalions being held in support and reserve.

Advance to the attack was not to be simultaneous along the whole line ; in each brigade the right battalion would move forward first. The attack can be regarded as divided into two phases. In the first phase, on the front of the 68th Infantry Brigade the 12th Durham Light Infantry were to advance to capture the tangle of trenches and the sunken road east of Le Sars, while a simultaneous advance by the 9th Yorkshire Regiment on the front of the 69th Infantry Brigade would secure the portion of the village south of the central cross-roads. The accomplishment of these tasks would, it was calculated, prove of immense assistance to the action of the battalions detailed for the second phase. In this the 13th Durham Light Infantry would push forward between the leading battalions to attack and capture the northern portion of the village ; while the 11th West Yorkshire Regiment, advancing at zero plus twenty minutes, would capture Flers 2 north of the Bapaume road.

The infantry attack was to be supported by the artillery of the 23rd and 50th Divisions, in conjunction with that of the 47th Division on the right. Following preliminary bombardment, the advance would be covered by an 18-pdr. barrage, opening on a line 400 yards in advance of the forward assembly positions of the infantry, and moving forward at a general rate of fifty yards a minute. Special barrages had been arranged to protect the left flank of the 9th Yorkshire Regiment in the initial stages of their advance.

The attack would further be supported by the fire of machine-guns and Stokes mortars, and a tank was detailed to assist the operation of the 68th Infantry Brigade.

Rain continued on October 4, but the weather cleared on the 5th, and during that and the following day the ground dried rapidly. Hostile artillery fire was heavy and continuous during these days preceding attack, and some idea of the close quarters at which the infantry of the front line were living with the enemy can be gained from the relation of an incident that occurred on the morning of the 6th.

Lieutenant Courage and Private Laughran, who were in the front line near the Bapaume road, detected some of the enemy moving in the village. A Stokes-gun was brought into action for the benefit of this party, which speedily scattered, six of them rushing forward to take cover. These Lieutenant Courage called on to surrender. As they did not at once comply, Laughran immediately rushed at them with so terrifying an aspect that all six promptly gave themselves up and were brought in.

These prisoners added to and confirmed valuable information that had already been procured from messages picked up from a German signal-lamp, which had been read and translated by Captain Lambert of the 8th Yorkshire Regiment. The only one of these messages preserved in the records of the 23rd Division is worthy of quotation, as indicating the ingenuity, as distinct from the language qualifications of the translator :—

"DIVISION DIVISION SUCH AUSKUNTIMBIFZ SHADT—U—V—2— LINIE FINIE RDGRSTER STELLUNT OFFIZIER—4—4—E."

Unfortunately the records do not contain the translation of what a casual perusal suggests might be the stormy remonstrances of the German Higher Command. One is left to wonder what was to happen to the " Stellunt offizier " if he didn't do it !

At 1.45 P.M. the attack opened. On the right the 12th Durham Light Infantry advanced in four waves, preceded by the tank. The tank, moving against the tangle, successfully cleared the trenches for occupation by the infantry, and then turned left along the edge of the sunken road to assist the left of the battalion's attack. At this point it was unfortunately struck by a shell and put out of action. The battalion came under heavy fire from the sunken road, and enfilade machine-gun fire from both flanks. The tangle had been captured, but the further advance of the 12th Durham Light Infantry was for the time checked. Throwing back their right to protect their exposed flank, they awaited developments that would favour the resumption of attack.

On the left the 9th Yorkshire Regiment, advancing close under the barrage, had entered and stormed the southern end of the village. Here the enemy, still seeking cover from our bombardment, were completely surprised. The more ready among them, rushing hastily to their machine-guns, fell to the bombs of the attacking infantry, while others were bayoneted as they swarmed from their dug-outs. But before the attack had gained the cross-roads in the centre of the village, the enemy's resistance stiffened, and the rate of advance slackened.

To assist the advance of the 13th Durham Light Infantry, an officer's patrol of this battalion had been sent forward to keep touch with the flanks of the two leading battalions, between which the 13th Durhams, it will be remembered, were to pass to carry out the second phase of the attack. An exaggerated report, to the effect that the 9th Yorkshire Regiment was "held up," was received by the officer commanding this patrol, and forwarded by him to his commanding officer. The O.C. 13th Durham Light Infantry immediately ordered one of his companies to advance from the south on the cross-roads, detailing a second company to support the movement.

The attack had now been in progress for half an hour. The leading company advanced in two waves. Heavy machine-gun fire met the advance ; Captain Blake, the company commander, was killed, and the first wave was stopped. Reinforced by the second wave, they commenced to engage the enemy with rifles and bombs. At this stage Captain Clarke, commanding the supporting company, intervened. Carrying forward the attack, he brought the companies of the 13th Durham Light Infantry to the cross-roads simultaneously with the 9th Yorkshire Regiment, who had by now fought their way through the village. Over 100 of the enemy were killed or captured at this point.

The opportunity for which the 12th Durham Light Infantry had patiently waited had now arrived ; the enemy's position in the sunken road which faced them had been turned, and they rushed forward and occupied it.

While these events had been in progress, the 11th West Yorkshire Regiment had advanced, as planned, at zero plus twenty minutes, to attack Flers 2 north of the Bapaume road. Two companies, forming the front line of attack, had assembled in Flers 1 ; two companies, in support, advanced from Destremont Farm. The forward and rear

H

attacking lines in their advance both encountered an overwhelming fire from machine-guns on their front and left flank ; the hostile artillery also inflicted heavy casualties. Of the two companies in support, advancing from Destremont Farm, only two unwounded officers and thirty men reached Flers 1. This first attack failed. But a bombing attack simultaneously carried out on the left up Flers 1[1] succeeded in driving the enemy back some fifty yards, and securing the entry to two communication trenches leading to Flers 2.

Attempt was now made to gain Flers 2 by bombing up these communication trenches from Flers 1 ; but the Germans continued to put up a stubborn resistance, and these efforts also failed to reach the objective.

A company of the 10th Duke of Wellington's was now sent forward to reinforce the West Yorkshire Regiment. The 9th Yorkshire Regiment, under direction of Major Barnes, had secured their position in the southern half of the village, and were in a situation to assist in the capture of Flers 2. A combined attack was accordingly arranged.

This third attack on the left of the 23rd Division's objective met with instant success. Worn by the fierce fighting it had already endured, the defence broke. Demoralisation seized the Germans, who had hitherto defended the position with such tenacity, and, abandoning Flers 2, they streamed back across the open, or sought safety in concealment. Those that fled were mown down by the fire of artillery, rifles, and machine-guns, and few escaped. Some 70 or 80 were completely annihilated by Lewis-gun fire from a position at the Le Sars cross-roads. Lieutenant R. E. Hobday of the West Yorkshire Regiment seized a German corporal, and forced him to assist in collecting and obtaining the surrender of his men. Over 100 of the enemy surrendered to this officer alone. 2nd Lieutenant Symes of the 69th Machine-Gun Company pursued and captured 20 Germans, while a further 40 gave themselves up to a party of our machine-gunners.

The 11th West Yorkshire Regiment had suffered severely, and Lieut.-Colonel Barker's sadly reduced numbers were now reinforced by a further two companies of the 10th Duke of Wellington's. Shortly afterwards Lieut.-Colonel Haynes, commanding the latter battalion, moved for-

---

[1] Flers 1, it must be remembered, was still in the hands of the Germans on the *left* of the 23rd Division front.

ward his headquarters, and, being senior to Barker, assumed command of the combined battalions. A company of the 8th Yorkshire Regiment had in the meantime been placed at the disposal of Lieut.-Colonel Prior, commanding the 9th Yorkshire Regiment. The remainder of the former battalion and the 8th York and Lancaster Regiment (from the 70th Infantry Brigade) were still held in reserve to the 69th Infantry Brigade.

The objective allotted to the 69th Infantry Brigade for October 7 had been captured, and the work of consolidation was now taken in hand.

While this fierce and stubborn fighting had been in progress on the left of the Division's attack, little opposition had been met on the front of the 68th Infantry Brigade. So far, the events on this flank have been related up to the point at which Captain Clarke carried forward the attack of the two companies of the 13th Durham Light Infantry to the cross-roads. Learning of the death of Captain Blake, he immediately assumed command of the two companies, and undertook the direction of operations in this quarter. Leaving one platoon in the sunken road to consolidate and gain touch with the 12th Durham Light Infantry, Captain Clarke advanced with the remainder through the north-eastern portion of Le Sars. Very little resistance was encountered. To protect the rear of the advance, bombers were dropped to deal with dug-outs where the enemy might still be lurking, and the farther extremity of the village was reached without difficulty.

Patrols were sent out to points of vantage, from which a clear view of the Butte de Warlencourt and the surrounding country could be obtained. At 3.40 P.M. it was reported by these that no sign of the enemy could be seen. A third company of the 13th Durham Light Infantry was then sent forward to assist in establishing a chain of strong posts to guard the village against counter-attack from the east and north-east. By 7.50 P.M. these posts had been established and connected up with the 12th Durham Light Infantry, whose defence in the sunken road had been strengthened by two machine-guns and two Stokes mortars.

Connection had, however, not yet been secured with the posts established by the 69th Infantry Brigade, which secured the north-western flank of the village. To fill the gap which occurred between the two brigades, a company of the 11th Northumberland Fusiliers and two machine-guns were sent forward before dark. Le Sars was now firmly held.

Farther east the attack of the 47th Division had succeeded on its right, but had failed to secure the left of its objective, where it had been opposed by the formidable position of the Butte de Warlencourt.

The night following the capture of Le Sars was spent by the infantry and Royal Engineers in improving the defences, and in preparation for the next day's operations. In this work great assistance was given by two companies of the 8th Seaforth Highlanders, who carried forward water and all kinds of stores throughout the night under heavy fire and circumstances of the greatest difficulty. The only practicable communication trench to the front—26th Avenue—had been badly broken up during the battle. Two companies of the 9th South Staffordshire Pioneers completely cleared this trench during the night, in spite of the congestion of traffic and the bad weather conditions that prevailed.

The task to be carried out by the 69th Infantry Brigade on October 8 consisted of the capture of the portions of Flers 1 and Flers 2 still in occupation of the Germans on the left flank of the 23rd Division, so as to effect junction with the Canadians, who were to make a simultaneous attack. A quarry situated in advance of this point of junction was also to be seized. Considerable progress along these trenches on their left had already been made by the 69th Infantry Brigade in the fighting of the 7th.

" A " and " D " Companies of the 8th York and Lancaster Regiment, attached to the 69th Infantry Brigade, took over the left of the line during the night, with a view to carrying out the attack. A Stokes mortar was placed at the disposal of each of these companies for the operation of the following day. A barrage was maintained throughout the night on the objectives in Flers 1 and Flers 2 by the Divisional Artillery.

At 4.50 A.M. the Canadians attacked. Simultaneously, the artillery barrage lifted, and the York and Lancaster companies commenced to bomb up the two trenches. The attack met with instant success ; fifty prisoners were taken, together with three machine-guns, and contact with the Canadians was established. A patrol sent forward to the quarry found it unoccupied. But it was realised that a garrison placed at this position would be exposed to the enemy's fire and isolated during daylight.   The quarry was accordingly left unoccupied in favour of a more suitable point, from which it could be overlooked.   Later in the day an enemy counter-attack forced the withdrawal of the Canadians, leaving the left of the 23rd Division somewhat exposed ; but no counter-attack was attempted on this open flank, and the position gained by the Division was maintained.

The 23rd Division had completed the capture to the last yard of the objectives assigned to it.

11 officers, 517 other ranks, and 8 machine-guns were captured by the Division on October 7 and 8.   The casualties of the Division during the same period amounted to 627 all ranks, killed, wounded, and missing: of these, 92 killed, 318 wounded, and 18 missing were of the 69th Infantry Brigade.[1]

The artillery, to whose support in the attack infantry brigadiers paid a high tribute, more than confirmed the confidence which it had already inspired in previous actions.   The success of the Division had, in no small degree, been due to the unceasing labour and self-sacrifice of those responsible for the work of maintaining communication.   During the seven days from October 2 to 8 the constant heavy shell-fire had made their work a matter of extreme difficulty and danger.   Wires were continually cut, frequently in several places at the same time, and their repair in darkness, rain, and deep mud demanded the most arduous work.   But so well did the linesmen work that never during the battle, except for the shortest periods, were brigade headquarters cut off from their battalions.   Forward of battalion headquarters messages had to be sent by hand, the runners being called on to cross open country under a heavy barrage ; yet messages were delivered in excellent time.

No officer who passed through the Great War can remain unmoved by the recollection of the British runners—mere lads, as often as not, who had nothing but their loyalty and high courage to urge them on their solitary passage through the hell of battle.   No leader ever earned from his men a deeper worship than the faithful runner inspired in the officer he served.

[1] The exact casualties in a particular action are somewhat difficult to determine.   The total given here is derived from Divisional records.   The records of the 68th Infantry Brigade show 309, making a total of 737.

The evacuation of the wounded had to be effected across the open under heavy shell-fire, but the efficiency and bravery of the medical officers, stretcher-bearers, and personnel of the Field Ambulances saved many lives and the suffering of wounded left untended. The fine example of Captain Riddell, R.A.M.C., attached to the 11th West Yorkshire Regiment, and of Captain Blake, R.A.M.C., attached to the 9th Yorkshire Regiment, was but typical of the action of those responsible for this work.

No true account of the action of the Division at Le Sars could, perhaps, better convey its complete success than the very erroneous impression gained by an outside observer. ' The Times ' correspondent reported that "the capture of Le Sars was effected without difficulty, the enemy surrendering freely."

But the following messages of congratulation were more highly appreciated by those who had experienced and overcome the particularly stubborn resistance put up by the Germans in many places :—

From G.O.C. III. Corps : Please convey to the troops of your Division engaged to-day my congratulations on their gallant and successful attack on Le Sars.

From III. Corps—G. 426—General Rawlinson wires as follows : Please convey to all ranks 23rd Division my congratulations and best thanks for their fine performance yesterday. The capture of all their objectives and 480 [1] prisoners is a feat of which they may be justly proud, especially after all the fighting that they have already been through during the battle of the Somme.

From 50th Division—G.A. 1, dated October 8 : Congratulations from all ranks 50th Division on your excellent fight and subsequent capture of Le Sars.

From G.O.C. 15th Division : Hearty congratulations on your success.

The following message received in the middle of the battle of Le Sars, and carefully preserved by the late General Lambert, must take its place in history :—

69TH BRIGADE.

Your return of tents, &c., on charge due at 12 noon to-day not yet received. Expedite. Urgent.

23RD DIVISION (Q).

----

[1] Total of prisoners first reported.

SUPPORTS MOVING UP—SOMME BATTLE, 1916.

It is feared that on receipt of messages like the above, which had escaped the vigilance of a much harassed staff, the officer inexperienced in staff work too often pictured the A.A. and Q.M.G. fuming and fretting over returns, oblivious of the battle that was raging. It was not always realised that a clockwork routine was necessary to secure these returns, and that the adjustment of this routine to the circumstances of a battle was no easy matter amid the hundred cares and anxieties of the moment.[1]

The attack and capture of Le Sars is conspicuous in the history of the 23rd Division as being the first offensive action which was, in the fullest sense, a Divisional operation. The Divisional Artillery, it is true, had supported previous attacks, and infantry brigades carrying out former operations had been reinforced by units of other brigades. The first attack on Contalmaison might be taken, too, to contravert this statement ; but the action of the 68th Infantry Brigade on that occasion, conspicuous though it was, had been subsidiary to the main attack of the 24th Infantry Brigade.

In the battle for the capture of Le Sars the attack had been made on a Divisional front by two infantry brigades, whose tasks had been co-ordinated by the Division. Once launched, as will always be the case where the Divisional reserve is not called upon or events demand a special co-operation with flank divisions, the control of the battle was in the hands of subordinate commanders. But the action of Le Sars provides more than one example of that intelligent co-operation which a spirit of comradeship is unable to achieve without a full grasp of the plan as a whole.

The action of the two centre battalions of the Division—firstly, in the manner in which the 9th Yorkshire Regiment, by their advance, facilitated the movement of the 13th Durham Light Infantry ; later, the immediate and unpremeditated attack by the latter on the cross-roads, when it was reported that the 69th Infantry Brigade's advance through the village was held up—showed an appreciation of the general plan, as distinct from the idea of a blind rush of units to their own objectives. When the strength of the defence in the sunken road became apparent, the 12th Durham Light Infantry also showed judgment in not pressing their attack till the position was turned.

---

[1] This, of course, does not apply to the late General Lambert, who had passed the Staff College, and could appreciate a joke against the staff at its true value.

If the plan and intention are made clear, unit commanders will, almost unconsciously, act in furtherance of the plan as circumstances require. The attainment of this instinctive co-operation of units must be placed to the credit of the Divisional command. The battle of Le Sars can be taken as illustrating that the unbroken success of the 23rd Division throughout its career could not be attributed solely to Fortune or to the valour of its troops. Fortune would have deserted the Division, and valour would have been of no avail, without the personal influence of the commander and the clear conveyance of his orders by the staffs of the Division and of subordinate formations.

With the battle of Le Sars the 23rd Division had seen the last of the mud and slaughter of the Somme battlefields. Its whole future in the France and Flanders theatre of war lay in the Ypres salient—that front which every British soldier was anxious to visit, but which, having experienced for the shortest period, he no less sincerely longed to quit.

On October 9 relief of the Division (less artillery) was carried out by the 15th Division. Our gunners were once again to be left behind.

PART III. FLANDERS

THE THIRD YEAR

CHAPTER I.

On completion of relief the Division concentrated in the neighbour- Map No. 1.
hood of Albert, with headquarters at Montigny. Here orders were
received for its transfer to the X. Corps of the Second Army.

The move was made in three stages. On October 11 and 12 the
Division moved to Ailly-le-Haut-Clocher area. The second stage brought
them by road to the S. Riquier area on October 13. Entraining again
on the 14th and 15th, the Division was assembled in the Second Army
area on October 15, with headquarters at Busseboom. Infantry brigades
were accommodated close at hand in or about Poperinghe, with the
exception of the 10th Northumberland Fusiliers and the 12th Durham
Light Infantry, who were placed at Ypres and Zillebeke respectively,
in readiness to commence the relief of the 2nd Australian Division in
the left sector of the 1st Anzac Corps. This sector lay at the point of
the salient formed during the past two years by the desperate efforts
of the Germans to capture the town of Ypres, and the resolute refusal
of the British Army to surrender it.

At this period of the war Ypres stood supreme as an example of
the devastation that could be wrought by modern artillery fire. Those
who had fought in the battles of the Somme had become accustomed
to the sight of ruined villages, to standing helplessly among mere heaps
of débris in a vain endeavour to identify the mairie, the school, and the
curé's house shown on the map provided for their guidance by a thought-
ful staff. But the complete annihilation of a town of the size of Ypres,
the wide area of ruin and desolation where, but little over two years

before, 18,000 citizens had lived in prosperity in a town of unrivalled beauty, brought home with a fuller force than the humbler villages of the Somme the sufferings of the civil population and the hideous waste of modern warfare.

When one considers the cost of a single heavy shell, one wonders whether the money and labour expended on the destruction of Ypres did not exceed the sum total of that expended on its creation and of that required for its reconstruction.

But though by no argument can the Germans justify the violation of Belgium, the destruction of Ypres can only be taken as part of their original crime. War having been carried into Belgium and to the gates of Ypres, the destruction of the town became inevitable. Blame cannot be justly laid on Germans for this act in itself.

On the outbreak of war the towers of Ypres overlooked the surrounding country. As the meeting-point of many roads, the town, moreover, had a special military importance in a country where traffic, after heavy rain, was restricted to the highways.

To this latter cause was the ceaseless shelling of the ruined town mainly attributable. It was not for the destruction of observation-posts, nor, except to a limited extent, for the harassing of the troops in billets, that the German guns made Ypres at the close of 1916 still a place in which it was unwise to tarry. The towers of the Cathedral and Cloth Hall had fallen to artillery fire in 1914 ; the houses where troops found billets in the first winter lay in ruins after the second battle of Ypres ; but the British communications still led through the town as inevitably as they had in earlier days.

The sector to be taken over from the 2nd Australian Division had a frontage of some 3500 yards. The centre of the front line was situated in Sanctuary Wood, about one mile east of Zillebeke. From this point the line fell back on the right south-west to a point 500 yards north-east of Zwarteleen. North of Sanctuary Wood the left flank of the line ran north-west, to include the Ypres-Menin road, which it reached at a point 250 yards west of Hooge.

The left of the two sections into which it was divided included two-thirds of the Divisional front ; on this flank, except at Hooge, where a post was thrown forward, the hostile line was at a distance of 500 yards. In the right section, on the other hand, with its shorter frontage,

THE CLOTH HALL, YPRES.

(From an etching by Lieut.-Colonel B. Buchanan, 23rd Divisional Artillery.)

the German line was in no place more than 100 yards distant, and at certain points was less than 50 yards from our own. On this flank, moreover, saps ran forward from the enemy's front line.

Each section was to be held by one infantry brigade, with two battalions in the front-line defence. Of the remaining battalions of the right brigade, one would be placed behind Zillebeke at Zillebeke Bund, the other at Ypres in Divisional reserve. The remaining battalions of the left brigade would be accommodated in the Infantry Barracks at Ypres, one being held in brigade, the other in Divisional reserve. Headquarters of both brigades were situated in Ypres.

The third infantry brigade would remain in Corps reserve in Winnipeg, St Lawrence, Montreal, Erie, and Toronto Camps, near Poperinghe.

The defence scheme arranged for the siting of machine-guns about the support line in positions from which overhead or indirect fire could be brought on the front ; they were no longer placed, as in earlier days, in the front line, where Lewis-guns now reinforced the fire of the riflemen.

Relief of the 2nd Australian Division commenced on October 17, and was completed on the 20th, when General Babington assumed command of the sector, with headquarters at Reninghelst. The 70th Infantry Brigade was placed in the right, the 68th Infantry Brigade was placed in the left section. North and south of the 23rd Division the line was held by the 55th and 47th Divisions respectively.

Our own artillery being still on the Somme, the 47th Divisional Artillery took over on October 23 from the 2nd Australian Divisional Artillery, which had hitherto covered the sector. About the same date the X. Corps took over the front line from the 1st Anzac Corps.

The weather had turned cold, but remained fine during the first few days, and the sector was very quiet. Rain came before the end of the month, and the enemy's bombardment became more active, particularly in the right section. Generally speaking, the enemy's artillery in this sector was directed chiefly behind the line, while his trench-mortars dealt with our front-line defences.

On October 31 a party of thirty Germans made a sudden raid on the listening-post of six men of the left battalion, which was posted on the Menin Road close to Hooge. This small post was forced to withdraw, but succeeded in gaining the Culvert in rear, with the loss of one man missing and four wounded. The post was immediately reoccupied.

The next few weeks in the line were uneventful. Shelling on both sides was continuous but seldom violent, though the arrival of German shells from every direction, except the immediate rear, was always a disconcerting feature of life in the Ypres salient.

Everything possible was done by the " Q " Staff of the Division, working in conjunction with the Y.M.C.A., for the comfort of the troops during the approaching winter. Coffee-stalls were established at Zillebeke and at the Lille Gate at Ypres for the refreshment of the men coming down from the trenches. Three recreation-rooms, two baths, and a laundry were soon in working order in Ypres. Here also improvements were carried out in the Y.M.C.A. reading-room, where, if the opportunity for quiet study could not always be found, warmth and a cheering contrast to trench life could be reckoned on.

On November 4, Field-Marshal H.R.H. the Duke of Connaught, accompanied by General Sir Herbert Plumer, commanding the Second Army, visited Divisional Headquarters and the headquarters of the 68th Infantry Brigade in Ypres.

November 20 found the 69th Infantry Brigade holding the right section of the line. It was decided to attempt a raid against the enemy that night in front of Clonmel Copse, which lay on the left of this section.

The objective selected was a German sap, with two horns curling to the north and south, which was situated in front of one of our listening-posts at a distance of thirty to thirty-five yards from our front-line parapet. The point to be attacked was protected by a belt of wire, twenty to thirty feet wide, covered by a light apron fence with a width of seven feet. The operation was assigned to the 10th Duke of Wellington's, who detailed a raiding party of forty, under the command of Captain Kelly. The raiders were organised into three parties : an assault party of twenty-five, under 2nd Lieutenant Davis ; a communicating party of six, under 2nd Lieutenant Millward ; a reserve party of six, under the command of Captain Kelly himself. A flanking party of three men of the 11th West Yorkshire Regiment with a Lewis-gun would co-operate from a sap on the left. The operation was to be supported by the fire of eighteen 18-pdr. guns, one 4.5 howitzer battery, one medium trench-mortar, two Stokes mortars, and two Lewis-guns.

Special arrangements had to be organised for dealing with the formidable obstacle of the wire. The night was still and dark. Sappers of the 128th Field Company R.E. cut a passage through the apron fence without difficulty. At 9.15 P.M., 2nd Lieutenant Cope, moving from a point some thirty yards south of the objective, crept forward obliquely to the wire, accompanied by two sappers with a Bangalore torpedo. Their movement was covered by bursts of Lewis-gun fire. Flares rose continuously from the opposing line, but the enemy were otherwise inactive.

At 11.18 P.M. the attack party left their trenches and commenced to creep slowly forward in two columns towards their objective. By this time Cope and his men, working with great courage and determination, had pushed their torpedo through twenty-two feet of wire. It was then obstructed, and could be pushed no farther. Thinking it must be against the enemy's parapet, Cope, at 11.34 P.M., fired the torpedo. The assaulting infantry dashed through the gap, but found eight feet of wire still uncut. The point of the torpedo had dropped, and was lodged in a shell-hole. Davis, with the leading men, got to work with wire-cutters, but in the bombing fight which now ensued several became casualties. There was no cooler or more determined leader in the 23rd Division than Kelly, but he was quick to realise that further progress was impossible. At 11.43 P.M. he gave the signal for withdrawal, and the party returned, bringing in its wounded. Communication with the artillery had been cut, and the guns continued their programme, evoking fierce retaliation from the German artillery and trench-mortars for close on an hour after the return of the raiders.

The result of the raid was disappointing. The failure of the operation could justly be attributed to ill-fortune. Thanks, however, to the judgment of Captain Kelly, the casualties had not been so heavy as they might have been but for the timely withdrawal. In the Duke of Wellington's, 2nd Lieutenant Millward and 10 other ranks were wounded ; in the 11th West Yorkshire Regiment, 2 other ranks were killed and 2 wounded.

The first experience the Division had had of the sector had scarcely accorded with the terrifying traditions of the Ypres salient. The weather had been fair on the whole ; the trenches were dry, and the comparative quiet of the front can be gauged by the casualties for the month of November : the 68th Infantry Brigade had lost 9 killed and 24 wounded ; the 69th Infantry Brigade 7 killed, 33 wounded.[1]

[1] Compare with casualties in the last tour in the Noulette sector in the preceding June, when the Division, in less than a month, lost 89 killed, 433 wounded.

The 70th Infantry Brigade had relieved the 69th in the right section during the last week of November. A second raid was now planned for the night of December 2/3, to enter the enemy's trenches just north of Clonmel Copse, close to where the attack had been delivered on November 20.

The plan was to enter the trenches close to a German sap, bomb down the sap, kill Germans, clear dug-outs, and secure prisoners.

The two officers and fifty other ranks of the 8th York and Lancaster Regiment detailed for the operation were organised in three parties. Lieutenant Fitzherbert, with one N.C.O. and two men, was to be responsible for clearing a gap in the wire with a Bangalore torpedo ; thirty-four N.C.O.'s and men, under Lieutenant Spalding, were to form an assault party ; these would be followed by a carrying party of one N.C.O. and twelve men.

At 12.15 A.M. on December 3 the torpedo party left their dug-outs in the front line, and started to creep across No Man's Land by a circular route to the point selected in the enemy's wire. Shortly afterwards the raiders followed through the same gap, silently taking up a position on two knolls to await the report from the torpedo party.

From the first, Lieutenant Fitzherbert's party encountered great difficulties. The night was very still ; the frozen ground to be crossed was pitted with shell-holes and pools of water ; the enemy seemed anxious and alert. Reaching the point selected, the party got to work. They were repeatedly fired on. Corporal Murphy, the leading man, was shot through the jaw at a range of twenty yards, but continued his work, pushing the torpedo through the wire till ordered back by the officer, when he withdrew to the raiders, and requested that he might join them. For close on four hours Fitzherbert lay close in front of the enemy's line working the torpedo into position. Frequently fired on, he was eventually hit. At 4 A.M. the Germans seized the far end of the torpedo and tried to pull it through. Fitzherbert at once fired it, clearing a gap of fifteen yards, and, though wounded, sprang forward and attacked the enemy with his revolver.

Immediately the torpedo was fired, the assault party, led by Spalding, who throughout exhibited the utmost bravery, pushed through the gap. A German, rushing up from his dug-out, thrust his bayonet through the leg of Sergeant Jurley, who was one of the first to gain the trench.

Before he could withdraw it Jurley smashed his head with a knobkerrie ; then, pulling out the bayonet, continued to fight.

The raiders bombed down the trench, right and left of the point of entry, and established blocks, while a special party worked down the sap. Some six or seven dead and a number of wounded Germans were found in the trench ; the remainder of the garrison dispersed.

But shortly after, the Germans reorganised and returned along the top of the trench, hoping to attack our men from above. To meet this, Spalding ordered his men up from the trench, and a stiff bombing fight ensued. The enemy was being steadily reinforced, and, to avoid being surrounded, Spalding now ordered a retirement to the British line. The withdrawal was steadily conducted, and the raiders regained their lines, having suffered the comparatively light casualties of 3 other ranks killed, 2 officers and 4 other ranks wounded.

The enemy continued to bombard our trenches for the next hour with artillery, trench-mortars, and rifle-grenades. As was usual in this sector, however, the bulk of the bombardment fell well in rear of the front line, where the party was assembled, and no further casualties were sustained. The fire of our own artillery and of the trench-mortars of the 69th and 70th Infantry Brigades replied to this bombardment, till at length it ceased.

The weather was variable during December—bright frosty days alternating with rain and occasional snow. The enemy's artillery became more active as the year drew to a close. Casualties were not heavy, but constant anticipation of bombardment, almost equally with the dis-comfort of the bombardment itself, imposed a continual strain on the troops in the trenches.

The sort of thing that became a constant recurrence is thus reported by an officer of the 70th Infantry Brigade : " We were having tea in the dug-out in Lovers' Walk when the enemy started shelling ; the whizz-bangs came along with a noise like a small whirlwind, and on bursting gave out nasty fumes. We crouched in the corner of our shelter. One shell burst on the doorway, and another on the roof, without doing much damage. At 6 P.M. we started an artillery ' strafe ' on our right. The Huns replied, and soon the air was humming with the rush of shells in all directions. I tried to hide behind my tin hat, and ' had the wind up ' properly, as I expected to be hit any moment. After seventy minutes

I

the shelling ceased, and on inspection I found the trench blown in in four places, but not a man hit. . . . I had a most enjoyable dinner that night, though the meat was a bit tough." The tough meat is but part of an experience which will recall a very common incident of trench life to those who spent their days in the front line during the war.

A daring piece of patrol work was carried out on the night of December 6 by 2nd Lieutenant Barber, 11th Sherwood Foresters, and Corporal Burton, 9th York and Lancaster Regiment, who had volunteered to destroy a German listening-post opposite the right of the sector. Carrying with them a 12 lb. Ammonal bomb, they crawled from the trenches at 11.45 P.M., and slid into a crater just in front of the post, which was situated at the rear of a sap. In the bright moonlight they could see that the sap was empty, so with the idea of entering it they crawled up the side of the crater, only to find the sap heavily wired. They were forced to reconnoitre it from outside, but could see that it was well built and solidly revetted. They then hurled the bomb, which fulfilled expectations with a terrific detonation, and scrambled safely home.

Shortly before 7 A.M. on December 15 sentries in the front line were surprised to hear bells ringing in the enemy's lines. Any unusual occurrence of this kind in trench warfare used to give rise to wild conjecture, particularly after the first German gas attack. On this occasion the sequel followed very shortly.

At 7 A.M. a trench-mortar shell falling in Sanctuary Wood heralded an intense hostile bombardment. Guns and trench-mortars fired for three hours with ever-increasing intensity on the right section of the front, occupied by the 68th Infantry Brigade ; while three aeroplanes, flying low over our trenches under the fire of our Lewis-guns, appeared to be directing the bombardment and reconnoitring the front and support lines. At 9.50 A.M. fire slackened, and by 10.30 A.M. all was quiet. The damage done to the trenches was tremendous.

The front line had suffered severely. On the right, where it was occupied by the 10th Northumberland Fusiliers, it was damaged beyond recognition, and a portion, including two saps, had been isolated. Support and communication trenches had been rendered impassable in many places, and several entrances to dug-outs had been blown in. But the casualties totalled only two wounded.

The day remained quiet till 4 P.M., when suddenly the German bombardment reopened on previous lines, but was now extended to place barrages on communication trenches, approaches, and roads as far back as the Lille Gate of Ypres. At 4.18 P.M. the enemy's barrage lifted off the portion of our trenches which had been isolated, and a party of fifty Germans, raiding one of the saps, succeeded in bombing their way down to the front-line trench. An S.O.S. signal sent up from the centre company of the 10th Northumberland Fusiliers was seen by two batteries and by a look-out officer posted north of Zillebeke.

The two batteries immediately opened fire on S.O.S. lines, and, the signal having been communicated, a heavy barrage was quickly placed on No Man's Land and the German front line.

The infantry at the point of attack, though cut off, put up a stubborn defence, and, with the loss of one man killed and two wounded, succeeded in driving back the enemy, who suffered severely from the artillery barrage, which intercepted them from their trenches. Three dead Saxons of the 204th Division were left in our trenches. By 5 P.M. artillery fire on both sides ceased, and all was again quiet. Further very serious damage had been done to the trenches, but the men, working strenuously all night at clearing and wiring, established communication between companies, and secured the position before dawn.

It is difficult to determine what had been the intention of the Germans on this occasion. The infantry action which followed such formidable preparation gave rise in the evening to the reflection " Parturiunt montes nascetur ridiculus mus." Their three-hour bombardment in the morning served mainly to give warning of possible attack, and to demolish trenches and render untenable points where they proposed later to secure prisoners. The shelling of communications right back to Ypres seemed unnecessary, unless some far bigger attack was intended than that actually developed.

The 23rd Division's second Christmas Day at the front was now at hand. The 69th and 70th Infantry Brigades were to pass it in Ypres, or in the neighbourhood of such familiar spots as Crab Crawl, St Peter's Street, Dormy House, or Yeomanry Farm, in none of which full justice could be given to a Christmas dinner.

The 69th Infantry Brigade, accordingly, celebrated their Christmas feast on December 21 before taking over the line. On the same day the 9th Yorkshire Regiment and the 10th Duke of Wellington's were inspected by the Commander-in-Chief on the Ouderdom-Vlamertinghe road. About the same time Sir Douglas Haig also inspected the 103rd Brigade R.F.A., who had just marched up from the Somme with the 23rd Divisional Artillery, who had been kept in that area for an exceptionally long period. The gunners were much heartened by the very complimentary and inspiriting words addressed to them by the Commander-in-Chief.

The more fortunate 68th Brigade, relieved in the line, found themselves in reserve near Poperinghe on Christmas Day. As the war dragged on, increasing effort was made to afford officers and men relief to the tedium of trench life and the horrors of war. Those who organised the amusements and comforts designed to give mental and physical refreshment to the British soldier played no small part in maintaining the *morale* of the British Army, which perhaps never stood higher and never proved a more important factor in war than in the year 1917.

In Poperinghe at this time there were clubs for officers and men ; divisional canteens, where all requirements could be satisfied ; and, last but not least, a theatre ! Here a caste of six men and one " girl " (which was frequently taken for a real one till it started to walk), together with an orchestra of six musicians, gave nightly performances. The performance was half concert, half cinema performance. The " girl " was the nucleus of the famous beauty chorus which graced the grand revues given by " The Dumps " in later days.

Then there was the second volume of ' The Dump,' the 23rd Division's Christmas Annual. There were thirty-four contributors to this year's number, including among many friends outside the Division such well-known names as Heath Robinson, Byam Shaw, Lewis Baumer, John Galsworthy, &c. Eight of London's best-known actresses [1] sent us their greetings, together with their portraits done by Miss Kathleen Shackleton.

The New Year opened with rain, which fell every day till January 14, when a hard frost set in, which continued well into February. Day after day the German shells, mostly 5.9 and 4.2, fell on the wretched ruins of Ypres. Sometimes the fire was intermittent ; sometimes it would continue all day without cease. Invariably it would break out at dusk to harass the transport moving up under cover of darkness

[1] Fay Compton, Gladys Cooper, Laura Cowie, Isobel Elsom, Julia James, Iris Hoey, Violet Loraine, and Nellie Taylor.

to replenish the line. Taking fourteen days at this period, one finds only four on which a bombardment of Ypres is not recorded.

On the right of the sector the opposing trenches were so close and the German infantry so clearly nervous that the greatest precautions had to be taken in carrying out reliefs, lest the enemy by detecting movement should become alarmed and make trouble. A company of the 9th York and Lancaster Regiment leaving the trenches after relief was caught in this way. A number of them were crowded in a shallow communication trench. Suddenly the air was lit with the flare of Véry lights, and a tornado of " whizz-bangs " and trench-mortar bombs swept over the trenches. Rushing down the muddy trench by the light of the bursting shells they gained the shelter of a deep trench, where they remained in meditation, soothing their nerves with a cigarette till the bombardment subsided.

No casualties were sustained, and the German official report stated that " East of Ypres a raid by English troops was stifled at birth by our batteries." So every one was satisfied.

The New Year's Honours List contained at least one award which brought the keenest satisfaction to the whole Division. General Babington received the K.C.M.G. in recognition of the services of the Division which he had trained and commanded.

Next to General Babington there was perhaps no officer more universally loved and respected or who had become more closely identified with the 23rd Division than Brig.-General Fasson, the C.R.A. Strictest of disciplinarians, exacting in the high standard of efficiency he demanded, he spared neither himself nor others, yet his sympathy and understanding were always apparent to his subordinates. There is no officer that served under him but speaks of him with reverence and a certain awe, none that remembers him save with the deepest affection. The magic of the secret message F.O.W., as it passed from battery to battery, will long endure in the recollection of those who learnt what " Fasson on the Warpath " portended.

General Fasson had only recently taken over command of the artillery covering the front on December 27. When, therefore, he left us on January 15 to take over command of the artillery of the XVIII. Corps, it was to the great regret not only of the gunners but of the whole Division. He was replaced by Brig.-General Sir D. Arbuthnot.

Another change in the staff of the Division occurred shortly afterwards, owing to the appointment of Lieut.-Colonel C. F. Watson to the command of the 1st Battalion of his regiment, The Queen's. First appointed to the 23rd Division as G.S.O. 2, Colonel Watson as G.S.O. 1 during the past twelve months had borne the responsibilities and heavy work of this position during the Somme battles. His energy, optimism, high courage, and loyalty were at all times most marked, and later earned him in another sphere of operations the command of an infantry brigade. On January 21 he was replaced by Lieut.-Colonel C. Evans, R.A.

On January 23 a raid was attempted on the enemy's trenches in front of Sanctuary Wood, opposite the centre of the right section. The raiding party consisted of one company of the Yorkshire Light Infantry, under command of Captain H. C. Bull. Snow lay thick on the ground, and the raiders were clad in white. Advancing at 9 P.M., they gained the enemy's front line ; but the Germans, anticipating attack, had evacuated it, and now opened a heavy trench-mortar bombardment on the line they had vacated.

The raiders suffered severely from this bombardment and from a shrapnel barrage placed on No Man's Land. Captain Bull and Lieutenants Dinsdale and Harwood were wounded, and the party withdrew. At the expense of 1 killed, 40 wounded, and 4 missing, the only result of the operation, which had been carried out as planned to the smallest detail, was an examination of the German trenches. These were reported to be seven feet deep, and in every respect inferior to our own. There were no trench-boards, and the garrison appeared to be dependent solely on " bee-hive " dug-outs constructed in their front parapet for protection against artillery fire.

On the following night Captain Donoghue was mortally wounded while searching No Man's Land for the missing men. In him the 8th Yorkshire Light Infantry lost an officer greatly loved by all. Over forty years old, he had come with the battalion from England as a junior subaltern. His never-failing enthusiasm and cheerfulness had set an example to all with whom he had come in contact.

Casualties in the Division during January showed a marked increase, and totalled 361 all ranks killed, wounded, and missing. In addition to the above there were 1169 sick. But reinforcements were coming

forward plentifully, the returns for the month showing 141 officers and
3674 other ranks.

On February 12 a thaw set in, and the ground, which had recently
become too hard for digging, was now converted into a heavy sticky
pudding, in which trench-boards became engulfed and the legs of weary
soldiers stuck fast.

It was about this time that General Babington was decorated with
the order of Commander of the Legion d'Honneur. The investiture
was held at Chateau Bryass by General Nivelle, the Commander-in-
Chief of the French Army, who was to meet with such ill-fortune so
shortly after.

Two small raids attempted on February 18 by the 69th Infantry
Brigade on the left of the right section found the enemy alert, and resulted in a bombing fight, in which 1 officer and 1 other rank were
wounded. A further raid on the following night opposite the right of
the same section found the German trench vacant. The raiding party
remained twenty minutes in the trench before returning.

The attitude of the Germans at this period showed extreme nervousness, and it had become a settled policy with them to anticipate raids
in certain portions of the front by vacating their front line. But such
tactics could not be reckoned on, as was proved by a big raid by the
47th Division on our right on February 20, in which 114 prisoners and
4 machine-guns were captured.

It had been hoped that there would be ample opportunity for training the British Army during the winter of 1916-17, and great preparations had been made for this. Experience can be gained in battle, but
the training of troops in accordance with the lessons learnt must be
carried out on the training-ground. Rest also was needed for the troops
in preparation for the 1917 campaign. Lord Haig explains how the
necessity for extending the British front in January as far south as
Roye precluded the possibility of giving the Army the rest and training
that it had been hoped would be possible.

Since the 23rd Division had taken over the trenches at Martinpuich
on September 18, they had now been continually in the line except
during the ten days during which their transference to the Ypres salient
had been carried out. More than half the winter had already passed.

The orders that the Division was at length to be relieved by the

38th Division, and to proceed to the Bollezeele and Tilques training areas, were therefore received with great satisfaction.

The relief was completed on February 25, and Divisional Headquarters were established on the following day at 35 Rue Carnot, St Omer, the Division being under command of the G.O.C. VIII. Corps. Brig.-General Colville was indisposed at this time. Major-General A. M. Stuart Wortley took his place as a temporary measure.

During the first three weeks of March the 68th Infantry Brigade remained in the Bollezeele area, 69th and 70th Infantry Brigades were accommodated in the Tilques area, Divisional Artillery in the Muncq-Nieurliet area.

A forward move, commenced on March 19 and 21, found Divisional Headquarters at Esquelbecq ; 68th, 69th, and 70th Infantry Brigades in areas about Elverdinghe, Poperinghe, and Houtquerque respectively ; Divisional Artillery moving to the Herzeele area, with headquarters at Wormhoudt.

The 68th Infantry Brigade, having relieved a brigade of the 38th Division in Divisional reserve, had temporarily come under the command of that Division. They were employed on the construction of earthworks and wiring in the rear defences, and on digging cable, in accordance with plans of the chief engineer, VIII. Corps. One battalion of the brigade occupied " L " line between Elverdinghe and Vlamertinghe, the remainder being disposed in camps in rear of this line.

These arrangements remained in force till April 1, when orders were received for the Division to revert to the command of the X. Corps, and to take over the Hill 60 sector.

The Division had had a clear month out of the line, of which full advantage had been taken to organise and train all units for the campaigns which were now in view. In the south during the winter the withdrawal of the Germans had followed as a sequel to the Somme battles, but the enemy was now firmly established in the Hindenburg Line. Russia was in the throes of revolution, and all prospects of peace without further heavy fighting had vanished.

The thoroughness of the month's training of the Division can be estimated by the detail in which it was carried out. It is recorded that a " man was even sent round to instruct company cooks in making potted ham and tongue without either ham or tongue." This surely exceeds the making of bricks without straw. What qualifications for a high and permanent post in the peace-time British Army !

The front to be taken over, which was at present occupied partly Map No. 6. by the 47th, partly by the 39th Division, lay astride the Zillebeke-Zwarteleen road, and extended from Henry Street on the right to St Peter's Street on the left. The front line, covering Verbrandenmolen on the right, crossed the deep railway cutting south-east of this village ; then, traversing the western slope of Hill 60 just below the crest, it turned east some 500 yards north of the hill to run to a point opposite Mount Sorrel. Hence it ran in a north-easterly direction to the left flank, which rested on Observatory Ridge, giving a total frontage of 2500 yards.

For 800 yards on the left the line would, therefore, be the same as that held on the right of the Division in its previous tour. Here we should be at the close quarters with the enemy which have already been described ; while in the new portion of the front to be taken over, the distance of the front line from the enemy varied between 50 and 150 yards.

The front was to be taken over by the 70th Infantry Brigade, with three battalions in the line, finding their own supports, and one battalion in reserve. In the left centre the front line had been so damaged as to be untenable, and for a space of some 800 yards would be unoccupied. In this portion of the front three platoons of the centre battalion were to be placed in a position behind Fosse Wood, 600 yards in rear of the front line.

On April 6 the 9th York and Lancaster Regiment relieved a battalion of the 39th Division on the left. The 69th Infantry Brigade was moved to Ouderdom the same day as Divisional reserve. The 68th Infantry Brigade, still detached, was in Corps reserve.

On April 8 the remainder of the 70th Infantry Brigade moved into the line, the 11th Sherwood Foresters and the 8th York and Lancaster Regiment taking over the Hill 60 section from the 47th Division, to form the centre and right respectively of the 23rd Division front. The Pioneer Battalion arrived in Ypres the same day.

On the night of the 8th/9th the 23rd Divisional Artillery relieved the left group of the 47th Divisional Artillery and three 18-pdr. and one 4.5 howitzer battery of the 39th Division.

To what extent the enemy was acquainted with these changes opposite his front it is not possible to say. But at 9 A.M. on Easter Monday,
April 9, when our artillery had just taken over and the front was still
strange to the infantry, the enemy opened an intense bombardment
with trench-mortars and guns of every calibre on the front and support
lines along the whole Divisional front. Except for a lull between 2 P.M.
and 3 P.M., there was no relaxation in the bombardment till 5.45 P.M.
It then ceased, and there was complete silence. The damage done was
appalling. The front line had been practically obliterated. In the
right and centre battalions, 8th York and Lancaster Regiment and
Sherwood Foresters, communication between battalion headquarters
and companies had been cut, and battalions and companies were cut
off from each other. In the right battalion, where there was no adequate
protection for the garrison, 90 casualties had occurred ; in the centre
battalion a large portion of the garrison was in deep dug-outs, but certain of these had been blown in, burying some 25 men ; the 9th York
and Lancaster Regiment on the left were fortunate in having adequate
protection, and had only sustained 18 casualties.

On the right of the Sherwood Foresters, Captain Whyatt, on the
cessation of the bombardment, succeeded in reaching Allen's Crater,
where a bombing and Lewis-gun post was situated. He found the gun
blown up, two of the team killed, and three wounded. One sergeant
constituted the garrison that remained. Captain Watts, who commanded the right company of this battalion, had succeeded in getting
a messenger through to battalion headquarters, reporting that the
entrances to the tunnel leading to our mining system had been blown
in, and giving the general situation. Two platoons in reserve at " Battersea Farm " and two at " Railway Dug-outs " were ordered forward to
reinforce this part of the line.

Suddenly at 6.43 P.M. an intense bombardment again opened. Colonel
Whatford, commanding the 8th York and Lancaster Regiment on the
right of the railway, was still cut off from his companies, but hearing
rifle and machine-gun fire he sent up the S.O.S. with his own hands.
Colonel Watson of the Sherwood Foresters ordered his adjutant, Lieutenant Cavell, to fire the S.O.S. signal. Cavell fell mortally wounded
as he left the dug-out to do this, and a few minutes delay occurred in
firing the rocket. The reply of the artillery on the right was instantaneous.

But the Germans had rushed forward to the assault, and succeeded in
entering the trenches of the left company of the York and Lancaster
Regiment. This company, reduced during the day from a strength of
152 to 47, with the assistance of the right company, thrust the enemy
out by counter-attack, and pursued him into No Man's Land, where
several of our men were killed.

In the meantime the Germans had advanced across the remains of
the front line opposite the Sherwood Foresters, and had penetrated to
Deep Support Line, 100 yards in rear.

During the pause in the enemy's bombardment Captain Watts had
been able to clear one of the entrances to the tunnel. The guards placed
over this had now been killed by a shell. The Germans, rushing to
this point, commenced to throw gas-bombs into the subway. Watts,
with a handful of men, succeeded, though partially gassed, in getting
out. Attacking the enemy with bombs, they drove them from the
trench. Further to the right, however, German bombers had advanced up Marshall Lane, parallel with the railway, where they
had succeeded in bombing entrances to subways, and were threatening
our main shafts. At the critical moment the reinforcing platoons
from Battersea Farm arrived on the scene. They were without
officers or N.C.O.'s, all of whom had become casualties ; but the
platoons immediately engaged the enemy, and drove him from Marshall
Lane.

The left company, cut off from the remainder of the battalion, suffered severely from the bombardment, but here the attack was not
pressed.

Against the 9th York and Lancaster Regiment, on the left of the
sector, the enemy did not advance till 7.45 P.M. The bulk of these were
repulsed by rifle, machine-gun, and Lewis-gun fire. A few who gained
the front line on the battalion's right flank were driven from the trench
by a bombing party with a loss of two prisoners. At the cost of very
heavy casualties the 70th Infantry Brigade had repulsed a most
formidable attack. Had the attack succeeded in its object, the
capture and destruction of our main shafts, it would have had
the disastrous effect, not only of losing the fruits of months of labour,
but of necessitating an entire alteration in offensive plans for the
future.

The casualties sustained were as follows :—

	Killed.		Wounded.		Missing.
	Officers.	Other Ranks.	Officers.	Other Ranks.	Other Ranks.
8th York and Lancaster Regiment	..	33	2	77	51
11th Sherwood Foresters . .	2	28	4	52	5
9th York and Lancaster Regiment	..	4	..	15	..
70th L.T.M. Battery . . .	..	..	..	1	2
70th Brigade Machine-Gun Company	..	..	..	2	..

Total casualties : 8 officers and 270 other ranks.

Certain of the missing were undoubtedly captured ; the bodies of others were later recovered, but it is feared that the greater number were buried or blown to bits by the bombardment.

The Germans left 36 dead in our trenches in the right and centre, 4 dead on the left.

A prisoner captured on April 30 gave an interesting account of the careful preparation of this attack. The troops carrying it out were the Assault Company and Pioneers of the 204th Division, assisted by a Flammenwerfer Battery. They totalled perhaps 350 men, under the command of Lieut.-Colonel Fleischleben of the 414 R.I.R. The objectives given to them were our mine-shafts and dug-outs. It is curious that, while this German considered that the flammenwerfers had played an important part in the operation, no mention of their employment is made in the official narrative of any of the three battalions in the defence.

The raiders' casualties had been officially given out to them as 10 killed and 18 wounded, but they had naturally been sceptical of these figures.

In connection with this fight, one Military Cross, two D.C.M.'s, and three Military Medals were awarded to each of the three battalions in the line. The officer of the 9th York and Lancaster Regiment to whom the Military Cross was awarded was 2nd Lieutenant Denyer, who had only joined the battalion on the previous day. To earn this decoration on one's second day at the front must surely constitute a record. Four Military Crosses and nine Military Medals were granted to the 1st Australian Tunnelling Company, who had taken a prominent part in the defence of their mining system.

Immediately after the ejection of the enemy on April 9, posts were established on the line of what, as far as could be judged, was the old front line, and the reconstruction of the defences undertaken. The damage done was enormous, and in the following days scarcity of labour, due to the many men required for work with the 1st and 2nd Australian and 2nd Canadian Tunnelling Companies, was keenly felt. But the activity of the hostile artillery was below normal, and in ten days' time the trenches were once again in fair shape.

On April 10 a strong enemy fighting patrol endeavoured to gain possession of a bridge which crossed the cutting in the Hill 60 section. Captain L. R. Halford of the 11th Sherwood Foresters, with a platoon and three Lewis-guns, drove back the enemy, and secured the bridge by the establishment of a strong-point.

A fortnight later the same officer was gassed during a gallant attempt to extricate a party who had been buried in a sap blown in by German artillery fire.

The 68th Infantry Brigade had now rejoined the Division, and on April 15 had relieved a brigade of the 39th Division in the Hooge section, so extending the sector to a two-brigade front, with one infantry brigade in reserve.

A promise of spring was in the air, and the discovery of a black-bird's nest with young birds augured better weather. The contempt shown by birds for artillery fire was always noticeable. In Nightingale Wood, near Dickebusch, the salvoes of our batteries and the whistling of shells would be greeted with a flood of song ; swans swam in the moat surrounding Ypres undisturbed by the German bombardment ; and many a man was lured by the wily partridge over ground pitted with shell-fire.

On April 28 verbal instructions were received that the Division was to be withdrawn at short notice. Relief by the 19th Division commenced the following day in bright warm weather, and was completed on May 2, when the 23rd Division was assembled in the Steenvorde area, with headquarters at Winnezeele.

On May 1 the Divisional Artillery suffered the loss of Lieut.-Colonel P. W. B. Henning, commanding the 103rd Brigade R.F.A., who was badly wounded outside his headquarters at the Lille Gate of Ypres. The fine fighting spirit of the brigade, which had earned the gratitude of the infantry times without number, had been inspired by the example of grit and cheery optimism set by this gallant officer.

The Division remained out of the line for just over a week. During this time the 69th Infantry Brigade (less Machine-Gun Company and Trench-Mortar Battery), the 101st Field Company R.E., and two companies of the 9th South Staffordshire Regiment were working in the forward area of the X. Corps.

The remainder of the Division was in hard training for operations in which it was shortly to be engaged. The nature of these operations, which was known to the Divisional Command, was not in accord with the " canteen rumour," which claimed that the Division was destined to be part of an " army of pursuit." This rôle, which had already been assigned to the Division by the same authority during the previous tour of training, made a strong appeal. The high-sounding title possessed an optimistic flavour, suggesting a hunt of demoralised masses of Germans with all the sting taken out of them.

Investigation of canteen rumours would prove an interesting study. They were always, even in the Army's darkest days, almost ludicrously optimistic. Their effect on *morale* was undeniably good ; for though it might be thought that when a rumour was not realised the effect might be depressing, it was so quickly covered by a fresh and more glowing rumour that no time was allowed for reaction. These yarns were seldom, if ever, promoted by official propaganda. Their sole origin, it is thought, lay in the incurable optimism of the British soldier. Prominent among their main promoters were the officers' servants. The association of these men with the officers gave them a claim to inside knowledge among their comrades in the ranks ; while the effect of a good yarn on an officer in low spirits was so beneficial that his servant would unblushingly concoct the most outrageous fabrications as part of his plain duty.

Like every one else, these soldier servants had their faults ; but their faults were few. For instance, an officer of the 23rd Division records that the nature of his servant, in other respects a paragon of virtue, was marred by one black spot. An excellent cook, a gallant soldier with considerable initiative, yet he would *never* bring the officer's tooth water unless specially ordered to !

There had just been time for a desperate contest in the final of the

Divisional Football Competition, in which, after being one goal all at time, the 69th snatched victory from the 70th Infantry Brigade in the last minute of extra time, when the army of pursuit theory received a severe blow. The Division was ordered back to the line.

On May 10 the 68th Infantry Brigade relieved the 57th Infantry Brigade in the Hill 60 section, and the 9th South Staffordshire Regiment (less two companies) relieved the pioneers of the 19th Division in Ypres. Artillery reliefs were carried out the following night. On May 12 the 70th Infantry Brigade relieved the 58th Infantry Brigade in the Observatory Ridge-Hooge section. On the same day General Babington assumed command of the sector, with headquarters at Busseboom.

The details of the task which lay before the 23rd Division can be left to the following chapter. Suffice it here that they were to prepare to take part in a grand offensive planned for the Second Army, and that the front of their attack would lie opposite Hill 60.

Instructions were now received from the X. Corps that all preparations for the projected attack were to be completed by the end of May. A large-scale offensive in position warfare at this period entailed a vast amount of work. Perhaps in no attack during the war were the preparations made in more minute and perfect detail as for the coming battle. Existing trenches had to be improved, assembly trenches and new communication trenches prepared, battery and trench-mortar positions completed, observation-posts and battalion battle headquarters constructed, communications secured by burying cable, tram-lines extended, and huge dumps of ammunition and stores organised.

Such activity could scarcely escape the notice of the enemy or fail to rouse his curiosity. The German artillery had for some days been paying particular attention to our batteries covering the Hill 60 section, and the front line and wire opposite Mount Sorrel had been simultaneously shelled by 5.9 and 4.2. Suspicion was roused, therefore, when, late on the evening of May 12, German officers were detected studying our lines. The precaution was taken of ordering the troops to stand to arms half an hour earlier than the usual time on the following morning.

At 2.50 A.M. on May 13 an artillery bombardment opened on our support line. Twenty minutes later trench-mortars opened on the

front line, and till 3.30 A.M. front, support, and reserve lines came under
an intense bombardment of shells of all sizes.

At 3.45 A.M. the enemy attacked in three parties, totalling about
fifty men. Smoke and dust concealed the raiders till close upon our
line. Six of their right party succeeded in entering the front line, but
were immediately expelled, though one of our men at this point was
found to be missing. The centre party was stopped by Lewis-gun and
rifle-fire when within ten yards of the line, and, leaving one man dead
in the wire, dispersed. Opposite the left of the attack a Lewis-gun
had been put out of action by a direct hit, but here also the enemy was
driven back by rifle-fire, leaving three dead in No Man's Land. The
second wave of the enemy's attack got no farther than half-way across
No Man's Land. At the cost of 6 other ranks killed, 1 officer and 18
other ranks wounded, and 1 other rank missing, the enemy's raid had
been repulsed. At the point where the enemy had attacked, the position, held by the 13th Durham Light Infantry, had little depth. No
S.O.S. signal had been sent up, and the Divisional Commander later
asked Colonel Clarke, who commanded the battalion, whether, in view
of the weakness of his position, it would not have been well to fire the
signal. His reply gave proof of the high spirit of this battalion. "The
13th," he said, "have never yet sent up an S.O.S."

Raids were carried out by us opposite Mount Sorrel on the 16th and
20th, but without result. In the first the enemy was prepared, and was
found strongly holding the narrow gap cut in the wire for entry. A
bombing fight resulted, in which one of our men was wounded, and the
party withdrew. In the second a party of 2 officers and 28 other ranks
of the 9th Yorkshire Regiment found the German front trench empty,
but in good condition ; 5 men of the party were wounded by rifle-grenades
during the withdrawal.

On the following night a small raid by the 8th Yorkshire Regiment
found an enemy sap near The Snout unoccupied. They were pushing
forward to the front line when the opening of a raid by the 47th Division
alarmed the Germans, who manned their parapet. Thereupon our raiders
withdrew without casualty.

During this period the 23rd Divisional Artillery was busy cutting
wire. The German guns were also active, particularly against our battery
positions and the eastern approaches to Ypres. Few artillery positions

east of Ypres were really "flash-proof" from the German artillery observers on Hill 60 and other vantage points, including numerous kite balloons. It was clear from the artillery map-boards subsequently captured on Hill 60, that the majority of our gun positions were accurately known by the German artillery. Battery after battery was singled out by the enemy for deliberate and destructive bombardment by his 5.9 and 8-inch howitzers. On May 20 some 600 shells were fired at A/103 Battery (Major Powell), and similar treatment was meted out in turn to most of our batteries. The loss of life and destruction of guns became a serious matter ; while the immense labour involved in getting up gun ammunition for the coming battle was increased by the incessant explosion, by day and night, of the dumps of ammunition collected at the battery positions.

After nightfall on the 28th, Major Shaw's battery (D/102) was heavily shelled in its position close to Transport Farm, and the cartridges in one of the howitzer pits were set on fire. Major Shaw, accompanied by Lieutenant Johnson (the Divisional Trench-Mortar Officer), 2nd Lieutenant Lapthorne, the battery sergeant-major, and one or two gunners, immediately entered the blazing gun-pit in a gallant attempt to extinguish the flames. Whilst thus engaged the entire store of howitzer shells inside the pit exploded with a terrific detonation. No member of the gallant little party survived, and no trace remained of the howitzer but a gigantic crater, some 30 feet in diameter and 16 feet deep. It was Major Shaw, it will be remembered, who first reported the evacuation of 26th Avenue (see Part II., Chap. III.). Johnson, an officer whose high character and modest unassuming gallantry had impressed all who knew him, had only recently taken over the duties of Divisional Trench-Mortar Officer from Major Britten. The latter, another gallant officer, had been killed in April whilst endeavouring to extinguish a fire in his battery position at Lankhoff Farm.

On May 30 the headquarters of the 68th Infantry Brigade at Railway Dug-outs were practically demolished by bombardment. A direct hit on the signal dug-out killed the operator and destroyed all the instruments. Fortunately none of the brigade staff was seriously injured, but Brig.-General Colville was very severely bruised by a shell splinter. Within one quarter of an hour two N.C.O.'s of the Signal Company had got all lines through to another dug-out.

During the whole period in the Ypres salient the Signal Company was engaged, owing to the heavy shelling, in an endless struggle to dig and maintain buried-cable routes and to keep the other lines through. Lieutenant Jameson, signal officer of the 70th Infantry Brigade, had a most remarkable escape about this time. While riding through the Lille Gate at Ypres his motor-bicycle received a direct hit from a 5.9 shell. The bicycle was smashed to atoms. The officer was untouched, and was later found fast asleep in a lorry within 100 yards of the scene of this occurrence. A tall story, but one which will be readily accepted by those who witnessed the sangfroid of this young officer throughout the war.

On May 14 the 24th Division had furnished an infantry brigade for the occupation of the left section, and the brigades of the 23rd Division were in turn practised in attack over shallow trenches, which had been constructed behind the line to form a replica of the Division's objectives in the coming attack.

As late as May 24 prisoners' statements showed that the Germans still had no anticipation of a big offensive, but believed that raids on a large scale were projected by the British. With the increasing intensity of our bombardment it seemed, however, unlikely that this attitude would be maintained by the enemy. Our mines were to play an important part in the battle, and our arrangements might be seriously disturbed by the German counter-mining operations discovering and destroying our galleries. In preparation for such an event the Hill 60 emergency scheme had been introduced. By this, should our galleries be threatened, our mine would be blown at two hours' notice, and a small attack would be made to occupy the crater.[1]

On May 31 a seven days' artillery bombardment preceding attack was opened on the enemy's trenches and wire. Hostile artillery retaliated heavily on back areas and various headquarters. Preparations for attack had now been in progress for three weeks, and were practically completed. Full instructions for the operation of the 23rd Division had been issued.

On June 2 a raid was attempted by the 13th Durham Light Infantry with the object of obtaining an identification of the enemy. It was

---

[1] Authority: Major A. K. Hay, Brigade Major, 23rd Divisional Artillery, at this period. No official record of this scheme, by its nature very secret, has been found.

THE CATHEDRAL AND CLOTH HALL, YPRES.

[Imperial War Museum—Crown Copyright.

timed for 10.30 P.M. Unfortunately, two minutes before zero hour, the enemy opened a heavy barrage on the front of attack, and the operation failed to effect its object. The raiding party had 1 officer and 5 other ranks killed, 1 officer and 17 other ranks wounded.

The big attack had been fixed for June 7. The difficulty and risk of moving and concealing troops were so great in the salient that it was decided to allow three nights for the relief of the 68th Infantry Brigade, in occupation of the line, by the troops who were to assemble for attack. These movements accordingly commenced on the night of the 4th/5th.

Practice artillery barrages were fired on the 3rd and 5th. During June 6 our guns continued their bombardment and wire-cutting. The enemy's artillery remained very quiet.

Divisional Headquarters were established at a farm about 1600 yards south of Vlamertinghe. On the same day, the 6th, zero hour for the attack was notified at 3.10 A.M. on June 7.

Concentration marches were carried through without a hitch. In the assembly of the troops the subways existing at Hill 60 and Mount Sorrel proved most useful, and the assistance given by the 1st Australian and 2nd Canadian Tunnelling Companies, in controlling and regulating traffic, prevented any possibility of confusion in the subways.

The 23rd Division was assembled for its entry into the first of the great battles of the 1917 campaign in Flanders.

CHAPTER II.

BATTLE OF MESSINES AND AFTER.

JUNE 7 TO SEPTEMBER 19, 1917.

Map No. 5.   YPRES had long since been destroyed. For close on three years the
German armies had endeavoured to tighten the strangle-grip which
had compassed the town's destruction that their feet might desecrate
its grave. The cost at which the town was saved from this final humilia-
tion may be read in the graveyards spread over the area of that deadly
salient in which the British Army held fast in its defence.

To appreciate fully all that the defence of this salient implied, and
the desperate efforts made by the British to wrest certain points from
the enemy, the ground should be seen. To many the Flanders Plain
still conveys the idea of a uniformly flat and featureless expanse of
ground. But the country, though generally level, is far from featureless,
and its very flatness adds importance to the high ground that occurs.

So it was that nowhere at the beginning of June 1917 had the British
trenches in the salient command over those of the Germans; while
the Messines-Wytschaete Ridge and its northward extension through
Hill 60 to Mount Sorrel gave to the enemy observation over Ypres and
practically the whole British area as far north as the Ypres-Menin road.

It was to secure these positions and to free Ypres and its defenders
from the desperate situation endured for so long that General Plumer's
Army (the Second) was to attack on June 7. By the occupation of these
positions the situation would be reversed; the Germans would find
themselves thrust out into an open plain overlooked by the British. But
here it should be noted that Hill 60, whose prominence from the western
side is now accentuated by the monument which crowns its summit,

while providing the British with perfect observation to south-west, south, and south-south-east as far as Wervicq, would not open up the ground to the south-east and east. To obtain observation over the latter ground it would be necessary to capture the Klein-Zillebeke Spur, which screens it from Hill 60.

The X. Corps was to attack as the left wing of the Second Army.[1] Of its four divisions, the 24th would be held in reserve ; the remaining three divisions would attack in order from right to left—41st, 47th, and 23rd.

It thus fell to the 23rd Division to undertake, in addition to the capture of the enemy's trenches on its front, the protection of the left flank of the whole vast attack, and the welding of the captured position to our old front line.

The frontage allotted to the 23rd Division in the attack was slightly over 2000 yards. Advance from our own trenches would be made between Windy Corner and Sap H on either side of the Ypres-Comines railway. The final objective given extended from the Verbrandenmolen-Hollebeke road, along the south-eastern edge of Battle Wood to Klein-Zillebeke, from a point north of which it was drawn back to join our old front line just north of Mount Sorrel. On the right of the railway the advance would be nearly level till the Caterpillar was reached, whence the ground descends rapidly through Battle Wood to meet the Ypres-Comines Canal at Lock 8 Bis. West of this lock, and on the front of the 47th Division's attack, a long high mound, constructed from excavations from the canal, had been strongly fortified by the Germans. This overlooked Battle Wood, and commanded its south-eastern edge in enfilade.

About 100 yards from the wood's south-western edge a narrow depression runs down its whole length ; a similar depression crossing the centre of the wood descends from the Hollebeke road (right boundary of the 23rd Division) to the railway.

The distance of the final objective in Battle Wood from the British front line was about 1400 yards.

The railway runs through a deep cutting between Hill 60 and the Caterpillar, whose summits are on about the same level. After emerging from the cutting, it continues for a space level with the ground on either flank, and is then carried on by an embankment which gains a height of

[1] Second Army—II. Anzac, IX. and X. Corps.

some 20 feet opposit᠂ Lock 8 Bis. Many dug-outs had been disclosed in this embankment, of which traces can still be seen on its eastern side.

On the left of the railway, Hill 60, with a wide summit, stands well above the ground on the Ypres side. The slope on this side was, however, in the hands of the British, whose line ran along or just below the north-western edge of the summit. The crest of the Klein-Zillebeke Spur, which follows the Zwarteleen-Klein-Zillebeke road, rises very slightly to a point half-way between these villages ; thence it continues level to Klein-Zillebeke, beyond which it commences a gradual descent to the south-east. Its south-western slope falls somewhat steeply to the railway.

A valley running up into the German line between the Klein-Zillebeke Spur and Mount Sorrel, about the centre of the attack, was wet and boggy ; its condition influenced the Division's plan of attack.

Lieutenant H. L. Oakley of the 8th Yorkshire Regiment, celebrated as an artist for his exquisite silhouettes, constructed a model of the Caterpillar and Hill 60 from maps and air photographs, showing the hostile trenches, railway, and the general detail of the ground. Study of this proved of immense value to officers and N.C.O.'s, who before the attack felt they knew the German trench system as well as their own.

Before considering the plan of attack, the articles carried by attacking troops at this period should be noted as influencing the task allotted to the infantry.

In addition to his rifle, bayonet, and ordinary equipment, the infantryman in the battle of Messines was to carry—

Steel helmet.
Water-bottle filled.
Entrenching tool.
Waterproof sheet.
One large tool to every other man (five shovels to two picks).
Tube helmet.
Box respirator.
Field dressing.
Two sandbags.
Two grenades (one in each top pocket of jacket, to be collected
    to form a reserve on gaining objective).
120 rounds S.A.A.
Two flares (every other man).
One iron ration.
One day's preserved meat and biscuit.

Certain men carried in addition wire-cutters, Véry pistols, and S.O.S. rockets.

The final objective to be captured was named the Black Line. To regulate the allotment of definite tasks to units, two intermediate objectives were selected, named the Red Line and the Blue Line.

The operation was to be divided into two phases. In the first the attack would be carried straight through to the second objective (Blue Line). Here there would be a pause of three hours to allow fresh troops to be brought forward for the last phase—attack for the capture of the Black Line.

The attack was to be carried out on the right by the 69th Infantry Brigade, reinforced by the 11th Northumberland Fusiliers and the 12th Durham Light Infantry ; on the left by the 70th Infantry Brigade.

The advance for the capture of the Red Line would pivot on the left flank of the 70th Infantry Brigade, so as to form a defensive flank from the British trenches to a point in the Red Line opposite the centre of the brigade's front. This point in the Red Line would then serve as a pivot, on which further troops would swing left to extend the defensive flank to the Blue Line in conjunction with the advance to capture the latter.

This first phase was to be carried out on the front of the 70th Infantry Brigade by the 9th York and Lancaster Regiment on the right, who would advance direct on the Blue Line, and by the 11th Sherwood Foresters on the left, who would be responsible for forming the defensive flank up to this point in the manner indicated.

The left of the Division's attack has been dealt with first, in order to make clearer the measures taken for this flank protection.

In the first phase, on the front of the 69th Infantry Brigade, which lay astride the railway, the 10th Duke of Wellington's, the 8th Yorkshire Regiment, and the 11th West Yorkshire Regiment, in order from right to left, were to capture the Red and Blue Lines. Of these, the Red Line covered the Caterpillar and Hill 60, being situated about 400 yards beyond the latter ; the Blue Line was placed at a distance varying from 70 to 250 yards beyond the Red Line.

The 9th Yorkshire Regiment and 12th Durham Light Infantry, in support during this phase, would move forward on the capture of the

Blue Line, in readiness to advance, respectively, through Battle Wood and between the railway and the Klein-Zillebeke Spur at the hour given for the opening of the second phase, which would culminate in the capture of the Black Line by these battalions. Co-operating in this advance, and keeping touch with both battalions, D Company of the 8th Yorkshire Regiment would move forward astride the railway with the special task of mopping up the dug-outs in the embankment.

In the second phase, on the front of the 70th Infantry Brigade the 8th York and Lancaster Regiment and the 8th Yorkshire Light Infantry (each less one company) were to advance for the capture of the Black Line. The right of the former battalion would move, roughly, along the crest of the Klein-Zillebeke Spur. The advance of the left battalion would constitute a half left wheel, in order to continue the defensive flank from the right of the 11th Sherwood Foresters.

Brigade reserves would be formed in the 69th Infantry Brigade by the 11th Northumberland Fusiliers, with headquarters in Larch Wood Tunnels ; in the 70th Infantry Brigade by one company of the 8th York and Lancaster Regiment and one company of the Yorkshire Light Infantry.

The 68th Infantry Brigade (less two battalions) was to be held in Divisional reserve about Zillebeke.

In considering the tasks allotted to infantry brigades it will be seen that the 70th Infantry Brigade, though called on to undertake the difficult and responsible duty of protecting the left flank of the attack, would find compensation in not being required to advance to any great depth except on their right.

The rôle of the 69th Infantry Brigade, on the other hand, advancing on a frontage slightly greater than that of the 70th, would be one of purely frontal attack, carried through to a considerable depth on its whole front.

To avoid the risk of delay in the initial advance which might be caused by the boggy ground in the valley which, it will be remembered, was situated about the centre of the attack, the inner flanks of brigades would move on either side of the valley, and would be so directed as to gain contact on the firm ground at the enemy's support line.

The total Field Artillery supporting the attack included 156 18-pdr. guns and 42 4.5-in. howitzers.[1]

These were organised into eight groups, of which three groups (66 18-pdrs. and 12 4.5-in. howitzers) would cover the advance of the 69th Infantry Brigade on the right ; five groups (90 18-pdrs. and 30 4.5-in. howitzers) would cover the 70th Infantry Brigade and the initial gap between brigades. They would be further responsible for the protection of the defensive flank on the left.

Support given by these guns would be by creeping and standing barrages. Standing barrages would also be formed on the Divisional front of attack by four 6-in., two 8-in., and two 9.2-in. howitzer batteries, while one 60-pdr. battery would search and sweep Battle Wood.

At the opening of the attack four Stokes guns of No. 3 Special Company R.E. would assist the 69th Infantry Brigade by firing thermit shell on the enemy's support line for ten minutes, and the 68th Light Trench-Mortar Battery would barrage the enemy's front-line trenches opposite Mount Sorrel, where they were too close to our own line for the Field Artillery to perform this service for the 70th Infantry Brigade.

In addition to the artillery and heavy, medium, and light trench-mortar batteries covering the advance, a machine-gun barrage would be provided by the 68th and 194th Machine-Gun Companies and by guns of No. 12 Motor Machine-Gun Battery (organised into six 8-gun batteries and two 6-gun batteries—total, sixty guns).

A flank barrage would also be formed by sixteen machine-guns of the 30th Division, which held the line on the left of the 23rd Division.

After years of labour and the ever-present danger from counter-mines, nineteen mines had been prepared under the German trenches along the whole front of the Second Army's attack.

The mines in this vast system, which covered a front of ten miles, would be simultaneously exploded at zero hour announcing the opening of the attack.

---

[1] Units composing 23rd Divisional Artillery Group :—

   102nd and 103rd R.F.A. Brigades of 23rd Division.
   106th and 107th R.F.A. Brigades of 24th Division.
   189th Army Field Artillery Brigade.
   298th Army Field Artillery Brigade (less D/298 + A/119).
   315th Army Field Artillery Brigade + A/277.
   148th Royal Field Artillery Brigade of 30th Division, attached for assistance on left flank.

At 2.30 A.M. on the morning of June 7 all battalions were ready
in their assembly positions. On previous nights the enemy had shown
signs of nervousness, and sudden intense barrages had been opened
on our front system. False alarms had perhaps created a false sense of
security ; to-night all was quiet.

The moment had arrived for which the tunnellers had toiled so long.
At 3.10 A.M. a terrific report announced the explosion of the mines. A
second detonation close at hand shook the strained nerves of those
assembled near the tunnellers' post. Major Henry, commanding the
1st Australian Tunnelling Company, having fired the mines under the
Caterpillar and Hill 60, had opened a bottle of champagne to drink
success to the 23rd Division.

Simultaneously, those far back behind the British front saw the
whole sky lit by the flashes of guns and bursting shells, then heard a
dull roar like the continued roll of mighty drums, as the artillery opened
the heaviest barrage yet put down in the course of the war. To those
in the attack the noise was terrific.

One minute later the infantry advanced. The enemy's artillery was
quick to reply, and within two minutes their barrage came down. But
by then our men had reached the German front line at nearly every
point.

The enemy, demoralised by the explosion of the mines and the sud-
denness of the attack, fled in all directions. Here and there it was impossible to restrain the troops from rushing through their own barrage
in pursuit of the flying Germans. Held up at length by the standing
barrage, some were thus isolated for a considerable time.

Only on the extreme left were difficulties encountered. Elsewhere
the enemy's wire had been most effectively cut ; but here some wire,
concealed by a hollow, was found intact. This obstacle disorganised the
advance of the left company of the Sherwood Foresters, whose position
in the attack was one of extreme importance. Anxious with regard to
the situation, but unable to get definite information, Major Hudson,
second in command of the battalion, went forward under heavy fire,
assisted in reorganising the company, and personally superintended the
consolidation of the position at this critical point.

At the head of the valley which separated the two brigades, and at
about their meeting-point, a party of the enemy put up a strong stand.

Volleys of rifle grenades, however, soon overcame this resistance and forced their surrender.

By 3.30 A.M., with the exception of a short length of trench on the extreme left of the attack, the whole objective of the first phase had been captured.

Example of the spirit of determination which animated the Division is afforded by the account given by Lieut.-Colonel Western, commanding the 8th Yorkshire Regiment, of the conduct of two of his officers. Captain B. L. Pearson, after capturing the Caterpillar, pushed on to his objective with three wounds and a broken collar-bone in spite of the expostulations of his company sergeant-major, who begged him to allow himself to be taken back. It was only when he fainted from loss of blood that he was removed. Captain N. Lambert was found by Colonel Western in the most advanced shell-hole that his company was consolidating. Though severely wounded in the lungs, he begged to be allowed to remain with his company. To the deep regret of all, this gallant officer was killed by a shell before reaching the dressing-station.

The leading troops of the 69th Infantry Brigade had suffered very light casualties, but the rear waves, which included battalion headquarters, signallers, &c., had sustained considerable losses from shell-fire.

The 8th Yorkshire Regiment now moved their headquarters to Hill 60, and undertook the consolidation of the mine craters here and at the Caterpillar, while special parties all along the front ferreted out those of the enemy who had concealed themselves from the leading waves of attack, and forced their surrender.

The completion of the first phase found the captured line occupied by the Duke of Wellington's in Battle Wood, the 8th Yorkshire Regiment astride the railway, with the West Yorkshire Regiment on the left of the 69th Infantry Brigade front. The line was continued on the front of the 70th Infantry Brigade by the 9th York and Lancaster Regiment, on whose left a defensive flank, thrown back to St Peter's Street in the old front line, was occupied by the Sherwood Foresters.

This day the 23rd Division had its first experience of the German "pill-box." The enemy had recently introduced this form of protection to hold strong-points in a country where water made the construction of deep dug-outs impossible. Small concrete forts, partly above and partly below ground, armed with machine-guns, they presented a strong defence against infantry attack.

Several of these " pill-boxes " had already been captured, and during the three-hour pause on the Blue Line which now ensued, battalion headquarters were moved forward to the protection of certain of these. Captured positions were consolidated, units reorganised, fresh ammunition supplies brought up, and touch gained throughout the Division front and with the 47th Division on the right.

Could the course of a battle be foreseen, the framing of plans for its conduct would be less difficult. There is small doubt that if, on June 7, the advance had been carried through without pause, the capture of the final objective could have been effected with greater ease and at smaller cost.

But an attack of this type, supported by a huge mass of artillery, and whose every phase has been prepared in minute detail, must necessarily be conducted on rigid lines. The complicated machinery of an artillery barrage is not adapted to a sudden change of plan. If one is to gain the advantage of an artillery barrage, one is committed to submitting to its regulating the rate of advance.

It was necessary therefore to remain stationary, and not possible to exploit the demoralisation into which the enemy had undoubtedly been thrown by the first attack. This three hours' respite gave the Germans opportunity for collecting and reorganising their shaken troops, and for preparing a stiff resistance to further advance.

At 6.50 A.M. the second phase opened. On the front of the 69th Infantry Brigade the 9th Yorkshire Regiment and 12th Durham Light Infantry advanced on the right and left of the railway, while D Company of the 8th Yorkshire Regiment moved forward in the centre to deal with the dug-outs in the railway embankments.

Pushing forward across the south-western slope of the Klein-Zillebeke Spur, the Durham Light Infantry's advance was never checked till they had gained their objective. The 8th Yorkshire company in the centre was equally successful. But in the broken ground, and among the shattered trees and undergrowth of Battle Wood, the advance of the 9th Yorkshire Regiment was greatly hampered by machine-gun fire. Their objective, too, lay some 300 yards farther forward than that of the remainder of the brigade. Fighting their way steadily forward, the battalion at length succeeded in gaining a line within 150 yards of their final objective on the edge of the wood.

Beyond this it was not possible to go ; for the troops of the 47th Division, attacking on their right, were held up in face of the mound on the canal bank. As has already been pointed out, while this position was in the occupation of the enemy the forward edge of Battle Wood would be denied to us.

The place was immensely strong. Dug-outs and covered machine-gun emplacements, spread along its length, converted the earth mound to a concrete fortress. The advance of the 47th Division against it lay down an open glacis slope completely commanded by this position, which even in its natural state might well be deemed impregnable to assault unless overwhelmed by the fire of siege artillery. Its natural strength will always be clear to the visitor to this spot. So long as the mound and surrounding ground remain in their present condition,[1] honeycombed with shell-holes, they will afford a striking example of the battle between concrete and siege artillery, which effected its capture some days later.

The 12th Durham Light Infantry had gained their objective without serious casualties, but these had been somewhat severe both in the 8th and 9th Yorkshire Regiment. Reinforcements were now sent forward to these battalions from the 10th Northumberland Fusiliers and the 10th Duke of Wellington's respectively.

While these events had been in progress on the front of the 69th Infantry Brigade, the 8th York and Lancaster Regiment and 8th Yorkshire Light Infantry had advanced for the capture of the final objective of the 70th Infantry Brigade. Both battalions had suffered rather heavy casualties from artillery fire prior to and during their movement to their forward assembly position in the Blue Line. " A " Company of the 8th York and Lancaster Regiment in particular suffered seriously, losing three of its officers, including the company commander and second-in-command, and many N.C.O.'s. The company was to form the left of its battalion, but in the disorganisation that resulted from the loss of its leaders it missed direction. Captain Barlow, who was acting as second-in-command of the battalion, immediately went forward, and, correcting the direction of its advance, led the company

[1] December 1921.

forward to its objective, killing many of the enemy and taking several prisoners. On the right the 8th York and Lancasters gained their objective in touch with the 12th Durham Light Infantry.

In the meanwhile the Yorkshire Light Infantry, wheeling as they advanced, had established themselves, in accordance with plan, in prolongation of the defensive flank.

The 70th Infantry Brigade had carried out the full task allotted to it. But just beyond the line carried by the 8th York and Lancaster Regiment lay a hillock, known as the Knoll, on which a party of the enemy had established themselves. The commanding position of this point made it essential that the enemy should be driven from it. 2nd Lieutenant Fraser, with a small party of men, charged the position, killed two officers, captured three prisoners, and put to flight the remainder of the Germans who had rallied here.

Shortly after the commencement of the advance for the capture of the Black Line, Lieut.-Colonel J. H. Bowes-Wilson, whose battalion (the 9th York and Lancaster Regiment) was established on the Blue Line in support, had gone forward to watch the course of the battle. About 7 A.M. this gallant officer was killed.

By 8 A.M., except on the extreme right, where the enemy's occupation of the mound made the complete penetration of Battle Wood impossible, the Division held the whole line of its final objective.

Orders had arranged for the consolidation of the Black Line as a front line, with a view to observation to the south-east, by which artillery and machine-gun fire could be directed on the enemy's gun positions, and of the Blue Line as a reserve line, covering back areas and previous observation posts.

The Field Companies R.E. and four platoons of the Pioneers were sent forward about 10 A.M. to carry out the latter task by the construction of a line of strong-points. It was on this day that Captain J. P. H. Ouchterlony, who had rendered splendid service to the Division during the past year in command of the 102nd Field Company, was killed. He was replaced by Captain D. G. Robb, who held command of the company until the end of the war.

Communication trenches across the old No Man's Land were pushed forward by the pioneers from Allen's Crater and Swift Street ; others were dug by the 2nd Canadian Tunnelling Company, under Major Brewster, to Mount Sorrel ; and by the 1st Australian Tunnelling Company on either side of the Verbrandenmolen road.

During the morning the 10th Northumberland Fusiliers were sent forward from Divisional reserve to reinforce the 70th Infantry Brigade.

The enemy now decided to make an effort to break in at the point where the advance had hinged on our front line.

At 10.30 A.M. a counter-attack was delivered on the front line immediately to the left of the 70th Infantry Brigade. By a determined effort a few Germans succeeded in entering the trench, but they were immediately driven out by the 2nd Bedfordshire Regiment of the 30th Division, who were holding the line on the left of the 23rd Division, and by parties of the 11th Sherwood Foresters and 8th Yorkshire Light Infantry. The counter-attack broke down with heavy loss to the enemy in killed.

Several times during the afternoon the enemy were observed massing as if for a counter-attack at various points on the Divisional front, but they were on every occasion dispersed by the fire of our artillery.

At 10.45 P.M. a large body of Germans was reported advancing on Klein-Zillebeke, with the apparent intention of recapturing the high ground north of the village. Every available machine-gun, Lewis-gun, and rifle opened, and a call to the artillery brought down a heavy barrage. Nothing further was seen or heard of this force till, at 11.15 P.M., a solitary wounded German N.C.O. crawled to our lines to surrender himself.

The excitement of an advance leaves little room for reflection. The sense of superiority experienced in the assault and capture of a position will stimulate men's *morale* for a considerable period. But the supreme test of discipline comes in the long hours that follow, when the early excitement has died down, and wearied men have more leisure to think of themselves.

Objectives this day had been captured early in the morning. Later the heat became very great, and throughout the day the captured positions were subjected to the most galling artillery fire. This fire was maintained throughout the night and following day. The troops holding Image Crescent and the Knoll, north of Klein-Zillebeke, suffered most severely ; but the line was held intact. Throughout the whole night of June 7/8 our Field Artillery maintained a barrage in front of the captured line.

During June 9 and 10 the enemy continued a heavy bombardment of the whole captured area, but no serious counter-attack was attempted. By this time relief had at last come to the weary troops. On the night of the 9th/10th the 24th Division commenced to take over, and by June 13 the 23rd Division had been withdrawn. No ground had been lost ; every trench captured was handed over.

The battle of Messines had been the most complete and overwhelming success yet attained in trench warfare. Along the whole battle front the advance of the Second Army had moved like clockwork. By noon the enemy had been swept from the Messines-Wytschaete Ridge, and later the deep advance in the centre of the army's attack had carried the German battery positions. On June 7 the Second Army captured 7200 prisoners and 67 guns.

Machine-gun barrages to cover the advance of the infantry, in co-operation with the artillery barrage, had already been introduced in the battle of Arras, but the machine-guns of the 23rd Division acted in accordance with these new tactics for the first time at the battle of Messines. Some idea as to the part they played can be gained from their ammunition expenditure. On June 7 the barrage machine-guns alone fired approximately 1,250,000 rounds.

On the other hand, the absence of hostile machine-gun fire was remarked by all who engaged in the assault.

The German artillery did very little counter-battery work. C/103 Battery was shelled for a short time ; B/103 was heavily bombarded in the afternoon, and had three gun-pits hit, one gun damaged, and a quantity of ammunition blown up ; D/103 was also shelled for a short time, but had no damage done to it.

In the course of the operations the 23rd Division captured 14 officers and 557 other ranks unwounded, and 58 other ranks wounded.

The casualties sustained by the two attacking brigades amounted to—

	Killed or died of wounds.		Wounded.		Missing.	
	Officers.	Other ranks.	Officers.	Other ranks.	Officers.	Other ranks.
69th Infantry Brigade .	12	195	40	728	..	149
70th Infantry Brigade .	8	175	23	730	2	156

In a single day the whole southern area of the salient had been thrust back, and Ypres freed from the threat of encirclement which had hung over the town for so long.

Some idea of the tremendous work thrown on the R.A.M.C. personnel of the Division can be gained by the detail of the casualties given above. Thanks to the perfect arrangements made by Colonel Blackham, the A.D.M.S., the skill and devotion of his officers, and the gallantry of the men of the Field Ambulances and of the regimental stretcher-bearers, the evacuation of the wounded was carried out without hitch.

Advanced dressing-stations were established on the right by the 71st Field Ambulance (Captains Hairsine and Picken) at "Sunken Road"; in the centre by the 69th Field Ambulance (Lieut.-Colonel Hammerton) at Railway Dug-outs; on the left at Zillebeke Bund by the 70th Field Ambulance, command of which had been taken over by Lieut.-Colonel Pye Smith in the previous November.

Relay posts were established for the conveyance of the wounded by hand to the dressing-stations, whence they were evacuated by trolley, on the right to Woodcote House, on the left and centre to Kruisstraat. Cars also assisted the evacuation in the centre from Railway Dug-outs, to which the wounded from "Sunken Road" had to be diverted by hand during the battle owing to the breakdown of the trolley line on the right.

Severe casualties were sustained. Captain Hairsine, leading forward his bearers, was killed. In the 70th Field Ambulance 11 N.C.O.'s and men, including the sergeant-major, were killed, and 20 wounded. But owing largely to the coolness and resource of Corporal Medley, who nobly supported his commanding officer in reorganising the work, the evacuation of the wounded continued without break.[1] Colonel Pye Smith himself set a magnificent example. Continually leading his bearers into the front line to rescue the wounded, who were lying under heavy shell-fire, he worked with the greatest heroism for sixty hours.

On relief the Division was withdrawn to the Berthen and Ouderdom areas, with headquarters at Berthen.

By June 13 all troops were back in rest, with the exception of the Royal Engineers, Pioneer Battalion, 68th, 70th, and 194th Machine-

[1] For their gallant conduct Lieut.-Colonel Pye Smith was awarded the D.S.O., and Corporal Medley the D.C.M.

Gun Companies, who remained in the line attached to the 24th Division. The machine-gun companies were withdrawn in the course of the next few days.

On the 14th news was received that the Germans had at length been driven from the mound on the canal bank which had threatened the right of the 23rd Division's attack on the 7th.

Not the least of the qualities of the British soldier as a fighting man is his quick recovery from the strain of battle. Following a success like the battle of Messines, the rest that was now enjoyed in perfect summer weather found the Division fit and ready again for battle in the space of a few days.

There were those in the Division, however, who never knew rest. For lack of a better term they may be called the " silent services." Their work was, perhaps, seldom quite appreciated or their existence recognised by units, till that which was normally accepted as "manna from heaven " failed to materialise. Then outraged brigadiers and C.O.'s, unmindful of past benefits, would turn and rend their hard-worked benefactors.

Prominent among these was the D.A.D.O.S. Major W. R. G. Bishop had held this appointment in the 23rd Division till February 5, 1916, when, on transfer to the 56th Division, he was replaced by Captain J. B. Oxenham, who remained with the Division till the end of the war.

The carefully kept war diaries of the D.A.D.O.S. provide in themselves a history of the development which marked the different phases of the war. In 1915 one finds the arrival of Lewis-guns, the withdrawal of respirators in favour of tube helmets, the issue of short rifles, the first consignment of thigh gum-boots, the receipt of steel helmets for trial.

In 1916 telescopic rifles and shovel-shields on trial arrive, while later Stokes mortars make their appearance.

In 1917 the raid is an established institution, and one finds a brigade clamouring for " Kukries " which " cannot be obtained."

Throughout, the purchase of hooks and eyes and buttons mingles with demands for 18-pdr. guns, and throughout comes the sad entry, " No car all day," or " No car till 5 P.M."

The diary of June 1, as giving the work of a typical day, may be quoted to vindicate D.A.D.O.S. for ever from the charge of spending his days in " joy riding " :—

To Bailleul for French medal ribbons for brooches required by noon. Bought iron and nuts for special stretcher fittings and flags for infantry brigade "moppers-up." Visited gun-park *re* 4.5-in. howitzers demanded, also shops *re* R.O. springs, &c., and D.S.C. *re* making fittings for stretchers ; railhead, where winter clothing receipts are practically completed. Asked brigades for distribution of surplus cutters and grenade carriers held by me. Bought torches, and also files for bayonets.

It is remarkable in the diaries of both D.A.D.O.S. and the Divisional Train that one finds work on days of big trench warfare battles pursuing its normal course without hitch. Beyond a casual entry, " Zero Day," one seldom finds reference to the battle.

Complete rest for the infantry was of short duration, as two battalions were required for work under the A.D. Signals and the Chief Engineer of the X. Corps. Battalions so employed were relieved at intervals till June 24, when orders were received for the 23rd Division to take over the Hill 60 sector from the 24th Division.

Brigade horse shows had been held during the rest period, and the opportunity was now taken of holding a Divisional horse show before moving forward. Judges at a horse show are always the subject of harsh criticism by all except prize-winners, but the Divisional show, held on June 25, proved an immense all-round success, and gave evidence of the care devoted to the animals and transport throughout the Division. The most popular judge on such occasions is the one who remembers that there are spectators as well as competitors. On this day there was a very close competition between two horses in the jumping. General Babington, the chief judge, decided that these should be given a second run, adding *sotto voce*, " . . . and C—— must go again, because he amuses the troops." Captain C—— played up in generous fashion. Midst the wild enthusiasm of the soldiery the first fence was negotiated in excellent style. Then the expected event occurred. At the second fence, a post and rails, the horse stopped dead, and, to a howl of delight from the crowd, Captain C——, sportsman and great horseman as he was, described a graceful parabola over the fence, landed on the far side with a thud reminiscent of the explosion of the Hill 60 mine, and rose smiling, with his eyeglass still firmly attached to the peak of his cap. For the troops it was the star turn of a great day !

The first infantry brigade to move forward was the 70th, which proceeded on June 26 to Chippewa Camp, near Reninghelst. This brigade relieved the 24th Division in the Mount Sorrel (left) section of the front on the night of the 27th/28th.

The 69th Infantry Brigade followed on June 28, and took over Battle Wood (right) section on the night of the 29th/30th.

On June 30 General Babington assumed command of the sector, with headquarters at Zevecoten Camp, near Reninghelst. The 68th Infantry Brigade moved in Divisional reserve the same day to Micmac Camp, one mile south-west of Dickebusch.

The front taken over, which extended from the canal in front of Battle Wood, past Klein-Zillebeke, to Davison Street, had a length of some 2500 yards.

At 2.30 A.M. on July 1 a strong German fighting patrol attacked under a shower of rifle grenades, and forced the temporary withdrawal of a post at Klein-Zillebeke. About an hour earlier a similar attempt on another post had failed, with the loss of one prisoner of the 6th Jäger Regiment of the 195th Division.

Though with the capture of the Messines-Wytschaete ridge the enemy had been deprived of observation from the south and south-east of Ypres, he still held commanding positions to the east and north-east, from which, as well as from the Pilckem ridge to the north, he still overlooked the ground in this quarter.

Future operations had been planned by which the Fifth Army was to attack with a view to thrusting the Germans from these positions.

In the initial operations of what was later to constitute the third battle of Ypres, the 23rd Division was not to be engaged. Their work now lay in preparations for the attack of the 24th Division, which was to form the right of the Fifth Army.

On July 3 the 47th Division took over the right section, which extended as far north as Klein-Zillebeke, and the 69th Infantry Brigade, thus relieved, was withdrawn to the Steenvoorde area. At the same time, the 70th Infantry Brigade extended its left to take over the line as far as Observatory Ridge from the 30th Division. This rearrangement gave a frontage of about 1400 yards to the 23rd Division, which

LE MONT DES CATS.

(From an etching by Lieut.-Colonel B. Buchanan, 23rd Divisional Artillery.)

now came under the II. Corps of the Fifth Army, whose southern boundary became the right boundary of the Division. The 68th Infantry Brigade was placed in support near Dickebusch ; the 69th Infantry Brigade being now held in Divisional reserve.

On July 4 H.M. the King passed Divisional Headquarters, and the men of the 68th Infantry Brigade lined the road to cheer him as he drove on his way to Vierstraat.

The 23rd Divisional Artillery on July 5 completed the relief of the 24th Divisional Artillery, which had hitherto been covering the front.

Work advanced steadily, though frequently set back by the damage caused by artillery fire, which at times was very severe, and by heavy rain showers, which played havoc in the clay soil where trenches still lacked revetment and drains.

Preparations for attack on a large scale involve the bringing forward of quantities of ammunition and material. In the Ypres salient the transport employed on these duties moved night after night through the bottle-neck of Ypres, and thence forward by the few existing roads and tracks, all of which were shelled by the enemy. Each morning disclosed gruesome evidence of the heroism of the drivers who nightly passed through this nerve-wracking ordeal. It is difficult to do proper justice to the British driver and his horses, for, however heavy the shelling, they never failed to deliver their loads at the appointed places.

On one of these occasions the ammunition waggons of D/102 had to pass through very heavy shelling to reach their battery near Zillebeke, and suffered many casualties to drivers and horses. Captain W. R. Pasteur, who was in charge of the teams, although himself slightly wounded, continued to supervise the work until finally struck by a shell which shattered both his legs. This gallant officer persisted, nevertheless, in giving directions to the last ammunition waggon until he died.

The 18th Division now relieved the 30th Division on our left, and the 68th Infantry Brigade replaced the 70th Infantry Brigade in the line.

On the night of July 7, 2nd Lieutenant Frederick Youens of the 13th Durham Light Infantry was wounded while on patrol duty. He had returned to the trenches to have his wounds dressed, when a heavy hostile bombardment opened, and a report came in that the enemy were preparing to raid our trenches. Youens, regardless of his wounds, immediately went forward and commenced to rally a Lewis-gun team, which had become disorganised by the heavy shell-fire. While he was engaged in this an enemy bomb fell on the Lewis-gun position. Youens seized it and hurled it over the parapet before it exploded. It was followed very shortly by a second bomb. This, too, he picked up. But before he could throw it clear the bomb exploded in his hand, severely wounding him and some of his men. Not only, however, had the gallantry of this officer saved the lives of several of his men, but his example had steadied the troops, who drove back the German raiders.

By his action Frederick Youens earned the fifth Victoria Cross awarded to the 23rd Division, but the wounds he had received proved mortal, and he did not live to wear the decoration.

On July 13 a party of 40 men of the 12th Durham Light Infantry, under Lieutenant Weightman and 2nd Lieutenant Freeman, raided an enemy post at Klein-Zillebeke. The capture of 1 wounded and 4 unwounded men of the 8th Jäger Regiment showed the 195th Division to be still on this front. The casualties of the raiders amounted to 7 wounded, including Lieutenant Weightman, and 3 men missing. The same night Lieut.-Colonel Lord Robert Manners was shot through the thigh while visiting some working parties of his battalion, the 10th Northumberland Fusiliers. He calmly remarked : " Friday and the 13th of the month ; I might have known it." This most gallant officer was, to the lasting regret of his battalion and all who knew him, killed by a shell a few days previous to the battle of the Menin road.

Both the German artillery and aeroplanes now showed an increased activity, and it was at this period that mustard-gas shells made their appearance. Their effect was to blunt the sense of smell and blister portions of the body which happened to be moistened with perspiration. The eyes were also affected, but blindness was not caused, as had been feared at first.

Our observation balloons had a rough time from hostile aircraft, and parachute feats by the unfortunate observers were of daily occurrence.

Aircraft action was apt to be depressing to our infantry in the trenches, who continually saw our slow artillery machines being harassed by the German fighters with but little retaliation by us. The greater part of the work of our fighting machines was carried out well behind the German line, unseen by our infantry. The policy of taking the war into the enemy's country, and so forcing him to retain fighting machines for defence, was undoubtedly sound ; but it was natural that the infantryman should judge from what he saw, and that he should accordingly not always appreciate the work that was being done. It had been generally felt earlier in the year that the enemy had got the better of us in the air, but on July 16 it is recorded that " our airmen show superiority in air fights."

The time had now come for the 24th Division to take over its offensive front. Relief of the 23rd Division (less artillery) commenced on the 22nd, and was completed on July 23, Divisional Headquarters being transferred that day to Merris, while units of the Division were accommodated in the Berthen area.

In addition to the artillery, which remained with the 24th Division, the 101st Field Company and 9th South Staffordshire Regiment were left in the forward area for work under the II. Corps.

The Division now came under the X. Corps of the Second Army.

The following letter was received when this transfer was carried out :—

II. Corps G.T. 2596, dated July 22, 1917.

.   .   .   .

On the eve of leaving II. Corps, the Corps Commander desires to thank Major-General Babington and all ranks of the 23rd Division for the good work they have performed while under his command.

A good division is one that fights hard and works hard. The 23rd Division came to the II. Corps with a fine fighting record from their recent exploits at the battle of Messines ; they leave it with a record of hard work, accomplished with zeal and determination in the face of many difficulties.

The Corps Commander desires to thank the 23rd Division for their services, and trusts that he may at some future date have the good fortune again to have them under his command.

(Sd.)   S. H. WILSON, B.-G. General Staff, II. Corps.

On July 31 the Fifth Army offensive opened. The day opened with Map No. 6. a drizzle, which before night had developed into heavy rain. Despite the unfavourable weather, the whole ridge which formed the objective of attack was captured, and observation denied to the enemy over the Ypres plain. On the left and in the centre of attack final objectives were in most cases captured ; but farther south the opposition encountered at Inverness Copse, Stirling Castle, and Lower Star Post held up the right of the attack. In reading the reports of the attack it could not be foreseen that the future would find the Germans still in stubborn possession of these positions and the 23rd Division attacking in this quarter.

For four days following the attack heavy rain continued without cease. The country became waterlogged, and the continuance of operations on a large scale became impossible. Once again the weather had favoured the enemy.

In the meantime the Division was in hard training, partly in the Second Army training area near Wizernes, partly about Meteren in the X. Corps area. The 101st Field Company was still working in the forward area, the 102nd was employed on the construction of rifle ranges.

On August 9 the Division was transferred from the Second to the Fifth Army, and headquarters, which had previously been transferred from Merris to Wizernes, moved to Eperlecques.

On this occasion General Babington received the following letter :—

HEADQUARTERS, 2ND ARMY,
August 7, 1917.

DEAR BABINGTON,—I am sorry to say the order has come for your Division to be transferred from the Second Army. Before the Division leaves I should like you to assure all commanders and staffs that I fully appreciate the good work that has been done by all the troops during the period they have been with us.

I am confident that they will carry out in the future, as they have done in the past, any duties that may be entrusted to them with credit to themselves and to you.—Yours sincerely,

HERBERT PLUMER.

About this time Lieut.-Colonel R. Stephenson, who was to remain as a notable figure in the Division till the end of the war, replaced Lieut.-Colonel Lush in command of the 9th South Staffordshire Regiment.

On August 15 the Divisional Artillery were transferred to XVIII. Corps, and moved to the north of Poperinghe, where they were held in reserve.

On August 16 the Fifth Army offensive was resumed. Again progress was made on the left of the attack, and Langemarck was captured,
but the right of the attack, which was directed against the north-west
corner of Inverness Copse, was unable to overcome the enemy's resistance, and beyond the capture of Westhoek and some small gains
on the western border of Glencorse Wood, little progress was made
either here or in the centre of attack.

The General Staff diary of this period is filled with good news from
other fronts. At Verdun the French had attacked and taken 2000
prisoners. The Italians, attacking on a forty-mile front, had captured
7000 Austrians. But it seems the only event in the 23rd Division worthy
of record in the diary at the time was that " Lobo of ' A ' Mess gives
birth to three puppies (her first family)."

On August 23 the 70th Infantry Brigade was moved to an area just
north of Reninghelst, where the Division on the following day took
over the headquarters occupied during the previous winter. The 68th
and 69th Infantry Brigades were moved forward at the same time to
the Ouderdom and Wippenhoek areas.

On the same day, the 24th, a German counter-attack against the
14th Division drove back their line for some distance between Glencorse
Wood and Inverness Copse. The 70th Infantry Brigade was held in
readiness as a reinforcement, and the 23rd Division was ordered to relieve
the 14th astride the Menin road. The orders for General Babington
to take command of this sector remained unaltered, but on the 25th
it was intimated that the 41st Infantry Brigade would remain in occupation of the line under his command. Two battalions of the 70th Infantry
Brigade would be placed at the disposal of the G.O.C. 41st Brigade ;
the remainder of the 70th Brigade and the 69th Infantry Brigade would
be in reserve in the neighbourhood of Divisional Headquarters, which
were to be established half a mile north of Dickebusch.

When General Babington assumed command on the morning of
August 26, the situation on the left of the line was somewhat obscure.
The enemy, with flammenwerfer and under an intense artillery barrage,
had attacked four posts on the left flank at dawn. It was later learnt
that only one of these had been forced back.

Just before daybreak on the following day an attempt was made
by two half-companies of the 41st Infantry Brigade, assisted by two

tanks, to capture 600 yards of trench running from the Menin road through the western edge of Inverness Copse. The weather, combined with the appalling condition of the ground, defeated the enterprise. Both tanks were ditched at Clapham Junction, and the operation failed.

Incessant rain throughout August had reduced the ground to a state which made it essential to postpone large-scale operations. The continuance of these had been planned for early September, and the G.O.C. II. Corps had intended nursing the 23rd Division for the part they were to play in them. But the indefinite postponement of these operations made the relief of the 41st Infantry Brigade, reduced by continual fighting and exposure, imperative.

On the night of August 27/28, during the course of their relief by the 70th Infantry Brigade, the Germans again attacked the posts on the left of the line. Hand-to-hand fighting ensued ; the enemy was driven back with heavy loss, and two prisoners of the 177th Regiment of the 32nd Division were secured.

Two days later the 25th Division took over the line. The relief of the 70th Infantry Brigade was carried out under cover of a terrific barrage put down by every gun in the line in reply to an S.O.S. call, the origin of which was never discovered. There was high tension on both sides at this period, and a relief was a lively undertaking. The adventures of an officer of the 9th York and Lancaster Regiment, though they occurred a few months before this time, serve to illustrate the conditions under which reliefs in the salient were normally carried out at this period. " Out of the line to near Ouderdom. On the way we encountered lachrimatory shells : I was riding Peggy. Trying to put on my respirator, I lost my tin hat and control of the horse. Got off the horse, and found my hat in the darkness ; put on my respirator ; lost the horse ; took off the respirator to find the horse, and to get a breath of air ; mounted horse again ; by this time I had lost all my men, who had marched down the road ; finally, I decided to risk the gas, and, taking off my respirator (without losing my tin hat), trotted after the company."

The detached R.E. and pioneers had now rejoined the Division, but the Divisional Artillery still remained detached to the XVIII. Corps. The C.R.A. of the 23rd Division at this time assumed command of the artillery covering the 58th Division front, consisting of the 102nd, 103rd, 155th (Army), 240th, and 241st Brigades.

Following relief of the 70th Infantry Brigade, command of the sector passed to the G.O.C. 25th Division on September 2. Two days prior to this several hostile aeroplanes appeared over Divisional Headquarters in the early afternoon. They dropped bombs on Dickebusch and the Café Belge, causing many casualties among the horses of the 128th Field Company. In other units four other ranks were killed and four wounded by this bombardment. The German air-craft were very active at this period, harassing back areas nearly every night. Steenvoorde, to which Divisional Headquarters moved on relief, was bombed on the night of their arrival, and again on the following night. Lederzeele, to which a further move was made on September 4, proved no more immune to the enemy's night bombing than Steenvoorde or Dickebusch.

On September 3 the Division was transferred to the X. Corps. A warning order was received the same day from this Corps with reference to the coming offensive in which the Division was to take part. All preparations for the attack were to be completed by September 18. On the front of attack of the 23rd Division, which was given as a line running roughly north and south, whose northern extremity rested on the Menin road at Clapham Junction 1300 yards east of Hooge, the 24th Division would, for the time being, undertake all preparations while the 23rd Division was in training for the attack.

On September 6 the Divisional Artillery was withdrawn from the line. A few days later the 102nd Field Company and three companies of the Pioneer Battalion were attached to the 24th Division to assist in the preparation for the attack.

On September 13 Sir D. Arbuthnot relieved the C.R.A. of the 24th Division in command of the group artillery covering the offensive front. This artillery, which was to be increased before the battle, included the 103rd R.F.A. Brigade.

On the following day General Babington assumed command of the sector, and established his headquarters at Burgomaster Farm, near Dickebusch. The 68th and 70th Infantry Brigades moved the same date to the Dickebusch area, and the 69th to Westoutre.

The day of the attack was now close at hand. The plan of operations had been drawn up, boundaries in the attack fixed, and orders and instructions given out for all the details of the attack. The final operation order alone remained to be issued.

The weather during the past weeks had greatly improved, but on several days heavy rain had fallen.

On September 15 aeroplane photographs, which were minutely studied every day, disclosed a somewhat disturbing development on the front of attack allotted to the 23rd Division. A group of artificial lakes, forming what was known as the Dumbarton Lake area, would face the advance. It was now seen that our artillery fire had broken the banks of these lakes at certain points, and had also caused a damming of the streams which connected them. As a result, the lake area had been converted to a swamp. It was necessary at once to alter the plan of attack in this area in a manner which will be fully explained in the next chapter.

On September 15 the 70th Infantry Brigade took over the line from in front of Clapham Junction to a point at the south-eastern corner of Bodmin Copse. Next day the 41st Division occupied 200 yards of the southern portion of this line, so reducing the 70th Infantry Brigade's front to the 1000 yards fixed for the battle front of the 23rd Division.[1]

On every day preceding the attack our artillery kept up a harassing fire throughout the whole twenty-four hours. The hostile artillery, in reply, persistently searched our battery areas all day. On September 18 C/103 Battery received direct hits on two pits, but no casualty resulted. Practice barrages were also fired daily, causing the enemy to disclose his own barrage line in the fierce retaliation these evoked.

Under cover of the practice barrages raids were carried out in the early morning of September 17 and 18. In the first, a party of 2 officers and 30 other ranks of the 9th York and Lancaster Regiment rushed a dug-out in Dumbarton Wood, and captured 1 prisoner without sustaining any casualty. In the second, Lieutenant Fraser and 2nd Lieutenant H. G. Brown, with 40 other ranks of the 8th York and Lancaster Regiment, penetrated Inverness Copse to a depth of 300 yards, and brought back 24 prisoners. One of these suddenly drew a bomb from his box-respirator and flung it at a party of our men ; he was promptly killed

---

[1] The forward line of assembly of the Division as shown on different maps varies considerably. The left of the actual line on Zero day was some 300 yards forward of Clapham Junction and was situated close to the western edge of Inverness Copse.

for his treachery. Of the raiders, 1 man was killed, Lieutenant Fraser and 2 other ranks wounded.

All preparations had been completed to the smallest detail by September 18. At 8 P.M. that evening attacking brigades were to take over their battle fronts in readiness to advance on September 20, to engage in what was to prove to be the greatest battle in the history of the 23rd Division.

CHAPTER III.

THIRD BATTLE OF YPRES (BATTLE OF THE MENIN ROAD).

SEPTEMBER 19 TO OCTOBER 1, 1917.

Map No. 6. THE strength of the resistance developed by the enemy in the neighbourhood of the Menin road, which was referred to in the previous chapter, had decided the Commander-in-Chief to extend the flank of the next attack southwards.

Any extension of the already wide front of attack for which the Fifth Army was responsible was deemed undesirable. On the other hand, to divide between two armies the control of the attack on the main ridge was equally inadvisable.

The left of the Second Army had accordingly been extended northwards, so as to entrust the attack upon the whole high ground crossed by the Menin road to General Plumer as a single self-contained operation, to be carried out in conjunction with the attacks of the Fifth Army farther north.[1]

The attack on the Second Army front, which had been fixed for September 20, was to be carried out by the 19th Division, X. Corps, and Australian Corps.

The X. Corps was to attack on a front of about 2500 yards between Groenenburg Farm, one and a half miles east of Zwarteleen and Clapham Junction on the Menin road, with three divisions—the 39th, 41st, and 23rd.

Three objectives, named the Red, Blue, and Green Lines, were laid down for the attack, which would be carried forward on the Corps front

---

[1] Sir Douglas Haig's Despatches, The Campaigns of 1917, Para. 47.

to a depth of from 1500 to 2000 yards. The distance between these objectives was, roughly, equal.

The 23rd Division, on the left of the X. Corps, was to attack on a frontage of 1000 yards, with the intention of capturing, as their final objective, a trench line running northwards along high ground from a point just south of the Menin road, 500 yards west of Gheluvelt, to the Reutelbeek.

The direction of the Division's attack, as of those of the 41st and 1st Australian Divisions on its right and left, would be due east.

The first and final objectives were of about equal length ; the second objective was slightly longer than these.

On broad lines the problem was simple, and its solution was found in the following straightforward plan.

The attack would be carried out by the 68th Infantry Brigade and 69th Infantry Brigade (strengthened by four guns of the 70th L.T.M. Battery) on the right and left respectively.

A half-section 3rd Canadian Tunnelling Company would be attached to each brigade. The 70th Infantry Brigade (less M.G. and four L.T.M.) would be held in Divisional reserve at and west of Zillebeke, whence, as the attack opened, two battalions—the 9th York and Lancasters and 11th Sherwood Foresters—would move forward to positions vacated by attacking troops.

Attacking brigades would both employ one battalion for the capture of each of the three objectives, their fourth battalion either being held in brigade reserve, or its companies utilised to strengthen attacking battalions.

In accordance with this plan, the 11th Northumberland Fusiliers and the 11th West Yorkshire Regiment were to capture the Red Line ; the 10th Northumberland Fusiliers and 9th Yorkshire Regiment the Blue Line ; the 13th Durham Light Infantry and 10th Duke of Wellington's the Green Line (final objective).

In the 68th Infantry Brigade one company of the 12th Durham Light Infantry would be at the disposal of each of the 11th and 10th Northumberland Fusiliers. In the left attack two companies of the 8th Yorkshire Regiment would be attached to the Duke of Wellington's.

One battalion (less two companies) would thus remain available in each brigade as a reserve.

But though the allotment of tasks to units presented no great difficulty, the carrying out of these tasks would be greatly complicated by the nature of the ground to be covered on the right of the advance.

Stiff fighting could be looked for all along the line, but north of the Menin road the advance would be made over fairly firm, level ground. South of the road it would be otherwise. Here the attacking troops would almost at once start to descend to the valley of the Bassevillebeek, which was fed by the stream which flowed through the two upper Dumbarton Lakes, and on which was situated the lowest lake, a large circular piece of water with an island in the centre.

Beyond the Bassevillebeek the ground rises sharply to form the western face of the Tower-Hamlets Spur, a flat-topped ridge running south from the Menin road till it falls somewhat abruptly to the junction of the Bassevillebeek and Gheluvelt Valleys. The eastern slope of this ridge falls more gently to the Gheluvelt Valley.

The natural strength of the Tower-Hamlets Spur against advance from the west was considerable, and before it was reached the attack would encounter the serious obstacle of the Dumbarton Lake area, the condition of which has been described in the previous chapter. A direct frontal advance to the second objective would be impossible on the front of the 68th Infantry Brigade.

To meet the difficulty presented by the marsh and streams which would confront them, it was directed that the 10th Northumberland Fusiliers should advance north and south of the flooded area, half following in rear of the right of the 69th Infantry Brigade attack, and half in rear of the attack of the 122nd Infantry Brigade of the 41st Division. When past the flooded area these battalions would converge to capture the objectives.

One hundred and two 18-pdr. guns, thirty 4.5-in. howitzers,[1] and forty-two guns and howitzers of the heavy artillery would cover the advance of the infantry on the 1000 yards front allotted to their attack.

Support was to be given by a succession of creeping barrages arranged in depth. Of these, A, B, D, and E barrages would be formed by guns and howitzers ; A and B by the Field Artillery ; D and E by 6-in., 8-in., and 9.2-in. howitzers and 60-pdr. guns.

---

[1] Field artillery under command of the C.R.A. 23rd Division : 162 Brigade (less C Battery), 315 Army Brigade (less D Battery), 189, 95, 103 Brigades, and 242 Army Brigade.

Emergency defensive barrages, consisting of all possible heavy artillery, were further arranged to cover the Red and Blue Lines, and the whole of the artillery would combine to place a protective barrage in front of the final objective after capture.

Arrangements were also made for smoke barrages in rear of the first and final objectives during the infantry advance against these.

Three 18-pdr. and one 4.5-in. howitzer battery were retained for special tasks ; of these, one 18-pdr. battery was placed at the direct call of each infantry brigade.

In addition to the artillery barrages, a fifth barrage, "C," was to be formed by sixty - four guns of the 19th, 248th, 194th, and 70th Machine - Gun Companies, under the direction of Major H. V. Combs, the Divisional machine-gun officer. These had been organised into eight 8-gun batteries, of which six would cover the advance for the capture of the first and second objectives. Of these, two would then stand fast, while four would move forward to join the remaining two batteries in forming a barrage to cover the advance to the final objective. Rates of fire would be one belt per four minutes during the infantry advance, one per eight minutes during intervening periods, and one per two minutes for ten minutes in reply to an S.O.S. signal.

To assist in clearing any strong-points from which the enemy could not be ousted, four tanks were to be attached to the 69th Infantry Brigade. Two of these would move along the Menin road, and two to the north of Inverness Copse. Later, they were to follow the infantry as far as possible towards the Green Line.

Divisional Headquarters were established at Burgomaster Farm, Dickebusch. Battle Headquarters were taken up by the 68th Infantry Brigade at Torr Top, the 69th in Sanctuary Wood, and the 70th at Bedford House, one and a half miles south-west of Zillebeke. Assembly positions had been selected for the 10th and 11th Northumberland Fusiliers south of Stirling Castle, for the 13th Durham Light Infantry at Torr Top, for the 12th Durham Light Infantry near Maple Copse. Battalions of the 69th Infantry Brigade were to assemble, the 11th West Yorkshire and 9th Yorkshire Regiments east of Clapham Junction, the 10th Duke of Wellington's in rear of these in the northern end of

M

Sanctuary Wood, and the 8th Yorkshire Regiment between Maple Copse and Sanctuary Wood.

The positions for the leading battalions in the attack had been chosen well forward in order to escape the enemy's barrage, which it was expected would fall some little distance in rear of our front line.

Heavy rain was falling on the night of September 19 as the infantry moved forward to take up their assembly positions, but about 1 A.M. the weather cleared. All preparations were carried out without hindrance ; the enemy's artillery remained fairly quiet ; there was no indication that attack was expected.

Dawn broke about 5.30 A.M. All was still calm. The morning was dark, and mist hung over Inverness Copse and the flooded area about Dumbarton Lakes.

During the ten minutes that remained till zero hour it grew sufficiently light to see 80 to 100 yards. At 5.40 A.M. our guns opened. The infantry closed on the barrage which crashed on the German line, and three minutes later advanced to the assault.

Despite the dense artillery barrage, an enemy strong-point in Dumbarton Wood remained immune. From this a withering fire was opened on the 11th Northumberland Fusiliers as they advanced on the right against the western edge of the wood. Pressing forward, they swept the enemy from this position, but not before many casualties had occurred.

A stream running between the Dumbarton Lakes now lay before them, and the difficulty of finding crossings further delayed the advance on this flank. The battalion was unable to keep close to the barrage, and sustained heavy casualties, including all its company commanders.

A German strong-point, moreover, situated on a knoll 100 yards west of Herenthage Chateau, threatened the battalion's left. Special attention had been drawn by the Divisional Commander to the necessity for clearing this point, which lay on the front of the 69th Infantry Brigade, and for dealing with the ruins of Herenthage Chateau.

A platoon of the 11th Northumberland Fusiliers had, therefore, advanced with the 11th West Yorkshire Regiment, with the special duty of capturing these positions as a protection to the left of its battalion. Under cover of 6-in. Newton mortars directed on this danger-point, the chateau and knoll were successfully carried.

The remainder of the battalion had in the meanwhile crossed the stream, and, despite all difficulties and the loss of their leaders, now captured their objective on the Red Line within a few minutes of the scheduled time.

D Company of the 12th Durham Light Infantry, detailed to form an advanced ammunition dump on the 68th Brigade front, had followed the 11th Northumberland Fusiliers, and, becoming involved in the fighting, had assisted in carrying the position.

While this attack was in progress on the front of the 68th Infantry Brigade, the 11th West Yorkshire Regiment, under command of Major H. H. Hudson,[1] had advanced on the left against Inverness Copse.

Arrangements had been made for the 69th Light Trench Mortars to assist the attack on this flank—two, under 2nd Lieutenant Bottomley, moving forward on the right, and three on the left, under Lieutenant Rushton and a sergeant. Five minutes before zero hour the sergeant's gun had been destroyed. Rushton's two guns now moved forward along the Menin road, but a heavy shell, bursting in the midst of the detachment, destroyed both guns and wounded the officer and all gun numbers. The sergeant, however, had by now procured a reserve gun, which he moved along the northern edge of Inverness Copse.

The infantry, pushing through the tangled undergrowth, were suddenly held up by fire from a strong-point. Observing this, the sergeant immediately brought his Stokes gun into action against the two dugouts which formed the strong-point, firing twenty-five rounds and obtaining a direct hit on the entrances. The infantry then rushed the position, where 35 Germans surrendered ; 2 had been killed and 5 wounded by the Stokes gun.[2]

The enemy now seemed thoroughly demoralised, and ceased to resist the attack. There was danger, however, as was to be proved later, that concealed in the tangle of dug-outs and trenches certain of the Germans might be passed over. This danger was increased by a slight loss of direction, which caused a gap to occur between the left and centre companies. But the gap was quickly filled by two platoons of the reserve company, which were thrown in on the initiative of Lieu-

---

[1] Lieut.-Colonel Barker had been required for duties at Brigade headquarters.
[2] It has not been possible to discover the name of the sergeant who performed this great service.

tenant Irving, whose courage and energy throughout this day were very marked.

Smoke-shell, mingled with the shrapnel barrage, now signalled that the first objective had been reached.

The Red Line had been captured, and by 6.10 A.M. consolidation had commenced. Parties were pushed forward as close as possible to the barrage to clear the ground of the enemy, and to discover crossings over the Bassevillebeke.

During the forty-five minutes' pause which had been ordered on the Red Line, the 10th Northumberland Fusiliers and 9th Yorkshire Regiment took up assembly positions in readiness to carry forward the attack.

Of the former battalion, half assembled in rear of the 9th Yorkshire Regiment between Herenthage Chateau and the Menin road, half in rear of the left flank of the 122nd Infantry Brigade. A and B Companies of the 12th Durham Light Infantry were each to follow one of these half-battalions. They had orders, however, not to become unnecessarily involved in the fighting in this second phase, as they were to be available, if possible, to assist the 13th Durham Light Infantry in the capture of the final objective.

By 7.8 A.M. the attacking infantry had closed up to the artillery barrage ; the barrage lifted, and the second phase of the attack opened. The earlier advance had been made at the rate of 100 yards in six minutes ; the barrage now slowed to 100 yards in eight minutes.

The task which lay before the 10th Northumberland Fusiliers was one of great difficulty. Following the inner flanks of brigades on either side to beyond the Bassevillebeke, the two half-battalions were then to wheel inwards, clear the ground rising from the far bank of the stream, and capture their objective on the Blue Line. A special 18-pdr. barrage had been arranged to assist this operation.

Early in their advance the left company lost all its officers, and failed to keep its direction ; but A Company, under Captain Steele, acting in support on this flank, took its place, and, after very stiff fighting, gained the objective, and effected the capture of some 80 prisoners, together with 2 field-guns and 2 howitzers. The right companies encountered fierce opposition, but forced their way forward to the Blue Line.

The 10th Northumberland Fusiliers had succeeded in the difficult task assigned to them, and the battalion, with its left holding Katinje

Cabaret, occupied the whole of the 68th Infantry Brigade's line on the second objective.

The companies of the 12th Durham Light Infantry had become inevitably involved in the severe and somewhat confused fighting which had taken place ; they were now assembled in a position in rear of the captured line.

To turn now to the 9th Yorkshire Regiment on the left flank. The assembly for attack had not been carried out without incident. As they pushed gradually forward through Inverness Copse to occupy shell-holes and what other slight cover could be found, dense clouds of smoke and dust, raised by the artillery barrage, combined to make it difficult to keep direction. Here and there isolated parties of Germans were still found in the copse ; now and again a despairing S.O.S. signal from one or other of these would rise from in rear of our advanced troops. These parties had been quickly overpowered.

During the pause on the Red Line the troops, in the highest spirits, had sat smoking captured German cigars, while the officers checked by compass-bearing the direction of their advanced assembly positions.

On moving forward to these, further small parties of Germans were found to have escaped the mopping-up parties of the 11th West Yorkshire Regiment in Inverness Copse. Many put up a stiff resistance, attacking our men with bombs, and inflicting numerous casualties at close quarters with machine-guns and rifles.

At least 60 Germans had been killed in this fighting before the battalion was formed up under the barrage in readiness to attack, and already 16 officers of the 9th Yorkshire Regiment, including 2 company commanders, had been killed or wounded when the battalion at 7.8 A.M. advanced for the capture of the Blue Line.

It had been anticipated that on the flat open ground to the north of the Menin road the main centres of the enemy's resistance would be found in a line of pill-boxes and dug-outs extending southwards from a concrete tower, situated about the centre of the 69th Brigade's area of attack, to a small pond just north of the road.[1]

---

[1] Strangely enough, the Intelligence Branch before the battle denied the existence of this tower. In December 1921 its remains still formed a prominent landmark, and around it and the pill-boxes which flanked it the débris of battle, British and German helmets, waterbottles, &c., still lay thick to testify to the desperate struggle which effected its capture.

This anticipation proved well justified. The dug-outs had suffered little from our artillery fire, and the severest fighting now ensued in this quarter.

Several hostile parties, realising that they were outflanked, abandoned their machine-guns, and, throwing down their arms, came forward waving small pieces of white cloth, with which their forethought had provided them. But many others engaged in fierce hand-to-hand fighting, and refused to surrender. These were all killed by bullet or bayonet, and some 40 dead were afterwards counted around the tower.

No fewer than 10 machine-guns were captured at this point, together with 15 flammenwerfer ; 5 trench howitzers and 4 trench mortars were found in the vicinity.

Whilst A and B Companies of the 9th Yorkshire Regiment were engaged in clearing this position, C and D Companies passed through them to capture the battalion's objective on the Blue Line. Only one officer remained with each of these companies, and of these one had already been slightly wounded. Casualties among the N.C.O.'s and men had also been heavy. It was an occasion when at many points the private soldier was left to lead himself.

So thoroughly did each man know his individual task that formations and direction were well maintained, and each section made independently for its objective, captured it, and commenced to consolidate it without further ado.

So north and south of the Menin road the second objective of the 23rd Division had been captured throughout its entire length.

Prisoners captured on the left flank stated that their regiment (Bavarian Ersatz) was now completely demoralised, and retreating rapidly in all directions. Large numbers of the enemy were, in fact, seen streaming across the ground to the left front in the direction of the Reutelbeek, and were heavily fired on by rifles and Lewis-guns.

Work on consolidation was much hampered by the fire of hostile machine-guns and snipers, but the ground was favourable to digging, and during the two hours that were to elapse before the advance was renewed, those that survived were able to provide themselves with good cover.

At zero hour the 13th Durham Light Infantry and the 10th Duke of Wellington's, destined for the capture of the final objective of the

THE TOWER.

(From a German negative, captured in the battle.)

Division (the Green Line), had advanced from their preliminary assembly positions to those vacated by the battalions detailed for the capture of the second objective. They were now moved forward to the Blue Line to assemble for attack.

To gain its position the former battalion had to move north and south of the lake area, the right half-battalion being followed by C Company of the 12th Durham Light Infantry.

B and D Companies of the 8th Yorkshire Regiment were attached to the 10th Duke of Wellington's. The latter company, moving forward on the left of this battalion, reached its position on the Blue Line without serious casualties, but the Duke of Wellington's suffered considerable losses from artillery fire during this approach movement. One of its companies (B) lost all its officers except one, but it was reorganised on the Blue Line by Captain Payne, together with his own company (A).

At 9.53 A.M. the final phase of the attack opened with the advance of the 13th Durham Light Infantry and the 10th Duke of Wellington's along the whole Divisional front.

The left of the Durham Light Infantry, whose advance lay across the broad summit of the Tower Hamlets Spur, now crossed the Menin road, which ran diagonally across the battalion's front.

They were soon engaged in stiff fighting among the remains of the scattered buildings which flanked the road. For a space the left of the battalion was held up by fire from a German dug-out. Company-Sergeant-Major Parker of the 10th Duke of Wellington's, observing this, attacked the dug-out from front and rear, and quickly captured it.

With their flank so secured, the battalion pushed forward all along the line. Making quick work of all further resistance, they captured 200 prisoners, and gained the line of their objective, with its wonderful observation over the plain which spread out below to the south and south-east.

Further to the right, on the front of the 41st Division, the attack had not been so successful, but before turning to this it is necessary to follow the fortunes of the 10th Duke of Wellington's.

From an observation-post established at the tower the advance had been watched till the troops disappeared in a cloud of smoke and dust just short of their objective.

On the left, Northampton Farm, which had been regarded as a possible seat of trouble, itself proved no obstacle. But just beyond it the attack was confronted by a line of over a dozen concrete dug-outs manned by machine-guns. These, combined with artillery fire, caused many casualties in the already reduced ranks, but failed to break the attack, which was pressed forward with the utmost determination.

The position was cleared and the final objective gained on this flank by Captain Tilly's company of the 8th Yorkshire Regiment and advance troops of B and D Companies of the Duke of Wellington's. A platoon and two Lewis-guns were now brought forward to protect the right flank of these troops, since touch had been temporarily lost between the centre and right of the attack. Here A and C Companies of the Duke of Wellington's had encountered stiff opposition among the concrete dug-outs of Veldhoek, and from a strongly held hedge which covered these. But the check was of short duration. 2nd Lieutenant Anderson's platoon, which had been delayed by a slight loss of direction, arrived opportunely; the centre of resistance was outflanked and captured.

Almost simultaneously 2nd Lieutenant Wilson, noticing the gap between the centre and right of the attack, pushed forward his platoon to fill it, so enabling the troops thrown out for protection here to be withdrawn.

It was due in no small degree to the skill of Major Borrow, 10th Duke of Wellington's, who was directing the attack, that the battalion and attached companies of the 8th Yorkshire Regiment had won their way forward.

The Green Line, the final objective of attack, had been captured along the whole front of the 23rd Division. Brigades were in touch, and on the left junction had been effected with the 2nd Australian Brigade (1st Australian Division).

But the situation on the 23rd Division's right was not so favourable.

The immense natural strength of the Tower Hamlets Spur has already been referred to. Fortified as it was, the capture of that portion of it which was included in the 68th Infantry Brigade's attack must rank as one of the finest achievements of the 23rd Division.

But the Germans undoubtedly had devoted their main efforts to strengthening the south-western end of the Spur round the buildings which gave their name to the Spur. Here was situated a mass of concrete dug-outs and pill-boxes. Against this position, and fully exposed to the fire of its rifles and machine-guns, the 122nd Infantry Brigade of the 41st Division was called on to advance : first, down an open slope west of the Bassevillebeke ; later, up the glacis of the western face of the Spur. From the moment of their departure from the Blue Line they came under the most galling fire. Despite terrible casualties they succeeded in pushing forward to within 150 yards of the final objective, but their most desperate efforts failed to capture the Tower Hamlets.

The right flank of the 13th Durham Light Infantry was thus danger-ously exposed. Realising this, D Company of the 10th Northumberland Fusiliers pushed forward from the Blue Line for the protection of the open flank. On being informed of the situation, Brig.-General Colville ordered forward a company of the 11th Northumberland Fusiliers further to assist in occupying the gap which had occurred north-west of the Tower Hamlets.

By 11 A.M. the machine-guns of the 68th and 69th Machine-Gun Companies had occupied the positions allotted to them, and captured machine-guns were employed to strengthen the defence. By 12 noon strenuous digging had secured sound defensive lines on the captured objectives, and the Field Companies R.E. and pioneers had been ordered forward for the construction of strong-points and other work in the new system. The 128th and 101st Field Companies had been detailed to the right and left brigades respectively. Each of these was responsible for the construction of two strong-points, the work on each point being carried out by one section R.E., one platoon pioneers, and two platoons attached infantry.

The 128th Field Company in addition made mat crossings over the swamp area, and later constructed temporary bridges.

The Pioneer Battalion was responsible for making, posting, and notice-boarding forward tracks.

The creeping barrage of the artillery and the machine-gun barrages had been faultless in covering the advance. The standing artillery barrage now no less effectively covered the work of consolidation, which was steadily continued while supplies of bombs, S.A.A., and wire were being brought forward by the carrying parties of the 12th Durham Light Infantry and 8th Yorkshire Regiment.

The fighting was not yet over, but the positions gained were to remain in the hands of the 23rd Division, and it may be well to pause here to consider the factors which had led to so complete a success.

In the defence the battle may be won before the infantry is engaged. The enemy's attack may be broken by the fire of artillery and machine-guns before their objective is approached.

In the attack ultimate success must lie in the hands of the infantry. But in a success such as had been obtained by the Division this day, all are conscious that the attainments of the infantry form but a true reflection of the efficiency of the Division as a whole.

The infantry may betray the other arms and services, but without their whole-hearted co-operation it cannot hope to succeed. The true spirit of co-operation is contained in the following letter to the 13th Durham Light Infantry from an artillery unit of another division, temporarily attached for the battle :—

To O.C. 13TH D.L.I.

We of the 33rd Divisional Artillery cannot let you go out without wishing you the best of luck and giving you our heartiest congratulations. Our F.O.O.'s, Battery Commanders, and all are full of the 13th D.L.I., and we all look on you as our own infantry. We all hope that we may again have the honour of supporting you and doing still more for you. We have had the best of good hunting together. I hope you will go off thinking half as much of the 33rd Divisional Artillery as they do of you.

(Sd.)   BERNARD BUTLER,
Lt.-Col. R.A.
Cmdg. 156th Bde. R.F.A.,
33rd Divisional Artillery.

September 24, 1917.

The Division in attack stands or falls by the action of its infantry ; pride in its infantry is derived from a confidence that they will repay in full measure all that has been done to help them to victory.

In a trench to trench attack conducted on a grand scale there are few whose responsibilities are greater or on whom the infantry are more dependant than the C.R.E.

At the outset, in the arrangements for the assembly of attacking troops, much lies in his hands : the preparation of tracks, the construction of battle headquarters, the organisation of dumps of engineer stores. The capture of the enemy's position is only half the battle ;

in the organisation for defence of the captured area which follows, the
Field Companies R.E. take an important part.

In the assembly for the attack on September 20 the infantry owed
much to Lieut.-Colonel Rooke, the C.R.E. ; and the work of the sappers
and pioneers in consolidating the positions has already been referred to.

Another branch of the Royal Engineers which was never known to
fail the Division was the 23rd Divisional Signal Company.

Communication proved very difficult on September 20.   Great
anxiety had prevailed before the attack opened owing to the breakdown of the big Corps buried system, on which all hopes had centred.
By great efforts Major Tillard, commanding the 23rd Divisional Signal
Company, had managed to get one line through to each brigade headquarters.   These lines by a miracle held up all day.

Brigade observers in pairs had been distributed at points of vantage
along the front, including the Tower.   But on the left brigade front
good visual signalling proved impracticable, and information had to be
sent back by runner.

The duties of a runner are as difficult and dangerous to perform as
they are easy to shirk.   Brig.-General Lambert, in his report of the
battle, pays a deep tribute to the loyalty of these men, but states that
the transmission of intelligence in face of great difficulties would have
been impossible on this front but for the excellent organisation and
preparation made by Lieutenant Cox, 8th Yorkshire Regiment, who
supervised these duties.

On the front of the 68th Infantry Brigade visual communication
was maintained between a post established in the Blue Line and advanced brigade headquarters.

Later in the day telephone communication was kept up fairly well
in rear of battalion headquarters, but wires run forward to companies
were constantly cut.

The gallant little pigeons, too, did yeoman service.

The carrying parties taking forward supplies, water, and material
to the troops in the captured positions worked manfully.

Those of the 68th Infantry Brigade, formed from companies of the
12th Durham Light Infantry and personnel of the 68th L.T.M. Battery,
made no fewer than three separate journeys from the old British line
to the Green Line.   On the left the work was done almost entirely by

specially formed Yukon pack teams, under Lieutenant Alnwick, 11th West Yorkshire Regiment. Referring to these in his report, Brig.-General Lambert writes :—

The manner in which these men—2 N.C.O.'s and 18 men from each battalion—worked day and night for their comrades, trudging under heavy fire, regardless of casualties, and cheerful to the last, is almost beyond description. . . . On the day of the attack I myself saw Yukon pack-men trudging stolidly and fearlessly right up to the front line over absolutely open ground to deliver water, S.A.A., and food to their comrades in need. This was not done by order, as they were intended to go only as far as battalion headquarters, but they went on their own initiative and without an officer.

No words could better convey the spirit which imbued the whole Division.

Nowhere was this spirit more apparent than with the medical services. One cannot speak for the German medical arrangements except from the experience of unfortunate British prisoners. It is certain that there was a greater distinction between friend and foe in the German hospitals than in ours. But, leaving the Germans aside, it can be truthfully said that no army in the war owed the debt to their medical officers that the British Army did, both with regard to organisation and personal devotion.

Even so, one is tempted to think that the 23rd Division was fortunate in the medical officers who served in it.[1]

The care of all others is to push forward ; their whole anxiety in battle lies with the up-traffic. The doctor's concern is with the down-traffic : to clear the way for the sad procession of wounded, and to administer relief to their suffering as early as possible.

But the A.D.M.S. of a Division is hampered by the knowledge that, should his arrangements interfere with the up-traffic, worse disaster than delay in the evacuation of the wounded may overcome his Division.

The arrangements of Colonel R. J. Blackham, the A.D.M.S. of the 23rd Division, worked perfectly on September 20. At one time danger threatened through lack of cars. Fortunately, the A.D.M.S. himself

---

[1] Names such as Pye-Smith, Hammerton, M'Kerrow, Riddel, Hairsine, Russell, MacIntyre, Pearson, will be remembered among many others.

was at the advanced dressing-station at Woodcote House, and he managed to procure twenty cars from elsewhere to help him out.

Nearly 2000 wounded passed through the main dressing-station, of whom 536 were stretcher cases.

Reflecting on the tasks which the attacking troops had accomplished, one concludes that that given to the 68th Infantry Brigade was the more formidable.

The descent to the marshy bottom of the lake area, necessitating skilful manœuvre under the full observation of the enemy, as distinct from the direct advance which had become habitual in former battles, the capture of the Tower Hamlets Ridge and the improvisation of protection to their right flank, called for skill in the leaders no less than staunchness in their men.

But while the advance of the 69th Infantry Brigade lay over more favourable ground, the positions to be overcome were no less formidable than on the right. Though the enemy held no commanding ground on this flank, the flat open ground gave a perfect field of fire to the machine-guns of his concrete defences. An inspection of the ground suggests that the Germans probably relied on the Tower Hamlets position, attacked by the 41st Division, and the group of dug-outs surrounding the tower, captured by the 9th Yorkshire Regiment, as their main centres of resistance.

The chief opposition to the attack had been from machine-guns. The hostile artillery was on the whole weak and ineffective. At the commencement of the attack it was mainly concentrated on our old front line. As the attack developed, the enemy barrage, in addition to being weak, was disjointed and erratic. Each successive barrage was weaker than the last, suggesting the withdrawal of guns. Only two or three batteries employed instantaneous fuzes, the greater part of the barrage consisting of smothered bursts of 4.2.

Earlier in this history it has been related how, with the introduction of the bomb, the rifle had been in danger of being regarded as the infantryman's badge of office rather than as his weapon. Following the Somme battles, great effort had been made in the Division to restore the confidence of the infantry soldier in his rifle.

On September 20, 1917, the results of recent training towards this end were made manifest. The great majority of the German dead had been killed by the bullet. Undoubtedly the machine-gun barrage had been very effective, and the machine-guns and Lewis-guns accompanying the advance had certainly inflicted many casualties. But the average expenditure of seventy rounds per rifle indicates the extent to which the infantry most closely engaged must have employed their rifles.

To return to the fighting which ensued after the capture of the Green Line.

At 2.45 P.M. large bodies of the enemy were observed from the Tower to be massing for counter-attack on a line south of the Reutelbeek. Artillery fire was immediately brought on to these, and the attack failed to materialise.

About 3 P.M. some hundred Germans advanced from the railway cutting north of Gheluvelt against the left company of the 13th Durham Light Infantry. This isolated effort broke down under rifle and Lewis-gun fire immediately after it was detected.

Later, a further concentration of the enemy west of Gheluvelt was dispersed by the fire of our artillery.

At 6.40 P.M. the 41st Division renewed its attack on the Tower Hamlets. The 15th Hampshire Regiment, on the left of the 122nd Infantry Brigade, succeeded in capturing their objective, together with 30 prisoners and a field gun, and gained touch with the right of the 68th Infantry Brigade.[1] The centre and right of the attack were, however, less fortunate ; touch was again lost, and a fresh attack was ordered for 9.30 A.M. on the 21st.

The 10th Duke of Wellington's Regiment had suffered heavy casualties during the day. The relief of their two left companies by the reserve company of the 8th Yorkshire Regiment was now ordered. The remainder of the 69th Infantry Brigade front was held by two weak companies of the 10th Duke of Wellington's, with one company of the 8th Yorkshire Regiment in close support. The relieved companies were placed in immediate reserve for the whole brigade front.

On the 68th Infantry Brigade front, the 9th York and Lancaster Regiment (70th Infantry Brigade), who had moved forward at zero to Torr Top, were now ordered to the Blue Line in relief of the 10th Northumberland Fusiliers, who were withdrawn to brigade reserve.

These reliefs were commenced during the afternoon under heavy

[1] G.S. War Diaries, 23rd and 41st Divisions.

hostile shelling. They were completed during the night, which passed
quietly.

Daybreak on September 21 found the infantry of the Division disposed
as under :—

	Left Section.	*Right Section.*
Green Line .	8th York and 10th Duke of W.	12th and 13th D.L.I.
Blue Line .	9th York	9th York and Lanc.
Red Line .	11th West York	11th North'd Fusiliers.
Reserve . .	11th Sherwood Foresters	10th North'd Fus. and
	(Sanctuary Wood)	8th K.O.Y.L.I.
		(Torr Top)
	8th York and Lanc.	
	(Railway Dug-outs)	

Headquarters 68th Infantry Brigade, Torr Top.
Headquarters 69th Infantry Brigade, Sanctuary Wood
                        (500 yards west of Stirling Castle).
Headquarters 70th Infantry Brigade, Bedford House.

During the previous afternoon one company of the 9th York and
Lancaster Regiment had established a defensive flank between the right
of the 13th Durham Light Infantry and the left of the 41st Division.

Two companies of the Yorkshire Light Infantry had been employed
during the night in carrying water and material to the front line.

At 8 A.M. on the 21st about 200 of the enemy attacked the left of
the 13th Durham Light Infantry, but were dispersed with heavy casualties by rifle and machine-gun fire, 1 German officer and 5 other ranks
being made prisoners.

The attack was repeated half an hour later, but again failed. Later,
an effort was made south of the Menin road with no better success, the
enemy suffering heavily from the enfilade fire of a platoon pushed forward
to a position north of the road.

The total casualties caused by these three attacks amounted only
to 2 killed and 6 wounded.

At 3 P.M., after an hour's artillery preparation, a fourth counter-
attack was launched, directed this time against the right of the line
from the Gheluvelt Valley. This also broke down under rifle and machine-
gun fire.

Finally, at 7 P.M., after a two hours' bombardment, the enemy was
observed massing south of the Menin road near Gheluvelt. The S.O.S.

was sent up, and the prompt reply of the artillery smashed this concentration before attack could be developed.

The right company of the 13th Durham Light Infantry had suffered heavy casualties and severe damage to their trenches from the hostile bombardment. To meet the threatened attack they had been reinforced by their battalion headquarter party and four Lewis-guns of the 12th Durham Light Infantry. These were withdrawn at 8.15 P.M. when the situation had quietened.

On the left of the 23rd Division the Australians had maintained their position. But on the right the Tower Hamlets position continued to give trouble. The left of the 41st Division in their attack at 9.30 A.M. had gained the Green Line, but the stiff resistance of the Germans south of the Tower Hamlets could not be overcome. Heavy enemy counter-attacks delivered throughout the day forced the withdrawal to the Blue Line of the troops who had gained their objective in the morning.

This withdrawal increased the defensive flank of the 23rd Division to over 700 yards.[1]

During the whole day the German artillery, assisted by aeroplanes, persistently shelled our battery areas, causing much damage to guns and ammunition.

On the night of the 21st/22nd the infantry was disposed as under :—

	Left Section.	*Right Section.*
Green Line .	11th Sherwood Foresters. 2 companies 8th York in close support.	8th K.O.Y.L.I.
Blue Line .	9th York and 2 coys. D. of W.	2 coys. 9th York & Lanc. 2 coys. 9th York & Lanc. (Defensive flank.)
Red Line .	11th West York.	2 coys. 12th D.L.I. 2 coys. 11th North. Fus.
Reserve .	2 coys. D. of W. 2 coys. 8th York.	2 coys. 12th D.L.I. 2 coys. 13th D.L.I.

---

[1] The actual situation in this hotly-contested area of the battlefield at any given time was never very clear.

Some troops of the 41st Division appeared to have gained the Green Line during the night. Messages recorded in the 41st Division War Diary report troops on the Green Line at 12.42 A.M., and again at 6.15 A.M. They show them at 5.30 P.M. and 7.2 P.M. clearly out of this line. At 9.2 P.M. one finds arrangements being made to establish posts on the Blue Line to gain touch with the 23rd Division.

By the morning of September 22 all strong-points had been completed and wired in, and the successive lines of defence thoroughly consolidated.

The German infantry remained inactive, but the artillery continued to shell our battery positions throughout the day, A/103, A/315, B/242 Batteries and those of the 156th R.F.A. Brigade suffering most.

The Division was now required to extend its front northwards to take over 600 yards of line from the Australians as far as Black Watch Corner road junction.

To effect this, fresh dispositions were arranged, by which the 70th Infantry Brigade (less 8th York and Lancaster Regiment), reinforced by the 68th Infantry Brigade (less Brigade Headquarters and the 11th Northumberland Fusiliers), would take over the right section, with a frontage of 1200 yards ; the 69th Infantry Brigade, plus the 8th York and Lancaster Regiment, would occupy the left section, with a frontage of 750 yards.

The reliefs necessary to this were carried out during the night 22nd/23rd.

Hostile artillery and aircraft were very active during September 23, and our batteries again suffered severely from the enemy's bombardment.

This died down on the 24th, and fortunately, for the relief of the Division had been ordered to commence during this day.

The 33rd Division was to take over the line north of the Menin road ; the 39th Division to take over south of the road.

Such reliefs as could be carried out during daylight were accomplished without difficulty. But in the case of the majority of units it was necessary to wait till dark. By then the enemy's artillery fire had increased, and continued heavy throughout the night.

Heavy shelling and the thick mist in the early morning combined to delay the relief, and at dawn the situation in the front line was somewhat obscure. Fortunately, casualties were not heavy, and by 9.30 A.M. the 69th and 70th Infantry Brigades were reported clear of the forward area.

Later, however, it was learnt that, shortly after relief had been effected in the front line, the enemy had counter-attacked, forced the withdrawal of a battalion of the 33rd Division to the support line, and recaptured a short length of the Green Line just north of the Menin road.

The 23rd Divisional Artillery remained in the line under command of the C.R.A. of the 33rd Division, and the 70th Machine-Gun Company was retained to strengthen the barrage of the 33rd Division.

Having handed over command to the G.O.C. 33rd Division, General Babington moved his headquarters to Westoutre. The Division was accommodated in the area about this village and Reninghelst, where the 69th Infantry Brigade Headquarters were established. The headquarters of the 68th and 70th Infantry Brigades moved to Hersen and La Clytte Camp respectively. The 9th South Staffordshire Regiment was placed rather farther forward at Dickebusch.

The following figures show the total casualties which had been suffered by the infantry of the Division between September 19 and 24 :—

	Killed.		Wounded.		Missing.	
	Officers.	Other ranks.	Officers.	Other ranks.	Officers.	Other ranks.
68th Infantry Brigade .	5	189	29	661	..	66
69th Infantry Brigade .	10	166	30	867	..	100
70th Infantry Brigade .	1	26	7	130	..	13
	16	381	66	1658	..	179

Grand total : 82 officers, 2218 other ranks.

The enemy had no opportunity of taking prisoners, and few, if any, of the missing had been captured.

Roughly, 600 German prisoners had been taken by the Division, the approximate number being—

By the 68th Infantry Brigade, 400 other ranks.
By the 69th Infantry Brigade, 6 officers, 190 other ranks.

Those captured on September 20 belonged mostly to the Bavarian Ersatz Division, those taken on the 21st to the 24th Division.

In addition, the following trophies were captured in the battle :—

	Field guns.	Machine-guns.		Trench-mortars.		Flammen-werfer.
		Heavy.	Light.	Medium.	Light.	
68th Infantry Brigade .	3	11	2	2	6	2
69th Infantry Brigade .	..	24	8	..	..	6
Total . .	3	35	10	2	6	8

The bodies of 597 Germans were buried on the front of the 69th Infantry Brigade alone.

In appreciation of the conduct of the Division in the fighting on September 20 and the following days, General Babington issued the following Special Order :—

The Divisional Commander desires to convey to all ranks his most sincere congratulations on, and warmest appreciation of, their excellent work and gallant conduct during the late operations.

The marked success which attended their efforts was largely due to the excellent relations which exist between all ranks, arms, and services of the Division, and to that readiness to co-operate with one another which they have at all times shown.

So long as this spirit continues, the Divisional Commander is confident that the 23rd Division will successfully carry out any task which may be assigned to it.

September 25, 1917.

Scarcely had the Division stretched its weary limbs to rest when, on September 26, disturbing news arrived. The 33rd Division had been subjected to heavy counter-attacks. Exhausted by severe and incessant fighting, it was to be relieved by the 23rd Division forthwith.

It had been intended to renew the offensive on September 26. The 33rd Division, now forming the left of the X. Corps, had been detailed to cover the right flank of the Anzac Corps in attack. The German counter-attacks of the 25th had rendered a modification necessary in the objectives of the British attack.

On September 26 assembly for attack had been hampered by fog, but the positions lost on the Menin road were recaptured. Farther north, however, no progress could be made till the afternoon, when Cameron House had been gained. The enemy again counter-attacked with some success. In the evening the last remaining battalion of the 33rd Division's reserve, the 20th Royal Fusiliers, was thrown into the fight.

The Germans had then delivered a heavy counter-attack along the whole X. Corps front, and Cameron House had been again lost.

On September 27 the 98th Infantry Brigade attacked once more to fill the gap which existed between the 33rd Division and the Australians. Fierce and confused fighting continued, till, at 3.50 P.M., the 98th Brigade reported that they were in touch with the Australians at Cameron Covert.

This, roughly, was the situation when the 23rd Division, after less than two days' rest, moved forward once more to relieve the 33rd Division on the night of September 27.

It was decided to hold the line with two infantry brigades, the 70th on the right, the 69th on the left. The 68th Infantry Brigade would be held in Divisional reserve in the Westoutre area, with two battalions placed at Ridge Wood, just south-east of Dickebusch Lake.

Relieving brigades, having moved by bus to the east of Dickebusch, marched to an area west of Clapham Junction and Stirling Castle. Thence after dusk they moved forward to the relief of the 33rd Division.

An ordinary routine relief is no easy matter in the dark; to take over the vague situation which generally exists after heavy fighting is trebly difficult. Fortunately, the relieving troops were familiar with the ground; reliefs were carried out successfully during the night, and the morning of September 28 found the sector occupied as follows :—

In the right section, which extended from the Menin road to a point about 450 yards due east of Northampton Farm, two battalions were distributed in depth for the defence of the forward area. Of these, the 8th Yorkshire Light Infantry, on the right, held one company in the front line, closely supported by two platoons of a second company; the 11th Sherwood Foresters, on the left, held a longer front, with two companies in the front line. The remaining companies of each of these battalions were placed either in support, on a line 1000 yards in rear of the front line, or in reserve, west and north-west of Dumbarton Lakes. The 8th York and Lancaster Regiment, in support of these forward battalions, was disposed in depth, with two companies about Stirling Castle, one company on the eastern edge of Sanctuary Wood, and their fourth company with battalion headquarters at the north-western corner of the wood.

The 9th York and Lancaster Regiment was held in brigade reserve at Bedford House [1] on the Ypres-St Eloi road. Headquarters of the 70th Infantry Brigade were situated just south-east of Sanctuary Wood.

---

[1] This, early in 1915, was known as Chateau Rosendal, and was said to be the property of the owner of Signorinetta, a Derby winner. It has not been discovered when or why the name was changed. Its site is now marked by a British cemetery.

The 69th Infantry Brigade, in occupation of the line on the left as far north as Cameron Covert, held the front line with three companies of the 8th Yorkshire Regiment, whose fourth company was disposed between Black Watch Corner and Carlisle Farm. The 11th West Yorkshire Regiment was in support in an area north of Inverness Copse. Farther to the rear, the 9th Yorkshire Regiment, in the north-eastern quarter of Sanctuary Wood, was also available for support. The 10th Duke of Wellington's Regiment was held in brigade reserve on the Ypres-Comines Canal, just west of Bedford House.

Five brigades of Field Artillery covered the front (156th and 162nd of 33rd Division, 102nd and 103rd of 23rd Division, and 242nd Army Brigade). These were organised in three groups, of which Lieut.-Colonel Badham Thornhill of the 23rd Division commanded the centre group.

At 9 A.M. on September 28, General Babington assumed command of the sector, with headquarters at Burgomaster Farm, Dickebusch. The 37th Division was now holding the line on the right of the 23rd Division ; the 5th Australian Division had taken over the sector on the left.

The 8th Yorkshire Regiment lost no time in sending out patrols after taking over the line. These succeeded in bringing in 24 prisoners.

The day passed fairly quietly till dusk, when the hostile artillery became more active, and a concentration of about eighty of the enemy was observed opposite our right. This was broken up by artillery fire, and the situation again quietened.

It was considered advisable to make a slight modification of the front during the night, an alteration which was to bring heavy fighting a few days later to the troops concerned. A spur running into Cameron Covert, which had been captured in the recent fighting and which was slightly in advance of the general line, was in the occupation of the Australians, though actually south of their southern boundary.

By an arrangement between the neighbouring brigadiers this spur was now taken over by C Company (Lieutenant M. Bennison) of the 9th Yorkshire Regiment, which had been placed at the disposal of the O.C. 8th Yorkshire Regiment for this purpose. Patrols sent out during the night by the Sherwood Foresters found the ground clear of the enemy for some distance on their front. Posts were therefore pushed forward on the left of the 70th Infantry Brigade front, and connected up before dawn.

Much work was needed on the defences, and great assistance was given in this by the 18th (Pioneer) Battalion Middlesex Regiment and the Royal Engineers of the 33rd Division, who had been lent to the 23rd Division at this time.

The most favourable time for work was early morning. The weather was warm, and sunny days were followed by bright moonlit nights. Concealment was best found in the thick white mist which gathered at dawn before the sun gained strength to disperse it.

Hostile shelling was constant during September 29, but not serious until the evening, when a very heavy barrage was placed by guns of all calibres on the ground about Black Watch Corner, south of Polygon Wood. A Vickers gun was destroyed, and the 8th Yorkshire Regiment lost some 25 killed and 15 wounded from this fire. At the same time, strong enemy forces were observed forming up for attack. Our artillery was brought to bear on these, but failed to check the movement of the Germans, who proceeded to advance. Waiting their opportunity, the defence then opened a withering fire of rifles and machine-guns, which completely demoralised the enemy, and drove back his attack in great confusion.

The German aircraft had been very active all day over our battery positions and back areas. At night the back areas were severely bombed. At night, too, our batteries were very heavily shelled by guns of all sizes, mainly from the direction of Wervicq. A great many mustard-gas shells were employed, from which C/102 and D/102 Batteries in particular suffered considerable casualties.

On the 69th Infantry Brigade front a few more prisoners and machine-guns were captured. In the right section a quiet night was spent in carrying out reliefs, by which the 9th York and Lancaster Regiment replaced the 8th Yorkshire Light Infantry, and the 8th York and Lancaster Regiment took over the line from the Sherwood Foresters.

At 4 A.M. on September 30 the country was shrouded in thick mist. At 4.30 A.M. a heavy bombardment opened on the front of the 70th Infantry Brigade. Trench-mortars, directed on the close support line, co-operated with the fire of the enemy's guns. Soon a dense cloud, formed by the smoke of bursting shells mingling with the mist, obscured the front.

By 5 A.M. this had cleared slightly, and a quarter of an hour later the enemy was disclosed close up to our trenches, advancing opposite the whole length of the brigade front. The attack was being directed in greatest strength against the 9th York and Lancaster Regiment just north of the Menin road.

Under the cover of liquid flames, hand grenades and smoke-bombs were showered by the enemy into our front-line trench. But the defence stood firm. Face to face with the Germans, our men hurled back bomb for bomb, while every rifle and Lewis-gun in the line opened rapid fire on the attacking waves. No Germans reached the trenches. The attack broke, and those of the enemy that survived fled in confusion.

The mist had prevented the artillery from answering the S.O.S. signal which had been sent up, and the runner sent back to report the attack took two hours to reach headquarters.

This formidable attempt by the enemy, preluded by artillery bombardment, had been repulsed by the infantry of the front line unsupported. The attack had extended to the Division on the right, where a post just south of the Menin road had been occupied by the Germans, but was immediately retaken by counter-attack.

Two prisoners of the 78th R.I.R. had been captured during the attack, and a machine-gun and flammenwerfer were later brought in. Some 80 German dead were counted on the front of the 70th Infantry Brigade.

Having regard to the strength of the attack, our casualties had been slight.

At 6 A.M. the enemy returned to the attack, but this second attempt met with no better success than the first.

Throughout the day hostile shelling continued intense over the whole Divisional front, and it was rightly conjectured that the enemy had not abandoned the intention of making a further effort to recover his lost positions.

During the night of September 30/October 1, by the light of a full moon, the 8th Yorkshire Regiment was relieved in the left section by the 9th Yorkshire Regiment, plus D Company of the 10th Duke of Wellington's, the whole being under the command of Lieut.-Colonel

R. S. Hart. Lieutenant Bennison's company of the 9th Yorkshire Regiment remained, as the left of the line, in the position it had already taken up north of Cameron Covert, in touch with the 110th Infantry Brigade, which had now relieved the Australian Brigade. D Company of the Duke of Wellington's was placed on its immediate right. South of these, two companies of the 9th Yorkshire Regiment held the line astride the Reutelbeek, while the remaining company occupied a position in support.

In the course of the night the R.E. and Pioneers of the 33rd Division completed an excellent communication trench, leading from FitzClarence Farm, close to the 9th Yorkshire headquarters, past Lone House, to within a short distance of Carlisle Farm.

About 5 A.M. a very heavy bombardment opened over the whole area of the 69th Infantry Brigade as far back as 1000 yards from the front line, and an intense barrage fell on the front line itself. Barrages were also placed in enfilade on the northern bank of the Reutelbeek, and on a line south of Black Watch Corner.

By chance an army practice barrage had been ordered for 5.15 A.M., and the fire of this on the 23rd Division front served opportunely as a reply to the enemy's guns.

From the first, communication between battalion headquarters and the front line was impossible. All wires were immediately cut ; dust and smoke prevented visual signalling ; no runner could pass alive through the hail of bursting shells. Pigeons were released, in the hope that these at least might carry back reports, but they alike failed.

Prior to taking over the line, Brig.-General Lambert had warned all ranks in his brigade that, suffer what they might, there must be no retirement from the front line, since any such withdrawal would make it almost impossible for him satisfactorily to deal with the situation. Lambert was not the man to issue heroic appeals without reason or to demand sacrifice without cause ; and his men knew it. Now for hours he was to be aware that the fiercest fighting was in progress, without being able to get any detail of how his front-line troops were faring.

At 5.30 A.M. the enemy was seen advancing in waves north and south of Cameron Covert against Lieutenant Bennison's company of the 9th Yorkshire Regiment on the left of the line. Rifle and Lewis-gun fire was immediately opened on the attack. North of Cameron Covert two of our Lewis-guns were almost at once put out of action by shell-fire, and the platoon officer in the front line was killed.

At 5.35 A.M. it became apparent that the troops of the battalion on the immediate left of the Division were being forced back, closely followed by the enemy. For ten minutes or more our left posts maintained a continuous rifle-fire, and a Lewis-gun was brought into action in place of those that had been destroyed. By this time, however, the enemy was well past the left flank and in rear of the position. It became necessary to withdraw the posts to a position some fifty yards in rear. Here they were reorganised by Lieutenant Bennison, with the assistance of 2nd Lieutenant Gibson of the 69th L.T.M. Battery, who had brought two Stokes guns into position the previous night near the edge of Polygon Wood.

These two officers now led forward their men to counter-attack. Unfortunately, both were hit, and a fresh attack by the Germans compelled a further withdrawal of 150 yards on the extreme left to avoid a complete envelopment. Here a determined stand was made, and contact was gained with troops of the Leicestershire Regiment of the 110th Infantry Brigade, who had come forward on the left.

While these events were in progress on the northern edge of Cameron Covert, the remainder of C Company of the 9th Yorkshire Regiment and D Company of the 10th Duke of Wellington's, in position further to to the right, south of a small marsh, had driven off two determined attacks.

Seeing that the enemy had obtained a footing in the trench on his left, 2nd Lieutenant Lewis of the Yorkshire Regiment led forward a bombing party, drove the Germans from the trench, and recovered the Lewis-gun of his platoon. Shortly afterwards this gallant officer was killed by a sniper.

Trenches only existed on the left in this portion of the front ; the men of the Duke of Wellington's were formed in scattered posts in shell-holes unprotected by wire.

A third attack was now launched against this position, but the Germans, finding they could make no progress, abandoned their efforts, and commenced digging in behind an old line of German wire opposite our position.

The enemy's bombardment, the most intense yet experienced in the war, continued without intermission till late at night. Much of it, directed from the south-east, raked the defences in enfilade. By 9 A.M. it had extended to the front of the 70th Infantry Brigade. On this flank the front line was to a certain extent immune, but the support line and area about battalion headquarters endured the most cruel and destructive fire. Lieut.-Colonel S. L. Whatford, commanding the 8th York and Lancaster Regiment, in a report on the shelling on October 1, states :—

> The Tower must have received at least thirty direct hits ; several enemy batteries appeared to be concentrating on it. Battalion headquarters appeared to have guns of all calibres concentrated on it—8 in., 5.9 in., and 4.2 in. It received a number of direct hits. One shell burst inside one of the rooms, killing three and wounding two of our men, and partially wrecking the inside. Two dug-outs in rear of headquarters were blown in and destroyed, killing and wounding a number of our men. . . . I am not exaggerating when I state that thousands of shells must have fallen around the Tower and battalion headquarters throughout the day.

These were the conditions under which commanding officers remained during the day ; weighed down by anxiety for their troops, as to whose situation they received but the most fragmentary information, but confident that their men would stand till the last.

Stubborn fighting continued on the left throughout the day. The noise of rifle-fire and bursting shells, combined with the fact that the spur running forward to Cameron Covert concealed all ground to the north, prevented any accurate knowledge being obtained by others of what was occurring on the extreme left.

The hostile aircraft showed great enterprise. Co-operating with their infantry, they continually swept low over our trenches, inflicting many casualties by machine-gun fire.

South of the spur the post established by Lieutenant Lewis's counter-attack, somewhat forward of the general line, held its own till every round of ammunition and every bomb had been expended. Then at dusk it was withdrawn to the line held by D Company of the Duke of Wellington's and all that were left of C Company of the 9th Yorkshire Regiment.

Captain Payne, commander of the former company, now established three forward posts on the left to secure his flank.

Throughout the operations the coolness and intrepidity of this officer and his subalterns, Lieutenant Waite and 2nd Lieutenant Ferguson, were an inspiration to their men. Cut off from each other by the heavy barrage and unable to communicate with battalion headquarters, Payne and Waite constantly went forward to inform themselves of the situation, and, acting on their own initiative, carried out to the letter the only orders they had received—" There must be no retirement."

At about 7 P.M. the enemy's barrage shortened on the front of the 70th Infantry Brigade, and much of it commenced to fall on the front line. At 7.15 P.M. an S.O.S. signal from the 69th Infantry Brigade gave warning of danger.

A few minutes later the 9th York and Lancaster Regiment, on the right of the Divisional front, detected the enemy massing on and to the north of the Menin road. Rifles, Lewis-guns, and machine-guns opened on the whole brigade front, and the S.O.S. signal was fired. The reply of the artillery covering the front was immediate. Overwhelmed by fire, the enemy failed to reach our trenches, and the attack completely broke down.

Nothing was to shift the 70th Infantry Brigade from the line they had taken over on the critical night of September 27. The main objective of the Germans on this flank had been the Menin road position. The honour of holding this position for three days and three nights against the enemy's repeated attacks had fallen to C Company of the 9th York and Lancasters, under command of Captain Wicke.

In the dusk of the evening the Germans could still be seen massing opposite the left of the Division. These Captain Payne's men, though themselves now enfiladed from the north by machine-guns, continued to subject to a heavy fire of rifles, Lewis-guns, and rifle-grenades. The ammunition expenditure on this flank during the day amounted to 220 rounds per man and 30 magazines per Lewis-gun, in addition to 4000 rounds of S.A.A. sent up from reserve.

With darkness the German efforts died down, and by midnight the situation was once more normal.

The line held by the Division was the same as before the attack, with the exception that, on the extreme left, it had been slightly drawn back, and now ran north from Cameron House to join the 110th Infantry Brigade. The determined attack of the enemy, supported by artillery fire of unprecedented intensity, had resulted in the loss to us of ground of no great importance on a front of 200 yards to a maximum depth of about the same distance.

What the day had meant to the Germans can be gathered from the following letter addressed by the Second Army to the X. Corps a few days later :—

SECRET.

Second Army,
353. G.
October 7, 1917.

X. Corps.

The evidence gained from captured documents all tends to show that the enemy intended to launch a heavy attack on the Second Army front on October 3, and that in order to gain a better footing a preliminary attack was made on October 1.

This was so heavily dealt with by 23rd Division that it so dislocated the further attack that General Von Finckenstein, commanding 4th Guards Division, who was in charge of the operations, evidently decided to postpone his attack from October 3 to October 4.

The result of this postponement is well known. The Army Commander wishes the 23rd Division to be informed of the far-reaching results of their determined resistance, and to congratulate and thank all ranks concerned on behalf of himself and the Second Army.[1]

(Sgd.)   C. H. Harington,
M.G.G.S.,
Second Army.

Prior to the receipt of the above letter, the congratulations of General Babington to the troops who had been responsible for these results, were issued in the following Special Order :—

The Divisional Commander most sincerely congratulates all ranks of the 69th and 70th Infantry Brigades on the highly satisfactory results of the last six days. Called upon to take over an important part of the battle front at short notice, and with but little time to reorganise after the battle of September 20 and the events of the subsequent days, these brigades have firmly held the ground won against repeated, and at times heavy, attacks by the enemy, all of which were repulsed with great loss to him, and comparatively small loss to themselves. This

---

[1] The 21st Division were subsequently included in this order.

very marked success is due to the able dispositions made by the brigade commanders and subordinate commanders, to the gallantry of officers and men in their determination never to give ground, and to the confidence the men now have in their rifles, and the use they made of them.

It has been clearly demonstrated to the enemy that against good troops he stands no chance, either in attack or defence.

DIVISIONAL HEADQUARTERS,
    October 3, 1917.

Finally, before closing this chapter, the words may be quoted of one whose great faith in his men is clear in every report he wrote, but who is found time and again amazed at the gallantry of the units under his command, and lost in admiration and gratitude for the manner in which his orders have been carried out. The late General Lambert, in his report on the fighting on October 1, 1917, states : " Never, I believe, have troops better understood or better carried out their orders."

CHAPTER IV.

LAST DAYS IN FLANDERS.

Map No. 6. RECALLED to the line to meet a critical situation, the 23rd Division
had during the last four days passed through an ordeal as severe as
any in its experience.

If it had before earned the rest which had been so rudely broken,
repose had now become doubly due.

During October 2 and 3 the defence of the sector was taken over
by the 5th Division, and the 23rd Division was withdrawn to the Berthen
area.

But at this time little complete rest could be looked for by any
British Division. The bright prospect that had opened earlier in the
year with the victories of Vimy and Messines had been already dimmed
by the unfavourable weather that had forced postponements, and hampered operations in the third battle of Ypres. Dark clouds now appeared on the horizon of the Allies. The collapse of Russia had set free
large hostile forces, which were being rapidly transferred to the Western
Front; the fighting capacity of the sorely tried French armies was at
this time seriously diminished by grave internal troubles; America
was not yet in a position to give any assistance on land.

The Russian debacle, it was realised, could not but affect the situation on the Italian front. But no great concern was felt with regard to
that theatre, where the Italians were not only holding their own, but
had, little more than a month since, inflicted a severe defeat on the
Austrians.

It was otherwise on the main Western Front. Here it was recognised that if the Germans were to be prevented from regaining the
initiative, the British armies in Flanders must continue to attack.

On October 1 the offensive was resumed, and troops of the 23rd
Division were required in various capacities to support the battle.
Though none except the Divisional Artillery, which had remained in
the line, were to be actually engaged, the disaster which overtook the
Germans this day resulted indirectly from the action of the 23rd Division
on October 1.

The postponement in their operations forced by the check received
that day had caused their main attack to be fixed for the 4th. The
British attack anticipated this by ten minutes ; the German infantry
forming for assault were delivered in unprotected masses to our artillery
barrage, and completely routed.

From 12 noon the 68th Infantry Brigade was held in readiness at
two hours' notice to reinforce the fighting line ; but they were not required. In the meantime the 10th Duke of Wellington's and 8th Yorkshire Light Infantry were despatched to the 2nd Anzac Corps for work
on light railways. On the following day the 21st Division was reinforced
by 300 men of the 11th Northumberland Fusiliers as stretcher-bearers,
and by the 12th Durham Light Infantry for burying cable.

Following this somewhat disturbed "rest," the Division received
orders on October 8 to relieve the 7th Division in front of Polygon
Wood.

The line to be taken over, about 2000 yards in length, ran from a
point on the Reutelbeek 1200 yards west of Becelaere northwards to
a point on the Broodseinde-Becelaere road, one mile north-west of the
latter village.

To ease matters for battalions, some of which had had little rest,
it was decided to hold the line with two composite brigades of six battalions each.

Relief was completed on the night of October 10/11, the 68th Infantry
Brigade headquarters taking over the right section, and the 70th Infantry
Brigade headquarters the left ; the headquarters of both brigades were
established at Hooge.

On the 11th General Babington assumed command of the sector,
with headquarters at Chateau Segard, one and a half miles east of
Dickebusch.

69th Infantry Brigade headquarters were held in reserve at Reninghelst.

On the right of the Division the line was held by the 14th Division, on the left by the 5th Australian Division.

On October 14 Brig.-General C. Cary-Barnard assumed command of the 68th Infantry Brigade in place of Brig.-General G. N. Colville, who had vacated the appointment on September 26 after commanding the brigade for just over a year.

The ground was in a terrible condition. Rain and incessant shelling had produced a quagmire through which it was already difficult to drag one's way; Polygon Wood and Nonneboschen were rapidly becoming impassable.

The approach to the line was made along almost obliterated tracks which led through a wilderness of shell-holes, surrounded by all the hideous wreckage of war, and filled with slimy water, which failed to hide the dead bodies of men and mules, which it had not been possible to clear from the field of battle.

Men would occasionally sink so deep and fast in the mud that it would take close on an hour for two of their comrades to drag them out ; laden mules would sometimes be drowned.

Casualties in severe numbers were continually sustained from the start, and the evacuation of the wounded was a matter of the greatest difficulty ; scarcely less difficult was the supply of rations and stores to the troops in the line.

Farther north the British still struggled through the mud in a renewal of the offensive, but on the X. Corps front action was confined to artillery co-operation to simulate attack.

The enemy's bombardment, both by artillery and aircraft, was incessant, gas and incendiary shells raining on the infantry and battery positions.

Nor were the back areas immune. On October 15 two bombs dropped on the camp of the 191st Company of the Divisional Train destroyed twenty horses.

On October 20 the headquarters of the 70th Infantry Brigade, which had been relieved in the line by headquarters of the 69th, moved to Hallines, together with the 8th and 9th Yorkshire Regiment, 11th Northumberland Fusiliers, and 8th Yorkshire Light Infantry.

The relief of infantry in the line by the 21st Division commenced on the night of October 21, and was completed by the 23rd, when all units of the Division, except artillery and R.E., were concentrated about Wizernes, where Divisional Headquarters were established.

Relief of the 68th Infantry Brigade (composite) had been started at 9.30 P.M., but, owing to the appalling conditions that prevailed, it had not been completed till 10 A.M. on the following morning. The 13th Durham Light Infantry lost 16 killed and 30 wounded in the course of relief ; among the remainder, fortunately, casualties were not very high.

During these eleven days in the line the Division suffered 1229 casualties, including 13 officers and 262 other ranks killed.

The 23rd Divisional Artillery were still covering the Menin road sector, where they had remained when the Division was withdrawn on October 1. On the 25th they were relieved, and withdrawn to the Westoutre area, where the Field Companies R.E. were now also accommodated.

The interest of all was fixed on the fighting in Flanders, and reports of what was occurring in the line were eagerly read. The capture of Gheluvelt and its later evacuation, among other reports at this period, became vivid to those who in September had fought their way to the outskirts of the village.

But the grim struggle that continued for the possession of the Paschendaele Ridge, and the mud and blood and slaughter of Houlthoulst Forest, have no place in this history.

For with these came reports of other events which were to affect the whole future of the Division.

Suddenly and unexpectedly the Austrians, reinforced by German divisions, had attacked the Eastern Front of the Italians. General Mackensen, who was in charge of the enterprise, claimed 10,000 prisoners and many guns.

General Cadorna, the Italian Commander-in-Chief, however, expressed himself as confident of holding up the enemy's advance. But on the following day, October 27, the total of prisoners had increased to 30,000, and Gorizia was threatened.

On the 28th a warning order was issued, of which the opening paragraph read : " The Division complete will be in readiness to move by rail forthwith ; destination unknown."

But the news which followed close on this order robbed it of much of its mystery. Gorizia had fallen, the Austrians had crossed the Italian frontier, the total captures had risen to 60,000 prisoners and 600 guns, and the enemy were sweeping across the plains of Venetia.

By the 29th, 100,000 prisoners and 700 guns were reported lost ; the Second and Third Italian Armies had been routed ; riots had broken out in Italy. Two officers of the Divisional Staff and the staff captains of brigades left for Paris the same night *en route* for Italy.

Training programmes, carefully drawn up for the rest period, were cancelled ; all energies were centred on musketry and marching to prepare for the work that seemed to lie before the Division at its unknown destination.

On October 30 the Divisional Supply Column and Ammunition Sub-Park entrained for Italy.

On the following day Field-Marshal Sir Douglas Haig inspected the infantry brigades and field ambulances north of Leulinghem.

At the close of the inspection the Commander-in-Chief addressed General Babington and his senior officers :—

Knowing, he said, all that they had been through in the past few weeks, he had expected to find a shaken and disorganised Division. But the appearance and discipline of the troops he had inspected would do credit to a fresh Division. He congratulated them, and thanked them for the good work they had done in France and in the recent heavy fighting in front of Ypres. In bidding good-bye to the 23rd Division, he was parting with one of his best divisions. He was sure that no matter what lay before them in Italy, they would uphold the good name of their Division and the great traditions of the British Army.

Thus released by the highest authority, the cat was out of the bag at last. Many officers, it is true, had already shrewdly guessed the unknown destination ; but to the rank and file the announcement came as an inspiring revelation.

Throughout the war there was an unreasoning, though natural, desire with all for a change of scene. Distance lent enchantment to the joys of other fronts. While the soldier scorching in the wretched wastes of Mesopotamia longed for the greater comforts of rest billets on the Western Front and the opportunity of a glimpse of his friends at home, his brother would have been glad to exchange the mud, gas, and shells of Flanders for the comparative peace which he imagined reigned in the Land of the Two Rivers.

Italy was new ground for British divisions ; the name of the country and the nature of the venture alike made a strong appeal to all. But for some days yet they had to possess their souls in patience. For two French and two British corps,[1] ten divisions in all, were to be thrown into Italy to meet the serious situation which had arisen.

Even under peace conditions the difficulty of transporting such numbers would have been considerable. To collect rolling-stock and organise such a movement while a battle of immense dimensions was still in progress in Flanders was a stupendous undertaking. Fifty-nine trains were required to transport the 23rd Division alone. The possibility, moreover, had to be reckoned with of units being required to enter battle almost immediately after detrainment, and the movement had to be organised on this basis.

For the bulk of the Division, now concentrated south of St Omer, two entraining stations were allotted at Wizernes and Arques ; the Divisional Artillery and Ammunition Column, No. 1 Company Divisional Train, Royal Engineers, and 9th South Staffordshire Regiment (Pioneers), who were in the Westoutre area, were to entrain at Godewaersvelde.

The movement was timed for each train to complete its journey in five days and four nights. On arrival in Italy the Division, as part of the XIV. Corps (Lord Cavan), was to be concentrated near Mantua.

The 68th Infantry Brigade commenced entrainment on November 6, and were despatched the following day. They were followed by the 69th Infantry Brigade on the 8th and the 70th Infantry Brigade on the 9th. By November 12 the leading troops had arrived at their destination, and all units of the Division had been despatched.

Prior to leaving Flanders the following message, addressed to the G.O.C. and all ranks of the 23rd Division, was received from Lieut.-General Morland, commanding X. Corps.

It is with much regret that I have to part with you from the **Xth** Corps.

The Division has served with the Corps for a year with a few short intervals.

---

[1] British XI. and XIV. Corps. British Divisions—5th, 7th, 23rd, 41st, 48th.

During this period it has taken part in the Messines operations and those of September 20 onwards.

The Division has done all that was asked of it, and has invariably retained the captured ground. Throughout, it has shown a fine fighting spirit and dash in the attack, and resolution and dogged determination in defence.

In wishing you good-bye, I am confident that you will maintain your fine reputation wherever you may be called upon to serve.

PART IV. ITALY
THE FOURTH YEAR

CHAPTER I.

THE MONTELLO.

THE journey to Italy repaid the Division for much of the hardships endured in past years. For who of the annual contingent who visit the Riviera to try their luck at the tables, or to qualify for their photographs in the society papers, can have enjoyed the sensations of these men transferred from the hideous desolation of the Ypres salient to the beauties of Southern France ? First, through the Rhone Valley, flanked by hills rich in their terraced vineyards, glorious in their autumn tints ; ruined castles crowning the hill-tops, churches and villages clinging to the steep slopes. Later, along the Riviera, flanked on the one side by the blue Mediterranean, on the other by verdant hills ; the line bordered by vines, orange-trees, and bright flowers.

An officer records in his diary : " Our morale has increased 50 per cent to-day ; the Riviera has revived our battered spirits as much as a tot of rum would have done. I feel quite tired with rushing from one side of the carriage to the other to see some new and wonderful sight." Reaction : few probably realised their hunger for beauty till it was satisfied.

But inspiration did not come from scenery alone. The war had not been brought so close to Southern France before, and at every station the troops were welcomed with a warmth which recalled to some the enthusiastic scenes in the north at the outbreak of war, before war had been accepted as the normal condition of life. Fruit, flowers, cigarettes, were lavished on the troops. Once again the British Army figured as moving to the help of the oppressed. For, despite the existence of an evil party to which the country owed its recent disasters, the true heart of the Italian people was deeply moved.

The spirit which prevailed can be gleaned from the following address, which is but typical of many which appeared in the towns of Italy :—

SOLDIERS OF FRANCE AND OF ENGLAND !

To you who pass through our country to the front, where the safety of Italy and the freedom of the world is being fought out, the citizens of Mantova with steadfast spirit send their warmest greetings. You are a guarantee to us of the victory which shall revenge on the barbaric invader both our dead and your own. And when the Armies of France and of England, proud of having fought with the Army of Italy, return to us full of the glory of having hurled back beyond the Alps the arrogant Hun—and may that day soon come,—then the people of Mantova will welcome you once more with gratitude and fraternal joy to march forward to the glorious destiny which is in store for our common fatherlands. Long live the Entente ! Long live the sacred union of civilised nations !

Owing to there being only a single line between Ventimiglia and Savona, it was necessary for the Divisional Artillery to detrain and perform this part of the journey by road along the Italian Riviera.

Map No. 7.   On November 11 Divisional Headquarters were established at Macaria, a small village fifteen miles west of Mantova ; and by the 16th the whole Division had been concentrated in the surrounding area.

On Italy's entry into the war the strategic disadvantage of the frontier which she had been forced to accept by Austria-Hungary became immediately apparent. To the north-east the natural barrier of the Alps was in the hands of the Austrians, and the frontier, overshadowed by these, lay in the open plains. To the north, by their occupation of the Trentino, the Austrians held the strategic door by which they could pass through the Brenner and Rezia Passes to the plains of Northern Italy. The Trentino was as a wedge driven through the natural protection which Italy should have found in the Alps.

Unless secure in this northern front, the Italian armies on the river Isonzo, behind which the Austrians had withdrawn on the north-eastern front, would be in constant danger of a descent by the enemy on their rear.

On the outbreak of war in May 1915, the Italians succeeded, after heavy fighting, in gaining ground on the Trentino front. Believing themselves now secure, they concentrated their main efforts in 1916 on the Isonzo front, with the object of breaking through to Gorizia and Trieste.

But in May of that year the Austrians opened a violent offensive on the Trentino front, and drove the Italians south of the town of Asiago. The whole of the Italian armies east and north-east of the Trentino became threatened with disaster.

Reinforcements were rushed back from the Isonzo ; the situation was saved, and the front once again stabilised. Though much valuable ground had been lost on this precarious front, the Italians again felt free to resume the offensive on the north-eastern front. This met with considerable success. The Isonzo crossed and Gorizia captured, the attack had been continued during the summer of 1917 on the rocky tableland of the Carso. At the cost of heavy casualties, the Italians gained such success that German troops were hastened to the front to save Austria from an impending debacle.

Then followed the disaster which had called the French and British to Italy's aid. A sudden counter-attack at Caporetto against the Second Italian Army, whose ranks, depleted in gallant fighting on the Carso, had been refilled by malcontents conscripted from munition factories, met with instant and overwhelming success.

Sixteen days had passed since the first blow had been delivered against the Italians. Since then the Austrian armies had penetrated deeply into Italy, but in the swiftness of their advance their strength had been for the time expended. The Italians had breathing space, and knew that their Allies in daily increasing numbers were now behind them. But the reinforcement of their shattered armies was urgently needed. The French army was already moving eastward, and the XIV. British Corps (23rd and 41st Divisions) was now ordered forward to deploy on the right of the French between Monte Geldala and Vicenza. The move was to be carried out in five marches, and to be covered by a tactical advanced-guard, under command of General Babington.

On November 19 the columns marched out through Mantua, whose streets, ablaze with the national flags of the Allies, were lined with cheering crowds.

On the 20th General Sir Herbert Plumer assumed command of the British Army in Italy, and established his headquarters at Legnago.

The route to be followed lay through Sanguinetto, Legnago, Montagnana, and Noventa. By November 23 the Division had covered sixty-four miles, and reached the line given as its destination. But events had occurred on the previous day which necessitated a further advance. A series of attacks had been made on the Italians in the vicinity of Mt. Tomba and Mt. Fenera,[1] and there were indications that further attacks might be expected. It was, therefore, decided to move the Anglo-French forces at once from the Vicenza line to within supporting distance of the Italian army ; the French forces to move in the general direction of Asolo, the British forces in the direction of Montebelluna.

The movement of the British was somewhat delayed. On the 24th the Division crossed the river Tesina, and on the 25th halted. The 68th Infantry Brigade, at the head of the Division, had by then crossed the river Brenta, and occupied the St Giorgio area; the 69th Infantry Brigade were at Grantorto ; the 70th Infantry Brigade at Presina. Divisional Headquarters were situated at Bevadore. Orders were now received that the XIV. Corps would probably be required to relieve the Ist (Italian) Corps on the river Piave on the Montello front, which lay between Nervesa and Rivaseca. In this event the 23rd Division would occupy the left sector of the front, with the 41st Division holding the right.

These orders were confirmed on November 27, and the march was resumed the following day, the movement being so conducted that troops could turn northwards at short notice, to co-operate with the French should hostile attack develop from that direction.

By the 29th the 68th Infantry Brigade had reached the Resana area ; the 69th and 70th Infantry Brigades were situated in the St Floriano and Albaredo areas respectively. Divisional Headquarters were established at Vedelago. Orders were issued for the relief of the 70th Italian Division, and reconnaissance parties of the 69th and 70th Infantry Brigades, which were to take over the line, proceeded to the Montello front on the following day.

---

[1] East of Monte Grappa.

The following letter was received shortly before the conclusion of the march :—

XIV. CORPS, S. 119/1.

23rd Division.

The Corps Commander, having seen all arms of your Division at different points of its historical march, congratulates you and all ranks over—
(1) The good march discipline maintained throughout.
(2) The smartness of the transport.
(3) The fine spirit of the men in spite of fatigue.
He was thoroughly satisfied.

(Sd.)   F. GATHORNE-HARDY, *Brig.-General.*
November 25, 1917.

Italy had become the victim of a most overwhelming and unlooked-for disaster. The bitterness of her defeat was increased by the feeling that she had been betrayed from within. The canker of evil propaganda had eaten into the heart of one of her armies, whose previous record in the war had been unsurpassed. Following the disaster of Caporetto, the armies on either flank had fought desperately, but in vain. The time came when the only road to salvation lay in retirement. To the demoralisation bred by a sense of betrayal was added that of continual retreat.

Not the least of the tasks of the Allies lay in restoring the *morale* of the Italian soldiers, who were passing westwards in sullen despair along the road by which the British moved forward. Our police and traffic controls had heavy work in clearing the way for our columns through these weary disheartened troops. It was work which, if not exercised with tact and good-humour, might have produced chaos. First impressions mean much ; and, in his heart, the British soldier knew it. With all modesty it is felt that the following testimony to the conduct of the British troops, at a time when this was an immense power for good or evil, must be recorded. It is contained in a letter, dated January 8, 1918, addressed to the Rt. Hon. A. J. Balfour by the British Ambassador at Rome :—

SIR,—The following quite unsolicited testimonial as to the impres-

sion which British troops are making in Italy will undoubtedly be of
interest.

The President of the Council observed yesterday that he could not
allow the opportunity to pass of expressing his unqualified admiration
of the British troops which had been sent to Italy. He had just
come down from the front, and in saying what he felt he was echoing
the opinion of General Diaz and also of the King of Italy. His Majesty
has said he could not find words adequately to express his appreciation
of these troops. There had not been a single case of indiscipline or any
subject of complaint.

I have also been shown a private letter from an Italian officer,
unknown to me personally, to a friend of his, in which he writes : " I
am at —— at the district headquarters, where you may send me a few
lines. I have almost all my time done service in the immediate neighbourhood of British troops. They are marvellous. I am not speaking
of their discipline, which is perfect, but of the singular delicacy of feeling which distinguishes officers and soldiers. When they leave a billet
which they have occupied not a chair is out of its proper place. Their
cleanliness is so great that you would not find a straw on the ground.
So also with their camps, where hundreds of waggons and quadrupeds
have stopped ; they do not leave any trace of their passage. No one
even takes a glass of water without asking leave."

Such exemplary conduct cannot fail to have the most beneficial
effect on relations, and I feel most grateful to the Supreme Command
in Italy for having inspired the forces sent to this country with such a
high ideal of their obligation.

I am sending a copy of this despatch to Sir Herbert Plumer.

I have the honour to be, with the highest respect, sir, your most
obedient humble servant.

The Rt. Hon. A. J. BALFOUR, O.M., M.P.,
&c., &c., &c.

The general course of the river Piave, behind which the retreating
Italian armies had taken their stand to check the Austrian pursuit,
runs south-east from the Southern Alps to enter the sea some thirty-
five kilometres north-east of Venice. But some four kilometres after
leaving the foothills of the Alps to cross the Venetian Plain, the river
meets an obstruction, which for a space of eight miles forces the stream
to flow in a direction due east before resuming its general course.

Map No. 8.   This obstruction is caused by the high ground of Il Montello, which,
rising from the plains, forms an isolated oval hill, with a length, east
to west, of roughly seven miles, and a maximum depth of four miles.
The highest point of the hill, which, owing to its gentle convex formation,

can scarcely be regarded as a "summit," is some 800 feet above the
river-bed.

With complete command over the river and opposite bank and over
the open plain which flanked it south-east and west the Montello
represented a position of immense strength.

The hill itself was covered with vineyards, with here and there a
patch of maize or wheat. Tobacco, too, had been grown by the more
enterprising crofters. Timber was plentiful, and copses of pine, acacia,
and mulberry grew in some profusion.

A remarkable feature of the ground was the presence of circular
depressions in fairly large numbers, which offered cover for infantry
and guns. Many of these measured more than 100 yards across, and
had a depth of from 50 to 60 feet.

Intersecting the Montello at right angles to its length were twenty-
one roads, leading from the southern plain practically to the river bank.
These were connected laterally by the Cliff Road on the bank of the
Piave, the military road on the southern (reverse) slope, and by the
main Volpago-Montebelluna road on the southern plain.

The area to be taken over from the 70th Italian Division included
the left or western half of the Montello and a narrow strip of plain,
one and a half to two kilometres wide, below its western slope. The
front line, which ran east and west along the right bank of the Piave,
had a total length of between seven and eight thousand yards.

The Italians, who for three weeks had been fortifying the position,
had done an immense amount of work. Three rows of well-revetted
trenches had been constructed parallel to the river bank, numerous
machine-gun emplacements had been formed, and dug-outs—not too
strongly constructed, it must be admitted—existed for the majority
of the troops in the line.

The river Piave, flowing not as one stream but split into as many
as ten different channels, in most of which the current was very swift,
represented No Man's Land.

Along the left bank, at a distance varying from a thousand to two
thousand yards, stretched the front line of the Austrian position, which
had a depth of some four miles. Generally situated on a plain covered
with trees and vines, the position was backed by low foothills; these were,
however, thrust forward on the east at Falze di Piave and on the west

at Vidor. The latter village, situated opposite a narrow point in the river which occurred just beyond the left of the Divisional sector, had considerable tactical importance. Further to the rear of the enemy's position rose the snow-covered peaks of the Alps.

The most complete observation over this area was obtained from the Montello. To a casual observer, looking out over the fresh fields and woods to the red-brick campanili of Moriago, Fontigo, and Sernaglia, it presented an aspect of smiling peace. The Austrian defences could not be seen. It was rarely that a gun was heard.[1] A lull had come in the fighting, and the only evidence of war was the absence of movement, though there were still many civilians living in the undamaged villages in the rear of the Austrian position.

In truth, this was a change from Flanders !

It was decided to hold the line with two infantry brigades, of which the right would hold the Montello on a front of about five kilometres, the left the extremity of the Montello west of Road 18 and the low ground which stretched back from the river between the hill and the village of Rivasecca.

Each brigade would place two battalions in the line, with one battalion in support and its fourth battalion in reserve.

The third brigade would be held in Divisional reserve in the area about Montebelluna, where Divisional Headquarters would be ultimately situated.

On the evening of December 2 the 69th Infantry Brigade relieved 135th Italian Regiment in the right section, and the 68th Infantry Brigade moved into reserve in the Montebelluna area.

During the night of the 3rd/4th the 70th Infantry Brigade relieved the 136th Italian Regiment in the left section. A certain amount of artillery registration by the enemy was in progress, but all reliefs were completed without casualty.

Most cordial relations had already been established with our Allies during the preliminary reconnaissance, and officers and men were received on relief with the greatest hospitality. It was a new and strange experience. Company and battalion headquarters were taken over in intact houses, where drawers torn open and floors littered with articles

---

[1] It is stated that a shell-hole was found on the Montello wired-in as a precaution against people falling into it.

of clothing and letters gave sad evidence of the recent flight of the
wretched inhabitants. Certain of the trench stores surprised the new-
comers. An officer records that among stores of various descriptions
for which he signed a receipt were four barrels of wine.[1]

The language question presented some difficulty, but unofficial
interpreters helped things out. Comparatively few Italian officers
speak English, though all speak French, and most of them German.
It was otherwise in the ranks, where the number of Italian soldiers
who had picked up English in the United States was remarkable. It
was amusing to note the change in his whole demeanour which came
over the Italian soldier when he switched from his own beautiful language and opened with a rich American accent. The language of the
States does not lend itself to graceful gesture, and the speaker would
rasp out catchwords with all the nonchalant aggressiveness of a prize-
fighter on Broadway.

After ten minutes' conversation with one of these worthies a staff
officer was electrified by " Waal, so long, Cockie ! " as his new acquaint-
ance moved off.

The subject of the recent catastrophe and the treachery connected
with it was occasionally referred to by the Italian officers with great
bitterness. They were confident that the stability of their armies would
soon be restored. For the Austrian troops they held no great regard,
ascribing the enemy's success to the half-dozen Prussian divisions which
had intervened, and for whom, one thinks, they entertained an exaggerated respect.[2]

On December 4 General Babington took over command of the sector
from General Grimandi. Divisional Headquarters, which had been
established on November 29 at Vedelago, moved on December 5 to
Biadene, and thence on the 7th to Montebelluna.

The Italians had not adopted the system of defence in depth with
its greater elasticity which had been developed by the opposing forces
in France and Flanders, but had adhered to the more rigid form which
had been in force in the earlier days of trench warfare both with our-

[1] Wine forms part of the Italian soldier's daily ration.

[2] The British felt no great enmity towards the Austrians, and it was at first difficult to
realise the bitterness which existed between them and the Italians.

At the conclusion of the Armistice the Austrian officers in the Trentino welcomed surrender
to the British (48th Division) to escape surrender to the Italians, which they bitterly resented.

selves and the Germans. The three trench lines were "en correspond-
ance "—replicas the one of the other,—and the front line was strongly
held both by infantry and machine-guns.

For greater convenience of relief the system was taken over in the
first place to a great extent on the Italian plan. But work was immediately undertaken to reorganise the defence in accordance with the
principles we had adopted in France.

This reorganisation aimed at establishing strong lines of Lewis-
gun defences on the lower slopes of the hill, with lines of machine-gun
defence on the middle and upper slopes, the latter being so sited as to
cover all spurs, while emplacements for trench-mortars were constructed
to enable these to bring fire on the valleys and other dead ground.

The front line would be held lightly by infantry posts to prevent
the approach of hostile patrols. At night they would be strengthened
for this purpose, and touch maintained by trench patrols. Lewis-guns
were to be sited on the Montello in three tiers, to bring enfilade fire on
the river-bed, the plateau immediately in rear of this, and the upper
slopes of the hill, across which ran our rearmost line of defence. One
machine-gun company was allotted to the right brigade ; two companies (each less a half-section) to the left brigade. Twelve guns of the
right company would be sited south of Cliff Road ; four held in brigade
reserve. In the left section thirteen guns would be situated in and about
the second line. Of fifteen guns held in reserve, nine, in case of alarm,
would occupy the lower western slope of the Montello, certain of which
would be capable of bringing direct fire on the river-bed ; two would
occupy a position to bring enfilade fire on the Brentellone Canal and
road towards Crocetta ; four would be held in mobile reserve.

Excellent as were the Italian trenches, they were very conspicuous,
and were regarded as more suitable for communication than for permanent occupation. The defence would rely mainly on the fire of carefully concealed Vickers and Lewis-guns, backed by infantry posted for
counter-attack.

The Field Artillery covering the front were organised in three groups,
consisting of the 103rd Brigade R.F.A. (Lieut.-Colonel Grove), the
102nd Brigade (Lieut.-Colonel Badham Thornhill), and the 14th Brigade
R.H.A. (Lieut.-Colonel Wickham), with one Italian mountain battery
of four guns.

TRENCHES ON THE MONTELLO.

The 14th Horse Artillery Brigade and the 103rd Brigade were situated in the cup-shaped depressions on the Montello, whilst the 102nd Brigade occupied well-concealed positions in the houses and orchards about Nogare and Crocetta. This brigade was well placed to fire down the river Piave across the front of the Montello position, whilst the guns on the Montello could similarly fire up the river across the front of the British trenches from Ciano to Rivasecca.

In addition, two British and three Italian Heavy Artillery groups supported the front of the XIV. Corps ; the 24th and 80th, each consisting of four siege and two heavy batteries, made up with the Italian groups a total of 96 heavy guns and 40 heavy or medium howitzers.

In connection with the reorganisation of the defence, much labour was devoted to the construction of shell-proof dug-outs and emplacements for machine-guns and trench-mortars. The Montello was very favourable to this work. By tunnelling into the side of a depression or under some small ridge, dug-out systems with several galleries could be executed. Timber for strutting was plentiful, and work continued day and night. In the flat gravel soil on the extreme left tunnelling was impracticable. Here defences of reinforced concrete were planned and taken in hand with equal vigour.

Conditions favoured work, the weather was fine, and the artillery remained generally inactive.

Night patrols to explore the river-bed and channels were undertaken from the outset. The first, sent out by the 70th Infantry Brigade on December 5, obtained no contact with the enemy. On the 8th patrols from the same brigade reached the main stream, which they reported deep, swift, and unfordable. Four days later, however, a party succeeded after great difficulty in fording this main stream, and locating an enemy post on the opposite bank.

To ford a river in Northern Italy in the winter requires a considerable degree of determination at any time.

The troops on our left at this time belonged to the Brigade Alpi, which was attached to the French. Their commander was General G. Garibaldi, a descendant of the great Italian patriot, whose character and charm he to a large degree inherits.

On December 11 there was a considerable increase in the enemy's artillery fire directed mainly on the flanks of the Montello, which seemed to indicate an attack. Just before dusk the Italians reported Austrian forces massing at Vidor. Our artillery searched the locality, and no attack materialised.

On December 19 the 68th Infantry Brigade relieved the 70th Infantry Brigade in the left section, and four days later the Division secured its first prisoner in Italy. At dusk on December 23 a party of 1 officer and 16 other ranks of the 10th Northumberland Fusiliers left the river-side village of Ciano, and, moving on a bearing true north, crossed the Piave. On reaching the opposite bank they encountered a small hostile patrol, one of whom surrendered, another narrowly escaping capture. The patrol then withdrew under cover of the fire of their Lewis-guns.

The prisoner proved to be a Hungarian of the 35th Division, and supplied a valuable identification.

December 25 was more like a real Christmas Day than any the Division had experienced for some years. All work was suspended, and the diet-sheet of one company that has been preserved gives an idea of the fare enjoyed. Breakfast—bacon and eggs ; dinner—roast pork and beef, potatoes, vegetables, Christmas pudding, fruit, beer, wine, cigarettes.

Our aviators celebrated the day by a trip across the line to the headquarters of a German Flying Squadron. Possibly the festivities of the latter were disturbed. Boxing Day saw the sequel. Some twenty-five enemy aeroplanes swept over our lines : an aerodrome at Istrana was bombed, Montebelluna was also damaged, and Divisional Head-quarters narrowly escaped. The enemy airmen behaved in the most reckless manner, leading to the belief that they had resumed their interrupted festivities before starting out. Their escapade ended disastrously for them. On the arrival of British and Italian machines, no fewer than eleven of the enemy were shot down without the loss of any of our airmen.

Christmas was also marked by the issue of the Divisional annual paper, ' The Dump,' and of a Christmas card, containing a cartoon representing the success of the Division in the battle of the Menin road.

On December 27, H.R.H. the Prince of Wales, as G.S.O. 3 of the XIV. Corps, paid his first visit to the sector. He was to be a regular visitor during the Division's tour in Italy.

A vast amount of work had been completed on the defences, and the Corps Commander paid a very high tribute to General Lambert and the 69th Infantry Brigade as regards the organisation of labour and the excellent manner in which it had been carried out to meet the tactical situation.

At the date on which the Division had taken over the Montello sector the year was far advanced, but the situation was still regarded as critical. For the Allies to maintain their position on the Piave, it was not only necessary that the line of the river should be firmly and stubbornly held : it was equally essential that no advance should be permitted to the Austrians on the mountain front. On and east of the Asiago Plateau the enemy were dangerously close to the Venetian Plain. A successful attack on that front followed by a descent in rear of the troops holding the Piave would threaten a disaster more overwhelming than any purely frontal attack on the river front could inflict.

All Italy prayed for snow to hold up operations on the mountain front. Normally this could be looked for in late November, but this year the snowfall had been long delayed. At last, on December 13, snow fell in the mountains, not very heavily, but sufficiently to bring a sigh of relief from the sorely tried Italians.

On the 20th, attacking with fresh heart, they recaptured Mt. Asolone.

On New Year's Day, 1918, the 47th French Division, in a brilliant attack on Mt. Tomba, captured all their objectives, together with 1500 prisoners. A week later there was a heavy fall of snow. Already, on January 7, it lay eighteen inches deep on Mt. Tomba, and was still falling. Serious operations in the mountains could be regarded as at an end until the coming spring.

In the meantime, on the Piave, work on the defences was steadily pushed forward, and night patrols across the river continued in weather which had become intensely cold.

Casualties in the Division during December had only amounted to 31 other ranks killed, 1 officer and 88 other ranks wounded. With the further protection gained by the development of the defences, the number of casualties greatly decreased during January. The total in the Division during this month was only 47, including 7 other ranks killed.

The patrol work was very severe. Men, stripped and with their bodies oiled as a resistance to the cold, would cross the first deep channel and drag across a boat carrying the patrol, dressed in white as camouflage against the snow, with their legs protected by thigh gum-boots. The patrol would then proceed to negotiate the farther shallower channels. If the swift current rose above a man's knees, it would be hard for him to keep his footing.

Early in January a patrol of the 68th Infantry Brigade of 1 officer and 15 other ranks succeeded in crossing the first three streams. The fourth stream was found to be very swift. In spite of all precautions every man was swept from his feet, and a Lewis-gunner was carried down-stream.

The gun was lost, but the officer struggled to the far bank, and succeeded in dragging the man out. The fifth stream was found impassable. The return journey was commenced. A chain of hands was now formed, but again both the officer and sergeant were swept downstream. Ultimately, with great difficulty, the whole party regained the right bank of the Piave safe and intact.

The channels were growing deeper every day. On January 17 an attempt was made to throw a swing-bridge across the main channel, but without success, and 2nd Lieutenant Cooper of the 9th York and Lancaster Regiment was unfortunately drowned during the operation. Efforts were also made to throw a rope attached to a grapnel across the channel, the grapnel being fired from a 2-inch trench-mortar.

About the middle of the month the 7th Division relieved the 41st Division in the right sector of the British front, and the 2nd Bersaglieri Brigade replaced the Acqui Brigade, which had previously taken the place of the Alpi Brigade on the left of the 23rd Division.

Hitherto Captain Bonte of the Italian Horse Artillery had acted as liaison officer to the Division. On January 19 this officer was required to attend a staff course, and was replaced by Lieutenant Count Corrado Emo Capodilista of the Alpine Artillery, whose services it was to be the good-fortune of the Division to retain till the end of the war. It was in Count Emo's house at Fanzolo that Lord Cavan had established the headquarters of the XIV. Corps.

Great services towards relieving the monotony of life on the Montello during the winter were rendered by the " Dumps," the Divisional Concert Party, whose entertainments in Montebelluna were given on a far more ambitious scale than in the old days.

A very successful revue, ' Remember Belgium,' was followed by a

pantomime, ' The Babes of Polygon Wood,' of which the caste is given
below :—

Bill		Robbers	Capt. W. W. Caithness, R.F.A.
Cyril	· · · ·		L/cpl. Hall, 8th Yorks.
Monty Belluna	· ·	A "Knut" · ·	Capt. Blackett, 11th N.F.
Marian · · · ·		Principal Girl ·	Sapper Pilling, R.E.
Landlord · · ·		of the Cowslip Inn	Sgt. Blencowe, 13th D.L.I.
Muriel · · · ·		Landlord's Daughter	Pte. Cronwell, York & Lancs.
Frank · · · ·		Another "Knut" ·	Pte. Prior, 9th Yorks.
The Villain of the Piece	· · · · ·		Pte. Schofield, 11th West Yorks.
Dame · · · · · · · ·			L/cpl. Glaves, 9th Yorks.
Babes of Polygon	Wood	Boy · · · ·	Pte. Fawcett, 9th Yorks.
		Girl · · · ·	Pte. Raynore, 8th K.O.Y.L.I.

These performances were largely attended by the officers of our
Allies, both French and Italian, among whom some of the more in-
genuous were led to believe that the British Army had imported certain
fascinating vivandières into Italy. The " book " must have proved
a severe test for their knowledge of our language—

> " I'm Monty from Montebelluna, the bounder from far Biadene,
> I'm a h—l of a fellow around the Montello,
> The road-hog of Road 17.
> I'm Prince of the River Piave, the pride of my bally platoon,
> And the girls of Padova all sigh and turn over
> For Monty of Montebellu —— na."

They were given their revenge at allied concerts, when half the
programme would be in French or Italian (Spirito Gentile—Romanza
per Tenore con Accompagnamento di piano, &c.) and half in English
(Cornet Solo—Sergeant Pell).

But the enemy did not allow us to overlook the fact that a war was
in progress. Night-bombing by aircraft was very severe, particularly
on Montebelluna and on Padua, where British G.H.Q. were situated.

Montebelluna was bombed on five nights between February 1 and 6,
and shelled on the 7th.

On January 3 the headquarters of a company of the 9th South
Staffordshire Regiment were demolished by a 12-in. howitzer, fortunately without casualty ; another of its shells made a crater of 27 feet
in diameter and 11 feet deep.

Despite these obvious indications of the enemy's power and intention of taking opportunity to bring harassing artillery fire on the area, a 16-target gallery range, in full view from the higher ground in the Austrian position, had been in regular use. This rifle-range had been built under the supervision and from the designs of Major A. W. C. Richardson, G.S.O. 2, who had been formerly on the staff of the School of Musketry at Hythe. It was situated about half a mile north-west of Biadene. Firing-points and targets had been carefully camouflaged, and, as far as is known, the range was never detected by the enemy.

A Divisional Rifle Meeting, lasting three days, was held here early in February. The various events provoked keen competition, and the prizes were presented at its conclusion by the Corps Commander.

In addition to these more serious distractions, one unforgettable feature of life in the sector was a bobbery pack, under the mastership of Lieut.-Colonel T. E. P. Wickham, 14th Brigade, R.H.A. This promiscuous assembly of pariahs were wont to pursue the wily hare on the Montello, under cover of convenient mists which shrouded the enemy's observation. The numerous kills claimed by the master could unfortunately never be verified, as the field, pumped and perspiring, was never known to be in at the death.

Shortly after, orders were received for the relief of the 23rd Division on the Montello by the 41st Division. This commenced on February 13 with relief of the Divisional Artillery, less A/102 Battery, which was to remain in the line with the 41st Division.

On the occasion of the relief, the following personal letter was addressed by the Corps Commander to General Babington :—

February 16, 1918.

MY DEAR BABINGTON,—I cannot let your Division leave the line without expressing to you my very sincere appreciation of the work they have done. It has been splendidly organised, and therefore methodically carried out.

The active spirit shown by all units in crossing the river is also most praiseworthy and very encouraging to our Allies.

Please let all ranks know how grateful I am to them for their accomplishments.—Yours very sincerely,

CAVAN.

Relief was completed by the 18th, when General Babington estab-lished his headquarters at Riese, about thirteen kilometres south-west of Montebelluna. The bulk of the Division was accommodated in the area about Riese, Altivole, and Vedelago. The 70th Infantry Brigade, however, were placed farther north at Crespano for work on what was known as the Costalunga line. This line, which was situated below Mt. Grappa on the foothills to the west of the river Piave, faced north, and would cover the left flank of the Piave position if the mountain positions were lost by the Allies. The 23rd Division, while in reserve, was to be prepared to occupy this line in case of emergency ; recon-naissance of the position was therefore carried out during the next few days.

It seems as if it had been the fate of the 23rd Division always to have its rest cut short by some unlooked-for event.

Affairs in Italy had by now assumed a calmer aspect. The sudden fierce onslaught which was to have put Italy out of the war had failed in its design. The divisions from France had arrived in time to sup-port their Allies, and the Italian front had stabilised. The Germans now had a vaster enterprise in preparation in the northern theatre, for which they were concentrating all their force. By the middle of February this had become clear to General Headquarters in France, and it was known that, in addition to twenty-eight divisions transferred from the Eastern Front, the Germans had brought back their six divisions from Italy.

This made it at the same time possible and advisable to transfer certain of the French and British divisions from Italy to the threatened front. It was decided to reduce the Franco-British forces in Italy to two French and three British divisions. The 7th and 41st Divisions [1] were accordingly ordered to be prepared to commence entraining for France on March 1. Sir Herbert Plumer was also to return to France after handing over command of the British forces in Italy to Lieut.-General Lord Cavan.

In order to prepare for these moves it was necessary for the 41st Division to be withdrawn from the line as early as possible, and the

---

[1] Later the 5th Division was substituted for the 7th, which remained in Italy with the 23rd and 48th Divisions. At one time the 23rd Division had been on the point of being ordered to France, but it was later decided to send the 41st.

23rd Division was ordered on February 23 to effect their relief on the left sector of the Montello front between February 24 and 27.

On the 24th the 68th Infantry Brigade moved forward from the Altivole area to the Montebelluna reserve area, and took over the left section of the line the same night. The 69th Infantry Brigade, moving from the Riese area, replaced the 68th Infantry Brigade at Altivole on the 24th, and took over the right section of the line on the night of the 25th.

By February 26 all reliefs had been completed, and Divisional Headquarters were once again established in Montebelluna.

The Austrian artillery were a good deal more active than during the Division's previous tour. This seemed to be due mainly to the rain and mist that prevailed, as it was noticeable that the poorer the visibility the more active would be the enemy's guns—a compliment to our counter-battery work.

Patrolling across the river was continued, but the water was rising daily, which made the work increasingly difficult. On March 1 a patrol of the 10th Duke of Wellington's got into touch with the enemy ; an officer having fired his revolver point-blank at an Austrian, and missed him, engaged in a hand-to-hand tussle. The man escaped, but left his cap behind, by which he was identified as belonging to the 1st Regiment 13th Schutzen Division. A week later the Piave had become impassable.

The present generation must always wonder how the British Army continued to exist before the introduction of football. Nowadays to throw a football to a British soldier is like giving a bone to a dog ; it will keep him content for hours, and ease his mind of the horrors and hardships he has endured.

Nowhere had it proved more valuable than in the ranks of the 23rd Division, recruited as it was from some of the keenest football centres in England. A further interest was now added to the game in Italy. Earlier in the year the annual Division competition had been keenly contested. In this, after beating the Royal Engineers 3 goals to 2 in the semi-final, the 68th Infantry Brigade had won the final in a match against the 70th Infantry Brigade by 3 goals to 0.

Lord Cavan had now offered a challenge cup to be played for by formations of the XIV. Corps. Having disposed of the XIV. Corps troops in the semi-final, the 23rd Division, in a great game played at Fanzolo on March 9, defeated the 5th Division by 1 goal to 0, and carried off the cup for the first year.

The Division's last tour on the Montello was to be of short duration. Orders had already been received that the 51st Italian Division would shortly take over the sector, and on March 11 relief commenced.

These reliefs between British and Italian divisions always proved somewhat complicated. A straight relief carried out between experienced British divisions could work like clockwork. But the different organisation of the Italian divisions, different methods in the conduct of relief, and the eternal language question made things more difficult.[1]

On this occasion the 23rd Division was organised into infantry brigade groups for the purpose of relief and withdrawal.

The relief was completed by March 14, when command of the sector passed to the G.O.C. 51st Italian Division, and General Babington withdrew his headquarters to Vigardolo, north-east of Vicenza.

On the same day a warning order was received from the XIV. Corps that the 23rd Division, as a temporary measure, would have to take over the whole of a new front of 8000 yards which had been allotted to the Corps on the Asiago Plateau. Relief of the 11th and 12th Italian Divisions on this front was to be completed by March 28.

Eventually the Corps front would be divided into two sectors, of which the left would be taken over by the 7th Division, leaving the 23rd Division in occupation of the right sector, with the French on their right flank.

By March 16 the concentration of the Division in its rest area northeast of Vicenza was complete, and the G.S.O. 1 and D.A.Q.M.G. proceeded to the Asiago front to arrange details of the forthcoming relief, which promised to be somewhat complicated owing to difficulties of transport in the mountains.

---

[1] See Appendix F.

CHAPTER II.

THE ASIAGO PLATEAU.

FIRST PERIOD : MARCH 23 TO JUNE 22, 1918.

THE AUSTRIAN ATTACK OF JUNE 15.

Map No. 9. IN the preceding chapter it was related how in May 1916 the Austrians had opened a violent offensive on the Trentino front, threatening the Italians with a disaster which was narrowly averted by rushing reinforcements from the Isonzo.

The line on which the Italians at that time re-established their front south and south-west of the town of Asiago was that which the XIV. Corps was now to occupy.

It has been said that the Montello position provided a contrast to Flanders, but such contrast was slight as compared to that presented on this mountain front.

Some sixteen miles north of Vicenza the Venetian plain is bounded between Caltrano and Calvene by the easterly course of the river Astico. North of this boundary the ground rises steeply, till at a height of about 4000 feet above the river-bed it gains the southern edge of the Asiago Plateau.

In winter the impression derived from a distant view of the precipitous slopes which lead to the snow-clad mountains which surmount the plateau is one of hopeless inaccessibility. The task of transporting several infantry divisions to these heights, let alone of maintaining them when there, appalled the uninitiated ; it was felt that Hannibal himself might well have quailed at the thought of dragging heavy artillery to support the defence on this mountain front.

But a closer investigation showed that though on the left Mt. Brusabo and Mt. Pau rose sheer from the valley of the Astico, the ascent to the mountains in the centre and on the right of the position extended over a distance of some four miles, and commenced on the right through foot-hills. Steep as the gradients were on the right and centre, it had been found possible to construct approaches for wheeled traffic. Fine metalled roads, cut in the mountain-side, gave proof of the acknowledged genius of the Italian engineer, equalled only by the nerve of the Italian drivers, whose Fiat lorries were met dashing at breakneck speed round hair-pin corners on the very edge of yawning chasms.

The Asiago Plateau, whose southern edge ran at a distance of 5000 yards from, and roughly parallel to, the allied front, forms a vast step, breaking the general slope of the Southern Alps. On gaining the plateau, the main road, which was to form the boundary between the British and the French, ran forward at a gentle slope through the allied defences to an open plain, where the war-ruined town of Asiago lay, half a mile in rear of the Austrian front line. Some 2000 yards to the north of Asiago the general slope of the Alps is resumed.

The term "plateau" conveys to many Englishmen the idea of an extent of flat or undulating ground. It may be as well, therefore, to correct an interpretation that would give an entirely wrong impression of the area to which the 23rd Division was now ordered. The Asiago Plateau has been compared above to a step. This step, far from being level, is covered on its southern half, in the area of the allied defences, by pine-clad hills, rising to a height of some 600 feet. But the bottoms of the valleys separating these hills run either level or at a gentle slope ; it had, therefore, been possible to construct forward and lateral lorry routes to run throughout the area at a moderate gradient.

The character of the northern half of the plateau, the area of the enemy's defences, was completely different. Here it took the form of an open undulating plain, which will be referred to as the Asiago Plain to distinguish it from the rugged area of wooded hills occupied by the Allies.

Between the opposing lines ran the dry bed of the river Ghelpac. Shallow and insignificant for the greater part of its course, the Ghelpac Valley deepened as it ran westward. Shortly after passing the centre of the Corps front, a sharp southerly bend brought it immediately below the Allies front line. From this point it resumed its westerly course as a steep ravine, finally joining the gorge of the Val d'Assa, just west of what was to constitute the left boundary of the British front.

Everywhere in the arrangements for the defence the skill and perseverance of the Italian engineer were manifest. Miles of trenches had been blasted from the solid rock to a depth in places of 10 feet. As an auxiliary to road transport, rack and pinion railways (funicular) carried ammunition and supplies up the steep mountain-side ; the teleferica, a cable stretching from the plains to the plateau's southern edge, on which ran small trolleys, performed similar service in mid-air. Properly speaking, the teleferica was not intended for human transport, but it was not unusual to see some daring spirit, who had ventured to take a short-cut to the mountains, marooned in space over a hideous chasm while a temporary hitch had occurred in the working of this ingenious contrivance.

The forward defences to be taken over by the British were situated on the northern slopes of the mountains in their descent to the valley of the Ghelpac. So situated, they would have been fully exposed to hostile observation but for the dense pine-woods, which provided concealment in the greater portion of the area. The front line ran level with or slightly above the open Asiago Plain, which was closed on the north by high mountains rising abruptly in rear of the Austrian positions.

The Austrian defences, with their front line at an average distance from our own of about one mile, spread east and west across the Asiago Plain. Viewed from the heights in rear of the Allies front line, the hostile trenches lay like a map at the observer's feet.

The slight elevations and the collection of shattered tree-stumps, which had been graced by the names of hill and wood in Flanders, had little in common with Italy's northern front. The arrangements for defence on the steep pine-clad slopes of Mt. Kaberlaba presented problems very different from those of the defence of Hill 60 and Battle Wood.

Consideration was due to the long experience of the Italians on this front. But in giving due weight to this, it had to be realised that their main principles of defence, as already instanced on the Montello, differed in certain essential points from those that we had adopted. Conditions on the Asiago Plateau, it is true, differed greatly from those to which our troops had become accustomed in France and Flanders. The distance of the enemy's trenches precluded all danger from such weapons as rifle-grenades and trench-mortars, and the covered approaches through the dense woods provided a novel factor.

But beyond this, the war had become stagnant. The continuous harassing fire of artillery, the perpetual action of patrols, and the frequent minor enterprises, which had become habitual in France and Flanders, had been unknown on this front. The intense cold and deep snow during winter and early spring, in fact, made infantry action nigh impossible.

In what was to form the right sector of the British front, ultimately to be occupied by the 23rd Division, the eastern portion of the defences was concealed by dense woods ; the western portion lay in the open. The Italian forward system of defence in this sector consisted of two strongly-built trenches running parallel to one another and heavily wired. Of these, the first-line trench was partly dug from earth, mainly blasted from rock ; the second, known as the second line, forming a parallel support trench at a distance of some 800 yards from, and at a height of between 400 and 500 feet above the front line, was blasted from rock throughout. Communication trenches were unnecessary in the wooded area on the right ; impossible on the steep exposed slopes of the left.

Heavy strips of wire, running obliquely to the front, connected the two lines, and trench elements had been constructed in places in rear of this wire. But there had been no serious provision for protracted defence between the front and support line. The scheme of defence was, therefore, somewhat rigid ; and the distance separating these two parallel lines was so great as to necessitate holding the front line very strongly.

It was thought that by organising a line of defence closer in rear of the front line, and by arranging for the manning of the oblique lines of trench elements in case of emergency, the defence could be rendered more elastic and the garrison of the front line be reduced.

But in estimating a reduction in the front-line garrison a very important point had to be considered. This was the lack of depth in the whole defensive system. The southern edge of the plateau was only 5000 yards in rear of the front line. If attacked, the Division would be fighting with its back to a wall, or, more literally, to a chasm. Once the front line was lost, artillery support would prove difficult. A further withdrawal would not only mean the loss of artillery support, but would risk capture of the guns themselves ; for the shifting of even one field-gun in this country entailed enormous labour.

There was, then, no question of an outpost zone and a battle zone. There was only one zone on the Asiago Plateau, and the loss of the foremost line of this would threaten the most serious results.

The first troops of the 23rd Division to move to the plateau were the Divisional Artillery, who on March 23 relieved the Italian artillery covering the right sector and came temporarily under command of the G.O.C. 11th Italian Division.

Hitherto the Allies' defence on the Asiago front has been considered chiefly from the infantry point of view. The novel conditions of the mountain front affected the gunner, perhaps, to an even greater degree than the infantryman. Artillery positions had to be found among the dense pine-woods which covered the steep slopes of the hills on the southern plateau. Everywhere shut in by lofty pine-trees, positions in many places were situated some hundreds of feet above the Allies' front line.

Under such circumstances the skill required for the selection of gun positions was equalled only by the labour of getting the guns into action. The field-gun, with its normally flat trajectory, had not been designed to operate in such country. To render it capable of giving close protection to the infantry in the front line, two courses were open : either the trajectory of the gun must be adapted to the circumstances of the positions, or the natural surroundings of the position must be adapted to the characteristics of the gun.

The Italians had adopted the first, and better, alternative. By the provision of reduced charges they had given the higher trajectory to their guns necessary to clearing the trees and to procuring the steep descent of the shell to close in front of the line to be protected. This method of coping with the difficulty was later adopted by us, but on first taking over, other means had to be employed.

Little trouble was experienced with the howitzers. Excellent positions for these were found in the valleys and also on occasional ledges on the reverse slopes of the hillsides. But the flat trajectory of the 18-pdrs. necessitated their occupying open positions on the forward slope, a "lane" being cut for each gun by sawing off the tops of the trees immediately in front of and below the gun position. The gun itself would be concealed, but few, if any, of the positions were strictly flash-proof. The flash, however, would only be visible to the enemy in prolongation of the lane, the high trees on either side of this preventing a definite location of the gun by cross bearings.

The rocky and precipitous nature of the ground made it difficult to find gun platforms. Consequently, guns of a battery frequently had to be dotted about with little regard to line or interval. The average distance of field artillery positions from the front line was about 1800 yards.

Both limbers and pack-mules were employed in the work of ammunition supply. As in the case of all animal transport in the Division, scarcity of water made it necessary for waggon lines to be established below the plateau.

Following the artillery the remainder of the Division was to move to the plateau by infantry brigade groups, marching first to the Thiene area, whence they would be taken forward by buses.

The first to move was the 68th Infantry Brigade group, which arrived on the plateau in the Carriola area on March 26, and, as a temporary measure, took over the left sector of the Corps front from the 12th Italian Division on the following day.

On the 28th the 70th Infantry Brigade group relieved the Italian troops in the right sector, and the 69th Infantry Brigade group moved to the reserve area on the plateau at Granezza, both coming under command of the G.O.C. 11th Italian Division.

On the 29th General Babington arrived at Granezza and assumed command. The sector was divided into two sections, the 70th Infantry Brigade remaining in the line in occupation of the left, while their troops on the right of the line were relieved by the 69th Infantry Brigade.

Completion of relief was celebrated at Divisional Headquarters by a luncheon party, at which General Babington and his staff were the guests of the G.O.C. 11th Italian Division.

The greatest cordiality prevailed, and the music of an Italian band combined with an excellent menu to induce a blissful oblivion to war. Suddenly conversation ceased : a distant but unmistakable moan had been detected. Rapidly increasing in volume, it was followed by a terrific crash and the abrupt cessation of the band. Valiantly the band resumed in the middle of the bar at which they had been interrupted,

but a minute later were dispersed by a second crash. A third shell—
and the luncheon party came to an informal end. The three shells had
burst within a hundred yards of where generals and staff had been
toasting the Entente.

The general policy of the Austrian artillery for months had been
one of "live and let live." These were the last shells fired on the Divisional front for perhaps a fortnight, and were undoubtedly intended
as a salute to mark the occasion. Such a coincidence was too remarkable to be attributed to mere chance.

The general strategic situation in Europe as affecting the policy
of the Comando Supremo in Italy does not lie within the province of
a history of the 23rd Division. But it is necessary to consider outside
events, and the wider issues involved, in so far as they affected the situation of the Division itself.

This period at which the Division moved to the Asiago front coincided with the darkest days of the Allies in the main theatre of war on
the Western front. So far as the British troops were concerned, Lord
Cavan, the British Commander-in-Chief, made it clear that every sacrifice
was to be made in favour of our armies in France and Flanders. Till
the situation improved in that theatre the British divisions in Italy
must expect no drafts, no reinforcements. Hitherto few casualties had
been sustained in Italy, and there had been little sickness ; units accordingly were well up to strength, and were formed of seasoned troops.
But to risk incurring casualties lightly or with insufficient reason would
be more than ever a crime.

The idle inaction of a purely passive defence, however, could not
but raise the *morale* of the Austrians, who it was known were being
urged by Germany to open a fresh offensive on the Italian front, and
would react on the *morale* and discipline of our own troops. Further,
if by a successful offensive a signal defeat could be inflicted on the
Austrians, the casualties incurred by the Allies would be justified by the
assistance that would be rendered by such a success to the armies in
France. A gain of ground, too, would deepen our own defence, and
relieve us from the embarrassing position of clinging with our eyebrows
to the edge of a precipice.

An offensive action on the Asiago front on a large scale, in which the
British and French were to take part, had accordingly been planned by

the Comando Supremo for the spring. It will be recounted later how
this large operation, which was continually cancelled and brought forward again in some modified form throughout the spring and summer of
1918, was finally abandoned in September. But the policy of the 23rd
Division on taking over the line was dictated largely by this project,
one of the first essentials to the success of which lay in placing the wide
No Man's Land separating our defences from the Austrian front under
British control. On the other hand, the approach of warmer weather,
with the possibility opened to the enemy for offensive operations, made
the organisation of the defence of more serious importance than it had
been during the winter months. It was decided to restrain during the
first few days the ardour of our artillery, those notorious disturbers of
the peace, till the Division had settled down to the new conditions of
the sector, and a scheme had been carried out to organise a defence on
less rigid lines than those of the existing system.

On taking over, the dispositions of the infantry in the line had been
so far affected by those of the Italian division relieved that the garrison
allotted to the front line, though not equal in proportion to that of the
relieved division, was still of much greater strength than had been
customary in France. The distance of the nearest supporting line and
other considerations already mentioned indeed made these dispositions
necessary.

The sector, which had a frontage of about 3600 yards, was divided
into two sections, each held by one infantry brigade, strengthened by
certain machine-guns of the 23rd Battalion Machine-Gun Corps, and
each supported by one brigade of Field Artillery. The defences of the
right section ran through dense woods, which extended beyond the
front line to form a belt of trees narrowing from right to left, greatly
restricting the field of fire. On this flank direct observation to the front
was further denied to the front line by the low Villa dal Brun-Guardinalti-
Poslen ridge, which, rising from the Granezza-Asiago road, ran roughly
east and west at a distance of between 200 and 400 yards forward of
the front line, Poslen, at the western point, being at a distance from the
front line of some 200 yards.

The defences of the left section, except for some 50 yards on the
extreme right, were sited in the open. An open glacis forward of the
front line provided an admirable field of fire throughout.

Q

The left of the Division rested on the dense pine-woods which clothed the slopes of Mt. Lemerle. The boundary of the sector, running down the northern slope of this mountain, descended steeply till the forward defences were reached, when the wooded ground sloped gently towards the valley of the Ghelpac.

The edge of these woods, which extended for a considerable distance beyond the front line of the left sector, ran forward at right angles from the point of junction of the two divisions. A hostile advance on this flank would accordingly be concealed from the left brigade of the 23rd Division.

It will be seen that the nature of the two sections was entirely different. In the right section the advantage gained by the concealment afforded by the woods was largely counteracted by the restricted field of fire, while in the left section, with its fine field of fire, movement by day between front and support line was in most places impossible, owing to the open nature of the ground and the steep rise in rear of the front line.

A somewhat detailed description of the sector has been necessary in order that the events of June 15, when arrived at later, may be better understood.

Before closing, special mention must be made of a prominent feature in the defence which was to play an important part that day. Immediately in rear of the right of the front line and parallel to it lay a steep razor-backed ridge some 800 yards in length, known as the San Sisto ridge. The forward slopes of this ridge were thickly wooded ; the rear slopes, bare or only sparsely wooded, fell some 80 feet below the summit to a rough road, which ran along the valley, separating the ridge from the main height, of which it was an underfeature. At its eastern end it fell steeply to the left boundary of the French, the Granezza-Asiago road.

The San Sisto ridge was the key to the position on this flank. Important to the British defence, it was still more vital to that of the French [1] on the right, whose position was open to enfilade fire from its eastern end.

The headquarters of the right brigade were established at Pria del Acqua, a road junction on the Granezza-Asiago road, those of the left brigade at Mt. Torle.

[1] At this time the 24th Division (General Priou).

Divisional Headquarters were established at Granezza, where were also located the headquarters of the C.R.A., C.R.E., and Machine-Gun and Pioneer Battalions.

Just prior to the Division taking over the new front a change had occurred in the Divisional Staff, owing to the appointment of Colonel Evans as Brig.-General on the General Staff in France. It is impossible to overrate the value of the work done by Colonel Evans during the fifteen months in which he had been G.S.O. 1 of the Division. The immense amount of detail with which the staff was called on to deal in the tremendous trench-to-trench battles of the 1917 campaign in Flanders added greatly to the labour and responsibility of one in Colonel Evans' position ; perusal of the Divisional operation orders of that period will alone convey some idea of the extent to which success was due to a staff officer who had gained the confidence and affection of his commander and all in the Division with whom he came into contact.

Colonel Evans' place had been taken by Lieut.-Colonel H. R. Sandilands, 5th (Northumberland) Fusiliers.

The reorganisation of machine-gun companies to form one battalion of sixty-four machine-guns was introduced in the 23rd Division on April 1. The 68th, 69th, 70th, and 194th Companies were placed under command of Lieut.-Colonel M. C. H. Barker, to form A, B, C, and D Companies of the 23rd Machine-Gun Battalion.

Lieut.-Colonel Barker, who was replaced in command of the 11th West Yorkshire Regiment by Lieut.-Colonel H. H. Hudson, only held his new appointment for a few days. His distinguished services to the Division had long since earned him recommendation for promotion, and on April 12 he left the 23rd Division on appointment to command a brigade in France.

He was succeeded in command of the Machine-Gun Battalion by Lieut.-Colonel Lindsay, whose place in command of the 13th Durham Light infantry was filled by Lieut.-Colonel E. H. Clarke.

On March 30 the 7th Division (Major-General Shoubridge) arrived on the plateau, and took over the left sector from the 68th Infantry Brigade, which was withdrawn to Divisional reserve, two battalions being placed at Granezza, and two battalions below the plateau at Mare. If called upon to support the defence, a long and arduous climb would have to be negotiated by these latter battalions, but their location was dictated by the severity of the weather, which demanded shelter for troops in reserve.

Accommodation on the plateau was scarce, and transport difficulties prevented the supply of more huts. Rival claims to the few huts available for the accommodation of the men in the forward area were soon presented for the arbitration of the Division Staff, and territorial rights were argued with all the vigour of a peace conference. The unfortunate arbitrator on such occasions cut a sorry figure, as a fair decision could only be arrived at by compromise giving full satisfaction to neither claimant.

The Division's first tour on the Asiago front passed comparatively quietly. The cold was severe, and clear bright days alternated with heavy snowstorms. Wood, however, was plentiful, and when it had been dried there was no lack of fuel. The health of the troops was excellent, and they very soon cultivated the wind and muscles of mountaineers.

During the first few days our artillery lay low in order not to disclose its presence on the front. Later, daily shoots on the enemy's defence evoked little reply. The Austrian artillery at this period seemed deliberately to decline to be drawn.

But despite the severity of the weather, and the necessity for getting accustomed to the novel conditions of the mountain front, the policy of a purely passive defence was not followed.

There were several small ruined buildings in No Man's Land which the Austrians were suspected of occupying at night. Such an outrage on neutral territory could not be countenanced, and the 70th Infantry Brigade immediately set to work to investigate matters.

On the second night in the line, March 29, 2nd Lieutenant Swire, 11th Sherwood Foresters, led a platoon against some buildings at Morar, and attacked an Austrian post that was found in occupation. Three prisoners were taken ; the remainder of the garrison were killed. The prisoners belonged to the 38th Honved (Hungarian) Division, not before identified on this front. In recognition of their bold and skilful leading in this, the first of many raids by the British on the Asiago Plateau, 2nd Lieutenant Swire and Sergeant Redfern were awarded the Italian Silver Medal of Valour.

On April 2 the 69th Infantry Brigade secured a deserter from the

WINTER ON THE ASIAGO PLATEAU.

Austrian artillery; two nights later 2nd Lieutenant Meikle and three other ranks of the 8th Yorkshire Light Infantry captured a prisoner while on patrol.

Another patrol, 2nd Lieutenant Walker and 15 other ranks of the 8th York and Lancaster Regiment, surrounded and captured an enemy post on the night of April 8, taking two prisoners and killing the remainder of the garrison. On the following night 2nd Lieutenants Flory and Mead of the 9th York and Lancaster Regiment, with 25 other ranks, attacked an Austrian post and secured two prisoners.

So within ten days of taking over the line the 70th Infantry Brigade had captured eight prisoners and had accounted for many more of the enemy in raids on their posts, honours being divided between the four battalions of the brigade. Things were beginning to stir on the Asiago Plateau, and the enemy, if he had been in any doubt before, now realised that there had been changes in the mountains.

For the rest, time was chiefly spent in reorganising and strengthening the forward lines of defence and in reconnoitring the rear defences. This reconnaissance was both arduous and difficult. The trenches, running up the mountain-side through dense woods, were in places filled with snow, and impossible to follow. The explorer, having missed the line, would often only rediscover it by finding himself up to his armpits in the soft snow which filled the trench.

With the expectation of milder weather there was anxious speculation as to which of two events would occur first: an Austrian offensive inspired by the German successes in France, or the allied offensive which was in contemplation on the Asiago front. On April 19 we received the first of many warnings of an Austrian attack. They were to attack the following day, but nothing came of it.[1]

Since the Division arrived in Italy four months had been spent in the line. Rest was now to be given to it.

On April 21 relief by the 48th Division commenced, and on the 23rd command of the right sector passed to Major-General Fanshawe.

On relief, the Division was withdrawn to the plains and placed in G.H.Q. reserve, Divisional Headquarters being established in the pic-

---

[1] The Italian intelligence was very well informed. It will be seen by Marshal Boroevic's letter, which appears later in this chapter, that it was the Austrians' intention to attack early in the spring.

turesquely situated palazzo of the Conte dal Porto at Trissino, over-looking the beautiful valley of the river Agno, in the neighbourhood of which the main portion of the Division was accommodated.

At first room could not be found for the whole Division in this area, and 68th Infantry Brigade Headquarters and two battalions were placed some distance away in the G.H.Q. training area at Torreglia, but later accommodation was found for them closer at hand at Piazzola.

The 69th Infantry Brigade was located in and about the small town of Cornedo, the 70th Infantry Brigade in the more important Arzignano. The Divisional Artillery occupied the village Montecchio Maggiore, which stands immediately below a high rocky ridge crowned by the ruins of two castles. Tradition claims these as the homes of Romeo and Juliet. One had undoubtedly served as a country seat to the family of Montecchio (Shakespeare's Montagu), but cold history must now shatter the illusions of our romantic gunners as to there being any stronger backing to the tales told to them by the local Giulettas of to-day.

The area as a whole was perhaps more " out of the war " and restful than any the Division had lived in since September 1914. Billets were good, and the inhabitants most friendly and hospitable, though the curse of Babel created occasional misunderstandings. For instance an officer who had been treated with the most cordial hospitality repaid it in all innocence by the most inconceivably churlish act. Every evening a smiling Italian maid would bring to his room a jug of hot water just before dinner. At last an evening came when, after having deposited the usual jug, she returned in a state of great excitement and distress, crying out frantically, " Brodo, brodo ! " The officer did his best to console her, but to no avail. Finally, wishing to get on with his toilet, he cheered her with " That's all right, old thing, don't you worry," pushed her from the room, locked the door, poured out his hot water, and com-pleted his toilet. He was, however, honestly anxious to help. So on arriving at the dinner-table he asked the Italian interpreter what the meaning of " Brodo " was. " Brodo," replied the interpreter, " why, broth ! " " Heavens ! " cried the officer in consternation, " I thought it looked rather dirty. I've washed in the family soup ! " So that family went supperless to bed.

It has been said earlier in this history that " rest " during the Great War was a comparative term. Purely as a " rest area " the Trissino district lacked nothing. Games could be played in the few fields left free of vines, and evenings be spent at the Arzignano Theatre listening to the latest performance of the " Dumps," without fear of interruption by hostile bombs.

But it lacked nearly everything that was necessary to a training area. The country was closely cultivated, and such things as rifle ranges, assault courses, &c., which formed part and parcel of a rest area in France, had still to be constructed. In view of the offensive operations which were projected for an early date, this was felt to be a great disadvantage. Practice in climbing, however, was at least possible in the Cornedo district.

On April 28 General Montuori, the commander of the Sixth Army, of which the British Corps formed part, accompanied by Lord Cavan and H.R.H. the Prince of Wales, inspected the 70th Infantry Brigade. It may be said here that during the six months that the Division formed part of the Sixth Army, scarcely a week passed in which General Montuori did not show his keen interest for the welfare of the British troops under his command. Typical of his kindliness was the presentation of a football cup to be competed for by troops of the XIV. Corps. As a result of this interest, the generous tributes which he paid to our troops were the more appreciated, since they were felt to be not merely formal compliments to an allied nation, but the true sentiments of a commander closely associated with his troops.

The Allies' offensive was now planned to take place early in June. The main attack on the Asiago front was to be delivered by the French on the right, the 23rd Division in the centre, and the 7th Division on the left. It was first necessary, however, to withdraw the 7th Division to rest.

It was arranged accordingly for the 48th Division to side-slip for the relief of the 7th Division in the left sector, while the 23rd Division simultaneously took over the right sector, within which lay their front of attack. These dispositions were completed by May 19.

It was in the course of moving forward to these reliefs that influenza appeared.

The 23rd Division claims, among other distinctions, that of having been the first British Division in the war to have encountered what later became the scourge of the armies in Europe. On the first march from the Trissino area no fewer than eighty men fell out on the wayside from one company of a battalion of the 70th Infantry Brigade. They had been billeted at Arzignano, a great centre of the silk industry, and the diagnosis of the rank and file attributed the catastrophe to a disease caught from silkworms ! With every respect to the medical profession, it may be said that the rank and file were at least unanimous in their diagnosis, while the disease as it spread first through the battalion and then through brigade, remained for some time a matter of controversy among the medical officers. The one would claim for it all the symptoms of influenza, while the other would hold that whatever the malady might be, at least it was *not* influenza.

It *was* influenza, not silkworms, and in view of the projected operations it created a very serious situation. At this time, fortunately, it took a very mild form. For three days only the victim was placed *hors de combat*, and recovery was quick. No means could be found of checking the spread of the epidemic. There appeared, however, to be no recurrence of the disease, and it could only be hoped that it would spread sufficiently quickly to render the Division immune before operations commenced.

During the next few weeks the disease attacked the Division regularly and methodically, unit by unit. It then spread to the 48th Division, who were most unfortunate in being weakened by this cursed sickness at a critical time when the 23rd Division had seen the worst of it.

Conditions on the Asiago Plateau had greatly changed since the Division's previous tour. The weather had become mild and pleasant, the snow had mostly disappeared, and the advent of spring had combined with the general provocation of our own and the French guns to rouse the Austrian artillery from their customary lethargy. Preparations were actively pushed forward for the projected offensive. Additional tracks for moving troops forward were made, advanced dumps of ammunition and engineering material created, battle headquarters selected, and forward positions for the artillery to support the attack were prepared. The attack to be carried out by the 23rd Division was a most formidable operation, though not perhaps as severe as the task allotted to the 7th Division, whose early advance would be faced by the deep gorge of the Val d'Assa.

In the early stages of the attack the advance would be supported by the fire of three Field Artillery brigades and of seventy-two pieces of British and Italian Heavy Artillery. No great difficulty was anticipated in the capture of the Austrian forward defences on the Asiago plain. But the line of the final objective ran along the lofty ridge of Mt. Mosciagh, which stood some 2000 feet above the plain overlooking the Val di Portule to the north. Infantry advancing against these heights would be faced by trenches sited on the steep wooded slopes of a wide reentrant formed by a rugged spur rising on the left to Mt. Interotto and the southern bend of the hills to Mt. Catz on the right. Mt. Interotto, on which some old Alpini barracks were situated, was to be captured by the 23rd Division ; Mt. Catz was to be taken by the French after carrying the town of Asiago.

For the Field Artillery to support the last phase of the attack, it would be necessary for the guns to move forward. This would be a laborious undertaking, and for a certain period the infantry advance would be covered only by Heavy Artillery, trench-mortars, and six batteries of Italian Mountain Artillery.

The capture of the final objective on Mt. Mosciagh would have been a most formidable operation, but one which Lord Cavan consistently held was not beyond the power of British troops.

The unique nature of the proposed operation, as far as the British army is concerned, lends a certain interest to the detailed instructions which were issued in preparation for the final operation order. But the narrow limits of a history do not admit of giving the details of an operation that never materialised. A point occurring in the artillery problem, which was of a nature both difficult and original, will, however, serve to indicate the sort of factors which had to be considered. When the infantry commenced to climb, distance as the usual basis of calculation for the rate of advance changed to height, the climbing power of the infantry being reckoned as from 150 to 200 metres per hour.

Though the scheme of this operation, which was in contemplation throughout the summer of 1918, was modified later on other fronts of attack, the final objective allotted to the 23rd Division remained practically the same.

On May 25 Brig.-General T. S. Lambert, who had served the 23rd Division in command of the 69th Infantry Brigade for over two years, was appointed to command the 32nd Division in France. General

Lambert had taken a prominent and distinguished part in every great victory the Division had won—Contalmaison, Le Sars, Hill 60, and the Menin road. His energy and initiative, his supreme confidence in himself and his men, and, above all, his unswerving loyalty to his Divisional Commander, had been in no small degree responsible for the unbroken success of the 23rd Division. His loss was keenly felt, but it was realised that it was only due to the tardy recognition of his merits that the Division had not been deprived of his services long before.

He was succeeded in command of the 69th Infantry Brigade by Lieut.-Colonel A. B. Beauman, a young officer who had earned promotion by distinguished services in command of the 1st South Staffordshire Regiment in the 7th Division.

At the moment this change in command seemed to occur at a most critical time. The most intricate phase of the projected attack had been allotted to the 69th Infantry Brigade. The front was unknown to Brig.-General Beauman, who had hastily to acquaint himself with the details of General Lambert's plans.

But events proved that his study of these plans was thrown away. On May 25 orders postponing the grand offensive *sine die* were received, together with an intimation that an attack on a less ambitious scale would probably be undertaken.

In the meantime night patrols had been active in No Man's Land, and had discovered that the Austrians had withdrawn their posts into or close to their own front line. It was here, then, that the identification of the enemy had to be sought.

A raid was planned for the night of June 1 by the 11th Northumberland Fusiliers against a group of three buildings, about 200 yards forward of the Austrian front line, known as South Ave. The raiders were organised into three parties : an eastern and western party, each under an officer, to rush the two forward buildings ; a third party, consisting of a section under the command of a lance-corporal, to attack a short line of trench east of the Ave road.

The operation was to be supported by the fire of 6-in. howitzers and the guns of the right (102nd) brigade of the Divisional Artillery.

At 11 P.M. the raiders were assembled at a point about 300 yards from their objective, and, on the signal of a whistle, advanced to the attack under an artillery barrage.

The eastern party rushed the house on the right, where the one Austrian found was made prisoner. The western party hurled bombs through the window of the second house, and, entering, discovered three of the enemy lying dead. The third building was unoccupied.

The greater number of the enemy were, unexpectedly, found in occupation of the trench. The lance-corporal led his party to a bombing attack against this, and succeeded in killing five and capturing two of the enemy. The whole party then withdrew with its three prisoners, who were identified as belonging to the 38th Honved Division.

In forwarding the report of this raid, the Divisional Commander remarked that "the accurate shooting of the artillery not only saved casualties by neutralising all rifle and machine-gun fire from the enemy's trenches, but also may reasonably be expected to have inflicted further casualties on them."

A week later a similar operation was planned on the 69th Infantry Brigade front against Morar, a group of houses about 1000 yards west of South Ave, situated, like the latter, just south of the enemy's front line, and suspected of harbouring an Austrian outpost.

D Company of the 8th Yorkshire Regiment, under command of Captain J. Tilly, was ordered to carry out the raid, supported by the 103rd Brigade R.F.A. (Lieut.-Colonel Curling).

The company was divided into three parties, with the idea of delivering a simultaneous attack from three sides. Captain Tilly and 2nd Lieutenant Wilkinson, with two platoons, were to attack from the east ; 2nd Lieutenant Lister's platoon from the south ; and 2nd Lieutenant Oldfield's platoon from the west.

The raiders left our lines on the night of June 8 to assemble for attack. An enemy working-party was detected in the position fixed for assembly, making it necessary to change orders and assemble slightly further from the objective on the southern side of the Ghelpac.

At zero hour the supporting artillery crashed on Morar, then lifted to clear the way for the infantry assault. The enemy were on the alert ; rifle and machine-gun fire immediately opened from Morar and the front line, and an attempt was made to put down a trench-mortar barrage.

The eastern party, slightly losing direction, arrived at a point south-east of the village. Tilly, moving forward to reconnoitre, was severely wounded. Wilkinson thereupon rushed forward, followed by his men, and, succeeding in forcing his way through the wire which covered the position, exterminated a post of three men.

Lister's platoon in the meanwhile had made repeated gallant attempts to force an entry from the south, but were held up by wire and by the machine-gun fire and bombs of the enemy. Though they failed to effect an entry, they, nevertheless, kept the garrison occupied while Oldfield's platoon rushed the position from the west. On this flank a double sentry post was encountered. One sentry was killed, the other taken, and a house at the south-west corner of the village was stormed. Here ten Austrians were made prisoners.

Thirty minutes had now passed, and 2nd Lieutenant Lister, to whom command of the company had fallen, gave the signal for withdrawal. The troops immediately disengaged, and gained the British line in good order, together with their eleven prisoners.

The enemy had offered a very stiff resistance to the attack, but casualties among the raiders were extraordinarily light. Three men had been slightly wounded. But though, numerically, the losses sustained by the 8th Yorkshire Regiment had been slight, they were rendered heavy by the death of the leader of the raid. Captain Tilly, whose gallant service to the 23rd Division has been recounted in previous pages of this history, succumbed to his wounds.

During the past weeks the hostile artillery had become increasingly active, giving colour to the persistent rumours that an Austrian attack was imminent. The idea of an allied offensive on a modified scale had, however, not been abandoned.

On June 12 orders were received for an attack on the Austrian position on the plateau. In this attack, which was fixed for June 18, the first objective to be captured by the 23rd Division was represented by a line running, roughly, west from the northern extremity of Asiago.

The proposed operation would greatly improve the situation of the French attacking on our right. But the 23rd Division, by advancing its line to the limited extent proposed, would be exchanging for a commanding position, largely concealed from observation, one whose forward defences and communications would be completely exposed, without any corresponding advantages beyond a slight deepening of the defence.

The 23rd Division was to attack on a three-brigade front. Orders were issued on June 13 for making the necessary dispositions preparatory to attack. In accordance with these orders, the 68th Infantry Brigade by June 14 held three battalions in their front line in place of the two battalions which ordinarily occupied the front line in defence. Certain battalions took up advanced headquarters which had been selected for the attack. Forward artillery positions had been selected for supporting the attack, some of these on the left being sited almost immediately in rear of the infantry front line. Many of the guns had already occupied these positions ; others were to move forward before dawn on June 15.

Late in the afternoon of June 14, while these arrangements were being continued, the most certain information was received that the Austrians intended to launch a heavy attack on the following day.

Very positive rumours of intended hostile attack had been frequent, and had hitherto proved vain. But on this occasion there seemed little doubt that the Austrians were, indeed, to make their supreme effort.

According to the information received, the attack would be preceded by a gas bombardment. On the Asiago Plateau the British front would be included in this bombardment, but not, it was thought, in the actual assault, which would probably not be delivered west of the French front.

At this time the 70th Infantry Brigade occupied the right section of the Divisional front, covered by the 102nd Brigade R.F.A. ; the 68th Infantry Brigade, in occupation of the left section, were covered by the 103rd Brigade R.F.A. The 22nd Brigade R.F.A. of the 7th Division, lent for the proposed attack of June 18, also supported the front.

The 70th Infantry Brigade held two battalions in the front line, one battalion in support in the second line, and one battalion in reserve, of which two companies were immediately in rear of the second line— one at Pria dell'Acqua, and one at Granezza.

The 68th Infantry Brigade held three battalions in the front line, the second line being garrisoned by one company from each of the flank battalions and one company from the battalion in brigade reserve. The remaining companies of the reserve battalion were placed at and in rear of Mt. Torle.

Till recently the infantry brigade in Divisional reserve had held three battalions on the plateau, two being in huts at Granezza, and the third further forward in camp in the Valle di Croce. Bad weather and sickness, however, had necessitated the withdrawal of this last battalion to Cavaletto just below the edge of the plateau. June 14 accordingly found the 69th Infantry Brigade with two battalions at Granezza, one at Cavaletto, and one, some 3000 or 4000 feet below the plateau, at Mare.

The French on our right, similarly to the British, had been occupied during June 13 and 14 in making dispositions for attack. The 23rd (French) Division (General Bonfait), in occupation of the French sector, had closed on its right, and three battalions of the 24th (French) Division, one of the 108th, one of the 50th, and one of the 126th Regiment, had been thrust in between the 23rd (French) Division and the 23rd (British) Division.

These three battalions of different regiments were temporarily under command of Colonel Bontemps of the 126th Regiment. The battalion of the 108th Regiment on the extreme left was in liaison with the Sherwood Foresters on the right of the 70th Infantry Brigade.

The remainder of the infantry of the 24th (French) Division was disposed at various points between the plains and the plateau, with headquarters at St Giorgio. General Bonfait commanded units of both divisions in the line.

The French were therefore in greater strength on the plateau than usual, but were at the disadvantage of being under a temporary organisation, by which both General Bonfait and Colonel Bontemps had units other than their own under their command.

The 48th Division was still in the left sector of the British front.

Following the warning that had been received, orders were issued to brigades in the line to be in immediate readiness to occupy battle positions, to watch the front closely with reconnoitring patrols, to keep " wire-watching " patrols particularly active, and to ensure that all precautions against gas were being observed. Battalions of the reserve brigade at Cavaletto and Mare were to be held ready to move at half an hour's notice. The Division thus warned, those to whom it was admissible retired to rest in complete confidence.

At 3 A.M. on June 15 a heavy hostile bombardment suddenly opened. Guns of both light and heavy calibre were employed by the enemy, and shells of every description—gas, shrapnel, and high-explosive—rained on the whole area from the front line to Granezza. The front line and the Kaberlaba Valley were heavily bombarded with gas ; shrapnel was mostly fired at the second line. Divisional Headquarters and the reserve area were subjected to rapid concentrations of gas-shell, followed by high-explosive shell in large numbers.

As an early result of the bombardment all forward telephone-wires were cut. These it had not been possible to bury owing to the rocky nature of the soil ; shallow trenches, providing the barest protection to the wires against shrapnel, were all that it had been possible to construct. Forward communication became dependent on runners, and for a considerable period the Divisional Commander remained in ignorance of the situation in the line. Rear wires, however, were unaffected, and the 8th Yorkshire Regiment was ordered from Mare to Granezza.

The 9th South Staffordshire Regiment (Pioneers) was ordered to withdraw for protection to the marginal line at the southern edge of the plateau, and to remain in this position till called on for its special duties.

Bombardment of the front system and reserve area continued with varying intensity. ˜Quickening at 4 A.M., it slackened at 5.15 A.M., quickening again at 5.45 A.M., and remaining intense.

In the meantime two night patrols sent out by the 68th Infantry Brigade from the left section had detected and reported the assembly of the enemy's infantry opposite the Divisional front, and had remained watching them closely. This report was communicated to the troops in the line in time for them to anticipate an assault on the Divisional front, which now seemed clearly to be included in the Austrian plan.

Day broke in heavy mist, and visibility remained bad throughout the day. The mist, while making it difficult for attacking troops to maintain touch and direction, favoured attack in safeguarding the early stage of advance from the rifle and machine-gun fire of the defence. The thick mist, too, made it impossible for the artillery to bring observed fire on to the attack.

The action of our artillery in the opening phase of the Austrian attack requires explanation. The question of when and where the artillery defensive barrage should be brought down on the British front in the event of a hostile attack had been the subject of considerable discussion. It was agreed that this barrage should be placed close in front of the front line. But if brought down on this line immediately on report of hostile assembly for attack, the barrage would cut off picquets posted in certain sections of the defence in advance of the front line. To allow for the withdrawal of these picquets and of such patrols as might be out in No Man's Land, it had been ordered that on report of a hostile assembly the artillery should open a counter-preparation scheme designed to break up the enemy's concentration by bombardment of his front line. While this was in progress our advanced infantry would withdraw to their front line. In the absence of information that the enemy were advancing to the assault, this counter-preparation scheme would be continued for a period of one and a half hours. At the conclusion of this definite period the artillery would sweep back across No Man's Land to the barrage line.

Now it will be remembered that the information received had suggested that the British front would be subjected to bombardment but not assault. Our artillery had replied vigorously to the hostile bombardment, but received no information of the enemy's assembly for attack, which was concealed by the thick mist which obscured the whole front. The intended assault on the British front had only become evident on the report of the infantry patrols who had detected his assembly. When wires were cut, the artillery detailed forward observing officers and runners. Though the work that these did was in every way admirable, it could, at best, only effect a very slow transmission of intelligence.

As a result, the report of the enemy's assembly was to such an extent delayed that the artillery were still employed on the one and a half hours' counter-preparation scheme when the enemy first advanced to the assault.

Suddenly at 7 A.M. two machine-guns under 2nd Lieutenant Skiller, posted on the right flank of the left brigade, detected and dispersed advanced parties of the enemy on Poslen ridge and about Casa del Bella. A few minutes later a British patrol, with all except the sergeant in command wounded, having withdrawn stubbornly in front of the advancing masses of the enemy, reached the front line. Immediately afterwards the Austrian infantry, headed by assault troops, bombers, flammenwerfer, and machine-gunners, were observed close at hand advancing to the assault along the whole front of the left brigade.

As the hostile infantry emerged from the mist they were met by a devastating fire from the rifles and machine-guns of the front line.

The Austrian storm troops, with unexpected gallantry, struggled for-ward regardless of heavy losses. On the right they were shot down by the 13th Durham Light Infantry on the wire protecting the front line. On the left a party of ten, with supreme determination, gained the front line trench itself, to meet instant death at the hands of the 11th Northumberland Fusiliers. On the front of the 12th Durham Light Infantry, in the centre, the attack was not pressed with the same vigour.

The advanced troops of the enemy had been annihilated ; the follow-ing waves faltered, then broke. The attack was completely checked. For close on three hours ineffectual efforts were made to rally the at-tacking forces to a further advance on the front of the 68th Infantry Brigade ; then at 9.45 A.M. the Austrians, having abandoned their first effort on this flank, were seen to be withdrawing to their own lines, or, thoroughly disorganised, to be seeking what shelter could be found in the folds of ground in No Man's Land.

The enemy had, however, in the meantime met with considerable success further to the left. Report had been received at 8.40 A.M. that the Austrians had succeeded in penetrating the front line on the right of the 48th Division, and were threatening to turn the left flank of the 68th Infantry Brigade.

To meet this danger Major Gill, in command of the 11th Northumber-land Fusiliers, had thrown back a defensive flank towards what was known as the Boscon Switch. Lieutenant Vizard shifted the position of his two machine-guns (L9 and L10) to support this change of front. The troops holding this flank remained heavily engaged, but the enemy's progress had been checked. The left flank of the Division had been secured by the initiative of its subordinate commanders.

It was in this phase of the action that the gallant conduct of Lieu-tenant J. S. Youll of the 11th Northumberland Fusiliers earned the Victoria Cross. Two accounts can be given of the behaviour of this splendid young officer, who was to lay down his life for his country before the close of the war. The first is the official report, which covered his re-commendation ; the second, a humble but human document,[1] which must form as glowing a tribute as has ever been paid to a soldier's gallantry :—

" For exceptional gallantry and conspicuous devotion to duty during

[1] Communicated by General Babington.

R

the enemy's attack on our line south-west of Asiago on June 15, 1918. This officer was in command of a patrol, and when the enemy's barrage opened it fell on the party. He, therefore, sent his men back to safety, himself remaining to observe the situation. On eventually returning to our line he 'found it impossible to rejoin his company, and reported to the right company of the Division on our left. When the enemy attacked he maintained his position with several men of different units until the troops on his left had given way, and an enemy machine-gun was firing at him from the rear. He then rushed the gun, and having himself killed most of the team, he opened fire on the enemy with the captured gun, and inflicted heavy casualties. Finding that the enemy had established himself in the front line of the Division on our left, he collected a small party of men, and during the morning led and carried out three separate counter-attacks. On each occasion he drove the enemy out of his position, but found that his left flank was exposed, and that the enemy were firing on him from the rear, and was each time forced to come into line with the troops on his left. Throughout the fighting, by his complete disregard of his personal safety and by his dash and gallantry, he set a magnificent example."

The second account is given in the following letter addressed to Lieutenant Youll :—

BRITISH RED CROSS
AND ORDER OF ST JOHN.

DEAR SIR,

    i am writing these few lines to you as i felt i must hoping you wont think me exceeding my duty as officers like you are worthy of the best recommendation and I should like to have one like you in charge of the platoon i was in for you are the sort of scrapper i like i could go anywhere with you and dear sir i think i am right i only heard some of the N.F. talking about different things and I took it you was the officer who come to where i was in charge of a section guarding a gap on our Batt. front when we found we were cut off on the 15th i believe you came in the Oxf and Bucks front if so you are the same i am pleased to have had the pleasure to see you in action for it puts heart in any man when they have a good officer and I have been in a scrap or too and it is some time since I saw one to equal you and Dear Sir you must excuse my writing as i have got one through the wrist and an explosive bullet in the calf of the leg and it has made a big hole in it and now dear sir i think this is all i remain,

Your obedient Cpl Stratford 18430

A Company 1/4 Ox & Bucks Lt. Infantry.

Sir i cant put my address as they keep shifting me all the time.

While these events had been taking place a most determined attack had been made on the right section, held by the 70th Infantry Brigade. Possibly by intention, but most probably owing to faulty arrangement, the attack was not launched on this flank till fifteen minutes after the advance against the left.

The enemy's bombardment had been very severe on the front line of the right section, the 11th Sherwood Foresters in particular suffering heavy casualties from enfilade fire directed from Gallio. In the right company of this battalion the company commander was killed, and all officers became casualties.

The front line of the 70th Infantry Brigade was covered by four officer's picquets, posted on the high ground west of Villa del Brun, and by four machine-guns, of which two (R1 and R2) were placed just south of Villa del Brun, and two (R3 and R4) just east of the San Sisto-Ave road. Picquets had orders to withdraw in face of a hostile attack in force.

The artillery defensive barrage line on this portion of the front, where the picquets were only a short distance in advance of the front line, had been placed, contrary to the general rule, outside the picquet line. This fact and the delay in the Austrian advance enabled B Battery (Major Stead) and D Battery (Major Antrobus) of the 102nd Brigade R.F.A. to get their guns on barrage lines before the enemy advanced to the attack.

At 7.15 A.M. the Austrian infantry advanced from their assembly positions.

Realising the serious nature of the attack, and being assured that the front line was prepared, three picquets withdrew. That on the left under Lieutenant Kempton, 9th Yorks and Lancs, unfortunately held on too long. Only two men of this picquet succeeded in regaining the front line to report that their post had been heavily bombarded, and later surrounded and overwhelmed by the enemy's infantry.

The French on our right at the same time withdrew their troops from the advanced work at Capitello Pennar, in accordance with their arrangements for meeting a heavy attack.

One of the machine-guns posted at Villa del Brun had been destroyed by shell-fire about 4.30 A.M.; the other, R2, now engaged the enemy with great effect. 2nd Lieutenant A. C. Higgins in command of this sub-section, although wounded and later badly shaken by a shell-burst, maintained the gun in action, firing 1000 rounds in all, till forced by an enemy bombing party to withdraw to the front line, where he continued for twenty minutes to engage the enemy with the rifle-fire of his detachment till compelled again to withdraw.

The machine-guns R3 and R4 (2nd Lieutenant Morrison) farther to the left observed the enemy advancing at 7.15 A.M. over the Guardinalti ridge, first in small detachments of six or seven in single file, later in larger parties of from twenty to thirty men. Heavy casualties were inflicted on them. The withdrawal of R2 had, however, laid open dead ground to the enemy, who, taking advantage of this, threatened at 8 A.M. to surround the position of the guns R3 and R4, which were accordingly withdrawn to the front line, where they continued to engage hostile infantry and machine-guns which were being brought forward over the Guardinalti ridge in large numbers.

Advancing across the open ground with great determination, the Austrian infantry gained the shelter of woods which masked the front line. The concealment afforded by the trees prevented a favourable target being offered to the rifles of the defence till the enemy came within close distance of the front line. Here, on the left of the 70th Infantry Brigade, the assault was stopped dead by the fire of the 9th Yorks and Lancaster Regiment. Over one hundred of the enemy were killed by this battalion in front of the wire, and many others wounded.

On the right things did not go as well. On this flank the casualties sustained in the bombardment by the 11th Sherwood Foresters had thinned out the garrison to a dangerous degree. Openings, moreover, had occurred in the very formidable wire obstacle which covered the front, caused either by the enemy's artillery fire, or by the failure of returning patrols to close gaps.

At this point some two hundred of the enemy obtained a footing in 150 yards of the front-line trench. Parties of these, with machine-guns and flammenwerfer, further succeeded in working up the steep wooded slope of the San Sisto ridge, which lay immediately in rear of this portion of the line, and in gaining a footing on the crest.

The battalion headquarters of Lieut.-Colonel Hudson, commanding the 11th Sherwood Foresters, were situated at the foot of the southern slope of the ridge. On being informed at about 8.45 A.M. of the penetration of the Austrians to the crest above, Hudson, realising the gravity of the situation, withdrew to the woods in rear of the road running south of the ridge. Here he collected the personnel of his headquarters and a few Italian trench-mortar gunners, and rapidly organised them for counter-attack. Advancing at the head of this small party he stormed the San Sisto ridge, capturing some twenty prisoners, together with a few machine-guns and flammenwerfer, and drove the remainder down the northern slope to the front line.

Accompanied by Sergeant Ellis and three men, Colonel Hudson followed up. Approaching the front line they caught sight of some Austrians in the trench. The sergeant rushed forward, but, quickly observing that the trench was filled with the enemy, he sprang to cover unseen by Colonel Hudson. Hudson ran forward, and, firing on the enemy, called on them to surrender. Believing, presumably, that large numbers were following him down the wooded slope, the Austrians held up their hands, and an officer, covered by Hudson's revolver, came forward to surrender. At this point one of the enemy threw a bomb, killing his own officer and severely wounding Colonel Hudson, who, unable to rise, rolled back to the cover of a communication trench and fell in. The enemy made no attempt to fire on him, and he was withdrawn later to safety.

Before advancing, Colonel Hudson had ordered forward two platoons of his reserve company, and asked for one platoon of the 8th Yorkshire Light Infantry to secure the defence of the San Sisto ridge. Though in great pain, before being taken from the field he gave instructions for the counter-attack to be continued.

The importance of the San Sisto ridge to the defence has been emphasised earlier in this chapter. A false report that it had fallen into the hands of the enemy, which reached Divisional Headquarters, for a time caused some anxiety. As a fact, the greater portion of this extensive position remained in the hands of the Division throughout, though, but for the prompt action of Colonel Hudson, the Austrians might well have succeeded in driving our scattered posts from the entire summit, and by their occupation of the ridge rendered the front line untenable on almost the whole front of the 70th Infantry Brigade and on the left of the French position.[1]

Colonel Hudson was not again to join the Division. The award of the Victoria Cross for his conduct on this occasion was a fitting culmination to a career in the 23rd Division which had been marked by a series of gallant actions at critical junctures.

For the time being the enemy remained in occupation of the gap which now occurred between the two front-line companies (A and D) of the Sherwood Foresters. There was also a serious gap between the left of the Sherwood Foresters and the right of the 9th York and Lancaster Regiment. This was opportunely filled by a party of fifty Italian trench-mortar men led forward by Maggiore Van Heuvel of the Italian Army, who throughout the day showed himself eager to assist the British defence in every possible way.[2]

About 9.30 A.M. large numbers of the enemy, who had emerged from the hostile lines about Sec, were observed advancing down the Asiago-Granezza road against the right of the Division. Machine-guns and a section of field artillery, opening on these, threw them into a state of thorough demoralisation. Reorganising later, they again attempted to advance—this time in extended order,—but were again engaged by machine-guns and dispersed.

By 10 A.M. the hostile advance on this flank had been abandoned, and the enemy remained in small scattered groups all over No Man's Land.

Visibility had now become better, and several of our batteries, assisted by a 6-in. howitzer, got splendid fleeting opportunities towards the Guardinalti ridge, while small parties of the enemy endeavouring to escape artillery fire offered themselves as targets to our machine-guns.

The only danger now was to the left flank of the Division, and it is necessary to return to the situation here, which remained somewhat critical.

By ill-luck, influenza was at its worst in the 48th Division on this day that the Austrians had chosen for their attack. The weakened

[1] The San Sisto ridge was held by C Company, 11th Sherwood Foresters, who found four posts on the 1000-yards crest of the ridge. It was between two of these posts that the Austrians obtained a footing on the crest.

[2] This Italian T.M. unit had taken up a position with a view to supporting the attack of the French on the 18th, who were to have taken over the San Sisto front prior to that date.

garrison of the left sector had been forced from the front line, and now held the strong line of the Lemerle Switch. This switch, running south-west from the Boscon Switch at a distance of from 300 to 1000 yards from the front line, linked up the front-line defence with the second line on the steep slope of Mt. Lemerle. The withdrawal had enabled the Austrians to capture one 4.5-in. howitzer battery of the 7th Divisional Artillery,[1] and to compel three 18-pdr. batteries, including part of A/102 (Major Burnyeat) of the 23rd Divisional Artillery, to cease fire and . withdraw their detachments.

Of these batteries, which were among those who had taken up forward positions in readiness for the British attack planned for June 18, the howitzer battery and A/102 were covering the front of the 68th Infantry Brigade, whose artillery support was accordingly greatly weakened. The 68th Brigade Ammunition Dump, situated at the junction of the Divisions, had also fallen into the hands of the enemy.

The 11th Northumberland Fusiliers still stubbornly held their front line, and the defensive flank thrown back along the Boscon Switch to connect with 48th Division was now occupied by their reserve company, brought forward from the second line. To replace the latter in the second line a company of the 10th Northumberland Fusiliers had been sent forward from the brigade reserve.

Between 10.30 and 11 A.M. No Man's Land on the front of the 68th Infantry Brigade was the scene of continual movement. Numerous carrying parties were observed moving forward, and stretcher-bearers were seen carrying back wounded in large numbers.

In rear of the enemy's lines bodies as strong as 3000 men were reported as being brought forward to reinforce the attack. The targets so offered to the artillery were engaged with great effect.

The intention of the enemy at this stage is not clear. Subsequent examination of prisoners failed to elicit anything beyond the fact that no orders of any kind had been given to them. Till they found themselves in the battle, reserve troops did not even know they were being brought forward to attack.

A tendency for the attack to swerve westwards in front of the 68th Infantry Brigade had been noticeable throughout, but the open exposed ground on this front might account for ill-disciplined troops seeking

[1] Attached to the 23rd Division.

the cover of the woods which lay before the right of the 48th Division.
It is probable that the intention of the Austrian Command was to renew
the attack on the 68th Infantry Brigade, and that such attacks failed to
develop owing to the disorganisation caused by our artillery fire and by
lack of clear orders. On the other hand, the idea of fresh attack on this
flank may have been abandoned in view of the casualties previously
sustained on the open glacis, and the reinforcements have been intended
to hold the 68th Infantry Brigade in position while exploiting the initial
success obtained on the right of the 48th Division.

Whatever the enemy's intention may have been, though desultory
fighting continued on the left of the 68th Infantry Brigade, no further
organised attack was made on this flank. The 48th Division firmly
held the Lemerle Switch, and the situation of the 23rd Division at this
period was that the front line remained intact with the exception of
150 yards of front-line trench in the right section, where the attackers
of the San Sisto ridge remained isolated.

An attempt to launch a fresh attack against the right section from
the Villa del Brun-Guardinalti ridge appeared to be made at 11.30 A.M.,
but an artillery defensive barrage prevented this attack from material-
ising.

To re-establish his front line about San Sisto Brig.-General Gordon
had sent forward from brigade reserve A Company (Captain Horsley)
of the 8th Yorkshire Light Infantry, reinforced by two platoons, for
counter-attack. This was delivered at 1.30 P.M. D Company of the
Sherwood Foresters still held the line on the left. On their right, the
Austrians were in occupation of the trench, while others lay in support
outside the wire. To the right again, the enemy were occupying a small
communication trench running back obliquely from the front line, while
an advanced post of some fifteen men had been placed in the open
between the front line and the communication trench.

The enemy had brought forward several machine-guns, which persuaded Captain Horsley to attempt a bombing attack from the left
flank rather than a frontal assault. A machine-gun under Sergeant
Campbell was placed so as to be able to cover the attack and also bring
enfilade fire on the communication trench.

Two platoons were employed. 2nd Lieutenant Meikle led the attack,
Captain Horsley following with the second platoon. The bombers

advanced with such determination that the Austrians for the most part commenced immediately to surrender, though here and there some showed fight.

Those outside the wire now began to cut their way through and advance to the assistance of their comrades. This was at once stopped by Campbell's machine-gun. Corporal Bennett with a Lewis-gun section dealt successfully with the advanced post in the open, five of whom were shot, the remainder surrendering. The enemy in the communication trench were now cut off ; all resistance ended, and 100 prisoners, together with several machine-guns, were captured.

During the morning, the battalion of the 108th Regiment on the right of the Sherwood Foresters had been reinforced by two companies of the 126th Regiment. One of these latter companies under Captain Fontan, by co-operating in Captain Horsley's counter-attack, rendered valuable assistance.

The gap which had occurred between the right of the Division was now filled, contact being gained with Lieutenant Gautier's company of the 108th.[1] The whole line was once again solidly held. On the front on which attack had been delivered against the Sherwood Foresters some 300 Austrians lay dead.

The defences of the Division were now clear of the enemy, the Austrian attack was exhausted, and the situation was steadily improving. Hostile artillery fire had quietened, and was confined to occasional short bursts of fire. During the afternoon the 48th Division by a successful counter-attack regained part of the ground lost, and the 18-pdr. batteries which had been silenced came into action again. The left defensive flank had been reinforced by the company of the 10th Northumberland Fusiliers previously sent forward to the second line, their place being taken by a second company of the same battalion from brigade reserve.

On the 23rd Divisional front large numbers of the enemy, including hundreds of dead and wounded, were still lying out in No Man's Land, but lacking any fresh large reinforcements, all fear of further attack had passed.

At 4.20 P.M. the 8th Yorkshire Regiment of 69th Infantry Brigade

[1] Lieutenant Gautier at a later date performed the duties of liaison officer to the 23rd Division, and for a time acted as A.D.C. to General Babington, during the absence in hospital of Lord Wodehouse.

was sent forward from Divisional reserve to reinforce brigades in the line, the battalion (less two companies) proceeding to the 68th Infantry Brigade, and A and C Companies to the 70th Infantry Brigade.

All troops of the 23rd Division through the long hours of attack had given splendid proof of their power of resistance. The guns of A and B Companies of the 23rd Machine-Gun Battalion had rendered valuable service. At the outbreak of attack they had been quick to pick up targets and inflicted heavy casualties on the advancing Austrians. Later, on the left, they had given great assistance on the threatened flank, Captain Toynbee, the commander of A Company, reporting in person to Major Gill, and, at the latter's request, employing such men as could be spared from the guns in bringing forward bombs to the hard-pressed infantry. At 10 A.M. Lieut.-Colonel Lindsay, commanding 23rd Machine-Gun Battalion, had been ordered to send forward ten guns from Divisional reserve at Granezza to certain previously selected positions in support. Of these, four guns gained their position in the right section without great difficulty ; the remainder, in their advance to the left section, encountered considerable shell-fire, but were all in position by 2 P.M.

The losses in the machine-gun battalion amounted to 1 officer and 4 other ranks killed, 3 officers and 31 other ranks wounded, 4 other ranks missing. Ten guns were destroyed, three damaged, five mules killed and ten wounded.

The Stokes guns also did good work in the defence. On the right Captain Wale's 70th Light Trench-Mortar Battery had four guns covering the front line, two on the San Sisto ridge and two covering the second line. The forward guns under 2nd Lieutenant Sulman fired 1400 rounds. The right gun was put out of action, the remainder being successfully withdrawn to the San Sisto ridge when the enemy penetrated the line on this flank.

The difficulties of the artillery at the opening of the attack have already been referred to.

As the day went on the field artillery did great execution ; certain guns in advanced positions were run out of their emplacements to engage the enemy at point-blank range. The detachments on the left, who were forced to leave their guns, made good use of their rifles at close quarters, and kept the enemy from approaching the guns.

RETURNING FROM THE LINE.

(Brigadier-General Cary-Barnard and Staff.)

The enemy's artillery had been strongly reinforced under cover of darkness during the previous night ; but concealed positions were difficult for him to find. Our counter-battery groups did great work, many batteries revealed in the open being quickly put out of action by our 6-in. howitzers.

The outstanding features of the day had been Colonel Hudson's brilliant counter-attack on the right and the magnificent fight put up by the 11th Northumberland Fusiliers on the left. This battalion had maintained its position against frontal and incessant flank attacks throughout the day. They had sustained rather more than twice the number of casualties inflicted on the remainder of their brigade, and at 7.10 P.M. they were relieved by the 10th Battalion, and withdrawn to brigade reserve.

The only disquieting feature which remained was that touch with the 48th Division had been again lost during the afternoon. At 8.40 P.M., however, report was received by Divisional Headquarters that the divisions were again in contact.

Except for desultory shelling by the enemy up till midnight, the night passed quietly. Both brigades sent out patrols. Those of the 9th York and Lancaster Regiment brought in 60 prisoners and 2 machine-guns before 10 P.M. At dawn Captain Tester of the same battalion led a patrol to Guardinalti and Ave, and secured two mountain guns. Though observed and sniped, they returned safely with their booty. The patrols of the 68th Infantry Brigade reported the ground to be clear of the enemy, except for dead and wounded, who were lying out in very large numbers.

Day broke on June 16 in mist and drizzle. During the morning the 48th Division regained the whole of their front line by counter-attack, and Divisional sectors were again adjusted. Complete quiet reigned on the front of the 23rd Division and on that of the French, who had maintained their line intact throughout the 15th.

The 23rd Division captured during the battle 230 unwounded prisoners, 127 wounded prisoners, 2 mountain howitzers, 24 machine-guns, and 15 flammenwerfer.

In view of the amount of hostile artillery fire brought on the defence the casualties suffered by the Division may be considered light. They amounted to 8 officers and 86 other ranks killed, 24 officers and 388

other ranks wounded, 1 officer and 48 other ranks missing—a total of
33 officers and 523 other ranks. At Granezza both the C.R.A. and C.R.E.'s
Headquarters were wrecked early in the day, fortunately without
casualty.

Had the enemy given a greater concentration to the very large number
of gas-shells fired early in his bombardment, the casualties inflicted would
probably have been greater.

The Austrian scheme of attack, as disclosed by a captured map,
was ambitious to the verge of lunacy, and could not be justified even
by the low opinion they obviously held of the fighting qualities of the
British and French troops. They looked to capturing the allied second
line and the heights of Kaberlaba by 9 A.M. At 10 A.M., having scaled
Mt. Torle, they were to pass through dense trackless woods to occupy
Mt. Langabisa an hour and a half later, whence they proposed to descend
on Divisional Headquarters and sweep the Asiago plateau clear of the
British troops in time for lunch at 1 P.M.

Further objectives towards the Venetian Plain appeared on the
map ; but the time allotted to these, dependent presumably upon the
length of the luncheon interval, was not indicated. It is possible to
gauge by a study of this ill-fated map, which discloses the optimism
of the enemy before the battle, the terrible blow which must have been
dealt to their *morale* by the resistance met in front of Asiago.

Those of their gallant storm troops who were not being carried cap-
tive to the Allies' hospitals were lying dead before the lines to which
they led the way. Never again during the long months which followed
did the Austrian infantry make the smallest attempt against the British
or French fronts, but lay anxious, night and day, in their trenches,
with a sinking *morale* engendered by a purely passive defence.

The following order of the day was issued by General Montuori,
commanding Sixth Italian Army :—

June 16, 1918.

Yesterday the army of the plateau sustained and repulsed the fierce
attack which the enemy, very superior in numbers, launched against
our front.

From Cesuna to Kaberlaba, from Pennar to the mountains of Val
Bella and Pizzo Razea, on the Cornone and in Val Brenta, British,
French, and Italian troops, emulating one another in gallantry and

valour, held and defended the lines which were entrusted to their bayonets.

The enemy attack, intended to overflow our defences and reach the edge of the plains, was contained and broken. The ancient foe of right and civilisation was once more shown the faith and spirit with which our troops are animated.

With the greatest pride and feeling I salute the British, French, and Italian troops and their commanders, both infantry and artillery, who struck consternation into the hearts of the enemy.

I would add a grateful tribute to our heroic dead, and, finally, I am sure that the army will join me in repeating from the bottom of their hearts the inspiring motto which is ringing to-day from the North Sea to the Adriatic : " Non si Passa ! "

(Signed)   L. MONTUORI, Lieut.-General,

Commanding Sixth Italian Army.

From the fact that the events which occurred on the front of the Map No. 7. 23rd Division in the battle of June 15, 1918, have been given in such detail, the reader must not be led to regard the Austrian attack as a local affair, delivered on the British and French fronts alone. The attack in this quarter was only part of a vast offensive delivered on a front of seventy-five miles from the Asiago Plateau to the sea, in which over fifty divisions were employed. Though it is incontestable that the greatest concentration was made against the Franco-British front, opposite which no less than sixteen and a half divisions had been massed, the attack was pressed vigorously on the whole front, and had succeeded in establishing the Austrians on the right bank of the Piave on and below the Montello.

Having abandoned the attack on the mountain front, the Austrians were enabled to move their reserves to the plains with a view to exploiting this initial success. During the following few days they made considerable progress, and the situation seemed serious.

From the shape of the allied front, as surely as a withdrawal from the mountains would force a retirement from the Piave, so surely would the enemy's progress on the plains, by threatening the communications of the mountain front, necessitate the most difficult operation of a descent from the Asiago Plateau. The sense of security brought by the defeat of the Austrians on the plateau was succeeded by a feeling of suspense as the possibility of attack from the rear was realised.

Fortune, however, favoured the Allies. The Italians brought forward reinforcements for counter-attack, and on June 20 the fickle Piave, rising in heavy flood, swept away such of the enemy's bridges as had escaped destruction by artillery or aeroplanes. The last hope of the Austrians had gone. But they realised it too late. Faced with the steadily increasing pressure of Italian counter-attacks, their retreat cut off by a treacherous river, they became involved in disaster.

Italian official estimates placed the total Austrian losses in their ill-fated offensive at 56,000 killed, 240,000 wounded, 24,000 prisoners.

At the root of the failure of this great Austrian attack lay the enmity which existed between their two leading commanders, Field-Marshal Conrad Von Hotzendorf and Field-Marshal Boroevic Von Bojna, the first commanding the armies operating on the mountain front, the second those on the Piave.

Conrad, who had playfully described our position on the Asiago Plateau as that of "a shipwrecked man clinging to a board, who would immediately sink were his fingers chopped off," favoured attack on the mountain front. Boroevic looked to an attack on the Venetian Plains as the surest means of success.

Space does not allow of a discussion as to which of these two alternatives should have been adopted. But the weakness of the compromise forced by this antagonism is clear from the following letter,[1] written by Boroevic on June 29, 1918, to his friend, Francis de Bolgar, a former Secretary of State :—

DEAR FRIEND,—Under the lively impression of events, I should like to confide to you the plain truth, which, with the exception of yourself, is known only to Windisch-Graetz, who was with my command.

1. The offensive against Italy was "ordered" for May 20—for political reasons. The fixing of this date showed me that, in spite of countless scrupulously exact reports from me, there was not the faintest notion in Baden (a watering-place near Vienna, then the Austro-Hungarian G.H.Q.) of the condition of the army. From the beginning of February it had, in consequence of the almost total cessation of reinforcements, been starved to such a degree that the men dropped on ordinary marches.

The Archduke Joseph himself had to hear complaints from Hungarian soldiers that they were hungry. The horses were skeletons, and the artillery simply immovable. The outlook was hopeless. All this was reported over and over again with demands for immediate rein-

[1] Published in 'The Times' newspaper.

forcements, and that we should be helped out with four weeks' rations to put the men on their legs again.[1] Things looked just the same in Tirol. Yet the reinforcements did not begin to make their appearance till June 8, a week before the offensive, which was fixed to begin on June 15.

2. The main attack was planned from Tirol, just opposite the French and British sectors. When I learned this I opposed it with all my might. I risked my command by writing, " Don't take the bull by the horns." All in vain. Finally, a mean compromise was arrived at, the main force remaining at Tirol, and the attack being ordered simultaneously from the Piave as well. Still to begin on June 15. I moved for a postponement of three days. Conrad said he could not postpone, so it remained fixed for the 15th. It was characteristic that the chief command was split up on the 14th. There were four G.H.Q.'s—Baden, Waldstatten in Belluno, Arz in the Court train in Tirol, His Majesty at the telephone in the Court train. At 6 P.M. on the 14th I was asked over the telephone, " What happens to-morrow ? " I replied, " I attack as ordered by G.H.Q." " Good. Act on your own judgment, but on your own responsibility." At 2 A.M. on the 15th I was at my post of observation in Oderzo, and at 3 A.M. the battle began. At 7 A.M. I crossed the Piave ; at 10 o'clock I had already 12,000 prisoners, and was on the Montello. I was very well pleased. At noon I heard from the First Army in Tirol that all was going well, and that the first lines had been overrun.

At 11 P.M. His Majesty called me to the telephone, and said in a tone which betrayed his emotions, " The Tirol army is defeated ; the troops have lost everything they had won, and have been thrown back to where they started." I was thunderstruck. I was implored to hold my ground. I signified that we would do our utmost. At the same time I telegraphed to G.H.Q. for details. No reply came. It was not till the next day that I learned the truth from the Eleventh Army. At the same time, enemy reinforcements, which on the 14th were still at Verona, appeared on my front. They had been brought up by motor. The adversary was stronger than I.

3. A new resolution had now to be taken. For without an easing of my effort by Tirol, a farther advance on my part was madness, and would have led to disaster. Without asking any questions, I ordered the bridgeheads already won to be held at all costs, as I hoped that the Tirol idea would be at once abandoned, and that the superfluous divisions from there would be sent to me, or that a fresh attack would be made in Tirol. I announced this to G.H.Q., pointing out that a decision must be made immediately and some answer given to my innumerable requests. None came, and I went on fighting. On the 18th I returned to Udine

---

[1] Judging from the condition of prisoners captured on the Asiago front on June 15 this appears to be an exaggeration. Their physique, clothing, and equipment were good. Some of the prisoners taken in raids in later months were in poor condition, and those captured in the final offensive of the Allies in October for the most part presented a wretched appearance.

—for the sake of easier communications,—and received orders to come to Spilimbergo to His Majesty in the Court train. On the 19th I reported there, and, in a private talk lasting one and a half hours, gave my appreciation of the situation. I gave my frank opinion on all that had occurred, and developed a plan of operations, which was accepted. On my asking about commissariat and munitions, Arz replied that a colonel would give me information on that point in Udine in the afternoon! So they did not know. Meanwhile Diaz had already drawn reinforcements from Tirol, so that I had seventeen divisions to meet an enemy with thirty. I pressed for a decision, but in vain. The colonel told me that, owing to lack of food, the output of munitions would sink in a week to a ration of 4.9 rounds daily for each gun. Further, Colonel Zeynek reported from Baden that the armies could only be supplied till the 25th. Utter helplessness! General consternation.

I told Arz that war could not be carried on in that way, and I begged him to urge the Emperor to proceed immediately to Vienna. I would collect the Ministers there myself by telegram, and then we must have plain speaking and clear orders. Arz agreed, but had not the courage to make the proposal, so I did it. His Majesty ordered Windisch-Graetz by telephone to join me at Udine. It was thirty-six hours before he could arrive. Again no decision was taken. On the night of the 20th—four precious days having gone by, in which the enemy had grown to thirty-three divisions, and I had suffered heavy losses—I turned over in my mind what was to be done, and at 7 A.M. I called up the Court train to know whether His Majesty was still there. They told me that he was in Vittoria. I called up Vittoria. No one knew anything. I called the Court train again, and received the answer, " His Majesty is still here." Thereupon I telegraphed : " The failure of the Eleventh Army and its hitherto scanty progress—due to the underfeeding of the army group for months past—does not appear to justify a continuance of the offensive against Treviso. Inasmuch as the enemy is constantly growing stronger and I weaker, with a treacherous stream just behind the battle front, the smallest incident may entangle the army group in a catastrophe. A definite decision must now be made. As the monarchy has fulfilled its duty as an ally with the utmost loyalty and must not expose itself to the danger of becoming defenceless, and so losing its weight in the Alliance, I suggest that the army group retire to the east bank of the Piave, in order, if necessary, to renew the attack at a later date."

To this proposal there came at 7 P.M.—that is to say, twelve hours later—the order to evacuate the right bank of the Piave. The movement was carried out without its being observed by the enemy, and was, perhaps, the most difficult of all I had to execute during the war. If I had only had two more divisions I could have done the whole thing without a fault. Therefore it is not the Piave which is to blame for what has happened, but the lack of thought and concentration prevailing at G.H.Q. His Majesty has not a man in his entourage. As he has nobody of experience at his elbow, we are moving towards a very sad future.

Windisch-Graetz and Rakovsky know all this. I won't interfere any more. I am heartily sick of the affair.

It is also significant that the entire Court train was against His Majesty's going to me, and he had to insist in order to carry his point When I appeared in the Court train they would willingly have prevented me from being received alone—a point to which I attach no value. But His Majesty commanded me to come alone in his presence, and it was not till an hour and a half later that Arz and Waldstatten were summoned. For months the meat and flour supplies were lacking. Now they are working very well. The oxen arriving to-day were available months ago, so was the flour.

So here you have a big letter from a small man. I cannot help laughing when I hear about the intrigues which are being woven against me. Those people have no suspicion how hard they are working for me, who in these circumstances would be delighted to get away at the earliest possible moment. The problems that threaten our existence are, in my opinion, to be solved only by a strong, resolute, and independent man, who convinces the Crown that it has more need of good counsellors than of mere tools. I am in good health, and have grown very grey in the last few days. The lava boils, none the less, beneath the snow-capped summit.—Most heartily, your old

BOROEVIC.

The 23rd (French) Division had had the misfortune to receive a direct hit on their headquarters in the early morning of June 15. General Bonfait was untouched, but a member of his staff was killed, and his Chief of the Staff severely wounded. The French sector shortly after the battle was taken over by General Odry,[1] who had recently replaced General Priou in command of the 24th (French) Division.

The opportunity of coming to grips with the enemy had been denied Map No. 9. to the 69th Infantry Brigade in Divisional reserve, and on taking over the right section after the battle they were anxious to try conclusions with the Austrians. Two raids to be carried out simultaneously against Sec and the hostile front line behind South Ave were planned for the night of June 21/22. The artillery covering the two operations, consisting of field artillery and 6-in. howitzers, were to carry out a similar programme in each case. Bombardment would open at zero hour, 11.30 P.M. ; at 0.3 minutes the 6-in. howitzers would commence to lift

---

[1] This distinguished officer had risen to the rank of divisional commander from that of private soldier. Such high promotion from the ranks is, it is believed, very rare in the French Army.

back to a line 300 yards to rear of the enemy objective ; at 0.6 minutes
the field artillery would lift to form flank barrages, and the infantry
would assault.

B Company and two platoons of C Company of the 10th Duke of
Wellington's were detailed to carry out the raid on the South Ave front
under command of Captain Kelly, V.C. A hundred men of C and D
Companies of the 11th West Yorkshire Regiment under Captain Pitman
were to make the attack on Sec.

The right party, having formed up for attack, advanced at 11.30
P.M. on South Ave. This place was found to be lightly held. Such
of its garrison as had not fled were quickly dealt with, and the
advance was continued. When within one hundred yards of the hostile
front line a party of the enemy, either an outpost or a working party,
was encountered. Few of these escaped the bayonets of the raiders.
At 11.40 P.M. the enemy's front line was entered east of the Guardinalti-
Ave road on a front of 200 yards. A company had just concentrated in
preparation for relief, and the trench was found to be strongly occupied.

Very heavy casualties were inflicted on the enemy, who put up
a feeble resistance ; dug - outs were bombed, 31 Austrians were
made prisoner, and a flammenwerfer and 2 machine-guns were captured. Passing back through the enemy's barrage, the raiding party
returned with their prisoners and booty about midnight. Accurate
estimates of enemy casualties in night raids were always difficult to
obtain. On this occasion the number killed was calculated as being
between 50 and 80. The casualties sustained by the raiding party were
somewhat heavy, amounting to 1 other rank killed, 1 officer and 18
other ranks wounded, and 1 officer and 2 other ranks missing.

In the West Yorkshire Regiment's raid the attack was carried out in
two waves. Two parties of C Company, under 2nd Lieutenants Hamilton
and Dixon, advanced on the right of the Sec road ; two parties, under
2nd Lieutenants Liversedge and Watson, on the left of the road.

The trenches were found to be thinly held, but the enemy showed
fight, and stiff bayonet-fighting ensued. In the end, the garrison of the
trench was annihilated, no prisoners being taken. The casualties in
the raiding party amounted to 1 officer and 7 other ranks wounded,
four having been caused by the bayonet.

CHAPTER III.

THE ASIAGO PLATEAU.

SECOND PERIOD : WEARING DOWN THE ENEMY.

JUNE 23 TO SEPTEMBER 24, 1918.

AT this period there was great uncertainty as to the direction in which Map No. 9. events would develop in the near future. On June 23 rumour, derived from an official source, said revolution had broken out in Austria. For twenty-four hours we regarded the war in Italy as practically finished. But on the 24th an attack by the Allies was ordered for the 27th. On the 25th it was rumoured that the Austrians were about to attack us ; the Allies' offensive was cancelled. By June 28 information of the enemy's intention to attack had become so definite that a number of reserve machine-guns were moved forward to support positions. On the plateau the enemy did nothing to confirm these reports ; but the Allies' offensive remained indefinitely postponed.

These rumours of hostile attack, however slight their basis may have been, stimulated the efforts which were being made to strengthen the defences.

The events of June 15 had proved that the general plan of defence was sound ; but there was still room for much work in strengthening the defences themselves. Till now there had been no cover throughout the sector proof against bombardment by heavy artillery. The seemingly strong rock dug-outs constructed by the Italians had unfortunately proved in more than one case mere death-traps. What appeared from within as a solid rock roof was in reality just a stratum of rock suspended from a higher stratum by a layer of earth. Too frequently also there was a fatal defect in the rock known to the "trade" as a "Dolomite crack."

The Austrians had some very heavy pieces at their disposal. In particular, two 17-in. howitzers did great damage. On June 29 a machine-gun and its entire detachment were destroyed by one of these, and many casualties were later caused on the British front by the fire of these heavy howitzers. The code-word "Beetle" will be remembered by those who served on the plateau as the indication to our guns and sound-rangers that these objectionable monsters were firing on our front. But they were never located until after the Armistice.

The moral effect, apart from the material possibilities, of the burst of a shell in the rocky soil was immense. Huge masses of rock were hurled in all directions to a distance of 800 yards and more, adding to the danger of casualties from shell splinters. Protection against hostile artillery fire was urgently required throughout the whole area of the sector.

The Field Companies R.E. were fully taken up with the construction of an intermediate line of defence between the front and second line, and the formidable task of excavating dug-outs from the rock, proof against heavy artillery, was placed in the hands of Major Bullock of the 9th South Staffordshire Regiment, whose working-parties were reinforced by Italian specialists with rock-drills.

After the lesson of June 15 it was unlikely that the Austrians would again venture to attack without a far heavier and more prolonged bombardment. It also seemed probable that if they again attempted an offensive, special attention in the preliminary bombardment would be directed to the San Sisto ridge, where the only existing cover was represented by shallow trenches giving very inadequate protection.

This position was accordingly given priority, and the construction of deep dug-outs, proof against the heaviest artillery, was put in hand forthwith. The formation of the rock on the San Sisto ridge rendered it unreliable as overhead cover, and the alternative plan was adopted of creating large underground chambers for the garrison by blasting down from the surface, the dug-outs being then roofed by layers of heavy timber, iron, and concrete.

Major Bullock had spent some years in South America, where he had acquired, in addition to a considerable knowledge of rock work, a complete vocabulary of Latin expletives. These served to extract work at high pressure from our Allies no less effectively than the original methods he employed for stimulating the British soldier. It was a big conception, involving immense labour; but two of the dug-outs were completed and all chambers prepared before the Division left the sector.

It must not be thought from what has been said above that the Italian needs driving to obtain good work from him. Though the Italian soldiers employed on the construction of mountain roads had the happy knack of appearing to be doing very little, the roads developed in a miraculously short time. The upkeep of roads below the plateau was left in the hands of the old men, women, and children of the mountain villages, who worked from early morning till late in the evening practically without supervision.

The policy which dictated the strengthening of the British defences did not presume that the enemy should be left in undisturbed occupation of the opposing lines. The Austrians were incessantly harassed by artillery fire, and their weakened *morale* was further shaken by night raids on their positions at irregular intervals.

On the night of July 1/2 a most successful operation was carried out by a party of the 11th West Yorkshire Regiment, consisting of one company, supported by two platoons, under the command of Captain R. E. Hobday, covered by the artillery of 102nd Brigade R.F.A. The raiders were organised in four parties. Having carried the enemy's front line, the two other parties were to work east and west along the line, while those in the centre attacked a string of dug-outs located along the Sec-Asiago road in rear of the front line.

The hostile position was entered without difficulty. 2nd Lieutenant Glynne, moving eastward with the right party, found two dug-outs, where casualties were inflicted and 15 prisoners taken. Captain Hobday led a party along the east of the road, while 2nd Lieutenant Ward with the other centre party co-operated on the west of the road. A great number of dug-outs were found, but only four proved to be occupied. From these 25 prisoners were secured. The left party, under 2nd Lieutenant Frost, had, in the meantime, moved westward along the front line, to find it practically deserted for a distance of 500 yards.

Lamp communication had been established with an advanced battalion headquarters at Villa Del Brun. Fifteen minutes after zero hour report was received of the success of the raid; fifteen minutes later the raiders, bringing with them a captured machine-gun and 1 officer and 42 other ranks of the enemy, were back in the British lines. The remarkable success of this enterprise, carried out at the cost of one man slightly wounded, was largely attributable to the accurate co-operation of the artillery. It was an outstanding example of what could be obtained from careful preparation, clear orders, and good leading.

On July 12 a parade was held at Granezza for the presentation of decorations by Lord Cavan and General Graziani, the commander of the French Corps. The troops parading were selected from those who had fought side by side on June 15, and were represented by two companies of the 11th Sherwood Foresters, two companies of the 108ᵉ Regiment, and a detachment of the 126ᵉ Regiment. On this occasion Major-General Babington received the decoration of the French Croix de Guerre with palm, and the D.S.O. was presented to Lieut.-Colonel Bontemps, commanding the 126ᵉ Regiment.

Yet another raid on the enemy's defences at Sec was made on the night of July 15/16, on this occasion by A Company of the 10th Northumberland Fusiliers, under the command of Captain Alexander. Three objectives were given, entailing a penetration of some 400 yards beyond the hostile front line to deal with certain dug-outs which had been disclosed in the hollow Sec-Cassordar road in rear of the line. The French artillery co-operated with our own in support of the operation. The enemy was found to be in a most demoralised condition. Their front trenches were strongly held, but the garrison fled as the first party of the raiders reached the line, and were caught in the barrage of the 18-pdrs. The artillery barrage having again lifted, the second party advanced up the sunken road, bombing the shelters and dug-outs found there. A number of the enemy climbed from these refuges and surrendered. It was learned from these that the officers of the garrison had on the first alarm plunged straightway into the deepest dug-outs they could find. The third objective was found unoccupied, and the signal for recall having been observed, the parties withdrew to their own lines, bringing with them 16 unwounded and 7 wounded prisoners. The casualties sustained by the raiding parties amounted to 4 other ranks missing. Severe casualties had undoubtedly been inflicted on the enemy by the artillery fire, in addition to the many sustained from cold steel and the bombs thrown into the dug-outs.

The second tour of the Division on the plateau was now drawing to a close, orders having been received for its relief in the right sector by the 48th Division, who had been replaced in the left sector by the 7th Division, and withdrawn to rest shortly after the Austrian attack. Before leaving, it was decided to satisfy the curiosity which had been roused concerning a section of the enemy's front line of defence. Opposite the centre of the British front three spurs ran south from the Austrian lines. Across the easterly two, named Post Spur and Coda Spur, which lay directly opposite the left of the right sector, the hostile front line coincided with the line of the Asiago-Canove railway, whose track, clearly observable on either side of and between the spurs, disappeared into deep cuttings in traversing the spurs themselves.

This spot had been the scene of great activity on June 15, and aeroplane photographs had disclosed the presence of many dug-outs.

The 69th Infantry Brigade had planned a raid on the enemy's line at this point for the night of the July 19/20.

The operation, which was carried out by two companies of the 9th Yorkshire Regiment, and which might have obtained large results, unfortunately only met with partial success. The raiders were divided into two parties, the right party to enter Coda cutting from its eastern end, the left party to gain the hostile front line between the spurs, and then, turning right and left, to attack Coda cutting from its western end, and to exploit the Spur cutting from the east.

Unfortunately, the advance of the right party on approaching its objective was broken by artillery and rifle-fire, and became very disorganised. The only members of this party to gain the front line were Captain Greenwood, M.C., 2nd Lieutenant Edwards-Crate, Lance-Corporal Watts and Private Lowther. These did not, however, abandon the enterprise, but, turning left into the Coda cutting, found the enemy lining the southern edge of the cutting, firing to their front in expectation of an assault from that direction. The small party of four, attacking from the rear, inflicted heavy casualties on the enemy with revolver and rifle, and then proceeded to clear ten large shelters and dug-outs of the enemy, killing a considerable number, and forcing the remainder, ignorant of the strength of their attackers, to emerge from their cover and surrender.

The lance-corporal at this juncture was shot dead at point-blank range. The others, incapable of dealing with the large number of enemy who had surrendered, were forced to withdraw, but took with them twelve prisoners. The left party, in the meantime, had succeeded in gaining the front line in face of strong opposition. Dividing at this point, as planned, a portion was led by Lieutenant Sharpe against the west end of Coda cutting, the remainder turning left under Lieutenant Bingham towards Post Spur. The former were held up by strong enemy bombing parties ; the latter succeeded in capturing one prisoner, but suffered considerable casualties from machine-gun fire. Lieutenant Bingham was wounded, and no progress could be made on this flank.

As a result of the raid, the enemy's casualties were estimated at over 50 killed, in addition to the 13 prisoners brought in. Useful information had been obtained with regard to the Coda cutting, where a continuous line of banked dug-outs and shelters had been located in its southern bank for the accommodation of the strong garrison which were found to be occupying it. The casualties sustained by the raiding party amounted to 2 other ranks killed, 1 officer and 14 other ranks wounded, and 3 other ranks missing.

During this period both the 7th Division on our left and the French on our right were similarly engaged in carrying out minor enterprises against the Austrian lines, and the enemy on the Asiago Plateau was kept in a condition of continual suspense. The French coup-de-main was generally a very much larger affair than the British raid. It was not indulged in so frequently, and on account of the enemy's tendency to clear from his trenches on threat of attack, did not always succeed in bringing in more prisoners than the raid ; but if the enemy awaited attack, a successful coup-de-main sometimes achieved very big results.

The 23rd Division's second and last tour in the right sector ended in July with relief by the 48th Division, now commanded by Major-General Walker.

The Division on relief was withdrawn to G.H.Q. reserve, and again accommodated in the Trissino area. This area had by now been more thoroughly organised for training, but manœuvre of anything but the smallest units was still difficult owing to the vines and cornfields which covered every inch of the rich soil. An excellent training-ground for this purpose was, however, found in the somewhat remote hills of St Margerita, where a detached battalion was placed under canvas.

The heat in the plains was now very great ; solar topis had been ordered for British troops on descending from the plateau, and the hours for outdoor work approximated to those of an Indian hot weather.

But the lot of the British soldier at rest in Italy compared favourably with that of his comrades in France, let alone those other theatres of war where relaxation was taken on a patch of desert among a plague of flies and incessant dust-storms.

In their quest for a place in the sun, the Germans, during the years preceding the war, had all but converted Lake Garda into a German colony. Its shores were dotted with German villas and hotels. Now empty and abandoned, certain of these hotels at Sirmione, a village at the point of a narrow peninsula on the southern shore of the lake, were taken over as a rest-station for the British troops. No more perfect place could have been designed for the refreshment of the war-worn soldier from the line. Separate hotels were arranged for officers, non-commissioned officers, and men. Here, far from the clatter of motor-lorries and safe from the not too enterprising Austrian aeroplanes, the days could be idled away bathing, fishing, or taking trips by motor-launch to islands or neighbouring villages. The evenings were spent at the theatre or at open-air concerts organised by Captain H. J. Ratcliffe, 11th West Yorkshire Regiment, whose able management of the rest-station did much for the welfare of the British troops in Italy throughout the summer.

In these days the only shadow which overhung the British troops in Italy was the situation in France. On July 16 news was received of the great German offensive in Champagne ; the development was awaited with keen anxiety. On the following day it was realised that the attack had failed to progress, and that the French were holding firm. Then came the news of the grand French counter-attack, and, as days went by, of the steadily increasing disaster which had overtaken the enemy.

The spirits of all rose to a pitch of high enthusiasm, the more since it was realised that the successes in France could not but react on the situation in Italy ; that the hour of defence was closing ; and that now the frequently postponed offensive against the Austrians would not longer be delayed. As will be seen later, these anticipations were somewhat premature.

There was perhaps no direction in which the British Army more favourably impressed their Allies than in the matter of transport. Our heavy draught-horses were the subject of constant admiration; and our turn-out, though not considered necessary in the same degree by the French and Italians, was a vanity which they often openly envied.

A Divisional Horse Show, held on a large open space at Trissino on August 10, provided an opportunity for our Allies to judge what the 23rd Division could do in this line, and proved an immense success. Officers of both the French and Italian cavalry entered for the open events, and Lord Cavan presented the prizes at the end of this very English holiday held in the midst of the vineyards of Northern Italy.

The Division in G.H.Q. reserve had to hold itself in readiness to occupy the "intermediate line" and "line of the hills" between plateau and plains in case of necessity. The lines had already been reconnoitred at the end of April, and provisional orders issued for the dispositions of the Division if called on to occupy these defences. An alteration in divisional and corps boundaries in the rear defences at this time demanded a revisal of the scheme, and a fresh reconnaissance was carried out by the staff and by commanders of units. The Division was further called on to reconnoitre lines of defence which had been organised in the plains along the river Astico. Sound principles certainly demand careful preparation to meet every eventuality, but the urgency with which these reconnaissances were insisted on seemed to point to the Higher Command not having abandoned the idea that the Austrians might even yet attempt a grand offensive to assist their Allies, now hard-pressed in France.

In the meantime, preparations for the long-postponed Allied offensive on the Asiago Plateau were once again ordered. The changed situation in France had made it possible to expect drafts for the units in Italy, and a promise of tanks was to introduce a new factor into the operations. From the description that has been given of the Asiago Plateau, it will be understood that the action of tanks would be greatly restricted on that front. But there were great possibilities for these weapons on the open plain surrounding the town of Asiago on the front of attack allotted to the 23rd Division ; and it was calculated that their climbing power would enable them even to operate on the Mt. Interrotto spur to the west as far north as the underfeature of Mt. Rasta. If their presence could be concealed before attack, the mere moral effect of their sudden appearance on the scene would be very great.

For an anarchist to form a secret store of bombs is a comparatively easy matter ; but to hide a fleet of tanks in a densely populated country like Northern Italy is a different matter. It was eventually decided that on arrival the tanks should be detrained at night and taken to the unfrequented hills of St Margerita.

But in the end the tanks, like many other things in this theatre of war, failed to materialise.

A difficulty in the preparations for the attack now contemplated was that while divisions were to attack on the fronts previously mentioned, it was necessary for the 7th Division to be withdrawn to rest prior to the operation. This necessitated the 23rd Division taking over the left sector, while the 48th Division remained for the time being in the right sector—*i.e.*, on the front of attack of the 23rd Division.

By an elaboration of the original scheme, the 48th Division was now to co-operate in the attack by passing through the 7th Division, and carrying the later objectives on the left flank. When the time came the various reliefs necessary to place the divisions in position prior to attack would, therefore, be somewhat complicated. Further, it became necessary for all preparations in the nature of construction of dumps, laying of communications, &c., for the 7th and 48th Divisions to be carried out by the 23rd Division, while the 48th Division became responsible for similar preparations for the attack of the 23rd Division on the right. In short, the most whole-hearted co-operation between divisions would be essential to the success of the operation. In the following weeks, during which preparations for the attack and arrangements for reliefs were made, the advantage of a permanent army corps were very apparent. The members of the several staffs of the British divisions in Italy had become as intimately acquainted with each other as with members of their own division. Friction or misunderstanding were unknown.

The 23rd Division relieved the 7th Division in the left sector on August 19. Divisional Headquarters were established at Kerr's Camp on the south-eastern slope of Mt. Carriola ; headquarters of the right

infantry brigade were situated just below the crest of Mt. Lemerle ;
those of the left infantry brigade at Magnaboschi. The reserve infantry
brigade was disposed between Mt. Carriola and the southern edge of the
plateau, with headquarters a short distance in rear of those of the
Division.

Earlier in this chapter it has been explained how the ground fell
sheer from the plateau to the plains in rear of this sector. Approaching
from Caltrano, infantry and pack-animals could reach the plateau by
steep mountain paths ; but wheeled transport had to make a long detour
to the west, zigzagging up the south-western slope of Mt. Pau, and then
skirting round its western and northern slopes to reach the plateau.

The general nature of the sector was similar to that of the right
sector, and was similarly divided into two brigade sections. But there
were two factors which demanded a certain difference in the dispositions
on the left of the British front. These were the different distribution of
forest and open ground, and the course and character of the river Ghelpac
opposite the left sector.

The front line on this flank of the British front ran throughout in
dense woods. But while the area of the right brigade, backed by the
steep slopes of Mt. Lemerle, was entirely covered with these pine-woods,
the ground in rear of the front line on the left was completely open and
exposed to hostile observation. This open rolling ground extended
westward to the area of the Italian Bersaglieri Division (General Monesi),
which held the neighbouring sector on this flank.

The slight depression which had indicated the dry course of the river
Ghelpac in front of the right sector had here deepened to a considerable
ravine. Continuing its westerly course, it ran through open ground
north of the woods which covered the immediate right of the left sector.
A sharp southerly bend then brought it to a point some 200 yards from
the centre of the front line of the right brigade, from which it again ran
west, parallel to the front line. At about the point of junction of the two
brigades, the front line turned sharply north to meet the Ghelpac, and
then continued west along the southern brink of what was now a precipitous densely wooded ravine. Covered by this deep ditch, the left
was secure, though it was necessary to arrange for the ravine to be
searched by high-angle fire should occasion demand. Trench-mortars
formed a prominent feature of the front-line defence in this quarter.

THE VAL D'ASSA AND BROKEN BRIDGE.

It was otherwise on the right and in the centre. Here it had been found necessary to establish picquets to cover the front line. On the front of the right battalion these were placed on the near edge of a clearing in the woods which restricted the fire of the front line. Farther to the left the picquet line crossed the Ghelpac as it turned south, and continued west along the high open ground on the right bank of the ravine till a point was reached immediately opposite that at which the front line, in its northerly bend, gained the left bank. On the extreme right the picquet line was drawn back to the front line along the easterly edge of the woods, so as to cover the open ground on the front of the right sector.

The second line, at a distance of some 1200 yards in rear of the front line, was situated on the forward slope of Mt. Lemerle, and connected north-east and north-west to the front line by the Lemerle and Cesuna Switches, of which the former ran through wood, the latter being strongly sited on high open ground. A defensive quadrangle was thus formed, whose southern side had a length of about 800 yards, and northern side (front line) a length of 3000 yards. The enemy on penetrating the front line in this sector on June 15 had been held in this quadrangle. The depth of his penetration had been due to the absence of any intermediate line of defence between the front and second lines. As a precaution against a repetition of this, the construction of a line of posts at a distance of 400 yards from the front line was now commenced simultaneously with the work of preparation for the attack of the 7th and 48th Divisions.

The Austrian artillery at this period became particularly active. The village of Magnaboschi, where the headquarters of the 70th Infantry Brigade and a reserve battalion were situated, was heavily bombarded on August 21. Some sixty casualties were inflicted on the battalion in the space of a few minutes, two 17-in. shells being responsible for the greater number of these. The site of brigade headquarters procured for them a measure of safety, but after this bombardment the reserve battalion was withdrawn to Mt. Magnaboschi, half a mile in rear, where it was encamped under the concealment of the woods.

The enemy, in addition to shelling the forward positions, carried out frequent bombardments on the Carriola valley and on the roads, which were very exposed in this sector. The protection of these roads from hostile artillery observation entailed an enormous amount of labour. Miles of high camouflage screens had been erected for this purpose. Owing to the frequent storms, which swept these away, they needed constant attention. Roads descending from rear to front had to be hidden by screens slung overhead like a series of triumphal arches. But the most elaborate arrangements could not always conceal from the Austrian observation posts the high dust raised by motor transport; water alone could do that, and water was scarce on the plateau.

Intelligence gained by previous divisions concerning the enemy's lines made it unnecessary for units in the line to feel their way to the same extent as had been necessary on first taking over the right sector. No time was lost, therefore, in obtaining identification of the enemy on the new front.

On the night of August 24/25 a raiding party under command of Captain Dakin, composed of 2nd Lieutenant Parker, 2nd Lieutenant Hinds, and 40 other ranks of the 8th York and Lancaster Regiment, crossed the Ghelpac valley on the front of the left section, and after one and a half minute's artillery preparation rushed the enemy's trenches at Ambrosini some 800 yards north of the river. Effecting a complete surprise, they inflicted many casualties on the enemy, and after remaining twenty minutes in the enemy's line, withdrew with four prisoners : one man of the party was killed, and one wounded by machine-gun fire.

On the night of August 26/27 a most successful raid on a large scale was carried out by the 10th Duke of Wellington's Regiment on the right flank against the enemy's position on the Vaister Spur, in conjunction with a simultaneous operation by the 48th Division farther to the east.

The objectives selected for attack were situated at a distance of over 2000 yards from our trenches. The first of these was represented by the hostile front line astride the upper end of the Vaister Spur. Further objectives given were a railway cutting situated some 300 yards in rear of the front line, and a quarry between the front line and the railway. The frontage of attack was about 700 yards, and all dug-outs lying in the area between the front line and the railway were to be searched.

Lieut.-Colonel Lethbridge, in arranging the operation, detailed three platoons from each of the four companies of his battalion, organising the whole into three parties of about equal strength. The attacking troops, totalling 14 officers and 350 other ranks, were placed under command of Captain Payne, and divided into the following parties :—

" A " Party.—2nd Lieutenants Simpson, Thomson, Bain, and Pass,
      and 110 other ranks.
" B " Party.—Captain Bolton, Lieutenants Neill and Jackson, 2nd
      Lieutenants Sugden and Ison, and 120 other ranks.
" C " Party.—Captain Payne, Lieutenant Edwards, 2nd Lieutenants
      Waite, Wood, and Garside, and 120 other ranks.

" A " party was to attack on a short front on the extreme right, " B " and " C " in the centre and on the left respectively. The operation was to be supported by the 102nd Brigade R.F.A.

At dusk a patrol was sent out to watch No Man's Land till zero hour, while the raiders were given a hot meal to prepare them for the work which lay before them.

More than any other operation in war, a night raid depends on surprise for success. Surprise is the very essence of the undertaking ; without it the whole advantage lies with the defence.

On this occasion it was not effected. The assembly of the raiding party was successfully carried out, but on advancing against the hostile position, they found the enemy fully prepared. In the face of severe opposition, and despite many casualties, the troops advanced in the most determined fashion and gained the enemy's trenches. Here fierce fighting ensued for thirty minutes, during which no fewer than 5 officers and 65 other ranks of the enemy were captured, together with two machine-guns. The skilful leading of Captain Payne and the gallantry of his men had converted what might well have proved a catastrophe to a brilliant success. The spirit of the troops was exemplified by the conduct of one of their company sergeant-majors. This warrant officer, though shot through the lung early in the fight, continued to command his party till the end, and, refusing all assistance, returned unaided to the British trenches together with the remainder of the raiders.

Sixteen stretcher-bearers had accompanied the raid, and a relay post had been established at battalion headquarters. It was well that these arrangements had been made, for casualties were heavy : 2 other ranks were killed, 5 officers and 43 other ranks wounded, and 1 officer and

5 other ranks missing. Severe as were these casualties in relation to the time the troops were engaged, they totalled less even than the number of enemy captured, while it was estimated that no fewer than 80 of the Austrians had been killed during the struggle in the trenches.

The artillery support of the raid had been most excellently carried out, but the number of guns had proved somewhat insufficient for so extensive a front of attack in position warfare.

This raid was on the largest scale of any carried out by the 23rd Division. Delivered against a fully prepared enemy, it had been accomplished in detail as planned. The raiders might well congratulate themselves on the results when they returned to the hot tea and rum that awaited them in the British trenches.

The operation carried out by the 48th Division had proved equally successful. In little more than half an hour the Austrians on the British front must have lost some 300 men, killed, wounded, and captured.

During the following fortnight, work on the defences was steadily continued, and the preparations for the big Allied offensive were practically completed.

Suddenly, on September 9, came news which upset all plans. The British divisions were to be transferred at the earliest opportunity to France, and owing partly to this and partly to lateness of the season, the idea of an offensive on the Asiago Plateau was to be definitely abandoned.

After all the thought which had been given to the Asiago offensive, all the time which had been spent in drawing up orders, and all the labour that had been expended in preparation for carrying them out, the cancellation of this operation came as a great disappointment. But a deeper disappointment to all in the 23rd Division came with the order that the number of battalions in infantry brigades was to be reduced to three, and that the 13th Durham Light Infantry, 9th Yorkshire Regiment, and 11th Sherwood Foresters, were to be transferred to France forthwith.

Even before the necessity arose in France for the reduction of brigades, very few divisions in the British Army had maintained their integrity. Not only had the composition of divisions changed, battalions also had in many cases been exchanged between brigades during the past few years.

Apart from the reorganisation of the field artillery, by which certain batteries had been taken to form army field artillery brigades, the 23rd Division stood to-day as it had been formed in England in 1914. Glancing at the back pages of this history, one can imagine the thoughts which came to the commander under whom these battalions had served for four long years with the news that he was now forced to part with them. Recollections of the 13th Durham Light Infantry sweeping through Le Sars or across Tower Hamlets ridge ; of the 9th Yorkshire Regiment's valiant attacks on Contalmaison and Battle Wood ; of the 11th Sherwood Foresters swinging on to their objectives in the battle of Messines, and resisting the enemy's counter-attacks at the hinge of the great attack—these can have been but a few of the reflections of General Babington in this hour of separation from battalions who had never failed him. Scarcely less bitter was it for ьhe battalions to part from the Division whose proudest achievements they had shared in the war.

The 70th Infantry Brigade was at this time occupying the left section, and the 11th Sherwood Foresters were determined to bid farewell to Italy in their own fashion.

A few days earlier, 2nd Lieutenant Hotson of this battalion had led an offensive patrol after dusk against the enemy's position about Ambrosini. On the information gained on this occasion, it was decided to raid the hostile front and support lines at this point with two companies on the night of September 9/10.

C Company (Captain Gibson) and D Company (Captain Spicer) were selected for the operation. The platoons, averaging 28 men, were commanded by Sergeant F. Ward, 2nd Lieutenant Hotson, Lieutenants Swire and Swale, 2nd Lieutenants Rose, Branker, Chester, and Wilson.

The attack was to be supported by the artillery of the left group under the temporary command of Major Abbey, who explained to all ranks, with the assistance of a large-scale map, the exact details of the action to be taken by the guns covering the raid.

Two areas were defined for the attack. A area, including Raid and Cameron Trenches, was allotted to C Company ; B area, containing Cornwall Trench in rear, was to be dealt with by D Company.

At 11.30 P.M. the infantry advanced from their assembly positions under an artillery barrage. The enemy opened on the attack with machine-guns, rifles, and bombs, but few awaited the assault.

T

As Gibson's company rushed Raid and Cameron Trenches, the majority of the Austrians fled from this line, which had been reduced by artillery fire to a shallow ditch little more than one foot deep. A machine-gun and its detachment were, however, captured, rifles in considerable numbers were found abandoned all along the line, and many of the enemy were killed by rifle and Lewis-gun fire as they endeavoured to effect their escape.

At zero plus 11 minutes, Spicer's party passed through C Company, and three minutes later, on the artillery lifting, assaulted Cornwall Trench. This trench was in better condition, and it was here the enemy had sought shelter. But the position was carried, and in the fighting that ensued many prisoners were secured before the withdrawal was ordered. During the withdrawal 2nd Lieutenant Hotson, to whose patrol work the success of the raid was largely due, and whose bravery and good leadership had been prominent in this night's work, was unfortunately killed by a stray bullet.

Twenty-seven prisoners and three machine-guns were brought in. The casualties of the raiding party amounted to 1 officer killed, 1 officer and 13 other ranks wounded, 2 other ranks missing.

On receiving the report of this operation, General Babington conveyed his congratulations to the Sherwood Foresters in two words— "Well done."

That brief message could have been appropriately applied to the whole record of the battalion in the 23rd Division, and equally to the services of the other battalions who were to leave us.

On September 11, brigadiers and commanding officers assembled at Divisional Headquarters to meet the Commander-in-Chief. Lord Cavan had come for two purposes : firstly, on behalf of General Montuori, to decorate General Babington in the presence of his officers with the Order of Savoy awarded to him by the King of Italy ; secondly, to meet the officers of the Division on the occasion of the departure of the three battalions.

Having performed the first ceremony, he gave a short address to the officers present, thanking them for their services, and then bade farewell to those who were leaving the Division, expressing his great regret that circumstances in France demanded their separation from the 23rd Division.

THE VAL D'ASSA AND MONTE INTERROTTO.

(From the air.)

General Babington proceeded on leave to England the same night, with every prospect, it seemed, of rejoining in France. On the following day, the 13th Durham Light Infantry, 9th Yorkshire Regiment, and 11th Sherwood Foresters left the plateau en route for France, where they were to form part of the 25th Division on its reorganisation.

The 7th Division was expected to entrain for France at a very early date ; the 23rd Division was to follow immediately afterwards. Dates of transfer depended solely on when rolling-stock became available.

With the cancellation of the grand offensive, the departure of these battalions, and the whole change of plan, there came a sense of anti-climax. Interest in the Asiago Plateau waned, and no incident of note occurred during the Division's last days on the mountain front.

Relief by the 20th Italian Division was ordered to commence on September 24, and was completed by the 27th. Thus briefly recorded, it might be thought that the relief was the most simple and eventless proceeding. It was far from this. The different organisation of an Italian division always made a straight relief impossible on such occasions, and in the Italian Army the corps staff concerned itself in details which in the British Army were left entirely at the discretion of division. Staff work, accordingly, became somewhat complicated.[1] A further difficulty on this occasion occurred through the hour selected on September 24 for artillery reliefs coinciding with the hour fixed for a minor offensive operation by the Italian division on the left. The postponement of this operation appeared to be impossible, but it was suggested that Austrian retaliation would fall on the area of the offending division. Previous experience, however, gave no assurance of this, and it was considered wise not to trust in it. By a great effort the artillery reliefs were completed before the hour of attack. Had this not been done, the Divisional artillery, as it proved, might have suffered severely, since the entire Austrian retaliation for the Italian operation was directed on the British front, the 23rd Division's sector being subjected to a bombardment of quite exceptional intensity.

Since March 29 the Division had spent just over four months on the Asiago Plateau. During this period they had captured 691 prisoners, including 20 deserters, in raids on the enemy's trenches, attacks

[1] See Appendix F.

on his patrols, and in the course of the Austrian attack on June 15.
The distribution of these captures is shown below :—

	Austrian attack.	Raids and patrols.
Units of 68th Infantry Brigade . .	121	32
„ 69th „ „ . .	3	170
„ 70th „ „ . .	320	45
	444	247

Details of the prisoners taken by other British divisions have not
been obtained. The 48th Division in their counter-attack on June
16 captured a very large number, and both this division and the 7th
Division had carried out incessant raids. The total taken on the British
front during the six months, April to September, may be estimated at
not less than 2000. Artillery fire had been continuous, and to take four
men killed or wounded to one captured would form a conservative
estimate. It can be taken, then, that the Austrians suffered no fewer than
10,000 casualties at the hands of the British during the spring and
summer of 1918.

Though the stupendous undertaking of the grand offensive against
the Austrians' mountain positions had failed to mature, the 23rd Division
could feel, as they turned their backs on the Asiago Plateau, that the
months spent on the mountain front had not been spent in vain.[1]

[1] A small trophy of the tour of the 23rd Division on the plateau has been preserved in the
following interesting manner :—
From time immemorial every Peer who passes through Oakham (Rutland) for the first time
must give a horse-shoe to be hung in the ancient castle, now used as an Assize Court. The
collection includes those given by Queen Elizabeth, Queen Victoria, King Edward, the Duke of
Connaught, and Viscount French.
A new horse-shoe has now made its appearance there, the donor being Lieut.-General the
Earl of Cavan. In the centre is a small shoe, and a tablet bearing the inscription : "This shoe
was taken off an Austrian pony captured in the trenches near Asiago, Italy, by a raiding party
of the 23rd Division."

CHAPTER IV.

THE BATTLE OF VITTORIO VENETO AND THE DEFEAT OF AUSTRIA.

SEPTEMBER 25 TO NOVEMBER 4, 1918.

IT had been expected that the 7th Division, in occupation of the Trissino Map No. 7. area, would entrain for France before the descent of the 23rd Division from the plateau. Difficulties in obtaining rolling-stock, however, had detained them in Italy, and it was necessary to allot a fresh area, east of Vicenza, to the 23rd Division, with headquarters at Costa Bissara.

From the purely residential point of view, the new area had many recommendations. Billets were good, and the Division enjoyed a well-earned rest during a week of perfect weather. But the projected transfer of the Division to France, where the armies had broken away from the old trench lines, made training in the tactics of open warfare an urgent matter.

The new area had not been organised for training, and the close cultivated country round Costa Bissara made it most unsuitable for practice in open warfare. Orders were therefore issued by G.H.Q. for the Division to change places with the 7th Division, who had now been training for a considerable period in the Trissino area.

On October 7, while this move was in progress, Lord Cavan drove to Divisional Headquarters at Costa Bissara, where he secretly informed Brig.-General Byron, in command of the Division during General Babington's absence, that a sudden complete change of plan had been made by the Comando Supremo. The grand attack on the Asiago Plateau having been definitely abandoned, it had been decided to open an offensive on the Piave front. The transfer of British troops to France had been cancelled, and the 7th and 23rd Divisions were to take part in the projected operations.

The strictest secrecy was to be maintained ; no hint was to be given that the move to France had been cancelled. The training that would be necessary would be in conformity with the idea that it was in preparation for the fighting on the French front, but it needed to be strenuous, as little time would be available. The troops were to be prepared for the long marches that it was anticipated would follow initial success on the Piave, and the direct co-operation between the smaller units of artillery and infantry was to be practised.

This practice was required particularly in the case of the mobile 6-in. mortars. These weapons were simply 6-in. Newton mortars whose barrels had been sawn in half and converted to screw guns, and beds cut up to adapt them to pack transport. Credit for their invention was due to Major V. E. Cotton of the 23rd Divisional Artillery, who had realised the value that could be gained by pushing forward a weapon with the devastating effect of a 6-in. trench-mortar in a mountain attack where the movement of field artillery would be a slow and laborious undertaking.

Owing to the cancellation of the mountain attacks the mobile mortars had had no opportunity of proving their worth. Infantry officers knew little of them, and, for various reasons, service in the mobile trench-mortar batteries had not been popular with the personnel of the 23rd Divisional Artillery detailed for the work. In the end, time was, unfortunately, not available for the practice in co-operation which was so much needed. The mobile trench-mortars were, therefore, to enter the coming battle under great disadvantages ; but they were destined, at the eleventh hour of their existence in Italy, and under conditions totally different from those for which they had been invented, to more than justify their introduction, and to become a source of pride, not only to their consistent supporters, but to all who were concerned with them.

On October 12 orders were received for the move of the Division to a position behind the Piave front. On the following day General Babington returned from England.

Lord Cavan had now established his headquarters at Casa Marcello, south of Treviso. At a conference held here on October 14 he explained the outline of the projected operations and the methods by which it was intended to carry out the offensive against the Austrian position on the Piave.

Lord Cavan himself had been appointed to command the Tenth Army, which was to consist of the XIV. (British) Corps and the XI. (Italian) Corps. His place in command of the XIV. Corps was to be taken by General Babington.

The general plan for the Allies' attack was to advance across the Piave with the Tenth, Eighth, and Twelfth Armies against the Fifth and Sixth Austrian Armies, forcing the Fifth Army eastwards and threatening the communication of the Sixth Army running through the Valmarino Valley. The Eighth Italian Army directed on the town of Vittorio Veneto would then be driven as a wedge between the two Austrian Armies.

After forcing the passage of the Piave and securing bridgeheads on the first day, the Tenth Army was gradually to swing eastwards and advance on the river Livenza in protection of the right flank of the Eighth Army in its move northwards. It was calculated that this further advance of the Tenth Army would also force the withdrawal of the enemy from the line of the Piave farther to the south, and so enable the Third Italian Army on its right to effect the crossing of the river unopposed.

The frontage allotted on the farther bank of the Piave to the XIV. Map No. 10. Corps, on the left of the Tenth Army, would extend from Cimadolmo to Casa Tonon. On this front the Corps was to attack with the 7th Division on the right, the 23rd Division on the left. A period of three days was named as the probable duration of the operations, and objectives in the several phases were given. But these were given as a basis on which corps and divisions could submit their proposals rather than as part of a definitely settled plan of attack.

The enemy's front line represented his main line of resistance. Protected by the obstacle of the river, its capture appeared likely to be the severest task that lay before the Allies, or at any rate the British. With the forcing of the Piave and the capture of the front line, it was anticipated that the enemy's resistance would weaken. But though the task of the fighting troops might prove lighter in the later phases, it was realised that the river would for some days heavily impede the work of supply, and that the difficulties of the services responsible for this work would increase as the advance was pushed forward.

Except in times of exceptionally high flood the river Piave does not present an unbroken expanse of water, but, split by numerous shoals and islands, runs in channels of varying depth. Certain of these, where the water is swift and deep, it would be necessary to cross by ferry or bridge, though normally the greater part of the river is fordable in October. But, as bad luck would have it, recent heavy rain-storms had brought down the Piave in high flood. The channels which must be forded were shown by calculations based on the records of hydrometers to be too deep to be crossed, and the date of attack was therefore governed by the fall of the river.

A detailed description of the front of attack of the 23rd Division may be left till we come to consider the matured plan of attack. An important point, however, which materially affected the plans of the XIV. Corps, required immediate decision.

On the front of attack of the XIV. Corps, at a distance varying from 300 to 700 yards from the right bank of the river, lay the island of the Grave di Papadopoli. This island, of a length of three miles and a breadth at its widest point of about one mile, was held by the Austrians as a strong detached post in front of their main position.

The G.O.C. XIV. Corps was called on to decide between alternative plans for the capture of the Grave di Papadopoli. The island could either be regarded as the first objective in the opening attack on the Austrian position, or its capture could be effected by a distinct and separate operation on a date prior to that of the main attack.

By following the first alternative there would be a greater probability of gaining the immense advantage of finding the Austrian main line of defence unprepared. But any hitch in the delicate operation of crossing to and capturing the Grave might, by indefinitely delaying the co-operation of the British troops in the main attack, prove disastrous.

By adopting the second alternative more time would be available for the assembly on the Grave of the troops detailed for the main attack, and opportunity would be afforded for reconnoitring the channels between the Grave and the left bank of the Piave. But the adoption of this course would probably neutralise the efforts which had been made to render the main attack a surprise, as it was unlikely that the Austrians would accept the seizure of the Grave as an isolated operation with nothing further in view.

1918.] THE BATTLE OF VITTORIO VENETO. 297

General Babington was never in doubt as to the advisability of adopting the second alternative. He even regarded it as vital to the success of the whole operation on his front. The wisdom of this decision, which was endorsed by Lord Cavan, undoubtedly contributed largely to the subsequent success of the Allies.

From the conference at which these matters were discussed, General Babington returned to Trissino to spend his last night at the head-quarters of the 23rd Division. The entrainment of the Division for the Noale area, south of Treviso, had commenced during the day, and was now in full progress.

The three entraining points allotted to the Division were at a considerable distance from billeting areas. Communication on the railway was faulty, the arrival of trains at entraining points was greatly delayed, and, owing to the distance of these points from billets, troops had frequently moved off before information had been received of delay on the railway. Heavy rain, falling continuously throughout the afternoon and night, flooded all roads. On one of these a bridge was swept away during the night, making the selection of another route necessary—a difficult matter in the pitch-dark. The troops, awaiting entrainment in the soaking rain, suffered the direst discomfort.

By the following morning half the Division had been despatched, and the movement continued more smoothly during the day.

On October 15 the Division parted with the commander under whose care it had been formed, and under whose leadership it had fought for the past three years. It was an event which affected all under his command, for to every man in the Division the name of General Babington had become a household word. In the earliest period of the Division's formation, over four years before, his pride in his command and jealousy for its good name, his justice and sympathy, had procured for him an immense influence : this influence, strengthened by his long and successful tenure of command, had become, one ventures to think, unique. His faith in the Division was bred of the confidence which he himself inspired in others. None who served in the 23rd Division would wish to make a prouder boast than that the spirit of the Division formed a true reflection of the spirit of its first commander. Regret at his leaving was tempered by the knowledge that the Division was to remain under his command in his higher appointment.

The following Special Order of the Day was published on the occasion of his departure :—

October 17, 1918.

It is with no ordinary feelings of regret that Major-General Sir J. M. Babington, K.C.M.G., C.B., relinquishes the command of the 23rd Division, with whom he has served since it was embodied more than four years ago ; no commander has ever received more whole-hearted support from all ranks than he has during that entire period.

By their exemplary conduct in billets, and most marked gallantry in the field, the Division have made a name for themselves of which they may well be proud ; in more than three years of hard fighting they have never once failed to gain their objective in the attack, or lost any ground in the defence.

Major-General Babington thanks all ranks from his heart for their devoted services, and, in bidding them farewell, assures them that his pride in them is only equalled by his affection for them.

General Byron, C.R.A., assumed temporary command of the Division on General Babington's departure.   Divisional Headquarters moved the same day to Noale village.   The concentration of the Division continued during the 15th, and was completed on the following day.

To divert the enemy's attention from the British concentration in the plains, the 48th Division, still on the mountain front, continued during this period to advertise the presence of British troops on the Asiago Plateau by constant raids on the enemy's trenches.

The continual postponement of offensive operations earlier in the year, when our armies were facing a critical situation in France, had been very galling.   Now, the feverish haste with which preparations were being pushed forward gave rise to anxiety lest sufficient time should not be allowed for the Division to be in readiness to undertake a difficult operation on an unknown front.

The Piave, however, was still in flood, rain continued to fall, and a few days' grace at least could be expected.

Reconnaissance of the front of attack allotted to the Division, which extended from Zandonadi to Casa Tonon on the left bank of the Piave, was carried out by all officers during the next few days.   It was conducted in Italian uniform—a disguise which was quickly penetrated by the quick eyes of the Italian soldier, but doubtless concealed the presence of the British from the Austrian observers.

To those who had become accustomed to the minute observation of the hostile position which had been possible from the heights overlooking the Austrian trenches on the Asiago Plateau, reconnaissance on the Piave front presented a depressing contrast. Having crossed the dead flat country which lay behind the Italian position, they approached the front line by the intricacies of unknown communication trenches. Gaining the front-line trench, they looked out through mist and rain across an apparently limitless expanse of water, shoals, and shrub-covered islands.

The Austrian front line ran along a high " bund," which marked the opposite bank of the river. Everywhere most difficult to locate, it was completely concealed where the Grave di Papadopoli intervened. The flat ground in rear of the front line was, moreover, entirely hidden by the " bund."

Reconnaissance on the Piave was useful in giving a general idea of the task that lay before the Division, but it did not assist in determining the details of attack. These it would be necessary to work out on the map.

The ferry-boat was to play an important part in the operations. Boating experience in the Division had for the most part been confined to holiday trips in the *Saucy Susan* at watering-places on the east coast of England. Such boisterous experience was calculated to be dangerous if applied to a small ferry-boat, packed tight with seven soldiers in fighting order, and all but gunwale-under in a swift stream. Practice in embarking and disembarking and in the suppression of the *Saucy Susan* spirit during transit was very necessary.

The Division had now been ordered to take over its offensive front from the Italians. Staging areas for the forward march were provided in the Sambughe-Preganziol area and at Treviso. A convenient stream close to Treviso afforded opportunity for boating practice, and it was arranged for brigades to carry this out under expert Italian instruction in the course of their forward move.

The 69th Infantry Brigade moved from the Noale area on October 19, and took over the offensive front of the 23rd Division on October 21, coming temporarily under the command of the G.O.C. 7th Division, whose troops were already in occupation of the line on their front of attack. The 68th Infantry Brigade followed on October 20, and moved up to take over the left of the Divisional front from the 69th Infantry Brigade, whose front was shortened by this relief on October 22.

Very careful preparation was needed for the co-operation of the Divisional artillery in the attack. No indication of the presence of British guns on the front was to be given to the enemy. Artillery positions were to be selected, but guns were not to be moved up to these till the latest possible moment. No registration was to be carried out ; all calculations were to be based on information supplied by the 6th Field Survey Company R.E. as to the height and position of certain datum-points on the front. The movement of guns across the river following capture of the hostile forward system, and the subsequent action of the artillery also, called for careful preliminary arrangement. The personal supervision of the C.R.A., and the command of artillery brigades by their own commanders, were regarded as very necessary to the success of these arrangements. General Byron's position in command of the Division did not permit of this, and though Major-General H. F. Thuillier, C.B., C.M.G., had now been appointed to command the 23rd Division, it seemed improbable that he would arrive from England before the commencement of operations.

On the other hand, little dislocation in command would occur through the appointment to temporary command of the Division of Brig.-General H. Gordon, whose wide experience during the war gave him high qualifications for Divisional command. A combination of circumstances made it possible immediately to fill his place in command of the 70th Brigade by Lieut.-Colonel Whatford, an officer long recommended for brigade command, and at this time unemployed.

It was in consideration of the above circumstances that the corps commander decided that General Gordon should take over temporary command of the Division from General Byron on October 20.

On October 21 General Gordon attended a conference at Corps Headquarters, returning late in the afternoon to hold a Divisional conference at Noale. Simultaneously with the assembly of the Divisional conference, General Thuillier arrived from England. Command of the Division had changed hands five times in little over five weeks !

Major-General H. F. Thuillier had already held varied and important commands. Joining the Royal Engineers in 1887, he had taken part in the expedition for the relief of Chitral, 1895. During the Great War

Major-General H. F. Thuillier, C.B., C.M.G.
G.O.C. 23rd Division.
Oct. '18 - Mar. '19

he had served as C.R.E., 1st Division, from May to September 1915, subsequently taking command of the 2nd Infantry Brigade, which he commanded throughout the battle of Loos and subsequent operations. In March 1916 he was given a special appointment at G.H.Q. as Director of Gas Services, and in June 1917 he took command of the 15th (Scottish) Division. In October 1917, owing to his special knowledge of the work, he was appointed Controller of Chemical Warfare at the Ministry of Munitions.

To take over command of an unknown division with an unknown staff immediately before a large operation on a strange front must have been a severe ordeal to the new commander. General Thuillier's immediate grasp of the details of the operation, and the entire absence of friction which characterised his command from the outset, were proof of his high qualities as a commander. He placed his trust in the Division, and immediately received their confidence.

At his request, the conference now assembled was presided over by General Gordon, while he sat aside and listened to the plans which had been formed.

Preliminary to the final operation order, separate instructions had already been issued giving the general plan of attack. The present situation was now put before the conference, and the final orders to be issued for the forthcoming operations were explained and discussed.

The river was still too high to be crossed, and the weather remained unsettled. The date of attack could only be defined as " Z " day. All preparations that were possible before this day were now complete.

As already stated, the ultimate objective of the Tenth Army in the immediate operations was to be the line of the river Livenza. The portion of this line allotted to the 23rd Division extended northwards from a point directly south of the town of Sacile.

The island of Papadopoli, whose north-western extremity lay opposite the front of attack of the 23rd Division, was to be captured by troops of the XIV. Corps prior to the main attack. Attacking troops of the 23rd and 7th Divisions were to be assembled on the eastern shore of the Grave on " Y/Z " night, preparatory to advancing to attack.

On the left of the 23rd Division, and above a point where the Piave narrowed to a width of about 400 yards, the 58th Italian Division was to bridge the unfordable channels on their front during " Y/Z " night, and advance to attack simultaneously with the 23rd Division. There would, however, be a gap of 5000 yards between the right of this division and the left of the 23rd Division in their attack on the Austrian front line.

The whole success of the attack of the 23rd Division would depend at the outset on the satisfactory assembly of attacking troops on the Grave di Papadopoli. The passage of troops to this point accordingly assumed an immense importance.

Before turning to the arrangements for the passage of the Piave by the 68th and 69th Infantry Brigades, it is necessary to describe more closely the river on the front of the 23rd Division.

It has been stated that the course of the river was split by numerous shoals and islands, and of these the Grave di Papadopoli has already been referred to. Normally, the main channel of the river lay to the south of the Grave. This channel was swift and unfordable. On the northern (farther) side of the Grave the channels were fordable except in flood time, though the current would at this time of the year be swift. All arrangements were based on these facts. It was not unknown, however, for the Piave to change its course after flood. If the main channel should now be changed to the northern side of the Grave, all preparations would be rendered abortive. This contingency was remote, and since it was not possible to provide for it, it was to be chanced.

Close to the right bank, and already connected to the mainland by foot-bridges, lay the small island of Cosenza. The breadth of the main channel between Cosenza and the Grave was some 200 yards. The distance from the northern shore of the Grave to the left bank of the river was about 1300 yards.

The material available for passing troops from Cosenza to the Grave consisted of 35 ferry-boats, of which 12 only could be employed at one time, and material and boats for the construction of a foot-bridge for infantry in single file. Each ferry-boat was capable of carrying 7 men. The rate of transit by 12 boats was estimated at 100 men per hour.

To regulate the crossing of the troops, two preliminary assembly areas were to be established, " A " area on the mainland for the crossing to Cosenza Island, " B " area on Cosenza for the further crossing to the Grave. To avoid dangerous crowding, a special officer in telephone communication with Brigade and Divisional Headquarters would superintend

the assembly in " A " area and the crossing to Cosenza. The further
passage from Cosenza was to be controlled by brigades in co-operation
with the officer commanding the men of the 18th Italian Bridging Company detailed as ferrymen. Passage by ferry-boat was to be commenced
at dusk, and continued by foot-bridge immediately this was constructed.

The attack of the 23rd Division in the earlier phases of the operations
was to be carried out by the 69th and 68th Infantry Brigades, on the
right and left respectively, the 70th Infantry Brigade being at this stage
held in Divisional reserve. To each attacking brigade would be attached
one company 23rd Battalion Machine-Gun Corps, one section field company R.E., one mobile (pack) section 6-in. trench-mortar battery, and
the personnel of one standard 6-in. trench-mortar battery for bringing
captured guns into action. In addition, one battery of Italian 65 mm.
mountain artillery was to be placed at the disposal of the G.O.C. 68th
Infantry Brigade.

The ultimate objective to be gained by these brigades would be the
line of the Campo Cervaro - Casa Colleton-Borgo Saccon road, some
2000 yards beyond the river Monticano. This line, it was thought,
might be reached on the second day of the operations.

The limit given to the advance on the first day was the road running
east and west through Borgo Malanotte from Tezze to the Casa Tonon-
Casa Dalmadella road. An intermediate objective, named the Red
Dotted Line, was given about midway between this line and the Austrian
front line.

The great distance which would intervene in the early stages of the
attack between the 68th Infantry Brigade and the right of the 58th
Italian Division called for special measures. The direction of advance
of the latter Division would be oblique to that of the 23rd Division,
and junction was to be ultimately effected at Casa Gerre 6000 yards
north of the river. Though the encirclement threatened by this gradual
approach of the two divisions might eventually manœuvre the enemy
from the intervening ground, the possible advantages to him of this gap
in the Allies front could not be disregarded. The area lying between the
flanks of the divisions was to be searched by artillery fire, and later
to be mopped up by the Italian troops detailed for the purpose ; but
to ensure that the advance of the 68th Infantry Brigade would not be
delayed after the capture of the first objective, it was advisable for the

brigade itself to be prepared to guard against the possibility of counter-attack on an exposed left flank.

The obstacle presented by the river Piave seriously affected the question of artillery support. It would be possible for the field artillery on the right bank to support the infantry advance up to and for a short distance beyond the objective given for the first day's operations. But beyond this, till such time as it should be found possible to bring the field artillery into action on the left bank of the river, the infantry advance would be dependent for support on the fire of heavy artillery and of the trench-mortars and mountain artillery attached to infantry brigades.

The passage of wheeled transport would eventually be made possible by a pontoon bridge connecting Salletuol with the southern portion of the Grave and by the construction, later, of short lengths of bridge to span the more distant channels. But not only would the Division be dependent on this one defile for the passage of all its wheeled transport, but the bridge would have to be shared with the 7th Division, and might even have to be made available for Italian troops.[1] Careful calculation had to be made to determine the priority given to guns, ammunition, R.E. stores, ambulances, supplies, &c. It would be useless for more guns to cross than could be supplied with ammunition ; it would be worse than useless to hold up S.A.A. waggons, and so risk the infantry on the far bank being found with empty pouches. Finally, it was realised that Divisional control of the artillery on both banks of the river would be out of the question. As batteries crossed the Piave, they were to come under the direct command of the infantry brigadiers whose brigades they were supporting. Divisional control of the artillery would only be resumed, if found necessary, when all artillery brigades had crossed to the left bank.

So far, the task allotted to the 68th and 69th Infantry Brigades for the capture of the line Campo Cervaro-Casa Colleton-Borgo Saccon has alone been dealt with.

During the progress of these operations the 70th Infantry Brigade in Divisional reserve was to cross the Piave by the Grave di Papadopoli, and close up on the leading brigades on the night following the capture

---

[1] It will be seen later that this bridge had to be made available for the passage of the 56th Italian Division on the night following the first day's attack.

of their final objectives, in readiness to advance at dawn next day for the capture of the line of the Livenza. The brigade would be strengthened by the attachment of certain machine-guns, trench-mortars, and pioneers, and its advance would be supported by such of the Divisional artillery as had become available.[1]

Such was the plan of operations explained at the Divisional conference held on October 21.

A scheme which contemplated forcing the passage of two rivers [2] and advancing to a depth of fifteen miles in three days might well appear ambitious. But it must be realised that the *morale* of the enemy was known to have reached a very low ebb. It was reckoned that if driven from their defences on the left bank of the Piave the demoralisation of the Austrians would be so complete as to render them incapable of further serious resistance.

On October 23 Divisional Headquarters moved to St Bartolomeo, and General Thuillier took over command of the left sector of the XIV. Corps front.

The hour of attack was now fixed for 6.45 A.M. on October 25. During the night of October 23/24 the 7th Division captured the northern half of the Grave di Papadopoli by a surprise attack. The operation, which was most skilfully carried out, was effected without artillery co-operation ; some 300 prisoners were secured. The opportunity for assembling troops on the Grave was immediately seized, and by dawn one company of the 11th West Yorkshire Regiment had been ferried across from Cosenza Island.

Casa Catena, the only intact and suitable building in the whole Divisional area, had been selected as Divisional Battle Headquarters. An elaborate system of telephone line had been laid to connect this building with the headquarters of the various units of the Division, and it was intended to establish Divisional Headquarters here on October 24.

At this juncture an incident occurred that exemplifies the little difficulties that are apt to be met with in an Allied army.

An Italian balloon section was found at the critical moment to be comfortably ensconced in Casa Catena. A young British officer had

---

[1] The detail of troops so attached is given later.
[2] The Piave and Monticano. Orders did not include the *crossing* of the Livenza.

been sent forward to take over the premises. His inexhaustible tact was hardly equalled by his knowledge of the Italian tongue, and he completely failed to evict the tenants. Tact with the O.C. balloon section stood second to the fluent Italian, in which he made it forcibly clear that he declined, point-blank, to budge.

Here was a pretty state of affairs at the eleventh hour before attack ! Visions of the Divisional commander conducting the battle through a megaphone from an open field brought back the young officer, flushed with argument and defeat, to call up the Divisional reserves of tact from St Bartolomeo. These were furnished on such occasions by the Italian Mission, whose head, Count Emo, was an adept at translating a British outrage into an act of cordial friendship. He could bring a blush to the cheek of the most hardened virago or sweet reasonableness to the most stubborn of his compatriots.

On this, as on other occasions, the Italian Mission prevailed. Divisional Headquarters moved into Casa Catena, and the Italian balloon section courteously withdrew into the pouring rain.

For the promise of better weather had been falsified. Rain had been falling heavily throughout the day, and was still falling when, at dusk, the crossing of troops to the Grave was resumed. Two days only had passed since the river had been declared unfordable ; the prospect for the morrow looked black.

One company of the 8th Yorkshire Regiment had been successfully ferried to the Grave when orders were received from the XIV. Corps cancelling the further passage of troops, and postponing operations. The river was again rising.

Divisional Headquarters returned to St Bartolomeo, attacking brigades again took up defensive positions, and the 70th Infantry Brigade, which had been brought forward to a position about the village of Catena, returned to Treviso and St Angelo. Such guns as had moved into position were concealed. The two companies now marooned on the Grave with troops of the 7th Division were in a most unenviable position. Exposed to the weather and hostile artillery fire, their supply might prove difficult if the flood continued.

But, though the crossing of troops to the island had proceeded smoothly on the previous night, experience had shown that passage by ferry-boat was a slow process. It was, therefore, decided to continue the passage of troops to the Grave during the night of the 25th/26th. Headquarters and two more companies of the 8th Yorkshire Regiment were ferried over before dawn.

Troops of the 7th Division completed the capture of the southern half of the Grave at the same time.

Now, fortunately, the weather at last took a favourable turn ; the river was again falling, and orders were received on October 26 for the attack to be delivered at 6.45 A.M. on the following day. Divisional Headquarters returned to Casa Catena, and the 70th Infantry Brigade in Divisional reserve was again brought forward. The captured positions on the Grave di Papadopoli were heavily shelled throughout the day ; but otherwise the front remained quiet. Hitherto there was no indication that the Austrians expected attack.

At dusk the remainder of the Divisional artillery moved into position, and the transfer of troops to the Grave was again resumed. Battalions in the first line of attack were given priority, reserve troops of each brigade being held back till these had passed over.

An Austrian searchlight which swept the Piave on the front of the 23rd Division greatly endangered the safety of the crossing. Fortunately, a detachment of the 3rd Italian Searchlight Company had been placed at the disposal of the Division. Their searchlight had proved invaluable on previous nights in blinding that of the Austrians by the ingenious expedient of crossing beams, and was again employed to-night for this purpose.

At 7.50 P.M. the passage of troops was reported to be progressing satisfactorily. At 10.30 P.M. report was received that the 101st Field Company and Italian Pontieri had completed the foot-bridge between Cosenza Island and the Grave. There was little doubt now that the assembly of attacking troops on the Grave would be completed in good time.

Hitherto not a British gun had spoken. But before the assault it was necessary to deal with the Austrian wire, which, though not considered formidable, was sufficient to present a serious obstacle to the infantry attack. The success of the attack was more likely to be prejudiced by uncut wire than by the artillery retaliation which would undoubtedly follow our bombardment. At 10.30 P.M. the heavy artillery opened, and the Divisional artillery commenced a bombardment of the enemy's wire.

Up to this point there had been no enemy interference with the crossing, but now, as had been anticipated, the Austrian artillery brought fire to bear on the neighbourhood of the ferry and bridge. The passage of the troops was, however, never seriously hampered, and by 3.30 A.M. all attacking troops had been successfully landed on the Grave. The entire 69th Infantry Brigade (less brigade headquarters), together with attached troops, was assembled on the island. The G.O.C. 68th Infantry Brigade retained two companies of the 10th Northumberland Fusiliers under his own hand on the right bank, in order to be in a better position to deal with possible developments on his exposed left flank.

While credit for the complete success of this most delicate operation was due both to the supervision of the officers regulating it and to the discipline of the men concerned, it was due, above all, to the skill, devotion to duty, and unceasing labour of the boatmen of the 18th Italian Bridging Company, who, in darkness and under fire of the enemy, had ferried the British troops across a stream running at ten miles an hour.

Ninety-seven of the prisoners taken by the 7th Division in the capture of the Grave, whom it had not been possible to send back before, were now transferred to the right bank.

At 5 A.M. a heavy rain-storm swept over the Grave di Papadopoli, drenching the troops assembled for attack.

At 5.30 A.M. grave news was received at Divisional Headquarters. The bridging arrangements of the 58th Italian Division on the left had broken down, and they would be unable to engage in the attack.

The 8th Yorkshire Light Infantry of the 70th Infantry Brigade were immediately moved forward to Palazzo Rosso, and placed at the disposal of the G.O.C. 68th Infantry Brigade to enable him to protect his left flank, which would now be completely in the air.

The bund, along which ran the Austrian front line, lay some 400 yards back from the river. To sweep the intervening ground, an 18-pdr. barrage, opening at 6.25 A.M. along the water's edge, commenced to creep forward to reach the front line at 6.45 A.M., when it would jump forward to clear the way for the infantry assault. The barrage was thin—less than one gun to 75 yards,—but to counteract this it had been arranged to concentrate fire on the most probable points of resistance when the barrage reached the enemy's defences. The two 4.5-in. howitzer batteries were employed, the one in placing a smoke barrage in protection of the left flank, the other in firing a creeping barrage with H.E. shell, 106 fuze, on the left flank of the infantry advance. A standing protective shrapnel barrage from two 105 mm. batteries, in enfilade of the whole of the left flank of the advance, provided further protection in this quarter.

In darkness, bitter cold, and heavy rain, the troops moved forward from their assembly positions on the Grave to close up to the artillery barrage. Officers led their commands by compass bearing. It is no light task, even in broad daylight and without interference, for a heavily-equipped man to ford an unknown river ; cool heads and stout hearts were needed if this was to be accomplished in darkness, and in the teeth of the artillery and machine-gun fire which now opposed the advance.

Fording the swift current of the channels, waist-deep, men linked arms to safeguard their passage ; but several were swept from their feet and drowned. It was a desperate venture ; but the fine leading of the officers and the steadiness of their men assembled the 68th and 69th Brigades for attack in their appointed places on the far bank of the Piave.

The timing had been perfect. There had been no rush, no confusion. The troops quietly deployed in rear of the artillery barrage and awaited the moment of assault.

As the barrage lifted from the Austrian front line, the infantry of the 23rd Division rushed forward to the assault. On the right, the 69th Infantry Brigade, with the 8th Yorkshire Regiment on the right, the 10th Duke of Wellington's Regiment on the left, and C Company of the 11th West Yorkshire Regiment in the centre, stormed the hostile front line and overwhelmed the garrison. The remainder of the 11th West Yorkshire Regiment, who followed in brigade reserve, were pushed forward, and by 7 A.M. the 69th Infantry Brigade had captured its first objective and occupied the front trench.

On the left, the 68th Infantry Brigade, advancing with the 12th Durham Light Infantry on the right and the 11th Northumberland Fusiliers on the left, met with a stiffer resistance, and encountered uncut wire. The latter battalion experienced trouble, in particular from machine-guns on the open left flank, and from certain forward machine-guns that had escaped the artillery barrage. Lieut.-Colonel St Hill, commanding the battalion, was killed ; all remaining officers over the

rank of subaltern became casualties, and command fell to Lieutenant
J. Roberton. The battalion, nevertheless, pressed forward with the
greatest determination, and, overcoming all resistance, gained its objective.

In the meantime the advance of the 12th Durham Light Infantry
had been held up by uncut wire, which was swept through its entire
length by shell and machine-gun fire. The situation for the moment
was critical. The 11th Northumberland Fusiliers, with their left flank
already completely exposed, looked in danger of being isolated. Captain Gibbon of the 12th Durham Light Infantry rushed forward with
four of his men to cut the wire. Almost immediately the four men were
killed and the officer was wounded. Seeing this, Private George Brown,
though himself already wounded, crept forward to the assistance of his
officer, who was continuing his efforts to clear an opening. The initiative
and superb courage of this officer and his men saved the situation. The
wire was cut, and the 12th Durham Light Infantry, streaming through
the gaps cleared by their gallant comrades, stormed and carried the
trench line on their front. Severe as had been the casualties resulting
from the check, the delay had been but momentary, and the 68th
Infantry Brigade completed the capture of their first objective simultaneously with the 69th Infantry Brigade on their right.

At 7.10 A.M. the artillery barrage once more crept forward, and the
infantry advanced to the capture of their next objective, the Red Dotted
Line.

The barrage regulating the rate of advance now moved at 100 yards
in five minutes. The country to be traversed was dead flat, but the
surface of the ground was broken and sparsely covered with withered
vines and patches of high grass and scrub. The advance of both brigades
was opposed by considerable fire, mainly from machine-guns.

On the right, the outer flank of the 69th Infantry Brigade had become somewhat exposed owing to the troops on the left of the 7th Division having been delayed by difficulties in crossing the river. But these
were now pushing forward, and no anxiety was felt with regard to this
flank.

The situation on the left flank was not so satisfactory. In view of
the gap which would exist between the 23rd Division and 58th Italian
Division, two companies of the 10th Northumberland Fusiliers had been

detailed in the original scheme for the protection of the left flank. These companies, as the advance continued, succeeded in capturing many machine-guns and in establishing infantry and machine-gun posts to form a defensive flank. But owing to the failure of the 58th Italian Division to cross the river, exposure in this quarter had become far more acute than was anticipated by the original plan. Though, for the present, the flank was secure, increasing demands were being made on the resources of the 68th Infantry Brigade for the protection of its left.

The trench line which represented the second objective was heavily wired, and would have lent itself to a stout resistance in the hands of a determined enemy. But the Austrians, large numbers of whom had already surrendered, had been demoralised by the first shock of attack. Their infantry would not stand to check, let alone engage assault, and the withdrawal of the infantry enabled our troops to outflank the enemy's machine-guns, which at first showed a determined resistance. At this stage of the attack 2nd Lieutenant J. S. Youll, V.C., 11th Northumberland Fusiliers, fell mortally wounded. But casualties were generally light, and by 8 A.M. the 23rd Division had captured its second objective.

The two companies of the 10th Northumberland Fusiliers retained by the G.O.C. 68th Infantry Brigade on the right bank of the Piave were now sent forward to reinforce the remainder of their battalion in the defence of the left flank. He still held in reserve the 8th Yorkshire Light Infantry of the 70th Brigade, which had been placed under cover of a bund some twelve hundred yards from the river's edge. Two companies of this battalion were now brought up to the neighbourhood of 68th Brigade Headquarters, which had moved to Casa Zeoto.

At the commencement of the battle the headquarters of both attacking brigades had been established at Casa Rizzi. Here for the present the headquarters of the 69th Infantry Brigade remained.

After a pause of forty-five minutes the advance was continued along the whole line for the capture of the final objective of the day, the Tezze-Borgo Malanotte-Casa Dalmadella line. Little resistance was met during this advance of 1200 yards till the line of the objective itself was reached. Along this line ran a metalled road. Among the trees which skirted the near side of the road in front of Borgo Malanotte, short lengths of trench had been constructed and partially wired. On the far side of the road stood two buildings, looted by Austrian soldiers, but otherwise intact. The one, a small house, stood on the road itself ; the other, a larger house surrounded by a garden, stood back some fifteen yards from the road.

At this point, which lay opposite C Company of the 11th West Yorkshire Regiment in the centre of the 69th Infantry Brigade, it became apparent that the Austrians had decided to stand. But the West Yorkshires quickly drove in the half-hearted defence of the trench line, and, crossing the road, stormed the buildings. A few minutes sharp fighting, the Austrian resistance broke, and the buildings fell into the hands of the attackers.

It was now noon. On its right the 23rd Division was in touch with the 91st Infantry Brigade of the 7th Division ; on the left a defensive flank of 3000 yards had been developed northwards from the river. The final objective had been gained on the whole front of the XIV. Corps.

In under six hours the passage of the Piave had been forced, and the British had advanced from the further bank to a depth of over 3000 yards.

Fighting, however, was not yet over. At 1 P.M. information was received by the G.O.C. 69th Infantry Brigade that the Austrians, rallying opposite Borgo Malanotte, had recaptured the buildings by a counter-attack delivered in great force ; ammunition had run short, and the situation at that point was for the time somewhat precarious.

Ammunition was hastily sent forward to the fighting line, and A Company (Captain Hobday) of the 11th West Yorkshire Regiment was immediately ordered up from brigade reserve to attack and retake the village. This fresh attack, delivered at 4 P.M., proved completely successful ; the greater portion of the troops that had been engaged in the Austrian counter-attack were killed or captured, and Borgo Malanotte changed hands for the third and last time.

As a result of the day's operations hundreds of prisoners had been captured, together with a large number of machine-guns, trench-mortars, and artillery pieces of various calibre.[1]

Considerable trouble had been experienced after capture of the final objective from machine-guns on the exposed left flank. To deal

[1] The total of prisoners, &c., captured by the 23rd Division between October 27 and 31 is given at the end of this chapter.

with this, both 4.5-in. howitzer batteries were ordered to creep forward and back along this flank firing H.E., 106 fuze. This did not serve entirely to reduce the enemy's fire, and the whole 103rd Brigade was brought into action along this flank, while the 102nd Brigade opened out the lines of fire of its 18-pdrs to cover the Divisional front. By the evening the enemy's machine-guns had been silenced except in the neighbourhood of Casa Dalmadella,[1] where they continued to harass the left of our line, till nightfall brought quiet to the whole front.

Two forward observing officers from each artillery brigade had been detailed to each infantry brigade in the attack. They had led their parties across the Piave with the infantry, and had been in constant communication with their headquarters by telephone, wires being attached to the footbridge to clear the swift deep channel between Cosenza and the Grave. Arrangements for visual signalling had been made, but it was not necessary to fall back on this.

Communication, under most exceptional difficulties, had been well maintained throughout the Division, and both Brigade and Divisional Headquarters had been in touch with the situation from start to finish. Cable, wireless, and visual were all established at an early hour. The success in this direction was largely due to the splendid efforts of Captain Jameson of the Divisional Signal Company ; nor did this officer confine himself to the establishment of communication. Always in the forefront of the battle, he found time to send back clear and concise reports of the situation, which were of the greatest assistance to the Divisional Commander. Major Tillard, commanding the Signal Company, whose careful arrangements were in the first place responsible for the excellence of the communication, in writing of Captain Jameson, says : " No words are adequate to express the gallantry of this officer, who during the course of two years was awarded the D.S.O., M.C., and two bars. He was absolutely fearless, and always to be found where the shelling was heaviest."

The following incident serves to illustrate the conditions under which communication was established and maintained :—

A party of the 23rd Divisional Signal Company was engaged in

---

[1] The accuracy of our artillery fire on an unregistered objective was proved by finding later that three direct hits had been obtained on this house—a very creditable performance on the part of all concerned.

laying a telephone wire across the Piave. The course of the river was still being swept by heavy machine-gun fire, but they had succeeded in crossing an island shoal in safety, when they were faced by a deep channel close to the far bank. The first men to attempt the crossing were swept from their feet and drowned. On witnessing this, Sapper Charles Robson, who formed one of the party, took from three of his comrades a heavy drum of cable and entered the stream alone. After narrowly escaping being drowned, by a supreme effort he gained the far bank with the drum, and the cable was laid. Then, though the whole surface of the water was being whipped by the strike of bullets, he immediately returned across the stream to the assistance of his comrades. Later, he carried more heavy drums across the river, and maintained the line under heavy shell-fire.[1]

A bridgehead had been secured by the XIV. Corps, but farther advance would be impossible till measures were taken to relieve the sorely taxed 68th Infantry Brigade of the responsibility for holding the defensive flank which they occupied on a front of nearly two miles, in addition to the line of the objective they had captured.

Such measures were now possible. On October 26, under circumstances of the greatest difficulty, the Royal Engineers, including the 128th Field Company, had, with the assistance of Italian Engineers, completed the pontoon bridge across the flooded channel that swept between Salletuol and the Grave. On the 27th the 101st Field Company had been placed under the Chief Engineer, XIV. Corps, to increase the number on bridging work. During this day, under heavy shell-fire and the bombs of hostile aeroplanes, Salletuol crossing had been extended by bridging the further channels between the Grave and the left bank.

The XVIII. (Italian) Corps had now been allotted to Lord Cavan, with a view to its being passed over the British bridges and attacking westwards to clear the front of the Eighth Army. The 56th Italian Division of this corps was brought forward to cross the Salletuol bridge after dark, and then move westwards in rear of the forward positions held by the 23rd Division. During the night, the Como Brigade of this division relieved the troops of the 68th Infantry Brigade holding the defensive flank. At the same time, a brigade of the 33rd Italian Division crossed the river by the Cosenza foot-bridge, and advanced to

---

[1] Sapper Robson was later awarded the D.C.M. for his action on this occasion.

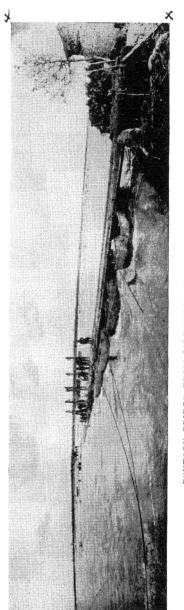

PONTOON BRIDGE FROM SALLETUOL TO GRAVE DI PAPADOPOLI.

PONTOON BRIDGE FROM GRAVE DI PAPADOPOLI TO AUSTRIAN BANK.

a position on the left bank, in readiness to operate on the left flank of the 56th Italian Division the following day.

The necessity for passing Italian troops over our bridges upset all plans drawn up for the crossing of British transport. This was being regulated by Major Owen, the D.A.A.G., Major Hilliard, the D.A.D.V.S., and 2nd Lieutenant Perks of the 223rd Employment Company, and controlled by Major Williams, the D.A.P.M. The scene at Salletuol at sunset on October 27 would have brought despair to the heart of a London policeman ; but Major Owen, dragged from his more legitimate duties, found himself in his element in the tangled mass of troops, waggons, and pack-mules.

The S.A.A. pack-mules and light trench-mortars had got clear away, and the 6-in. mobile mortars managed to cross to the Grave just before the flood of Italian troops, scarcely less formidable than that of the Piave itself, swept down on the Salletuol bridge. The experience of the 6-in. mortars serves well to illustrate the difficulties of the crossing. The two sections to cross over were those of X/23 and Y/23. The former was commanded by Captain Ballard, assisted by Lieutenant Graham, while Captain Dobinson, D.T.M.O., himself assumed command of Y/23, assisted by Lieutenant Copey. The trusty " Rabbit," a short-tailed mule who could climb a precipice or walk a tight rope, led the way, and soon the long line of mules, silhouetted against the red glare of the setting sun, was strung out over the pontoon bridge. They were followed by the two limbered waggons accompanying each section.

By the time the column had crossed to the Grave it was dark. The shingle of the island showed no tracks of the transport that had pre-ceded them, and such tapes as were found were old Austrian lines, which were useless as a guide. Off-loading the mules, the officers set out to attempt to find the crossings to the farther bank. Several times they struck a deep unfordable channel, and were beginning to despair when, attracted by the groans of some wounded Austrians, they fell in with a party of stretcher-bearers. These men informed them that the farther channels were not bridged,[1] and led them to a ford opposite Cimadolmo.

An orderly was sent back to bring forward the column. Simul-taneously with the column's arrival the Italian flood swept down and

[1] In this they were wrong.

threatened to submerge them. Mixed up in the dark with the Italian infantry, all for a time was confusion. At length our men got clear and plunged into the stream. The water was waist-deep and the current swift. The smaller ones experienced great difficulties, but were held up by the taller and stronger. More than once our men were swimming for a space before regaining a foothold. All the waggons got safely across except one, which stuck in a hole. One of the mules was twice carried under the water and all but drowned, and several of the smaller men were only just saved from being swept down-stream. Conspicuous among the men who were working manfully in the water were Captain Ballard, Lieutenant Graham, and Corporal M'Call.

Before the waggon had been extricated the Italian troops again came on the scene, and confusion reigned once more. Several of these were swept from their feet, but were saved from drowning by Corporal M'Call and the bigger gunners. At last a supreme effort by the mules, who were shoulder-deep in the water, shifted the waggon, and it was dragged ashore. The waggon-mules were found to be lame, so it was decided to dump the ammunition and send the waggons back empty to fill up and come forward the following day with fresh mules. It was then the duty of the commanding officers to set out and find the infantry brigades to which they were attached, while their detachments, soaked to the skin, found what rest they could in an open field.

The decision to return the waggons was, under the circumstances, a wise one. But as events turned out, they were never to reach their sections again till the operations were at an end, and the trench-mortars were to be dependent for ammunition on their pack supply.

Map No. 11.   At 9 A.M. on the 28th the Como Brigade attacked in a westerly direction, then, wheeling north, came into line with the 68th Infantry Brigade, in readiness to continue the advance on the left of the 23rd Division. As the Como Brigade wheeled, the 33rd Italian Division moved over the ground thus cleared and continued the westerly advance, taking in flank the Austrian defences against which the Italian attack of the previous day had failed to develop.

The necessity for awaiting the conclusion of these manœuvres, as well as the holding up of the British traffic on the Salletuol bridge, prohibited any possibility of gaining the objective originally planned for the 28th. The direction of the advance was now to change from north

to north-east. To effect this the advance ordered was to take the
form of a partial right-wheel ; the objective given to the left of the
68th Infantry Brigade was at a distance of some 3500 yards ; the
advance of the right of the 69th Infantry Brigade along the Tezze-
Vazzola road as the central point of the XIV. Corps would be
somewhat less.

At 11.30 A.M. Divisional Headquarters moved from Casa Catena to
Casa Rizzi close to the right bank of the Piave.

At 12.30 P.M. 69th and 68th Infantry Brigades advanced. Battalions
on the left of the line in each brigade had been relieved ; the 10th Duke
of Wellington's by the 11th West Yorkshire Regiment, the 11th by the
10th Battalion Northumberland Fusiliers. Otherwise, battalions were
placed as on the preceding day.

The enemy were found to be retiring covered by rear-guards. The
inhabited area had not yet been reached, but the zone to be crossed had
suffered little from shell-fire. Roads were in fair condition, and buildings, trees, and vegetation provided cover for the retreating forces, and
made ambush a probability to be guarded against.

The field artillery, still in action on the right bank of the Piave,
would only be able to cover the advance for a short space. Methods
practised against the limited objectives of a trench-to-trench attack
now required modification ; the training of the Division to meet a novel
form of warfare was to be tested. The test was well met ; the skilful
handling of platoons and sections and the initiative of individuals not
only prevented the enemy's tactics from delaying the advance, but succeeded in capturing large numbers of his infantry and machine-guns
before they could be withdrawn.

D Company (Captain Lawson) of the West Yorkshire Regiment
captured and cleared Borgo Villa, and later, Soffratta, taking many
prisoners.

Little opposition, however, was experienced on the right or centre
of the advance, the enemy's main resistance being brought against the
left flank, before which lay the longest advance.

As on the previous day, the chief trouble caused was by nests of
machine-guns supported by infantry. A centre of resistance of this
type had been organised in some ruined buildings near Casa Bravato.
An officer of the 10th Northumberland Fusiliers, with the personnel

of his company headquarters and one platoon, charged this position with the bayonet, captured 3 machine-guns, and accounted for 60 of the enemy killed or captured. A second platoon surrounded and captured 160 prisoners at another point.

It was on this flank, too, that Private Wilfred Wood of the same battalion earned the Victoria Cross. A machine-gun nest was holding up the advance of the platoon in which he was a Lewis-gunner. Creeping forward with his gun to a point from which he could bring the position in enfilade, Wood caused 140 of the enemy to surrender. Later, when the advance was again held up by the point-blank fire of a single machine-gun, this young soldier charged the gun single-handed, and, firing his Lewis-gun from the hip, killed the entire crew of the machine-gun ; then, pushing forward on his own initiative, he brought the fire of his gun in enfilade on a ditch crowded with Austrian infantry, who, believing their retreat cut off, surrendered to the platoon, which was now advancing against their position.[1]

The advance was covered throughout by the fire of heavy artillery. Compensation for the loss of field artillery support was found in the fire of the mobile trench-mortars attached to brigades, and also, on the left flank, by bringing into action certain of the Austrian pieces. The machine-guns of the 23rd Battalion Machine-Gun Corps also greatly assisted the advance by covering fire delivered from the upper storeys of buildings in rear of the infantry.

Early in the afternoon the 23rd Division gained the line of its objective from a point just south of Vazzola to about Casa Gerre. Casualties had been light, but included Lieut.-Colonel H. H. Hudson, who was wounded. His place in command of the 11th West Yorkshire Regiment was taken by Major C. L. Armstrong, whose brother, Major G. J. Armstrong, was called to brigade headquarters at the same time to act on the staff.

The movement had pivoted on the 7th Division, with which the 23rd Division had remained in close contact throughout the day. Touch with the Italians on the left was, however, lost, and was not regained till after the line of the Livenza was reached some days later.

[1] Wood's name is to be seen recorded at Euston Railway Station among those of the many employees of the L. & N.W. Railway who gained distinction in the war.

In the course of the day the headquarters of the 69th and 68th Infantry Brigades had been established at Borgo Malanotte and Casa Benedetti respectively.

On October 28 Lieut.-Colonel Rooke temporarily assumed the duties of Chief Engineer of the XIV. Corps. His place as C.R.E. was filled by Major Turner of the 102nd Field Company.

The river Monticano now lay across the line of advance at a distance of 3000 yards from the present position. The Monticano at this season ran between steep banks as a deep sluggish stream of an average width of some 30 ft. It was traversed by a stone bridge 1500 yards north-east of the village of Vazzola.[1]

On the morrow the 69th and 68th Infantry Brigades were to force the passage of this river and continue the advance to reach the line of the Campo Cervaro-Casa Colleton-Borgo Saccon road by 10.30 A.M.

The nature of the opposition encountered on October 28, and the indications of a general withdrawal of the Austrian forces, suggested the possibility of this line being reached without serious opposition. In this event the 68th and 69th Infantry Brigades having reached their final objective, the 70th Infantry Brigade group would move forward to pass through this line at 1 P.M., and, covered by such of the Divisional Artillery as it had been possible to bring forward, would attack north-east to carry the line forward during the afternoon to Colombo-Celotto-Bibano di Sotto-Borgo-Pianzano.

Detachments were pushed forward by both the 69th and 68th Brigades during the night of October 28/29, with a view to seizing the crossings of the Monticano before dawn. Parallel to, and 500 yards south of the river, ran a canal. A company of the 8th Yorkshire Regiment seized a bridge crossing this canal, mistaking it in the dark for the river bridge. A company of the 11th West Yorkshire Regiment obtained contact with the enemy at dawn on the near bank of the river, just north of Soffrata. A little farther to the left a detachment of the 12th Durham Light Infantry gained the Monticano just in time to drive back a party of Austrians who were about to destroy a wooden bridge which they had constructed at this point.

---

[1] The writer, unfortunately, has not had the opportunity of revisiting this front. He has been largely dependent on memory of such points as these in describing the Piave, Monticano, Sacile, &c.

Opposition was still strongest on the left, where fighting patrols of the 10th Northumberland Fusiliers were unable to make progress owing to hostile machine-gun fire.

At 6 A.M. the 70th Infantry Brigade, accompanied by the Pioneer Battalion and three mobile sections 6-in. trench-mortars, crossed the Piave by the Grave di Papadopoli crossing, and concentrated in the area about Casa Benedetti at 9 A.M. Here they were to remain in Divisional reserve pending developments. The brigade's first-line transport and attached machine-guns were to cross by the Salletuol bridge later in the morning. The bridge would to-day also become available for the Field Artillery.

At 8 A.M. Divisional Headquarters moved to Borgo Malanotte, where gruesome evidence remained of the price paid by the Austrian on the 27th in his efforts to cling to this position. The accumulation of filth in the buildings recently occupied by Austrian soldiers beggars description, and combined with the relics of battle to make Borgo Malanotte a spot that will live long in the memory of those who sojourned there.

The 69th and 68th Infantry Brigades advanced at 8.30 A.M., and reached the line of the river Monticano without difficulty. Here it soon became evident that the enemy was holding the line of the river in considerable strength.

It had been rumoured that the Austrians had planned a withdrawal from the Piave before the Allied offensive was delivered on October 27. The fact that no supply or ammunition dumps of any importance fell into the hands of the attack on the 27th is almost certain evidence that preparations for retirement had been made. For had such dumps existed, the rate of advance on the 27th would have made their withdrawal during the battle impossible for even the most highly organised troops.

Unfortunately the British advance had been retarded after the operations of the first day. The Austrians, realising that it was necessary to check the rate of the allied advance if they were to secure their withdrawal by the bridges of the Livenza, had taken advantage of the delay to rally their rear-guards and organise the defence of the Monticano. The line taken up by the enemy on the left bank of the river included many machine-guns, and was strongly supported by artillery.

At 10 A.M., after stiff fighting and under heavy shell-fire, the 8th

BRIDGE OVER THE MONTICANO, NEAR VAZZOLA.

Yorkshire Regiment on the right of the 69th Infantry Brigade succeeded in forcing the passage of the river by the stone bridge north-east of Vazzola. A company of this battalion, on gaining the farther bank, came under heavy rifle and machine-gun fire from the direction of a group of buildings. Frontal attack on this point would mean heavy casualties. Sergeant William M'Nally, selecting a favourable position for his platoon, instructed it to bring rifle and Lewis-gun fire to bear on the buildings to distract the attention of the enemy and keep down their fire, while he himself, creeping forward unseen to a point in rear of the buildings, rushed the position single-handed, killed or put to flight the entire garrison, and captured the machine-gun found there.[1]

The 8th Yorkshire Regiment, having now secured a footing on the left bank of the river, advanced in face of strong opposition, and gained the western outskirts of the village of Cimetta about 12 noon. The advance of the troops of the 7th Division on the immediate right of the 23rd Division had, in the meantime, been held up by the defence of this village, which was very strongly held by the enemy. The right flank of the 8th Yorkshire Regiment became heavily engaged at Cimetta, and Lieut.-Colonel Backhouse was eventually compelled to withdraw his battalion to the line of a brook 300 yards south of Cesiola. This line he continued to hold throughout the day against determined attacks delivered on his front and right flank. On the left of the 69th Infantry Brigade, Captain Douglas, whose company covered the advance of the 11th West Yorkshire Regiment, on reaching the southern bank of the Monticano, had been forced to hold up his advance till he could gain stronger support from Lewis-guns and machine-guns. On these becoming available, about 9.30 A.M., 2nd Lieutenant Buckwell with a handful of men dashed forward under cover of heavy machine-gun fire and secured a crossing near Casa Malta. The battalion followed, and by 12 noon, after heavy fighting, had captured Casa Balla.

During this period the 68th Infantry Brigade was encountering very strong opposition, and had not yet succeeded in crossing the river. To protect his left the G.O.C. 69th Infantry Brigade sent forward one

[1] This N.C.O. had distinguished himself by a similar act of valour on October 27, when he rushed a machine-gun post single-handed, killing the crew with his pistol and capturing the gun. For these acts of gallantry Sergeant M'Nally was awarded the Victoria Cross, the ninth and last awarded in the 23rd Division.

company of the 10th Duke of Wellington's from his reserve to establish
a defensive flank in the neighbourhood of Casa Bifis. At 1 P.M., however, the 12th Durham Light Infantry, on the right of the 68th Infantry
Brigade, at last succeeded in forcing the passage of the Monticano, and
in pushing forward to within 100 yards of their objective.

The area in which troops were now operating was inhabited, and the
country was blinded by stretches of vines, crops, and trees. To preserve
contact, even between platoons, was difficult enough. Battalions at
this point seem to have temporarily lost touch.

Reports received by Divisional Headquarters made it clear that the
three battalions on the right and centre of the attack had by this time
crossed the Monticano. But the officer commanding the 11th West
Yorkshire Regiment, unaware that troops had crossed on his left, believed that flank of his battalion to be completely exposed. Lieut.-
Colonel Holford, commanding 12th Durham Light Infantry, on the
other hand, was under a similar misapprehension with regard to his
right flank, and, being correctly informed that the 10th Northumberland Fusiliers on his left had hitherto failed to effect a crossing, was
under the impression that his battalion was holding a salient. As a fact,
there were at this time scattered parties of Austrians between the two
battalions, and actually in rear of the 12th Durham Light Infantry;
but, with a correct conception of the situation, the junction of the two
centre battalions of the Division could have been effected without great
difficulty. It may be accepted, however, that the situation was even
less clear to the enemy, except in so far that it must have now been
apparent to them that their resistance could not be maintained much
longer.

Owing to a report having gone astray, the G.O.C. 68th Infantry
Brigade had remained, for a considerable period, in ignorance of the
situation on the left of his brigade. On being acquainted with it, he
immediately determined to utilise part of his reserve to relieve the pressure on the left of the 12th Durham Light Infantry, and at the same
time to facilitate the crossing of the 10th Northumberland Fusiliers.
This task was allotted to the 11th Northumberland Fusiliers.[1]

The battalion was ordered to move to the left bank of the Monticano

---

[1] This battalion, owing to the heavy casualties suffered on October 27, had since been reorganised into two companies.

by the crossings already secured, and then, facing left, to clear the ground in rear of the 12th Durham Light Infantry, and take the enemy opposing the 10th Northumberland Fusiliers in flank.

In accordance with these orders, the 11th Northumberland Fusiliers crossed the Monticano, and, having gained touch with the right of the 12th Durham Light Infantry, turned at 4.15 P.M. to attack across the front of the 10th Northumberland Fusiliers, with their right on the Cervada stream and their left on the Monticano.

Many machine-guns were found still in action in the area over which the 12th Durham Light Infantry had passed, and the enemy, turning to meet this attack on their flank, put up a determined opposition. Overcoming all resistance, the battalion advanced across the open for a distance of 800 yards, sections alternately making short rushes and supporting the advance by rifle and Lewis-gun fire. Then, in a final charge, which completed the clearance of the front, they bayoneted 4 officers and 70 men, and captured 155 prisoners.

The Austrians had now been driven from the Monticano on the whole front of the Division, and the 10th Northumberland Fusiliers, crossing to the left bank, continued their advance.

In the meantime, the 91st Infantry Brigade of the 7th Division, after severe fighting, had overcome the enemy's resistance, and captured Cimetta about 3 P.M. This greatly relieved the situation of the 8th Yorkshire Regiment, whose whole reserves it had been necessary to throw into the fighting line to maintain the position taken up south of Cesiola. The 9th York and Lancaster Regiment of the 70th Infantry Brigade was now in a position of readiness to pass through the 8th Yorkshire Regiment. To close the latter battalion for farther advance would have entailed considerable delay ; the G.O.C. 69th Infantry Brigade was, therefore, permitted to employ the 9th York and Lancaster Regiment in carrying the right of his objective.

The enemy's resistance on the line of the Monticano had been broken, but it had served to delay the advance. The 70th Infantry Brigade had deployed in readiness to move forward and continue the advance ; but the day was too far spent to carry out this further operation. Orders were, therefore, issued for the 68th and 69th Infantry Brigades to consolidate the line gained.

The final position taken up during the night was the line of the

Campo Cervaro-Casa Colleton-Borgo Saccon road, which it had been hoped to reach by 10.30 A.M.

The stiffest resistance yet experienced had been encountered this day. On October 27 our infantry had advanced 5000 yards in five hours. This day they were fighting for over seven hours on the line of the Monticano before the crossings of the river had been secured on the whole Divisional front. The capture of Cimetta by the 7th Division had only been effected after six hours' heavy fighting.

It is improbable that the Austrians would have put up so stiff a fight had the attack been supported by artillery fire. But it can be taken that, in selecting the line of the Monticano, they were fully alive to the difficulties presented by the Piave to the forward movement of artillery ; and that they reckoned that attack, if delivered on the 29th, would be unsupported by artillery fire.

A/102 Battery, the first to cross the river, came into action west of Vazzola during the afternoon ; but the situation of the infantry was not sufficiently clear for its guns to be employed to full effect. The only artillery support to the left of the attack was that given by the 146th Italian Mountain Battery. The personnel of this battery, having carried their guns and ammunition across the Piave, had dragged them forward by hand in support of the 68th Infantry Brigade throughout the operations. Their support had proved invaluable, and Brig.-General Cary-Barnard spoke in the highest terms of the readiness with which they had met the severest demands.

The night passed quietly, and orders were issued for operations to be continued by the advance of the 70th Infantry Brigade Group on the following day.

The Brigade Group, under the command of Brig.-General H. Gordon, was constituted as follows : two 18-pdr. batteries (A and B, 102nd Brigade R.F.A.), 146th Italian Mountain Battery, three mobile sections 6-in. trench-mortars,[1] 70th Infantry Brigade, 23rd Machine-Gun Battalion (less two companies), 9th (Pioneers) Battalion South Staffordshire Regiment.

This small combined force was to advance to gain as a first objective the line Casa Brandolin (exclusive)-Orsago (inclusive), and, as a final objective, the line of the river Livenza.

[1] Sections of X/23, Y/23, and Y/48 (Lieut. Goodall) attached from the 48th Division.

During the night the battalions of the 70th Infantry Brigade were disposed as follows : the 9th York and Lancaster Regiment remained in the line on the right of the 69th Infantry Brigade, the 8th King's Own Yorkshire Light Infantry were in reserve to the 68th Infantry Brigade, the 8th York and Lancaster Regiment occupied a position of assembly in rear of the left of the line.

At 9 A.M. on October 30 these three battalions, to each of which was attached one section of pioneers, advanced as the forward line of the attacking force. They were followed by the artillery of the column, and by the pioneer battalion (less detached platoons) in brigade reserve.

Though preceded by the corps mounted troops, it was necessary for battalions to find their own advanced-guards. The advance lay through a densely populated agricultural area containing numerous farms and villages. Though the country was clear of the enemy, the task of advanced-guards was difficult, and progress was slow. At 11 A.M. an advanced Divisional Headquarters was established at Vazzola.

The 9th York and Lancaster Regiment on the right gained the line of the first objective by 1.35 P.M. ; at this hour the Yorkshire Light Infantry and 8th York and Lancaster Regiment, who had a greater distance to traverse, were still considerably in rear of the Casa Brandolin-Orsago line.

The 68th and 69th Infantry Brigades, in Divisional reserve, were now moved forward to the Godega and Borgo areas respectively.

At 3.15 P.M. General Gordon received information that a force of Austrian cavalry and infantry, attacking from the direction of Ronche and Sacile, had inflicted serious casualties on the corps mounted troops, and captured certain of their motor machine-guns.

By now the 9th York and Lancaster Regiment had advanced to the line of the Meschio stream. Orders were issued for this battalion to hold the southern bank of the stream with its left on the road culvert at point K 65, while the Yorkshire Light Infantry and 8th York and Lancaster Regiment pressed forward vigorously to prolong this line through Ponte della Muda to Cordignano.

These dispositions were taken up by 5.30 P.M. The Austrians, contenting themselves with the small success they had obtained, did not approach the line of the river Meschio, and the corps mounted troops were withdrawn behind the protection of the line occupied.

An advance of some seven miles had been made during the day, and the approach of darkness made further movement inadvisable. Orders were accordingly issued from Divisional Headquarters, now established at Bibano di Sotto, for the line of the river Meschio to be held for the night, advance to the river Livenza being postponed till the morrow.

A third 18-pdr. battery, C/102, had arrived during the afternoon, and had been moved to Orsago at 5.50 P.M.

The objective given to the 70th Infantry Brigade Group for October 31 differed slightly from that given for the 30th. The line to be gained, instead of extending from Sacile to Ronche and Col di Fer, was now to be taken west of Sacile to S. Michele and Caneva (inclusive).

Just before reaching Sacile the river Livenza takes a sharp easterly bend, dividing the town into a northern and southern quarter. Then turning south and west, it forms a loop round the southern quarter before it resumes its general course to the south, and passes under a railway bridge about 600 yards from the centre of the town.

Some large solid buildings were situated on the western outskirts of the southern quarter; south of these stood the railway station, facing the iron-girder railway bridge, which had been partially destroyed by the Italians in their retreat in 1917. The river was further crossed by two wooden bridges, the one in the centre of, the other just above, the town. The distance from the railway bridge below the town to the wooden bridge above the town was 1000 yards as the crow flies, but by following the easterly bend of the river this distance would be doubled. The streets in the central portion of Sacile on both banks of the river were narrow. In the neighbourhood of the central bridge, which was some forty yards long, the river, flowing swift and deep between embankments, was overlooked by tall buildings on either bank.

During the night of October 30/31 a patrol of the 9th York and Lancaster Regiment reached the outskirts of the town, which was found to be strongly held.

At 9 A.M. on the 31st the 70th Infantry Brigade advanced with the 9th York and Lancaster Regiment on the right, the 8th Yorkshire Light Infantry in the centre, and the 8th York and Lancaster Regiment on the left. As before, one platoon of pioneers was attached to each battalion, the remainder being held in brigade reserve. The advance of each battalion was supported by one 18-pdr. battery of the 102nd Brigade R.F.A.

The 9th York and Lancasters almost immediately came in contact with the enemy in front of Sacile, and by 9.30 A.M. were heavily engaged by the enemy holding the railway station. The 12th Durham Light Infantry of the 68th Infantry Brigade were now placed at the disposal of the G.O.C. 70th Infantry Brigade, and moved to a position in reserve about Point K 65. The 8th Yorkshire Light Infantry (Lieut.-Colonel Quirk) and the 8th York and Lancaster Regiment (Lieut.-Colonel Colley) had, in the meantime, reached the line S. Michele-Caneva without opposition.

The left of the 9th York and Lancaster Regiment, gaining the western edge of Sacile, succeeded by 12 noon in penetrating the outskirts of the town, and joining hands with the 8th Yorkshire Light Infantry on their left.

At this point the enemy withdrew across the river. By 12.30 P.M. the right bank was occupied, and the 70th Infantry Brigade had captured its objective along the whole of its front.

During the afternoon junction with the 7th Division was effected at the railway bridge, which was still passable by infantry. The wooden bridges in the centre of and above the town had both been destroyed just before our leading troops reached the river.

The enemy had abandoned an immense amount of material. The 70th Infantry Brigade alone, in addition to having captured some 500 prisoners, had secured 54 guns. The bulk of the Austrian forces was now flying in complete rout towards the Tagliamento ; but their rearguards still clung to positions on the left bank of the Livenza.

Sanction was given to the request of the O.C. 9th York and Lancaster Regiment to be allowed to force the passage and form a bridgehead at Sacile with three companies. It was proposed to construct a temporary foot-bridge from the débris of the central town bridge. But before this work could be undertaken it was necessary to subdue the enemy's fire.

A hostile battery firing into the western portion of the town was quickly silenced by 18-pdr. guns of the 102nd Brigade R.F.A. Machine-guns, however, kept up an incessant fire from the houses on the opposite side of the river. Stokes guns and 6-in. mortars were brought forward, and, co-operating with the fire of two machine-guns posted in houses on the near bank, soon silenced the enemy's fire.

A detachment of the Pioneer Battalion was then brought up to improvise a foot-bridge from the wreckage of the demolished bridge. In the variety of the work thrust on them, the pioneers of the Division had much in common with the Royal Marines. They could never foretell what would be asked of them next. Whatever the job proved to be, it never found them dismayed ; however stiff or unpleasant, it was invariably accomplished. They now set about the bridging of the river with customary zeal, but scarcely had they commenced work than a machine-gun opened fire from the steeple of Sacile Church, and wounded several of their men. Three direct hits by our artillery silenced the machine-gun, and the pioneers, resuming work, quickly completed the construction of a foot-bridge.

Crossing on the left bank, the 9th York and Lancaster Regiment proceeded to clear eastern Sacile. Sharp street-fighting ensued, but the enemy was eventually driven from the protection of walls and buildings, and a bridgehead was established.

Desultory firing continued for a space in the dusk of the evening ; then as night fell the Austrian remnants withdrew under cover of darkness, and all was silent. Suddenly a single shot rang out, fired, perchance, at nothing more solid than one of those shadows that take form and move before the eyes of a wearied sentry, but a shot none the less worthy of record, for it was the last fired in the Great War by the 23rd Division.

The front of the Division on the night of October 31/November 1 ran on the left bank of the Livenza from the railway bridge, south of Sacile, through the eastern outskirts of the town ; north of the town the line was drawn back across the river due west to S. Michele, and thence north-west to Chiaradia and Vellerher. The Division was in touch with the 7th Division and the XVIII. Italian Corps on the right and left respectively.

During the five days that had elapsed since the British troops crossed the Piave the strain on the supply services had been very great. The temporary blocking of the Salletuol bridge by the passage of Italian troops had thrown out of gear all carefully worked-out arrangements. Thanks, however, to the unremitting efforts of the " Q " Staff throughout the Division, and to the unceasing labour of Lieut.-Colonel Leese, commanding the Divisional Train, and of all others engaged in the work, supply arrangements were carried through amazingly well. In the 68th Infantry Brigade the situation had been to a large degree saved by the arrival of the mules of Mobile T.M. Section, which were used by Brig.-General Cary-Barnard to carry forward rations to the infantry, in addition to their legitimate employment. Similar improvisations had to be made for other units, and, under the circumstances, it was inevitable that the troops should suffer a certain degree of hardship. On the morning of October 30, after three days' incessant fighting, the 68th and 69th Infantry Brigades had been in urgent need of rest. But now they were completely refreshed and eager to press forward. There was nothing in the condition of the troops to prevent the advance being continued.

But though two bridges were now available for transport across the Piave, this advantage was discounted by the distance that intervened between the advanced troops and railhead. The question of supply made a halt imperative. The XIV. Corps accordingly held the line of the Livenza during November 1, while the transport and the remainder of the Field Artillery commenced to close up.

On November 2, Lord Cavan's Tenth Army, with the XI. Italian Corps on the right, XIV. Corps in the centre, and XVIII. Italian Corps on the left, commenced its advance on the river Tagliamento, twenty miles east of the Livenza. The line of the river Meduna was to be gained in the first day's march, and the 23rd Division, in reserve to the XIV. Corps, was ordered to move to the Porcia area, some six miles due east of Sacile.

The 69th Infantry Brigade crossed the Livenza at Cavolano, one and a half miles south of Sacile, and advanced by the somewhat circuitous Tamai-Palse road. The remainder of the Division (less the 103rd Brigade R.F.A., 102nd and 128th Field Companies, 69th Field Ambulance, and Sanitary Section) crossed at Sacile, and marched by the main Fontana

Fredda-Pordenone road. The 128th Field Company was still working on the Piave ; the 102nd Field Company and the pioneers were to remain at Sacile for the construction of bridges across the Livenza. Along the Pordenone road, which ran wide and straight through open country, there was terrible evidence of the loss in power of a river to save a routed army. Before war was carried into the air a defeated army, by placing a river between itself and pursuit, might hope to gain some respite to restore its shattered *morale*, but the deepest and widest river is of no avail against aircraft. The sights on the Pordenone road moved the victorious British troops to horror and to pity ; to the weary half-starved enemy, whose disorganised masses had blackened the broad high-road during the past few days, the vision of the fate which might at any moment visit them must have brought a terror which eclipsed even the bitterness of defeat. For mile after mile the road was flanked with wreckage of troops and transport, shattered guns and waggons, the mangled remains of drivers intermingled with those of the horses, corpses of infantrymen riddled by machine-gun fire. Recalling the scene, a witness has been moved to write that it " almost forced the observer to the conclusion that this form of warfare should be forbidden in the future." [1]

But the halt on November 1 had enabled those of the Austrians who had escaped destruction from our aircraft to withdraw to the Tagliamento, and contact was not obtained with the enemy by the Tenth Army on the 2nd. The advance was continued on November 3, but orders received for the forward movement of the 23rd Division were later cancelled, and it remained billeted in the Porcia area, with headquarters at Porcia. The 103rd Brigade R.F.A. rejoined the Division this day, and the 128th Field Company was ordered forward from the Piave.

It is dangerous to base general statements on particular experience, but the impression gained in the area now occupied, as well as in those through which the Division had passed during the past few days, was that the conduct of the Austro-Hungarian Army in occupation of Italian territory had been good. The enemy's troops had undoubtedly suffered severely from hunger in recent days ; the condition

[1] Article in the Army Quarterly, October 1921, by Major-General The Hon. J. F. Gathorne-Hardy, C.B., C.M.G., D.S.O., late M.G.G.S. Tenth Army.

✳ of their sick and wounded left untended in the hospitals was pitiable. ✳ The Italian population, on the other hand, though they had experienced for a whole year a sense of abandonment and the indignities of an enemy occupation, showed little sign of affliction from lack of food. Trivial incidents, however, sometimes form deep—and occasionally false —impressions. It is well, therefore, to relate two particular incidents which may have unduly influenced the opinion given above.

At the farm at Bibano di Sotto, where Divisional Headquarters were established on the night of October 31, commander and staff, tired out and hungry, assembled in a vast kitchen round a roaring fire. Some months before, it had been realised that if General Babington was to be preserved to the 23rd Division, he must be rescued from the tender mercies of the British soldier cook, and a first-class Neapolitan chef had been kindly supplied from the ranks of a neighbouring Bersaglieri division. This worthy was now busy preparing the inimitable macaroni and rissotto for which he had become justly famous, being regaled the while with tales of woe from the members of the household, which included two or three very beautiful peasant girls. Count Emo translated the gist of the conversation, which so moved the most tenderhearted of the staff that, when dinner was ready, he refused to touch food till the starving though protesting contadine had been served. A large bowl of macaroni was accordingly set before the girls. It was pitiful to see, not the ravenous assault on the dish that was expected, but the painful embarrassment with which the offering was accepted. They did their best, poor girls, but it soon became apparent, thanks to the tactless intervention of the staff officer, that they had only recently finished a good square meal !

On the other hand, it was related by an old peasant near Porcia, as proof of the atrocities the enemy were capable of, that, not content with eating his dog, the Austrian soldiers had eaten his cat as well. The old man himself looked remarkably hale and hearty.

By the afternoon of November 3 the Tagliamento had been crossed with little opposition, and bridgeheads secured by the Tenth Army between St Vito and Spilimbergo. Elsewhere the Italian armies had now advanced, carrying all before them. The 48th British Division on the mountain front had crossed the Asiago Plateau and penetrated the Trentino. With her armies defeated and disorganised, and revolution threatened in the interior, the position of Austria had become hopeless.

An armistice was signed on November 3, to come into force at 3 P.M. the following day, when troops were to halt on the line gained. At that hour the Tenth Army occupied a line of about one and a half miles from Basagliapenta to S. Daniele-Pinzano, at an average distance of one mile east of the Tagliamento.

The following is a summary of the terms of the armistice :—

1. The Austrian Army to be reduced forthwith to twenty divisions on a peace footing, to maintain order in the country. Demobilisation to take place at once.

2. All territory as defined in the Convention of London is to be evacuated by Austrian forces within fifteen days. All Germans in Austria to be cleared out at once.

3. Half of total war material of whole Austrian Army is to be handed over at once to Italian authorities, and concentrated at centres to be fixed by them.

4. Prisoners to be returned at once, without reciprocity.

5. Certain strategical points in Austria to be occupied by the Allied Forces.

6. Allied Forces will have the use of all roads and railways in Austria for an advance towards Germany.

7. The Allied Forces shall have the right of requisitioning stores and supplies in Austria on payment as required.

4/11/18.

So ended the last battle of the 23rd Division, named by the Italians Vittorio Veneto from the main strategic objective of attack, but which will always be connected in the minds of the British troops who took part in it with the name of the Piave. For, without undue presumption, it can be claimed that the forcing of the passage of the flooded river was one of the finest feats performed by British troops in the World War. Fortune favoured the venture—Fortune, let it be admitted, favoured the Division from the hour she gave them their first commander, —but no operation in the war had depended more for success on the qualities of the regimental officer and the troops. Leadership, high courage, and perfect discipline were essential to success, but the slightest mischance might have brought failure ; and it must never be forgotten that the operation as carried out would have been impossible but for the

AUSTRIAN PRISONERS RETURNING ACROSS THE PIAVE.

magnificent services of the Italian Pontieri. It is not too much to say that if the XIV. Corps had failed in its attack on the Piave on October 27, there would have been no battle of Vittorio Veneto. The Austrians had already arranged to withdraw, and had not the bridgehead been secured by the XIV. Corps that day, the enemy would have eluded the pursuit which brought them to disaster, and have effected, at comparatively small loss, a retirement to the Tagliamento or the frontier.

The total captures by the 23rd Division between October 27 and 31 amounted to 177 officers, 5934 other ranks, 93 guns, and some 200 machine-guns.[1]

Casualties amounted to : killed, 10 officers, 169 other ranks ; wounded, 34 officers, 692 other ranks ; missing, 95 other ranks. Total, 1000.

Now at last the Division was to take that "intensive " rest which has been claimed in previous pages to be the only form of intensity which they had not been called on to undertake in the past four years. The early submission of Germany seemed certain. With the end of the war in view mental rest had already been obtained, but before complete bodily repose could be procured it was necessary for the Division to retrace its steps across the Piave.

---

[1] Of the prisoners 2709 were claimed by the 68th, 2650 by the 69th, and 500 by the 70th Infantry Brigade.

68th Infantry Brigade captured 105 machine-guns.   70th Infantry Brigade and 69th Infantry Brigade rendered no return of these.

CHAPTER V.

THE LAST DAYS OF THE 23RD DIVISION.

NOVEMBER 5, 1918, TO MARCH 7, 1919.

THE conclusion of the Armistice found units of the Division located as
follows :—

Divisional Headquarters . . .	⎫
C.R.E.	⎬ Porcia.
68th Infantry Brigade . . .	⎮
71st Field Ambulance . . .	⎭
Divisional Artillery	Fontana Fredda.
101st and 102nd Field Companies .	⎫ Near Pordenone.
23rd Machine-Gun Battalion . .	⎭
69th Infantry Brigade . . .	Palse.
70th Infantry Brigade . . .	Rorai Piccolo.
9th South Staffordshire Regiment .	⎫ Rorai Grande.
70th Field Ambulance . . .	⎭
Divisional Train	⎫ Ronche
Mobile Veterinary Section . .	⎭ (near Fontana Fredda).
✷ 69th Field Ambulance . . .	⎫ Sacile.
Sanitary Section	⎭
128th Field Company, R.E. . .	Orsago (S.W. of Sacile).
223rd Employment Company . .	Casa Catena.

All except the three last-named places are in the neighbourhood of
Porcia.

Withdrawal commenced on November 8, for the most part by the
same roads by which the Division had followed in pursuit of the Austrians
only a week before. On the night of the 8th, Divisional Headquarters
were again at Bibano di Sotto, on the 9th at Vazzola. On the 10th,

Headquarters moved to Treviso, and the Division, crossing the Piave by the Caserta and Palazzon bridges, was billeted in the St Biagio, Carta Reale, Lancenigo area.

Distressing scenes were witnessed at the bridges which led across the Piave. Very strict orders had been issued forbidding the removal of any captured Austrian transport. But the more efficient a British transport officer is, the more strongly developed in him are the characteristics of the pirate and smuggler. Virtuous C.O.'s, realising this, too often turned a blind eye, it is feared, to the misdeeds of these subordinates, whose liberal and ingenious interpretation of the clearest orders would have excited the envy of a criminal lawyer. Samples of every sort of animal and vehicle arrived with most units at the Piave under the pretext that these particular samples could not exactly be classed as "transport," or could not precisely be said to have been "captured." By devious routes they had been brought to the bridgeheads, eluding the vigilance of the minions of the law. Here A.P.M.'s and their staff would be engaged in cheery conversation while a couple of shaggy ponies and a crazy country cart, painfully obvious among the solid British transport, approached the defile. But A.P.M.'s and their staff had been dealing with pirates and smugglers for four years now ; as the day went on a steadily increasing mass of sad-eyed ponies and nondescript vehicles parked on the left bank of the river, and crestfallen transport officers crossed the Piave empty-handed.

And here it may be mentioned the corps commander witnessed one of those actions typical of the British soldier. A very old man and a small girl, refugees—possibly grandfather and granddaughter,—came over one of the foot-bridges. It was evident that all they possessed were the rags they stood up in. One of our men took off his helmet and held it out, saying, " Here, lads, something for the old man and the child." The appeal met with immediate and universal response from those standing by.

On November 11 the Division (less artillery), with a limited amount of transport, entrained at Treviso to move to an area west of Vicenza. The remainder of the transport concentrated with the Divisional artillery about Mestre, twelve miles south of Treviso and close to Venice, whence they were to move by road. On the same day news was received that Germany had signed an Armistice. Every year since 1914 it had been declared that peace was to come before Christmas. The prophetic optimist had perhaps had a harder task during 1918 to convert others to his views than in any previous year. But peace now had really come, and his reputation as a seer was vindicated. "What did I tell yer ; didn't I say last June that this 'ere war wouldn't last beyond Christmas ? " "Yes, he did that," agreed a chorus of enthusiastic converts ; "'e's a wonderful clear thinker is old Nobby ! " Forgotten Nobby's prophecies at Aldershot in 1914 and in the Bois Grenier the following year ; his visions of triumph after Le Sars, and his stout declarations in the misery of mud and shell-fire on the Paschendaele Ridge that "these Boches are about finished ; they'll throw their hand in before Christmas." Even if remembered, none will grudge him his place among the prophets, for Nobby, like the greatest of these, had not believed so much in the truth of his forecasts as in his power to raise the spirits of his comrades.

The Palazzo at Trissino was always something of a bone of contention among the British divisions when more than one was at rest. It remained so no longer, as General Babington now selected it as the headquarters of the XIV. Corps. The headquarters of the 23rd Division were established on November 12 at Arzignano, where one infantry brigade was also accommodated. The Division had become well-known in the town, and the troops were accorded an enthusiastic reception on their return. The streets were placarded with notices in Italian and English, congratulating the British troops on their victory, and welcoming them back.

The question of accommodation was one of great difficulty, and close billeting became the order of the day. To those who were with the Division in these days awaiting demobilisation, it may be useful to recall the areas where units were placed. Infantry brigades, who exchanged areas periodically, were billeted in or about Arzignano, Montecchia di Crosara, St Giovanni, and, later, Veronella and Schioppo. The Divisional artillery, arriving on November 16, occupied Arcole and Gazzolo, some distance from Divisional Headquarters. The 23rd Machine Gun Battalion, first at Lobia, was later moved to Cologna Veneto, about sixteen miles south of Arzignano. The 9th South Staffords Regiment was at Chiampo ; 69th, 70th, and 71st Field Ambulances at St Giovanni, Schioppo, and Arzignano respectively, the 73rd Sanitary Section being with the last-named.

At first it was difficult to believe that after four long years of war
an almost certain prospect of peace had opened. The incredible fact
for a time was in itself sufficient to keep men's minds occupied. But
when its full significance was grasped it was quickly realised that a
heavy task lay before all concerned if the thousands of men who constituted the Division were to be kept happy and contented. Discipline
is easy to enforce with the British soldier when the necessity for it is
realised. While the war was in progress the value of discipline had
been clear to the common-sense of the men in the front line. Would the
need for it now be equally evident to them ? Idleness is a certain source
of evil. The men had never grudged the hours spent in training for
battle. Would they now as willingly spend their time in military
exercises while awaiting their return to civil life ? Wives and parents
were eager for the return of their husbands and sons. The men were
anxious as to their future and their prospects of employment in
civil life.

Those responsible for the demobilisation of the British armies had
before them a problem strangely akin to that presented to the General
Staff before the battle of the Piave. A bridge had to be constructed
over which millions of men had to pass from the Army to civil life, and
a carefully studied order of precedence had to be established for this
crossing. In the same way as it would have been useless to pass more
guns across the Piave than could be supplied with ammunition, or disastrous to have starved the infantry by blocking the bridge with non-
essential transport, so now it would prove fatal to pass men across the
narrow defile to civil life whose trades were dependent on the work of
more essential men denied a passage. Stampede or panic would lead
to certain chaos.

The scheme drawn up was masterly. If it had been strictly adhered
to, it is the opinion of the present writer that the demobilisation of
the British Army would have been carried out without a hitch. Any
soldier knows that while the poorest scheme stands a chance of success
if loyally supported, the most perfect plans, if interference forces a
change of orders, may end in disaster. Unfortunately the interference of certain organs of the Press, calculated to introduce the panic
which was at all costs to be avoided, forced alteration in the original
scheme. As a result, the stupendous undertaking of the demobilisation

of the British Army, though carried out in an amazingly short period, was marred by a good deal of dissatisfaction, and did not run entirely smoothly.

But there were yet some weeks before the earliest on the list of the 23rd Division could hope to return to civil life, months before others would be demobilised. Never before have British games so well served the British Army. Here was found an outlet for the men's superfluous energy and an interest for their minds. But one wonders if they knew the immense amount of hard work the organisation of these games entailed on the officers. Apart from the regimental officers, who laboured for the recreation of their units, the Division as a whole owed a great debt to Major Grimwade, the G.S.O. 2 of the Division. Originally with the 13th Durham Light Infantry, later brigade-major in the 70th Infantry Brigade, and on the Divisional Staff during the battle of Vittorio Veneto, Major Grimwade, by his tireless energy, great ability, and unfailing good-humour, had rendered conspicuous service to the Division throughout the war. His services in these post-armistice days were scarcely less valuable. Week in, week out, he never spared himself, working incessantly at the organisation of competitions in the Division and the training of the Divisional football team.

Military training was not made strenuous, but no relaxation in the smartness of drill or soldierly turn-out was allowed : the strong *esprit de corps* of the units of the Division was alone sufficient to maintain this. But it was felt that the opportunity should also be taken to replace training for war by preparing men for their future struggle in civil life. It was to this end that the Education Scheme was introduced. Battalion, brigade, and divisional education officers were selected, and classes held to give the instruction which the younger men had missed owing to the war. Lectures were arranged on various subjects.

The manner in which commanding officers would turn these lectures to their own advantage was illustrated in the case of one given on "India" to the battalion at Chiampo. The lecturer, having sketched the history of India and its place in the British Empire, gave a somewhat detailed description of the various races that inhabited the country and their religious prejudices. In the case of the Sikhs, he related the custom of never cutting the hair. At the conclusion of the lecture the C.O. thanked the lecturer for the many interesting facts he had told them ; then, looking round his men, he added, " I am afraid Colonel S. must think we have a good many Sikhs in this battalion."

The Division, now awaiting demobilisation, was in its components the same 23rd Division that had crossed to France in 1915 but for the reorganisation of the artillery [1] and the loss of the three battalions in the previous September. These last will always be regarded and regard themselves as part of the 23rd Division, whose traditions they so nobly upheld in France in the short period of their separation. The following letter, received by General Babington from the brig.-general whose brigade they formed, testifies to the spirit of these battalions remaining unchanged till the end.

74TH BRIGADE, FRANCE,
October 11, /18.

DEAR GENERAL,—The Yorks, Sherwoods, and D.L.I. of my brigade who recently left your Division have been in action during the last few days. I am writing to tell you how splendidly they have done. It has been a pleasure and an honour to command them. In seven days, in spite of strong opposition and notwithstanding heavy casualties, they have advanced about fifteen miles. The cheerfulness and keenness of the men is wonderful. Colonels Hart and Young [2] have come through all right, but Colonel Clarke, I am sorry to say, is severely wounded. Hart, Greenwood (D.L.I.), and Bird (Sh. Foresters) did specially well. But all ranks did splendidly, and it is invidious to mention names. I know you will be delighted to hear about the boys who were so long in your Division.—Yours sincerely,

H. M. CRAIGIE HALKETT.

But now the gradual parting of comrades which saddened the post-Armistice period was to commence. On November 19 orders were received for Brig.-General H. Gordon and the 8th York and Lancaster Regiment to proceed to Fiume as part of an Inter-Allied Corps of Occupation. The battalion, under Lieut.-Colonel Colley, entrained on the 21st for Venice, where they embarked for Fiume two days later. Here they were destined to remain till the following September, when a *coup-d'état* by the Italian poet, D'Annunzio, produced a Gilbertian situation which rendered the retention of British or French troops useless. The story of the occupation of Fiume has been included in a short but most

---

[1] See Appendix B.

[2] Colonel Young was later killed in France.

interesting history of his battalion by Captain A. C. Calvert.[1] In February 1919, Lieut.-Colonel Whatford, who had commanded the 23rd Machine-Gun Battalion since the Armistice, proceeded to Fiume and resumed command of his old battalion. There was no officer in the 23rd Division more highly respected or more greatly loved than Colonel Whatford. Joining the Division during the battle of the Somme to command the 8th York and Lancaster Regiment, he had passed through the severest ordeals unscathed. In September 1919, as commander of the British troops at Fiume, he proceeded to Italy to interview the Inspector-General of Communications. During his absence there were signs of serious unrest in the town. Hearing of this late at night, he immediately arranged to return by car to Fiume. The car overturned near Cremona, and Colonel Whatford, one of the most gallant officers that served with the 23rd Division, was killed.

The 8th York and Lancaster Regiment had left the Division as an intact unit ; the remaining units were gradually to dissolve as demobilisation progressed. But this process had not yet commenced, and the Division was still strong and representative when H.M. the King of Italy reviewed the British troops at Castelgomberto on November 27. The Division was represented by the 68th Infantry Brigade, and by troops from each of its other units. In the review, which was a magnificent spectacle, there was no more impressive figure than General Babington, who led the British troops past the King. It was good to be in the Royal enclosure that day, and to witness the enthusiasm of the many French and Italian officers who were among the spectators as the XIV. Corps marched past. The transport and the heavy artillery with their superb teams roused their admiration, perhaps, above all. None was more strongly moved than General Bonfait, a close friend of General Babington's, and commander of the 23rd French Division, which had been alongside us on the Asiago Plateau. Wildly he appealed to all around, as the lines swung past, to look, and again to look—had ever such troops been seen before ?

Later it was the privilege of some of the 23rd Division to attend the review of the French Division by the King of Italy. The contrast was as marked as that between the British and French temperament. The same attention had not been given to turn-out either in their equip-

[1] The York and Lancaster Regiment's Journal, ' The Tiger and Rose,' April 1920.

H.M. THE KING OF ITALY AT THE REVIEW.

(Also, General the Earl of Cavan and Major-General Hon. J. F. Gathorne-Hardy.)

ment or horses, and one did not see the rigidly dressed lines or exactitude of the British march-past. But the spectacle was warlike and extraordinarily impressive. The artillery, which led, looked grim and businesslike ; the infantry, following at a quick pace in mass, with its forest of bayonets carried at the shoulder, headed by the trumpeters whirling their clairons, and sounding blasts of martial music to the deep-noted drums, will never be forgotten by those who were present. French and British reviews differ so completely in character that comparison between them is impossible. But those in Italy were alike in being among the most inspiring experiences of those who witnessed them.

On December 12 General Thuillier was ordered to proceed to Taranto temporarily, to restore order among certain troops of the West India Regiment, among whom serious disorders had occurred. In the treatment these coloured troops had received there had been much that constituted very real grievances. By firmness and tact, and, above all, by his sympathetic handling of the situation, General Thuillier quickly restored order, and gained the confidence of the West Indians. It proved necessary, however, for him to remain at Taranto for some weeks. On his departure, Brig.-General Byron again assumed temporary command of the Division.

Home leave had been ordered, and the first peace Christmas found many officers and other ranks in England ; those remaining in Italy feasted with as great a gusto as in previous years, and with less fear of its proving to be their last chance in life of a good square meal.

Infantry brigades periodically carried out three-cornered reliefs, so assuring that each should have its turn at Arzignano, the metropolis of the area. Here the " Dumps " gave nightly performances to crowded houses at the theatre, under the management of Lieutenant Roberts, supported by Captain Blackett, Corporal Hall, a first-class comedian, and the other members of the troupe, who all worked nobly to lighten the long winter evenings. Near Arzignano, too, the Divisional football competitions were played off before large crowds of spectators.

Racing started modestly in the New Year with point-to-point races, which provided ample opportunity for immersion in ice-cold water, and culminated in two first-class race meetings. These provided great excitement. First came the lotteries, presided over by that sturdy veteran Lieut.-Colonel Lethbridge, whose persuasive geniality made him no less successful in disposing of horses with a 100-1 chance than it had been in leading his battalion in war against similar odds. The meetings themselves required a vast amount of organisation. The totalisator was undertaken by Captain Hely Hutchinson, who had been G.S.O. 3 of the Division since April 1918. Great and varied had been the tasks that he had been called on to undertake during his service with the Division, but this will probably rank in his memory as the stiffest of all. He was one of those fortunate (or unfortunate) people who could be relied on to take on any job and carry it through successfully. The races, which were attended by General Babington, General Montuori, and a large number of Italian and French officers, proved an immense success. Prominent among the jockeys were Brig.-General Beauman and Major " Tibet " Hilliard, the D.A.D.V.S. But the most successful was a " dark " rider who had replaced Major Owen as D.A.A.G. after the Armistice. It came as something of a surprise when the unassuming Major Booth, largely by his superb riding, swept the board with his horse " Fourteen Points." There were some great jockeys, too, among the other ranks, whose races provoked great enthusiasm among the crowds assembled on the high bank that provided a natural stand overlooking the course.

Before demobilisation had seriously started, the Division enjoyed a final triumph in the football field. For the third year in succession they won the Cavan Cup, open to divisions and corps troops of the British Army in Italy. The final, played against the 48th Division, was a magnificent game. Both teams were first-class, containing more than one international player, and the contest was watched in breathless excitement. In the nature of things there could be no keener partisan on the ground than General Babington, who knew every player in the 23rd Division and all about him, and it caused some amusement to watch the self-restraint he exercised in observing the strict neutrality of a corps commander. It fell to him at the end of the game to present the cup to the winning team. The cup was later given to General Babington by the winning team, and it now forms one of his most precious possessions.[1]

Our relations with the inhabitants during this period remained

[1] Dates of events in 1919 have proved unprocurable. General Babington had probably at this time assumed command of the British troops in Italy, as indicated later.

THE VICTORY HANDICAP STEEPLECHASE.

cordial. Irksome as the delay in demobilisation must have been to many of our men eager to start work again in civil life, it must have been equally so to the people who looked forward to getting their homes once more to themselves. That so little friction occurred will always be remembered gratefully as due to the hospitality of the Italian people. There were minor incidents, but these were of an amusing rather than a serious nature. That they were not allowed to develop into grave misunderstanding was greatly owing to the tact and good-nature of the Italian Mission attached to the division. The work of Count Emo Capodilista and his stalwart assistant Signor Pratesi was at times delicate, but their skill in pouring oil on troubled waters was unequalled.

As an example of Count Emo's methods, an incident at Divisional Headquarters may be quoted. The lady of the house where they were situated had been extremely hospitable, till in a rash moment one of the first-floor rooms had been made available for the instruction of a class of soldiers under the Education Scheme. This she regarded as an unpardonable outrage, and attacked the G.S.O. 1 in no measured terms. He, frankly funking the encounter, feigned entire ignorance of the Italian tongue, and referred her to the Italian Mission, at the same time hastily acquainting Count Emo of the situation. Such preparation proved all that was needed. On arrival at the office of the Mission, the lady was greeted by Count Emo, who, before she had time to commence her complaint, expressed himself as lost in admiration of her appearance, and hazarded a guess that she was bound for Rome. Allowing no interruption, he extolled her hat, her dress, her gloves, her entire turnout in general and in detail. The trick was done ; there was only a hesitating and feeble protest, and the signora returned graciously welcoming the whole British Army to her house.

But such trivialities weighed little against the true kindness and hospitality, which will remain as the recollection of the Italian people in their relations with the 23rd Division. It is only hoped that the Italians feel that the conduct of our troops served in some degree to establish these relations, and to lead to warm friendships formed and still kept up by many.

But with the progress of demobilisation in the New Year the billeting question became easier. Lord Cavan and his staff left for England, and command of the British troops in Italy devolved on General Babington. General Thuillier returned from Taranto, and was replaced by Brig.-General Cary-Barnard. The Division was gradually dissolving, and arrangements were made for Brig.-General Beauman to take over command when units had been reduced to cadre strength.

The following address was made by General Thuillier to the men on demobilisation, a copy being given to each W.O., N.C.O., and man before he left for home :—

You are about to be released from your service in the Army. You will have the satisfaction for the rest of your life of knowing that you have done your share in the Great War that is now over. That war —probably the greatest and most arduous in the world's history—was waged for the defence of our country, our homes, and our families, to save them from the horrors that overtook the peaceful populations of Belgium, Servia, and part of France, and, with the Armies of our Allies, to uphold the rights of all peoples to live in peace.

The Army and its commanders are well aware that our victory in that struggle has been due mainly to the efforts of yourself and men like you, to your labours, your perseverance, your endurance of hardship, your courage under the most adverse conditions. You have earned and obtained the gratitude of the nation.

I trust that during the rest of your life you will retain a kindly memory of your friends and comrades—both officers and men—of the 23rd Division, with whom you have been so closely associated in trenches and billets for so long. I hope also that the spirit of comradeship and mutual endeavour for the country's cause, which has been established by our experience in the war, will be maintained during the years of peace, and that we may all continue to put them into practice in our dealings with each other as citizens, and thus advance the general prosperity and welfare of all classes in the country.

In the name of the officers of the 23rd Division, I thank you for your services, congratulate you on being able to return to your home in safety, and wish you every success in the future.

By the first week in March, less than four months from the signing of the Armistice with Germany, the Division had been reduced to cadre strength.

On March 7 command of the troops of the 23rd Division still remaining in Italy was handed over to Brig.-General Beauman by General Thuillier, who left for England the same evening. Two days later General Babington, having handed over command of the British troops in Italy to General Walker, commander of the 48th Division, left for home.

Here the history of the 23rd Division as a fighting formation, united under a single command, must end. The thousands who had served with it were already scattered ; they are now spread throughout the world. The breaking-up in a few weeks of a formation like the 23rd Division, which, preserving its identity throughout, had been welded together by the tests endured through four years of war, might at first seem comparable to the sudden destruction of some huge but delicate machine for which no further use can be found. If nothing remained of the Division but its bare name, this dissolution might be taken to illustrate the absolute vanity of war. But though few have better reason to appreciate the curses and miseries of war than those who served with the 23rd Division, no others realise more clearly that a brotherhood can be formed in war stronger and more endurable than any formed in peace. If the past pages have failed to convey to the reader the spirit which carried the Division to its victories in the war, let him seek out those who served with it. Wherever they are found in the world, and whatever their sphere in life may be, he will find them still united in their pride of and affection for their old Division. These are no empty words ; they are written with conviction by one who, joining the Division in the last year of the war, was immediately and forcibly struck by the unity and keen *esprit de corps* that existed in the Division, who during the period in which this history has been written has found in the records at his disposal this spirit, strong in early days, developing with each successive victory won ; and who, in recent years, in association at home and abroad with members of the 23rd Division of every class, many of whom have been under his own command, has found the spirit still lives which united the 23rd Division in war.

This spirit of comradeship, confidence, and determination was fostered by Major-General Thuillier during his short and successful tenure of command ; it was inspired by one whose name must always stand for all that was greatest and noblest in the 23rd Division—Lieut.-General Sir James Babington.

23rd Division (Officers) Association.

President:

Lieut.-General Sir J. M. BABINGTON, K.C.B., K.C.M.G

Officers who served with the 23rd Division at home or overseas, and who have not yet had particulars of the above Association are asked to communicate with the Hon. Secretary :—

Major V. E. COTTON, O.B.E.,

"Langdale,"

Grassendale Park,

Liverpool.

The Membership of the Association is world-wide and has increased each year since the Association was founded in 1920. To-day, there are well over 400 members resident in 35 different countries. An Illustrated Year Book is published annually and issued free to members, giving names and addresses, Divisional and personal news, etc. An Annual Dinner is held in London in June.

APPENDICES

APPENDIX A. (Pp. 349-350.)

68TH INFANTRY BRIGADE.

Brigade Headquarters.
10th Northumberland Fusiliers.
11th Northumberland Fusiliers.
12th Durham Light Infantry.
13th Durham Light Infantry. (To 25th Division, 11/9/18

———

68th Trench-Mortar Battery.

ORDER OF BATTLE.

23RD DIVISION.

69TH INFANTRY BRIGADE.

Brigade Headquarters.
11th West Yorkshire Regiment.
8th Yorkshire Regiment.
9th Yorkshire Regiment.   (To 25th Division, 11/9/18.)
10th Duke of Wellington's Regiment.

69th Trench-Mortar Battery.

70TH INFANTRY BRIGADE.

Brigade Headquarters.
11th Sherwood Foresters.   (To 25th Division, 11/9/18.)
8th K.O. Yorkshire Light Infantry.
8th York and Lancaster Regt.   (To Fiume, 21/11/18.)
9th York and Lancaster Regiment.

70th Trench-Mortar Battery.

24TH INFANTRY BRIGADE.

Brigade Headquarters.
1st Worcester Regiment.
1st Sherwood Foresters.
2nd Northampton Regiment.
2nd East Lancashire Regiment.

24th Trench-Mortar Battery.

This brigade formed part of the 8th Division. On October 18, 1915, it joined the 23rd Division, its place in the 8th Division being taken by the 70th Infantry Brigade. On July 15, 1916, the two brigades exchanged places again, each rejoining its own Division.

DIVISIONAL TROOPS.

Headquarters, 23rd Division.
Headquarters, 23rd Divisional Artillery.
102nd Brigade, R.F.A.
103rd Brigade, R.F.A.
104th Brigade, R.F.A.   (Became an Army F.A. Bde. in February 1917.)
105th Brigade, R.F.A.   (Broken up on September 3, 1916.)
X/23 Trench-Mortar Battery.
Y/23 Trench-Mortar Battery.
Z/23 Trench-Mortar Battery.
V/23 Trench-Mortar Battery.
23rd Divisional Ammunition Column.
Headquarters, 23rd Divisional Engineers.
101st Field Company, R.E.
102nd Field Company, R.E.
128th Field Company, R.E.
23rd Divisional Signal Company.
9th South Staffordshire Regiment (Pioneers).
68th Machine-Gun Company.   (Joined from U.K., 3/3/16.)
69th Machine-Gun Company.   (Joined from U.K., 3/3/16.)
70th Machine-Gun Company.   (Joined from U.K., 15/7/16.)
194th Machine-Gun Company.   (Joined from U.K., 16/12/16.)
23rd Divisional Train (190th to 193rd Companies, A.S.C.)
69th Field Ambulance, R.A.M.C.
70th Field Ambulance, R.A.M.C.
71st Field Ambulance, R.A.M.C.
35th Mobile Veterinary Section.
223rd Divisional Employment Company.   (Formed in June 1917.)

} For successive reorganisations of artillery brigades, see Appendix B.

} Reorganised as 23rd Battalion Machine-Gun Corps on April 1, 1918.

Divisional Cavalry : H.Q., C Squadron, and M.-G. Section, Duke of Lancaster's Own Yeomanry.
Divisional Cyclists : 23rd Divisional Cyclist Company.

} Both these units were transferred to III. Corps Troops on May 13, 1916.

.

SUCCESSIVE REORGANISATIONS OF THE DIVISIONAL ARTILLERY.

BRIGADES.	ORIGINAL COMPOSITION, 1915.	FIRST REORGANISATION, 19TH MAY 1916.	SECOND REORGANISATION, 3RD SEPTEMBER 1916.	THIRD REORGANISATION, 18TH JANUARY 1917.
102ND BRIGADE R.F.A.	A/102 (4 18-prs.) B/102 (4 18-prs.) C/102 (4 18-prs.) D/102 (4 18-prs.)	A/102 (4 18-prs.) B/102 (4 18-prs.) C/102 (4 18-prs.) D/102 (4 4·5″ hows.—*late A*/105)	A/102 (6 18-prs.—1 *Section A*/105 *added*) B/102 (6 18-prs.—1 *Section A*/105 *added*) C/102 (6 18-prs.—1 *Section A*/105 *added*) D/102 (4 4·5″ hows.)	A/102 (6 18-prs.) B/102 (6 18-prs.) C/102 (6 18-prs.) D/102 (6 4·5″ hows.—1 *Section C*/104 *added*)
103RD BRIGADE R.F.A.	A/103 (4 18-prs.) B/103 (4 18-prs.) C/103 (4 18-prs.) D/103 (4 18-prs.)	A/103 (4 18-prs.) B/103 (4 18-prs.) C/103 (4 18-prs.) D/103 (4 4·5″ hows.—*late B*/105)	A/103 (6 18-prs.—1 *Section B*/105 *added*) B/103 (6 18-prs.—1 *Section C*/105 *added*) C/103 (6 18-prs.—1 *Section C*/105 *added*) D/103 (4 4·5″ hows.)	A/103 (6 18-prs.) B/103 (6 18-prs.) C/103 (6 18-prs.) D/103 (6 4·5″ hows.—1 *Section C*/104 *added*)
104TH BRIGADE R.F.A.	A/104 (4 18-prs.) B/104 (4 18-prs.) C/104 (4 18-prs.) D/104 (4 18-prs.)	A/104 (4 18-prs.) B/104 (4 18-prs.) C/104 (4 18-prs.) D/104 (4 4·5″ hows.—*late C*/105)	A/104 (6 18-prs.—1 *Section C*/104 *added*) B/104 (6 18-prs.—1 *Section C*/104 *added*) C/104 (4 4·5″ hows.—*late D*/105) D/104 (4 4·5″ hows.)	On 18/1/17, C/104 was broken up, a section being transferred to both D/102 and D/103. In February 1917, the 104th Brigade left the Division and became an Army F.A. Bde., a new C/104 and a third section to D/104 being added from outside sources
105TH BRIGADE R.F.A.	A/105 (4 4·5″ hows.) B/105 (4 4·5″ hows.) C/105 (4 4·5″ hows.) D/105 (4 4·5″ hows.)	A/105 (4 18-prs.—*late D*/102) B/105 (4 18-prs.—*late D*/103) C/105 (4 18-prs.—*late D*/104) D/105 (4 4·5″ hows.)	BRIGADE BROKEN UP	

TRENCH-MORTAR BATTERIES.

FORMATION.—X/23 and Y/23 were raised as Corps units in 1915, being known at that time as the 12th and 21st T.-M. Batteries respectively. The personnel were volunteers from R.G.A. and infantry. Their first armament was very crude, and fired jam-tins filled with explosive. Early in 1916 these two Batteries joined the Division and were equipped with 1½-inch mortars. Later they received four 2-inch mortars each, which fired a 51 lb. bomb with steel tail, usually called a "toffee-apple."

Z/23 and V/23 were formed from the Divisional Artillery in March 1916. Z/23 was armed with 2-inch and V/23 with 9·45-inch mortars. The latter fired a 152 lb. bomb, commonly called "the flying pig."

1ST REORGANISATION.—V/23 was disbanded in October 1917, before the Division left for Italy.

REARMAMENT.—In February 1918, X/23, Y/23, and Z/23 were rearmed with 6-inch Newton mortars.

2ND REORGANISATION.—Z/23 was broken up in March 1918, X/23 and Y/23 being raised to 6 mortars each. Later, one section of each Battery was made mobile by carrying the guns in two halves (on the "screw-gun" principle) on pack mules.

APPENDIX C.

COMMANDING OFFICERS AND STAFF, 23RD DIVISION.

DIVISIONAL COMMANDERS.   Approximate tenure.
Major-General Sir J. M. Babington, late 16th
Lancers . . . . Aug. 1914–Oct. 1918
Major-General H. F. Thuillier, late R.E. . . Oct. 1918–March 1919

DIVISIONAL STAFF.

General Staff Officers, 1st Grade :
Colonel D. J. M. Fasson, R.A. . . . April 1915–June 1915
Colonel A. Blair, K.O.S.B. . . . . July 1915–Jan. 1916
Lt.-Col. C. F. Watson, The Queen's . . Jan. 1916–Jan. 1917
Lt.-Col. C. Evans, R.A. . . . . Jan. 1917–March 1918
Lt.-Col. H. R. Sandilands, 5th Fusiliers . . March 1918–March 1919

General Staff Officers, 2nd Grade :
Major H. J. Bartholomew, Worcester Regt. . Sept. 1914–Feb. 1915
Major C. F. Watson, The Queen's . . . March 1915–Jan. 1916
Major F. H. Moore, R. Berks Regt. . . Jan. 1916–Feb. 1917
Major A. W. C. Richardson, Bedfordshire Regt. Feb. 1917–April 1918
Major A. K. Hay, R.A. . . . . April 1918–March 1919
Major H. N. Grimwade, D.L.I. (temporarily) . Oct. 1918–March 1919

General Staff Officers, 3rd Grade :
Major H. J. N. Davies, Connaught Rangers . Feb. 1915–May 1915
Major N. H. S. Fargus, Royal Scots . . June 1915–March 1916
Capt. T. O. M. Buchan, The Queen's . . March 1916–Nov. 1916
Capt. Sir J. V. E. Lees, Bart., K.R.R.C. . Nov. 1916–May 1917
Major R. H. Middleton . . . . May 1917–July 1917
Capt. H. W. Lester, 10th Duke of Wellington's July 1917–April 1918
Capt. J. Gray-Simpson, Cameron Highrs. . April 1918–July 1918
Capt. C. D. Hely-Hutchinson, R.A. . . July 1918–March 1919

Assistant Adjutant and Quartermaster-Generals :
Colonel E. W. S. K. Maconchy, Indian Army Oct. 1914–June 1915
Lt.-Col. R. O. Burne, R.A.S.C. . . . June 1915–March 1916
Lt.-Col. H. B. de V. Wilkinson, D.L.I. . . March 1916–May 1917
Lt.-Col. E. F. Falkner, R.A.S.C. . . . May 1917–March 1919

APPENDIX C.

Deputy Assistant Adjutant-Generals :

Lt.-Col. A. F. Randolph, R. of O. . . .	Nov.	1914–April 1917
Major H. C. Owen, Middlesex Regt. . .	April	1917–Dec. 1918
Major H. Booth, 3rd Hussars (S.R.) . .	Dec.	1918–March 1919

Deputy Assistant Quartermaster-Generals :

Capt. H. N. Young, Inniskilling Fusiliers .	June	1915–Sept. 1915
Major G. E. Hawes, Royal Fusiliers . .	Sept.	1915–Sept. 1917
Capt. G. V. Breffit, Somerset L.I. . . .	Sept.	1917–Sept. 1918
Capt. J. Gray-Simpson, Cameron Highrs. .	Sept.	1918–March 1919

ADMINISTRATIVE SERVICES.

Assistant Directors of Medical Services :

Colonel C. J. MacDonald	Aug.	1915–April 1916
Colonel R. J. Blackham	June	1916–May 1918
Colonel W. C. Croly	May	1918–July 1918
Colonel W. G. Wright	July	1918–March 1919

Deputy Assistant Directors of Medical Services :

Capt. C. R. M. Morris	Aug.	1915–March 1916
Capt. J. G. Gill	March	1916–Nov. 1917
Capt. W. J. Pearson	Nov.	1917–March 1919

Deputy Assistant Directors of Ordnance Services :

Capt. T. J. White	Dec.	1914–March 1915
Major W. S. G. Bishop	March	1915–Feb. 1916
Capt. J. B. Oxenham	Feb.	1916–March 1919

Deputy Assistant Directors of Veterinary Services :

Major F. L. Melhuish	Aug.	1915–Feb. 1917
Major J. J. Hilliard	Feb.	1917–March 1919

Deputy Assistant Provost Marshals :

Capt. E. J. Solano	Aug.	1915–Aug. 1916
Major G. A. S. Williams	Aug.	1916–Sept. 1918
Capt. C. E. Stearns	Sept.	1918–Nov. 1918
Major G. A. S. Williams	Nov.	1918–March 1919

Senior Chaplains :

Revd. Blakiston (*C. of E.*)		1915–March 1916
Revd. H. D. Oldfield (*C. of E.*) . . .	March	1916–Jan. 1919
Revd. McClimant (*Non.-C. of E.*) . . .		1917–Jan. 1919

PERSONAL APPOINTMENTS.

Aides-de-Camp to Commander :

Lieut. Lord Wodehouse, 16th Lancers . .	June	1915–Oct. 1918
Lieut. C. J. Aris, 16th Lancers . . .	Aug.	1915–Jan. 1916
Capt. L. A. Bampfield, 9th Yorks Regt. .	Feb.	1916–Oct. 1918
Capt. G. A. Crowther, 9th York and Lancs. Regt.	Oct.	1918–Feb. 1919

APPENDIX C.

23RD DIVISIONAL ARTILLERY.   Approximate tenure.

Commanders, Royal Artillery :
Brigadier-General F. B. Elmslie . . .	Nov.	1914–June 1915
Brigadier-General D. J. M. Fasson . .	June	1915–Jan. 1917
Brigadier-General Sir D. Arbuthnot, Bart. .	Jan.	1917–Aug. 1918
Brigadier-General J. Byron	Aug.	1918–March 1919

102nd Brigade, R.F.A. :
Bt.-Colonel E. Gunner	Dec.	1914–Feb. 1915
Lt.-Col. W. Faber	Feb.	1915–March 1915
Bt.-Colonel W. H. Connolly	April	1915–Aug. 1915
Lt.-Col. H. Biddulph	Aug.	1915–March 1916
Lt.-Col. M. C. J. Hartland-Mahon . . .	March	1916–Oct. 1916
Lt.-Col. G. Badham-Thornhill . . .	Nov.	1916–March 1919

103rd Brigade, R.F.A. :
Major E. M. Birch	Dec.	1914–Jan. 1915
Lt.-Col. D. J. M. Fasson	Jan.	1915–April 1915
Lt.-Col. P. W. B. Henning	May	1915–May 1917
Lt.-Col. Hon. B. J. Russell	May	1917–July 1917
Lt.-Col. E. W. Grove	Aug.	1917–Jan. 1918
Lt.-Col. Hon. B. J. Russell	April	1918–April 1918
Lt.-Col. J. Curling	April	1918–March 1919

104th Brigade, R.F.A. :
Colonel E. A. P. Hobday	Dec.	1914–March 1916
Lt.-Col. M. C. J. Hartland-Mahon . . .	March	1916–March 1916
Lt.-Col. R. G. Maturin	March	1916–Sept. 1916
Lt.-Col. W. A. Nicholson	Sept.	1916–Feb. 1917*

105th Brigade, R.F.A. :
Lt.-Col. R. C. Drury		Aug. 1915
Lt.-Col. W. A. Nicholson	Aug.	1915–Sept. 1916†

23rd Divisional Ammunition Column :
Lt.-Col. R. C. Drury	Aug.	1915–
Lt.-Col. V. J. Kuper		–March 1916
Colonel E. A. P. Hobday	March	1916–March 1916
Lt.-Col. H. Biddulph	March	1916–May 1916
Lt.-Col. B. G. Buchanan	May	1916–May 1918
Major W. H. Borwick	May	1918–Jan. 1919

23RD DIVISIONAL ENGINEERS.

Commanders, Royal Engineers :
Bt.-Colonel A. C. Foley	Nov.	1914–Aug. 1915
Lt.-Col. P. J. J. Radcliffe	Aug.	1915–Aug. 1915
Lt.-Colonel A. G. Bremner	Aug.	1915–Feb. 1917
Lt.-Col. E. H. Rooke	Feb.	1917–March 1919
Major R. A. Turner (temporarily) . . .	Oct.	1918–Nov. 1918

* When Brigade left the Division.   † When Brigade was broken up.

APPENDIX C.

Approximate tenure.

101st Field Company, R.E. :
Major I. J. Connor . . . . . Aug. 1915–July 1916
Major R. A. Turner . . . . . July 1916–March 1919

102nd Field Company, R.E. :
Major C. B. Bonham . . . . . Aug. 1915–June 1916
Major J. N. F. Armstrong . . . . June 1916–July 1916
Major J. P. H. Ouchterlony . . . . July 1916–July 1917
Major D. G. Robb . . . . . July 1917–Dec. 1918
Major R. G. Christie . . . . . Dec. 1918–March 1919

128th Field Company, R.E. :
Major H. W. Gordon . . . . . Aug. 1915–July 1916
Major P. de Fonblanque . . . . July 1916–May 1917
Major A. Podmore . . . . . May 1917–July 1917
Major M. Luby . . . . . . July 1917–March 1919

23rd Divisional Signal Company, R.E. :
Major F. A. Iles . . . . . . Jan. 1915–Sept. 1916
Major J. A. S. Tillard . . . . . Sept. 1916–March 1919

68TH INFANTRY BRIGADE.

Brigade Commanders :
Brigadier-General G. H. Ovens . . . Sept. 1914–Nov. 1914
Major-General B. J. C. Doran . . . Nov. 1914–May 1915
Brigadier-General E. Pearce-Serocold . . May 1915–Feb. 1916
Brigadier-General H. Page Croft . . . Feb. 1916–Aug. 1916
Brigadier-General G. N. Colville . . . Aug. 1916–Sept. 1917
Brigadier-General C. D. V. Cary-Barnard . Oct. 1917–Jan. 1919

10th Battalion Northumberland Fusiliers :
Colonel D. S. Stewart . . . . Sept. 1914–June 1916
Lt.-Col. Lord Robert Manners . . . June 1916–Aug. 1917
Lt.-Col. W. H. Middleton . . . Aug. 1917–Feb. 1919
Lt.-Col. B. C. M. Western (temporarily) . Oct. 1918–Nov. 1918

11th Battalion Northumberland Fusiliers :
Colonel H. Rose . . . . . Sept. 1914–Dec. 1914
Bt.-Colonel E. A. F. Carter . . . . Dec. 1914–June 1915
Lt.-Col. T. Thord Gray . . . . June 1915–March 1916
Lt.-Col. E. G. Caffin . . . . March 1916–Oct. 1916
Lt.-Col. G. M'D. Pratt . . . . Oct. 1916–March 1917
Lt.-Col. A. A. St Hill . . . . March 1917–Oct. 1918
Lt.-Col. B. C. M. Western . . . . Nov. 1918–Dec. 1918
Major W. H. Mosley . . . . Dec. 1918–Jan. 1919
Major W. K. Maclachlan . . . Jan. 1919–April 1919

12th Battalion Durham Light Infantry :
Lt.-Col. L. E. C. Elwes . . . . Sept. 1914–Sept. 1916
Major C. E. Cummins ⎱ (temporarily) . June 1916–June 1916
Major W. W. Macgregor ⎰ . June 1916–Feb. 1917
Lt.-Col. R. Tyndall . . . . Feb. 1917–Nov. 1917
Lt.-Col. J. M. Longden . . . Nov. 1917–April 1918

APPENDIX C.

	Approximate tenure.
Lt.-Col. J. H. E. Holford	April 1918–Dec. 1918
Major E. Borrow	Dec. 1918–Feb. 1919
Major P. L. Lincoln	Feb. 1919–April 1919

13th Battalion Durham Light Infantry :

Colonel G. A. Ashby	Sept. 1914–July 1915
Lt.-Col. J. R. O'Connell	July 1915–Aug. 1915
Lt.-Col. N. T. Biddulph	Aug. 1915–May 1916
Lt.-Col. R. V. Turner	May 1916–July 1916
Major G. White (temporarily) . . .	July 1916–Aug. 1916
Lt.-Col. M. E. Lindsay	Aug. 1916–Oct. 1916
Lt.-Col. C. E. Walker	Oct. 1916–May 1917
Major J. A. Downey (temporarily) . .	June 1917–June 1917
Lt.-Col. M. E. Lindsay	May 1917–Sept. 1917
Lt.-Col. D. H. Clark (temporarily till April '18)	Oct. 1917–Oct. 1918*

69TH INFANTRY BRIGADE.

Brigade Commanders :

Brigadier-General F. S. Derham . . .	Sept. 1914–March 1916
Brigadier-General T. S. Lambert . . .	March 1916–June 1918
Brigadier-General A. B. Beauman . .	June 1918–March 1919

11th Battalion West Yorkshire Regiment :

Lt.-Col. F. W. Evatt	Sept. 1914–Dec. 1915
Major R. F. Lush ⎫	Dec. 1915–Jan. 1916
Major S. B. Maufe ⎬ (temporarily)	Jan. 1916–Feb. 1916
Major H. L. Anderton ⎭	Feb. 1916–Feb. 1916
Lt.-Col. M. G. H. Barker	Feb. 1916–April 1918
Lt.-Col. H. H. Hudson	April 1918–Oct. 1918
Major C. L. Armstrong	Oct. 1918–March 1919

8th Battalion the Yorkshire Regiment :

Lt.-Col. E. G. Caffin	Sept. 1914–Oct. 1914
Bt.-Colonel C. J. Spottiswoode . . .	Oct. 1914–Oct. 1914
Lt.-Col. A. J. Stephen	Oct. 1914–Jan. 1916
Lt.-Col. E. L. Lowdell	Jan. 1916–May 1916
Lt.-Col. P. E. Vaughan	May 1916–Aug. 1916
Lt.-Col. B. C. M. Western . . .	Aug. 1916–Aug. 1917
Major A. C. W. Cranks ⎫	Jan. 1917–Feb. 1917
Major R. C. Grellett ⎬ (temporarily) .	Aug. 1917–Sept. 1917
Major E. Boys ⎭	Sept. 1917–Oct. 1917
Lt.-Col. M. R. C. Backhouse . . .	Oct. 1917–Nov. 1918
Major J. C. Bull (temporarily) . . .	July 1918–Aug. 1918
Lt.-Col. R. C. Grellett	Nov. 1918–March 1919

9th Battalion the Yorkshire Regiment :

Bt.-Colonel A. de S. Hadon	Sept. 1914–Oct. 1914
Lt.-Colonel H. G. Holmes	Oct. 1914–July 1916
Lt.-Col. H. A. S. Prior	July 1916–Oct. 1916
Lt.-Col. A. C. Barnes	Oct. 1916–Dec. 1916

* When Battalion left the Division.

APPENDIX C.

	Approximate tenure.
Lt.-Col. H. G. Holmes	Dec. 1916–Jan. 1917
Lt.-Col. H. A. S. Prior . . .	Jan. 1917–June 1917
Lt.-Col. R. S. Hart	June 1917–Sept. 1918*

10th Battalion Duke of Wellington's Regiment :

Colonel G. R. Crawford . . .	Sept. 1914–April 1915
Lt.-Col. H. J. Bartholomew . . .	April 1915–March 1916
Lt.-Col. S. S. Hayne	March 1916–Oct. 1916
Lt.Col. R. R. Raymer	Oct. 1916–Aug. 1917
Lt.-Col. F. W. Lethbridge . . .	Aug. 1917–March 1919

70TH INFANTRY BRIGADE.

Brigade Commanders :

Brigadier-General Sir D. Kinloch, Bart. .	Sept. 1914–Sept. 1915
Brigadier-General L. F. Phillips . .	Sept. 1915–Nov. 1915
Brigadier-General H. Gordon . .	Nov. 1915–Nov. 1918

11th Battalion Sherwood Foresters :

Lt.-Col. T. B. Hawks	Sept. 1914–June 1915
Lt.-Col. H. F. Watson	June 1915–July 1916
Lt.-Col. J. J. O'Sullivan . . .	July 1916–Aug. 1916
Major G. M'D. Pratt (temporarily) .	Aug. 1916–Sept. 1916
Lt.-Col. H. F. Watson	Sept. 1916–Nov. 1917
Lt.-Col. C. E. Hudson	Nov. 1917–June 1918
Lt.-Col. H. N. Young	June 1918–Sept. 1918*

8th Battalion King's Own Yorkshire Light Infantry :

Lt.-Col. H. T. Manley	Sept. 1914–Oct. 1915
Lt.-Col. H. E. Trevor	Nov. 1915–July 1916
Lt.-Col. C. H. M. Imbert-Terry .	July 1916–March 1917
Lt.-Col. T. H. Owen (temporarily). .	Nov. 1916–Feb. 1917
Lt.-Col. D. Quirk	March 1917–Feb. 1919
Lt.-Col. G. L. Pyman (temporarily) .	June 1918–Oct. 1918

8th Battalion York and Lancaster Regiment :

Lt.-Col. J. F. Wolseley . . .	Oct. 1914–Nov. 1914
Lt.-Col. H. S. Walker	Nov. 1914–Aug. 1915
Lt.-Col. M. L. Hornby	Aug. 1915–April 1916
Major H. P. Smith (temporarily) . .	April 1916–May 1916
Lt.-Col. B. L. Maddison . . .	May 1916–July 1916
Lt.-Col. S. L. Whatford . . .	July 1916–Nov. 1918
Lt.-Col. F. Colley	Nov. 1918–Feb. 1919
Lt.-Col. S. L. Whatford . . .	Feb. 1919–Sept. 1919

9th Battalion York and Lancaster Regiment :

Lt.-Col. A. J. B. Addison . . .	Sept. 1914–July 1916
Major A. E. Palmer } (temporarily) . . Major D. Quirk	July 1916–Nov. 1916
Lt.-Col. R. Ratcliffe . . .	Nov. 1916–Feb. 1917
Lt.-Col. J. H. Bowes-Wilson . .	Feb. 1917–June 1917
Major D. Lewis (temporarily) . .	June 1917–July 1917
Lt.-Col. S. D. Rumbold . . .	July 1917–March 1919

* When Battalion left the Division.

359

APPENDIX C.

PIONEER BATTALION.   Approximate tenure.

9th Battalion South Staffordshire Regiment :
Bt.-Colonel A. R. Loscombe	Sept. 1914–Aug. 1915
Lt.-Col. E. H. Thruston	Aug. 1915–Jan. 1916
Lt.-Col. R. F. Lush	Jan. 1916–July 1916
Lt.-Col. R. Stephenson	Aug. 1916–March 1919

23rd Battalion Machine Gun Corps :
Lt.-Col. M. G. H. Barker	April 1918–April 1918
Lt.-Col. M. E. Lindsay	April 1918–Nov. 1918
Lt.-Col. S. L. Whatford	Nov. 1918–Feb. 1919

23rd Divisional Train, R.A.S.C. :
Lt.-Col. A. Northen	Jan. 1915–March 1918
Lt.-Col. N. Leese	March 1918–March 1919

ROYAL ARMY MEDICAL CORPS.

69th Field Ambulance :
Lt.-Col. A. N. Walker	Aug. 1915–Sept. 1916
Lt.-Col. G. H. L. Hammerton . . .	Sept. 1916–July 1918
Lt.-Col. J. J. H. Beckton	July 1918–Jan. 1919

70th Field Ambulance :
Lt.-Col. M. F. Grant	Dec. 1915–Nov. 1916
Lt.-Col. C. D. Pye-Smith	Nov. 1916–May 1918
Lt.-Col. W. L. Robertson	May 1918–March 1919

71st Field Ambulance :
Lt.-Col. E. B. Pooley	Aug. 1915–July 1916
Lt.-Col. H. Gibson	July 1916–Sept. 1917
Lt.-Col. J. B. A. Wigmore	Sept. 1917–Nov. 1917
Lt.-Col. J. G. Gill	Nov. 1917–Feb. 1919

35th Mobile Veterinary Section :
Lieut. Percy	Feb. 1916
Capt. R. C. Allinson	Feb. 1916–March 1919

223rd Divisional Employment Company :
Capt. W. M. Edwards	June 1917–March 1919

Duke of Lancaster's Own Yeomanry :
Lt.-Col. R. H. Tilney (Headquarters) .
Major W. E. Boyd (C Squadron) . . .
Capt. H. W. Sanderson (Machine-Gun Section)

23rd Divisional Cyclist Company :
Capt. J. E. B. Bosville . . . .
Capt. T. O. M. Buchan . . . .

} During the period these units served with the 23rd Division.

APPENDIX D.

DECORATIONS AND DISTINCTIONS AWARDED TO THE
23RD DIVISION DURING THE GREAT WAR.

BRITISH	. . Victoria Cross	9
	K.C.B.	1
	C.B.	3
	K.C.M.G.	1
	C.M.G.	18
	D.S.O. (including 16 bars)	105
	O.B.E. (military)	19
	M.B.E. (military)	31
	Promotion, and restored to Active List for distinguished service in the field . . .	1
	Brevet rank	21
	Military Cross (including 38 bars and 2 second bars)	464
	D.C.M. (including 9 bars and 1 second bar) . .	279
	Military Medal (including 106 bars and 3 second bars)	1907
	M.S.M.	154
	Royal Humane Society's awards . . .	2
FRENCH	. . Legion d'Honneur—Commandeur . . .	1
	,, ,, —Officier	1
	,, ,, —Chevalier	1
	Croix de Guerre	16
	Médaille Militaire	4
ITALIAN	. . Order of Savoy—Officer	1
	Order of the Crown of Italy	3
	Order of St Maurice and St Lazarus . . .	4
	Silver Medal for Valour	31
	Bronze Medal for Valour	47
	Croce di Guerra	120
BELGIAN	. . Officier de l'ordre de la Couronne . . .	1
	Decoration Militaire	1
	Croix de Guerre	40
RUSSIAN	. . Order of St Anne, 3rd Class	1
	Cross of St George, 4th Class	1
	Medal of St George, 4th Class	1
MONTENEGRIN	Silver Medal for Valour	3

APPENDIX E.

THE OFFICIAL NAMES OF THE BATTLES FOUGHT BY THE
23RD DIVISION DURING THE GREAT WAR, 1914-1919.

*(Based on the Report of the Battles Nomenclature Committee
(Cmd. 1138)).*

THROUGHOUT this history of the 23rd Division, battles and engagements
in which it took part have been referred to by the geographical names
so familiar to members of the Division. Those who served in the Division may, it is thought, be interested to see the record of the Division
translated into the less familiar titles officially decided upon in the
" Report of the Battles Nomenclature Committee " (Cmd. 1138). As
time goes on, these official names are likely to be employed in the works
of future historians, and consequently this Appendix may prove useful
to those who utilise Divisional histories as books of reference in the
future.

For a complete understanding of the principles on which the official
names have been arrived at, reference should be made to the very excellent Report above quoted. The following explanations of the Table
(below) embrace only those points essential to its understanding.

Explanation of Table.—The Battles Nomenclature Committee classi-
fied the various types of military operations in each theatre as follows :
1. The Phase.   2. Operations.   3. Battles.   4. The Battle, with Tactical
Incidents of that Battle.   5. Actions, &c.   6. Miscellaneous Incidents.

With 5 and 6 the 23rd Division is not concerned, but the first four
may be briefly described as follows :—

1. *The Phase.*—The war on the Western front has been divided
   into seven phases.

2. *Operations.*—A series of military events, taking place in a
   certain area and between certain dates, having a common
   purpose or effect. The " Operations " column of the
   Table is intended to give a general outline of the course
   of events, and thus to form a guide to the list of engagements given in the columns following.

3. *Battles.*—This is used in the sense of a " Group of Battles."
   Thus " The Battles of the Somme, 1916," include twelve
   individual battles of the first magnitude and three actions.

4. *The Battle.*—A battle is one distinct engagement. By the use
of varieties of type the Report endeavours to indicate
the relative importance of battles. Certain battles include " tactical incidents." The number of tactical
incidents recorded is not necessarily any criterion of the
greatness of the battle itself. Incidents have only been
recorded when this could be done without risk of obscuring the greater issues involved.

As regards the " limits " given in the last two columns :—

Chronological.—A " day " is midnight to midnight. Preparatory
action is not included. Each engagement commences
from " zero day," but, on the other hand, the period of
consolidation after an attack is included.

Geographical.—The rear line approximates to the main line of
heavy artillery positions, but the flanks correspond with
the outside limits from which the infantry assault was
delivered, or within which the enemy's infantry advanced
to the attack.

| OPERATIONS. | BATTLES. | | ACTIONS, &c. | MISCELLANEOUS INCIDENTS. | LIMITS. | |
	NAME.	TACTICAL INCIDENTS INCLUDED.			CHRONOLOGICAL.	GEOGRAPHICAL.
	FRANCE AND FLANDERS.					
	PHASE III.—THE ALLIED OFFENSIVE, 1916.					
Operations on the Somme (1st July to 18th Nov. 1916).	**THE BATTLES OF THE SOMME, 1916.**	...	...	...	1st July to 18th Nov.	
	(i.) BATTLE OF ALBERT, 1916.	Capture of Contalmaison.	...	...	1st to 13th July.	The Combles valley to Hardecourt: thence the road to Maricourt—Suzanne—Bray—Albert—Bouzincourt—Hédauville—Forceville—Bertrancourt—Sailly-au-Bois (exclusive)—Hébuterne—Puisieuxau-Mont.
	(iv.) BATTLE OF POZIERES RIDGE.	...	...	...	23rd July to 3rd Sept.	Road Bazentin-le-Petit—Contalmaison — Fricourt — Bécourt — Albert (exclusive): thence the river Ancre.
	(vii.) BATTLE OF FLERS-COURCELETTE.	...	...	...	15th to 22nd Sept.	The Combles valley to Hardecourt: thence road to Maricourt—Fricourt—Bécourt—Albert (exclusive): thence the river Ancre.
	(viii.) BATTLE OF MORVAL.	...	...	...	25th to 28th Sept.	The Combles valley to Hardecourt: thence road to Maricourt— Fricourt — Bécourt—la Boisselle—Bapaume.
	(x.) BATTLE OF THE TRANSLOY RIDGES.	Capture of Le Sars.	...	...	1st to 18th Oct.	The valley from Sailly-Saillisel to Combles: thence road to Ginchy—Longueval—Martinpuich—Courcelette: thence the valley to Warlencourt.
	PHASE V.—THE ALLIED OFFENSIVES, 1917.					
The Flanders Offensive (7th June to 10th Nov. 1917.)	**THE BATTLE OF MESSINES, 1917.**	...	...	...	7th to 14th June.	Road Frelinghien—le Bizet—Petit Pont—Neuve Eglise—Dranoutre—Locre—la Clytte —Dickebusch—Kruisstraat: thence a line to Zillebeke—Gheluvelt.
	THE BATTLES OF YPRES, 1917.	...	...	...	31st July to 10th Nov.	
	(iii.) BATTLE OF THE MENIN ROAD RIDGE.	...	.	...	20th to 25th Sept.	The Commines — Ypres canal as far as Vormezeele: thence road to Vlamertinghe Chateau —Elverdinghe Chateau —Worsten—Bixschoote.
	(iv.) BATTLE OF POLYGON WOOD.	...	...	...	26th Sept. to 3rd Oct.	
	(vii.) FIRST BATTLE OF PASSCHENDAELE.	...	...	...	12th Oct.	
	ITALY.					
The Austrian Offensive, 1918.	**THE BATTLE OF THE PIAVE.**	The fighting on the Asiago Plateau.	...	...	15th to 16th June.	The Asiago Plateau, north of the line Conco—Cogollo.
The Italian Offensive, 1918.	**THE BATTLE OF VITTORIO VENETO.**	Passage of the Piave.	...	...	23rd Oct. to 4th Nov.	Between the railways Treviso — Conegliano and Treviso—Oderzo.

366   APPENDIX E.

NOTES.

1. In the above Table only those battles are included for which the
23rd Division appears to qualify, according to the spirit of the Report
and within the limits laid down. Operations are not included in which
the Divisional Artillery fought with other Divisions, nor are operations
in which the 70th Infantry Brigade fought as part of the 8th Division,
nor any other operations by units temporarily detached from the 23rd
Division.

2. Though the 23rd Division was holding the Bois Grenier sector
at the time, it does not appear to qualify for the " Action of Bois Grenier "
on September 25, 1915, which formed part of the Battle of Loos, since,
within the geographical limit laid down, the Division neither attacked,
nor was it attacked by the enemy, nor was there any period of consolidation. For similar reasons the Division does not qualify for the " German
attack on Vimy Ridge " on May 21, 1916, though its artillery qualify
under the Committee's acceptance of the principle " that all batteries
firing upon the front of attack should be held to have taken part in the
engagement."

3. In two battles for which the 23rd Division qualifies—the Battle
of Flers-Courcelette and the first Battle of Passchendaele,—its part
approximates more nearly to consolidation of an active front, within
the given limits, than to participation in the main attacks. The casualties
incurred and the appalling conditions endured in these " periods of consolidation " have rightly been held to qualify for the battle.

APPENDIX F.

ORGANISATION OF THE INFANTRY AND MACHINE-GUNS OF AN ITALIAN DIVISION.

ILLUSTRATING DIFFICULTIES OF RELIEF BY A BRITISH DIVISION IN A SECTOR OF DEFENCE.

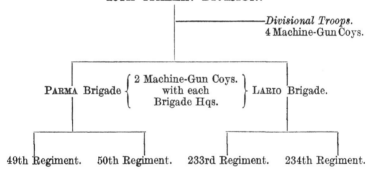

20TH ITALIAN DIVISION.

Divisional Troops.
4 Machine-Gun Coys.

PARMA Brigade { 2 Machine-Gun Coys. with each Brigade Hqs. } LARIO Brigade.

49th Regiment. 50th Regiment. 233rd Regiment. 234th Regiment.

NOTE.

Each regiment consists of 3 battalions, each of 3 infantry and 1 machine-gun companies, and from 2 to 4 light mortars.

A machine-gun company has 6 guns, giving a total of 48 guns to a brigade, and 120 guns to the Division.

INDEX.

372INDEX.

374

INDEX.

C. NAMES OF INDIVIDUALS.

376 INDEX.

NAMES OF INDIVIDUALS—continued.

378 INDEX.

INDEX. 379

D. GENERAL INDEX.

Victoria Cross Awards—*contd.*
  Youens, 2nd Lieutenant Frederick (13th Durham Light Infantry), 166.
  Youll, Lieutenant J. S. (11th Northumberland Fusiliers), 257.

Water—
  Scarcity on Asiago plateau, 239.

Y.M.C.A., 10, 126.
Yukon packs, 188.

E. MILITARY UNITS AND FORMATIONS.

23RD DIVISION.

Divisional Staff—
  Divisional Commander, 6, 298, 300, 353.
  G.S.O. 1, 16, 43, 134, 233, 243, 343, 353.
  G.S.O. 2, 7, 43, 134, 230, 338, 353.
  G.S.O. 3, 342, 353.
  A. and Q. Staff, Foreword, 25, 48, 119, 126, 162, 233, 328, 353-4.
  D.A.A.G., 315, 342, 354.
  A.D.M.S., 161, 188, 354.
  D.A.D.M.S., 354.
  D.A.D.O.S., 35, 162-3, 354.
  D.A.D.V.S., 38, 315, 334, 342, 354.
  D.A.P.M., 315, 335, 354.
  A.D.C. to Commander, 265, 354.
  C.R.A., 10, 16, 42, 50, 133, 243, 268, 298, 300, 355.
  Divisional Artillery Staff, 25, 42.
  D.T.M.O., 145, 315.
  C.R.E., 33, 186-7, 243, 268, 319, 334, 355.
  D.M.G.O., 177.

68th Infantry Brigade, 5-6, 10-2, 14, 16, 25-6, 32, 34, 40, 43-7, 49, 51, 53-4, 61-2, 65-6, 68-9, 72-5, 80-1, 83-9, 94, 97, 99, 100-1, 108, 110-1, 115, 117, 119, 125-7, 130, 132, 136-7, 141, 143, 145, 147, 152, 164-5, 169, 171, 175-7, 179, 181, 184, 187, 189, 190-1, 193-4, 196, 207, 209, 211, 218, 222, 226, 228, 232, 239, 243, 246, 253, 257, 263-4, 266-7, 292, 299, 302-4, 308-9, 310-1, 314, 316-7, 319, 320-5, 327, 329, 333-4, 340; Appendix A., 356.
  68th Infantry Brigade L.T.M. Battery, 153, 187, Appendix A.
  68th Infantry Brigade Machine-Gun Company, 53, 153, 161, 185, 243, Appendix A.
  10th Northumberland Fusiliers, 5, 40, 68, 94, 97, 101, 103, 123, 130-1, 157, 159, 166, 175-7, 180, 185, 190-1, 226, 263, 265, 267, 278, 308, 310-1, 317, 320, 322-3; Appendix A., 356.
  11th Northumberland Fusiliers, 5, 60, 71-2, 101, 115, 151-2, 175, 177-9, 185, 191-3, 207-8, 229, 250, 257, 263, 267, 309, 310-1, 317, 322-3; Appendix A., 356.
  12th Durham Light Infantry, 5, 53, 71-2, 74, 83, 88, 101-2, 111-3, 115, 119, 123, 151, 156-8, 166, 175, 177, 179, 180, 181, 183, 185, 187, 191-2, 207, 257, 309, 310, 319, 322-3, 327; Appendix A., 356-7.
  13th Durham Light Infantry, 5, 34, 37, 59, 72, 86, 88, 94, 99, 111, 113, 115, 119, 144, 146, 165, 175, 177, 180, 182-3, 185-6, 190, 191-2, 209, 229, 243, 257, 288-9, 291, 338-9; Appendix A., 357.

69th Infantry Brigade, 5-7, 11-2, 14-6, 25-6, 32-4, 40, 43-4, 46-9, 53, 61-2, 65-6, 68, 72-5, 81-3, 86-7, 89, 91, 95, 98-9, 100, 108-9, 111, 115-9, 126-8, 131, 135-7, 142-3, 151-3, 155-7, 160, 164-5, 169, 171, 175-8, 181, 189, 190-1, 193-8, 200, 203-4, 207-8, 211, 218, 222, 227, 232, 239, 244, 246, 249, 250-1, 254, 265, 273, 279, 292, 299, 300, 302-4, 308-12, 317, 319, 320-1, 323, 325, 329, 333-4; Appendix A., 357.
  69th Infantry Brigade L.T.M. Battery, 79, 86, 129, 142, 179, 201, Appendix A.
  69th Infantry Brigade Machine-Gun Company, 79, 86, 114, 142, 185, 243, Appendix A.
  11th West Yorkshire Regiment, 5, 29, 33, 47, 65-8, 72, 75, 79, 80, 90, 111, 113-4, 118, 126-7, 151, 155, 175, 177-9, 181, 188, 191-2, 197, 229, 243, 274, 277, 281, 305,

CHRONOLOGICAL RECORD.

2 B

Printed in Great Britain by
WILLIAM BLACKWOOD AND SONS.

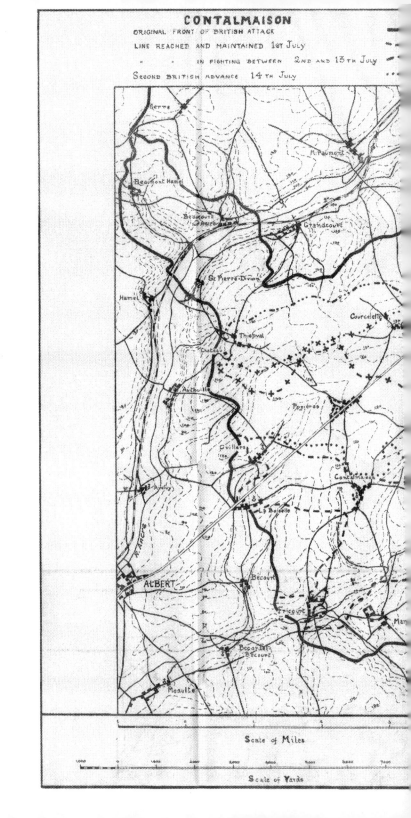

CONTALMAISON

ORIGINAL FRONT OF BRITISH ATTACK

LINE REACHED AND MAINTAINED 1st July

"   "   IN FIGHTING BETWEEN 2nd AND 13th July

SECOND BRITISH ADVANCE 14th July

Scale of Miles

Scale of Yards

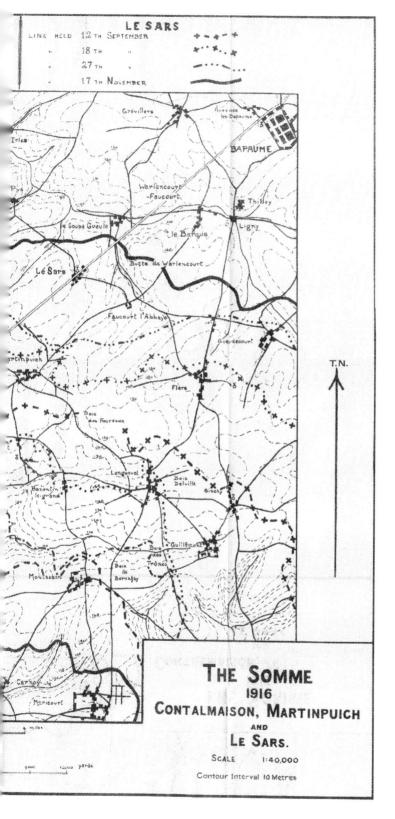

LINE HELD 12TH SEPTEMBER
"   18TH   "
"   27TH   "
"   17TH NOVEMBER

LE SARS

THE SOMME
1916
CONTALMAISON, MARTINPUICH
AND
LE SARS.

SCALE   1:40,000

Contour Interval 10 Metres

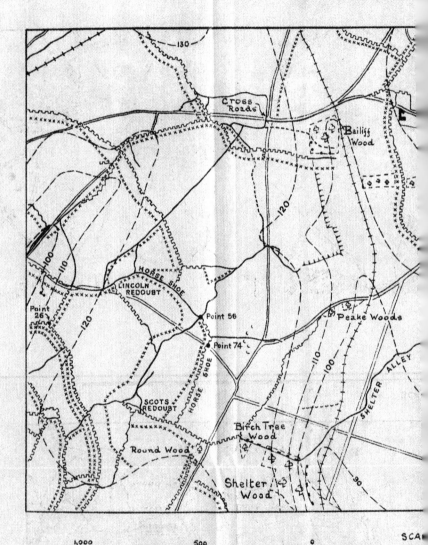

130

Cross Roads

Bailiff Wood

E

120

100

110

HORSE SHOE

LINCOLN REDOUBT

Point 26

120

Point 56

Point 74

Peake Woods

110

100

HORSE SHOE

SHELTER ALLEY

SCOTS REDOUBT

Birch Tree Wood

Round Wood

Shelter Wood

90

1,000   500   0   SCA

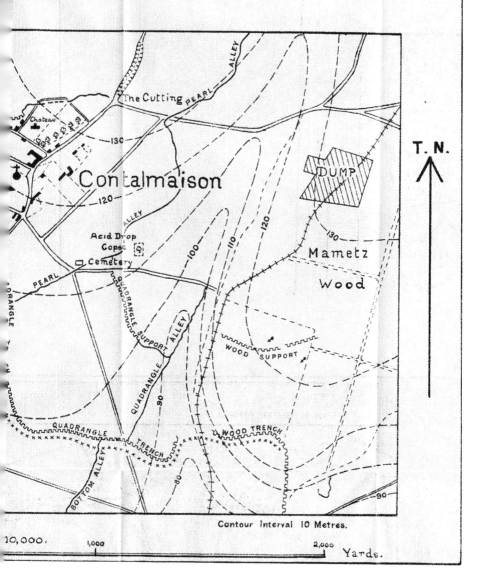

T. N.

PEARL ALLEY

The Cutting

Chateau

130

Contalmaison

120

DUMP

130

Acid Drop
Copse

Cemetery

Mametz

Wood

PEARL

QUADRANGLE SUPPORT ALLEY

WOOD SUPPORT

90

QUADRANGLE

TRENCH

WOOD TRENCH

BOTTOM ALLEY

80

90

Contour Interval 10 Metres.

10,000.   1,000   2,000
                                              Yards.

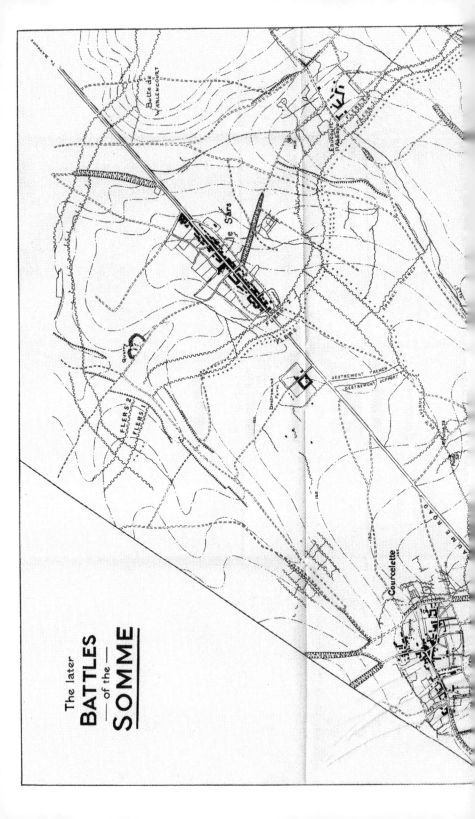

The later
BATTLES
— of the —
SOMME

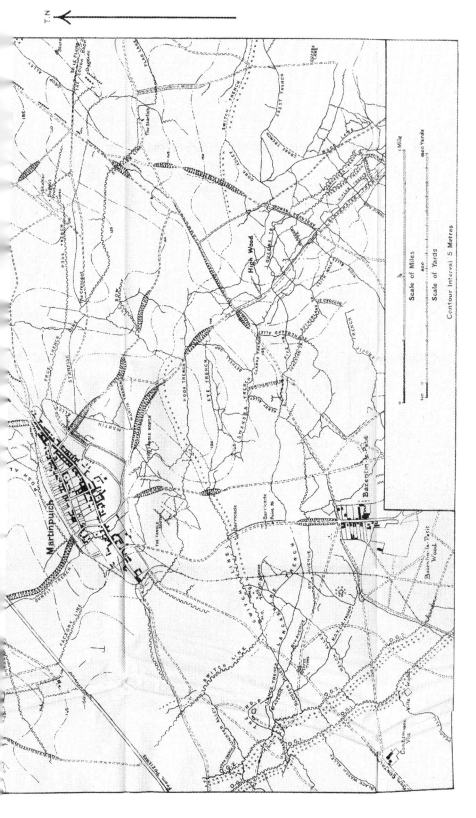

Scale of Miles

Scale of Yards

Contour Interval 5 Metres

High Wood

Martinpuich

Bazentin-le-Petit

Bazentin-le-Petit Wood

27   28   29

Larch Wood

Verbrandenmolen

Zwarte

La Chapelle

29

The Dump

Hill 60

The Caterpill

Thos

33   34   35

The Ravine

The Bluff

Triangular Wood

3   4   5

White Ch⁰

The Stables

Eikhof F^m

Oosthoek Estaminet

Cumberland Rd

Damm Strasse

Delbeke F^m

Pheasant Wood

9   10   11

Ravine Wood

Englebien F^m

Denys

Wood

2 Feet deep

G.S.G.S. 58·1.

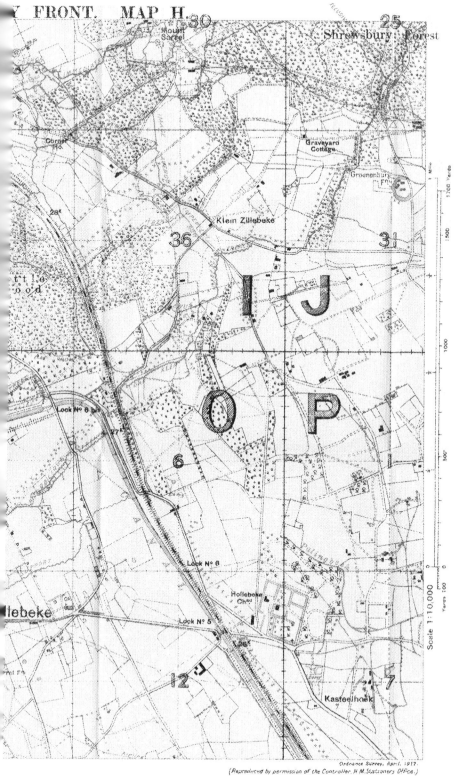

30

25

Shrewsbury Forest

Mount Sorrel

Graveyard Cottage

Groenenburg

Corne Ho.

28K

Klein Zillebeke

36

31

I

J

oo'd

O

P

Lock Nº 8 bi

6

Lock Nº 8

lebeke

Lock Nº 5

Hollebeke Chau

12

7

Kasteelhoek

Scale 1:10,000

Ordnance Survey, April, 1917.

(Reproduced by permission of the Controller, H.M.Stationery Office.)

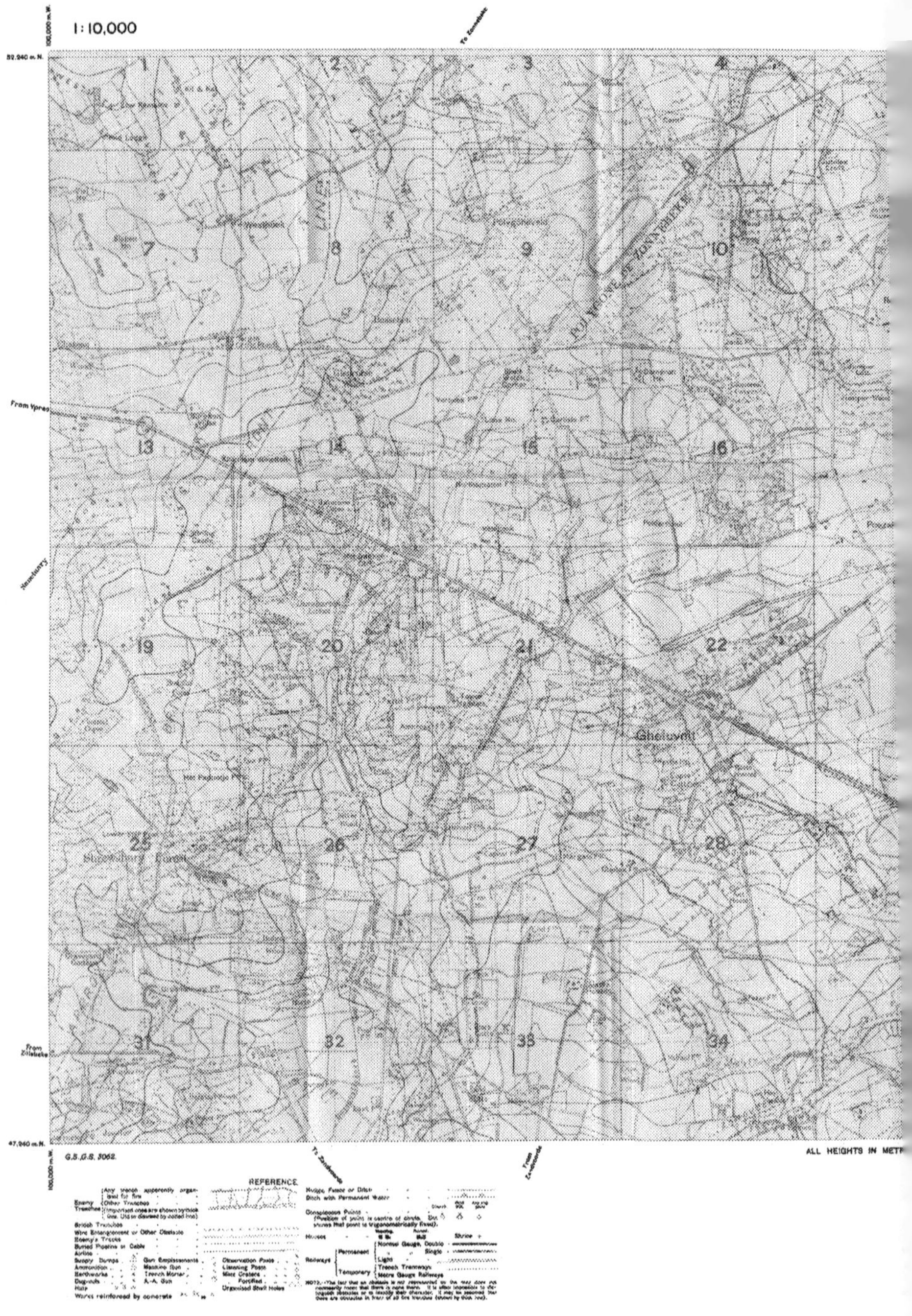

1:10,000
52,240 m.N.
To Zonnebeke
From Ypres
Sanctuary
From Zillebeke
47,240 m.N.
To Zandvoorde
From Zandvoorde
Gheluvelt
Shrewsbury Forest
Het Pappotje Fm.
1
2
3
4
7
8
9
10
13
14
15
16
19
20
21
22
25
26
27
28
31
32
33
34
ALL HEIGHTS IN METR
G.S.G.S. 3062.
REFERENCE
Enemy Trenches
Any trench apparently organised for fire
Other Trenches
(Important ones are shown by thick line. Old or disused by dotted line)
British Trenches
Wire Entanglement or Other Obstacle
Enemy's Tracks
Buried Pipeline or Cable
Airline
Supply Dumps
Ammunition
Earthworks
Dugouts
Huts
Gun Emplacements
Machine Gun
Trench Mortar
A.-A. Gun
Observation Posts
Listening Posts
Mine Craters
Fortified
Organised Shell Holes
Works reinforced by concrete
Hedge, Fence or Ditch
Ditch with Permanent Water
Conspicuous Points
Houses
Shrine
Railways
Permanent
Temporary
Normal Gauge, Double
Single
Light
Trench Tramways
Metre Gauge Railways

GHELUVELT

EDITION 9 A   TRENCHES CORRECTED TO 14-9-17.   28 N.E. 3.

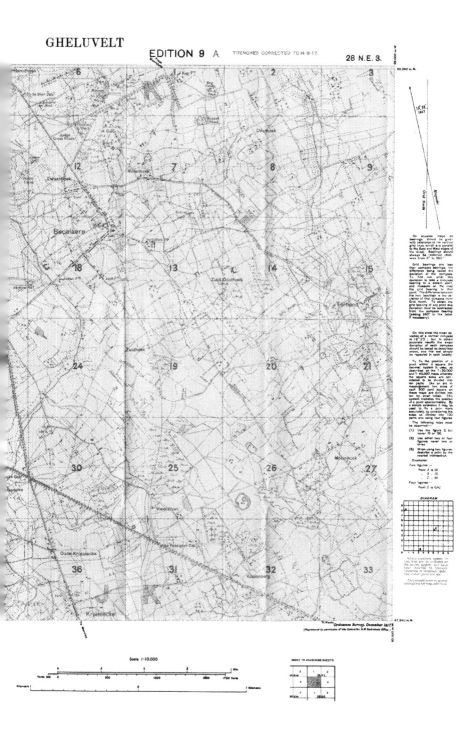

Scale 1:10,000

INDEX TO ADJOINING SHEETS

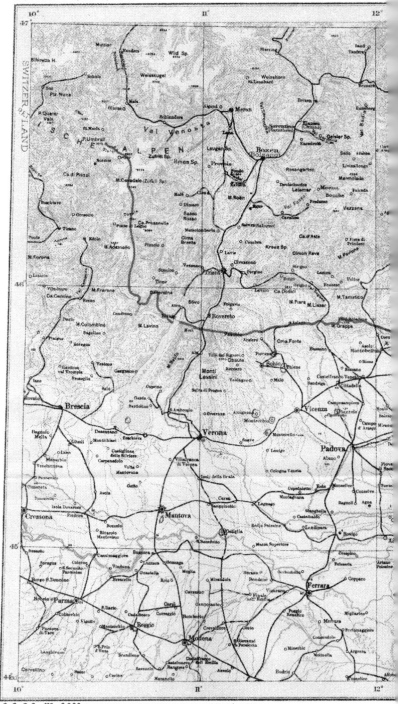

Austrian Front Line June 14th 1918.

Scale
Miles   10 5 0   10   20

1 Inch = 15·78 M

Kilometres   10 5 0   10   20   30

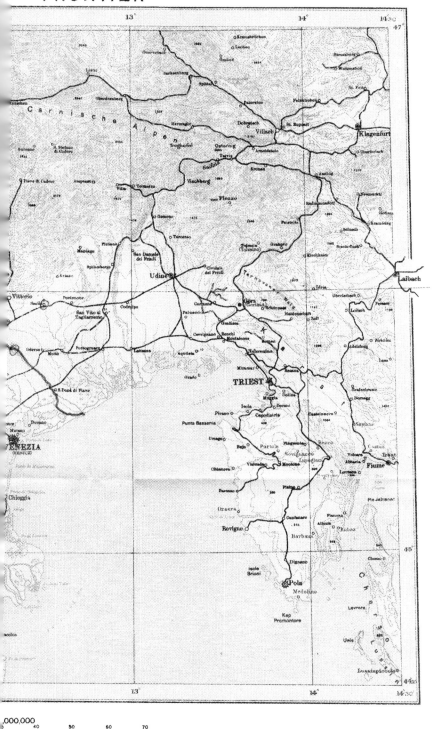

,000,000

40   50   60   70
                                        Miles

Millimetre · 1 Kilometre

0   60   70   80   90   100   110
                                        Kilometres

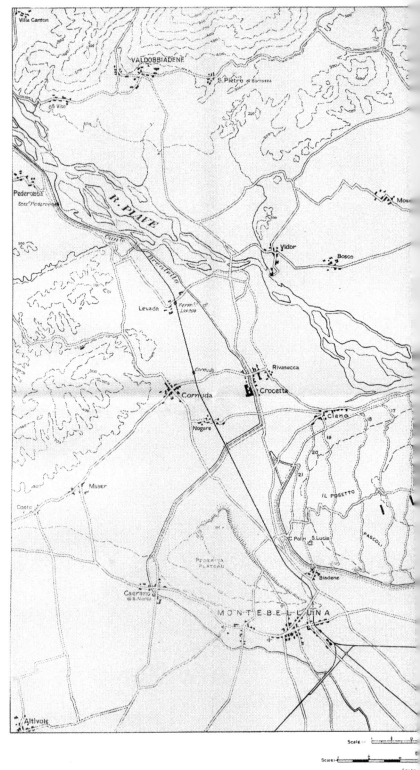

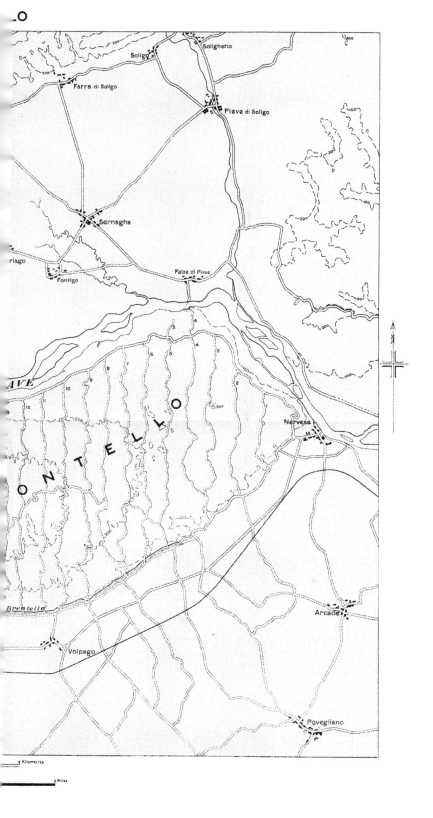

ASIAGO PLATEAU

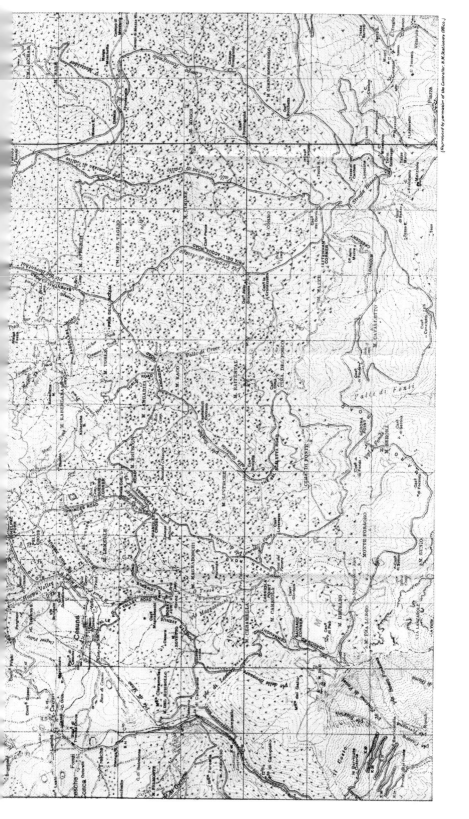

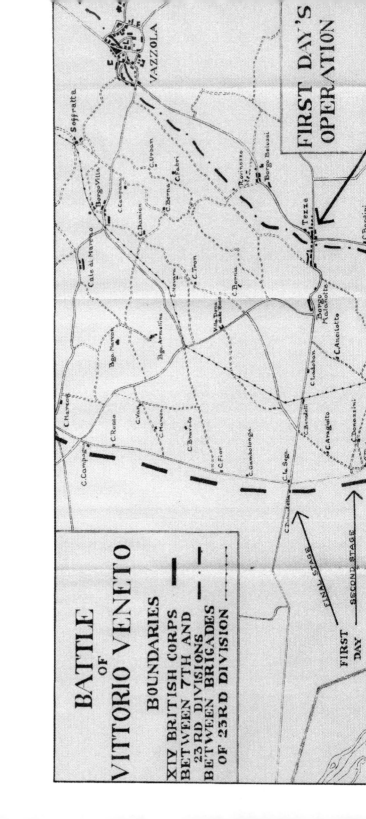

BATTLE
OF
VITTORIO VENETO

BOUNDARIES

XIV BRITISH CORPS ▬▬▬
BETWEEN 7TH AND ▬ ▪ ▬
23 RD DIVISIONS
BETWEEN BRIGADES ▪▪▪▪▪▪
OF 23RD DIVISION

FIRST DAY'S
OPERATION

FINAL STAGE

FINAL STAGE

FIRST
DAY

SECOND STAGE

FIRST

VAZZOLA

Soprrotta

C.Urpon
Borgo Villa
C.Coppero
C.Fabri
C.Damian
C.Berna
Rorchetto
Cale di Marzno
Borgo Beivosi
C.Norans
C.Trom
Terze
C.Bardini
C.Berna
Bgo.Narzon
Via Poze
Borgo
Bgo.Armellina
Malanotte
C.Anselotto
C.Martena
C.Rosso
C.Guadahan
C.Vieco
C.Merca
C.Bardini
C.Brovido
C.Angiotto
C.Campagno
C.Fior
C.Donatini
C.Gambalonga
C.Fighera
C.la Sga
C.Zenchetta
C.Meri villa

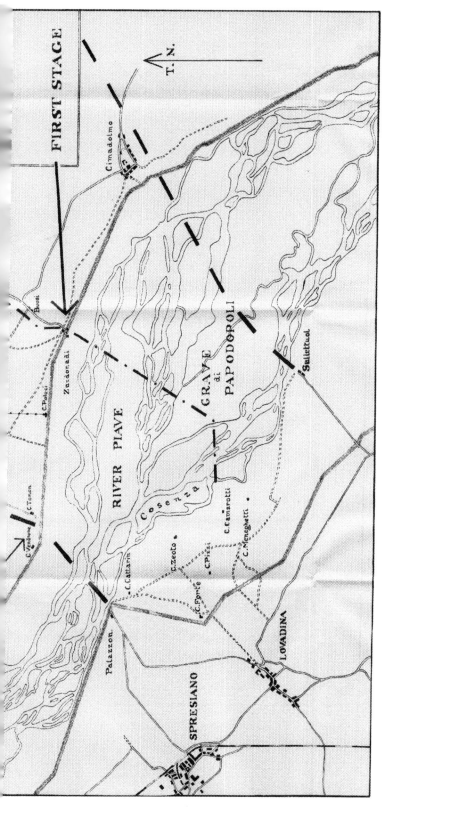

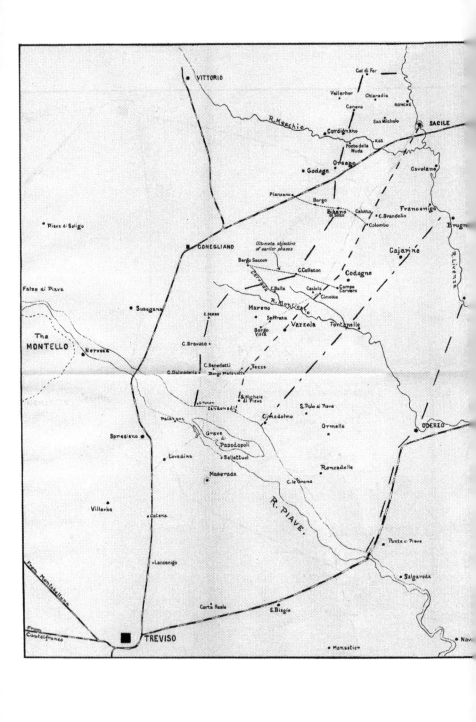

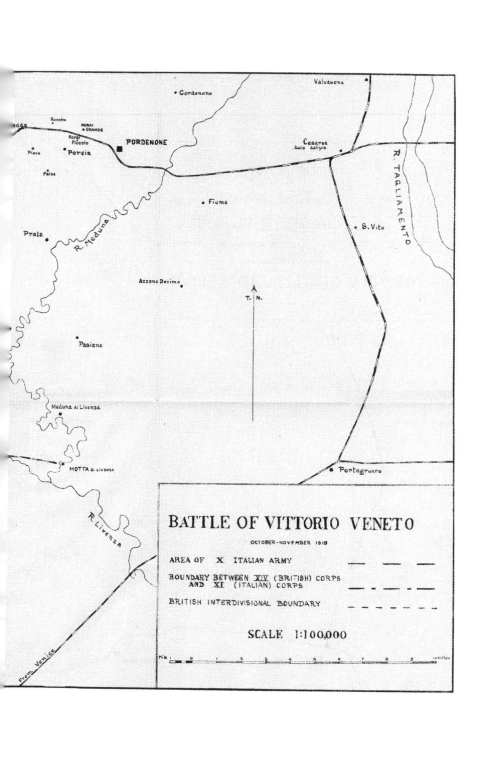

Gordenone

Valvasone

Ronche
RORAI GRANDE
Rorai Piccolo
PORDENONE

Porcia

Pieve

Paise

Casarsa
della delizia

R. TAGLIAMENTO

Fiume

S. Vito

Prata

R. Meduna

Azzano Decimo

T. N.

Pasiano

Meduna di Livenza

MOTTA di Livenza

Portogruaro

R. Livenza

From Venice

BATTLE OF VITTORIO VENETO

OCTOBER-NOVEMBER 1918

AREA OF X ITALIAN ARMY

BOUNDARY BETWEEN XIV (BRITISH) CORPS
AND XI (ITALIAN) CORPS

BRITISH INTERDIVISIONAL BOUNDARY

SCALE 1:100,000

Mis 1   0   1   2   3   4   5   6   7   8   9   kilométres

Lightning Source UK Ltd.
Milton Keynes UK
UKHW011833300121
377954UK00002B/40